Something to Live For

Something to Live For

The Music of

Billy Strayhorn

Walter van de Leur

OXFORD
UNIVERSITY PRESS
2002

OXFORD
UNIVERSITY PRESS

Oxford New York
Athens Auckland Bangkok Bogotá Buenos Aires Cape Town Chennai
Dar es Salaam Delhi Florence Hong Kong Istanbul Karachi
Kolkata Kuala Lumpur Madrid Melbourne Mexico City Mumbai Nairobi
Paris São Paulo Shanghai Singapore Taipei Tokyo Toronto Warsaw

and associated companies in

Berlin Ibadan

Copyright © 2002 by Oxford University Press, Inc.

Published by Oxford University Press, Inc.
198 Madison Avenue, New York, New York 10016

Oxford is a registered trademark of Oxford University Press

All rights reserved. No part of this publication may be reproduced, stored in a retrieval system, or transmitted, in any form or by any means, electronic, mechanical, photocopying, recording, or otherwise, without the prior permission of Oxford University Press.

Library of Congress Cataloging-in-Publication Data

Leur, Walter van de.
Something to live for: the music of Billy Strayhorn / Walter van de Leur.
p. cm.
Includes bibliographical references (p.) and index.
ISBN 0-19-512448-0 (cloth)   ISBN-13 978-0-19-512448-4
1. Strayhorn, Billy—Criticism and interpretation. I. Title.
ML410.S9325 L48 2002
781.65'092—dc21
2001037040

Book design & composition by Mark McGarry, Texas Type & Book Works
Set in the Scala family of types

9 8 7 6 5 4 3 2 1

Printed in the United States of America
on acid-free paper

Dedicated to the memory of Mark Tucker

Contents

	Preface	ix
	Acknowledgments	xi
	Introduction	xv
1.	Fantastic Rhythm: The Pittsburgh Years	3
2.	The Renaissance of Arranging: First Works for and with Duke Ellington	23
3.	The Strayhorn Effect: A New Way of Writing for Jazz Orchestra	44
4.	Thinking with the Ear: Strayhorn's Musical Fingerprints	65
5.	Writing and Arranging Companion: Credited and Uncredited Collaborations	85
6.	"He Is He and I Am Me": The Ellington-Strayhorn Collaboration	100
7.	Wounded Love: Away from the Ellington Organization	117
8.	Masterpieces by Strayhorn: Writing for Albums	131
9.	The Whodunit Game: The Mature Style of Billy Strayhorn	142
10.	North by Southwest: The Final Years	165
11.	Conclusion	179
	APPENDICES	
	A. Scores of Scores: Manuscripts at the Billy Strayhorn and Duke Ellington Collections	185
	B. Billy Strayhorn's Works on Record	194
	C. Billy Strayhorn's Works on Record (Posthumously Premiered)	255
	D. Billy Strayhorn's Compositions	262
	Notes	287
	References	309
	Credits	315
	Index	319

Preface

Unless stated otherwise, the musical examples in this book are not transcriptions but draw directly on the original autograph music manuscripts, at times condensed or edited to enhance legibility. The original manuscripts give detailed information about instrumentation and voicing, yet rarely include rhythm section parts, or dynamic and other interpretive markings—elements that the Ellingtonians usually worked out in rehearsals. Since the main focus here is on Strayhorn's use of harmonic, melodic, rhythmic, and structural composition, the absence of these performance elements does not affect the argument.

I have added four appendices for reference. Appendix A discusses the particularities of the autograph scores in the main manuscript collections, the Duke Ellington and Ruth Ellington Collections at the Smithsonian Institution, and the Billy Strayhorn Collection at the Strayhorn Estate. Appendix B lists the more than five hundred different autograph scores by Strayhorn that can be linked with certainty to known recordings. This appendix also serves as the reference discography for the book, that is, it lists reference recordings for all recorded works mentioned in the text. As much as possible I have listed current CD issues, but many recordings are out of print. They can be found in the Jerry Valburn Collection at the Library of Congress. Appendix C lists all Strayhorn compositions, and arrangements that were premiered after his death. The final appendix, D, lists all of Strayhorn's known compositions both recorded and unrecorded.

If a score is not known to be recorded, it is identified in the text by its full "official" title (as copyrighted), followed (between brackets) by the original manuscript title—if different from the official title—and its current archival location. Manuscripts discussed in the book to which Strayhorn did not contribute (and which therefore are not listed in Appendix B), are treated similarly: they are followed by their manuscript title and current archival location.

The following abbreviations refer to the main music manuscript collections that house Strayhorn (and Ellington) autographs:

BSC Billy Strayhorn Collection (Series 1-5), Strayhorn Estate, Pittsburgh, Pa. Materials in possession of BSC are currently not publicly accessible.

DEC Duke Ellington Collection (DE #301, Subseries 1A), Archives Center, National Museum of American History, Smithsonian Institution, Washington, D.C.

DH Manuscripts in private possession of Strayhorn biographer David Hajdu, New York. Currently not publicly accessible.

LOC Library of Congress copyright registration files.

REC Ruth Ellington Collection (RE #415, Series 2), Archives Center, National Museum of American History, Smithsonian Institution, Washington, D.C.

SIDE Sidemen's Parts, Duke Ellington Collection (DE #301, Subseries 1C), Archives Center, National Museum of American History, Smithsonian Institution, Washington, D.C.

Acknowledgments

This project has spanned almost a decade and would have been impossible without the help of many.

Instrumental in realizing my first Smithsonian Institution Fellowship were the late Mark Tucker, Sjef Hoefsmit, Leigh Landy (University of Amsterdam), and Steve Galloway (Amsterdam Conservatory). For my pre-doctoral fellowship at the Smithsonian, I owe much to the chairman of my dissertation committee, Rembrandt Wolpert (University of Amsterdam).

My thanks to the staff at the Smithsonian Institution Fellowships Program, most notably the late Mary Dyer, who ran the interns and fellowship office at the National Museum of American History in a most idiosyncratic way. Thanks also to those institutions that provided additional financial support: The Netherlands-America Foundation, Philip Morris Netherlands, and the Becker-La Bastide Foundation.

Among those who made my research at the Smithsonian Institution's Duke Ellington Collection successful are my advisor, John Edward Hasse, curator in American Music, and my archivist-friends at the Archives Center (which houses the Duke Ellington Collection), located in the National Museum of American History: Fitzroy Thomas, Deborra Richardson, Reuben Jackson, Ted Hudson, Scott Schwartz, Ben Pubols, John Fleckner, Wendy Shay, Vanessa Broussard-Simmons, Mimi Minnick, Fath Ruffins, Rob Harding, David Haberstich, and above all my dearest friend Annie Keubler, who continued to be my lifeline to the collection.

The discussions with my co-fellows and friends Bob Haddow, Helen Rozwadowski, John Gennari, Elizabeth White, Carolyn Goldstein, and Alan Berolzheimer taught me invaluable lessons for my research. After all the hard work, the Tuesday-night-at-the-Irish-Times crowd helped me wash away fatigue and loneliness. My special thanks to Pete Daniel, Grace Palladino, and Charlie McGovern.

During my first fellowship at the Duke Ellington Collection I met David Hajdu, author of *Lush Life: A Biography of Billy Strayhorn*. David played a crucial role in my research. I am indebted to him for sharing his tremendous knowledge with me, as well as his love for the music of Billy Strayhorn and Duke Ellington. His fathomless support, assistance, and camaraderie have been an important source of inspiration. (Our favorite game is "Strayhorn trivia": "You better get us a table in the back," he once told a waitress who seated us, "we might sing.")

This book and all its underlying research would have been impossible without the help of Dr. Gregory A. Morris, executor of Billy Strayhorn's estate and currently president of Billy Strayhorn Songs, Inc., and his spouse Thelma Lovette-Morris, who invited me to their home during my first fellowship. There I found a musicologist's paradise: an uncatalogued collection of hundreds of autograph scores by Billy Strayhorn, containing many unknown works. Greg and Thelma granted me unlimited and unconditional access to the materials in their possession, and saw to it that their home was my home. Words cannot express my gratitude.

Special thanks also to all the other Strayhorn heirs, most notably the members of the executive committee of Billy Strayhorn Songs, Inc.

My second fellowship at the Smithsonian called for the migration of my family. Our Archives Center friends helped us out with practical matters small and large, and made our stay during the snowy winter and spring of 1996 most pleasurable. Special thanks to Vanessa and Raymond Broussard-Simmons, Cooby Greenway, Deborra Richardson, Wendy Shay, Ted and Geneva Hudson, and Mimi Minnick.

The Dutch Jazz Orchestra was instrumental in putting Strayhorn's music in perspective. The orchestra's dedicated and patient work with hitherto unrecorded scores by Strayhorn and Ellington provided invaluable answers. Many thanks to my real heroes: Jerry van Rooijen, Ack van Rooijen, Jan Oosthof, Ruud Breuls, Erik Veldkamp, Mike Booth, Peter van Soest, Martijn Sohier, Ilja Reijngoud, Hansjörg Fink, John Ruocco, Albert Beltman, Hans Meijdam, Toon Roos, Ab Schaap, Nils van Haften, Rob van Bavel, Frans van der Hoeven, Jan Voogd, and Eric Ineke. The Dutch Jazz Orchestra's recordings of newly discovered works already have written history.

My dear friends Albert Beltman, the Dutch Jazz Orchestra's artistic leader, and Dick Kuijs, producer at Radio Netherlands International, deserve special mention. From the start, they saw the tremendous artistic and historic significance of Strayhorn's unrecorded work, which—against all odds—they sought to make public without compromise. Troopers.

The following individuals answered my questions, sent me tapes and articles, or helped me in other ways. They do not necessarily underwrite any or all of my conclusions and observations set forth in this book: Aaron Bridgers, Morris

Hodara, Jan Bruèr, Louis Tavecchio, Philippe Baudoin, Sjef Hoefsmit, Jack Towers, Laurenz Wiskott, Jeff Sultanof, theoreticians Boudewijn Leeuwenberg, Ab Schaap, Willem-Wander van Nieuwkerk (specialist on Debussy and Ravel), Clemens Kemme, Patrick Schenkius, and William Russo, musicians Allard Robert (specialist on the French horn), and Niels van Hoorn (specialist on mallet instruments), musicologists and historians Mark Tucker, Stefano Zenni (specialist on Charles Mingus), Andrew Homzy, Dan Caine (specialist on *Beggar's Holiday*), Don Rayno (specialist on Paul Whiteman), Keith Waters, and Loren Schoenberg. Thanks also to David M. Jellema (Center for Popular Music at Middle Tennessee State University), Wolfram Knauer (Jazz Institut Darmstadt), Sylvia Kennick Brown (Special Collections Librarian at Williams College), Jan Ophuis (Dutch Jazz Archives), and the staff at the Rutgers Institute of Jazz Studies. Thanks to members of the various groups that are dedicated to the music of Duke Ellington and Billy Strayhorn: TDES Inc. (New York), the Duke Ellington Society, Chapter 90 (Washington, DC), the Duke Ellington Society UK (London), and the Duke Ellington Music Society (Belgium).

As all my research started to take the form of a book I received invaluable support from David Hajdu, Christian de Pee and Chris Calhoun, and my editorial team at Oxford University Press: Maribeth Payne, Maureen Buja, Joellyn Ausanka, and Ellen Welch.

I am grateful to those who read early drafts of my manuscript: David Hajdu, Rembrandt Wolpert, Greg Morris, Mark Tucker, David Baker, Boudewijn Leeuwenberg, and Ab Schaap. They all provided important insights.

Christian de Pee assisted me with shaping the final manuscript. His keen eye for detail and his perspective on English as a second language helped me in important ways to improve my argument.

Thanks also to those who helped me secure the reprint permissions for the music in my book: Herb Jordan from Billy Strayhorn Songs, Yolanda Blum and Zoraya Mendez from Music Sales Corporation, Sally Warkaske from Hal Leonard Corporation, Matt Smith from International Music Publications, Cheryl Swack from Warner Bros. Publications, and Ray Kersaut from the Songwriters Guild.

Last, a special thanks to my parents, Johanna and Walter van de Leur-Leentvaar, and my in-laws, Mia and Wim Smeets-Van der Borgh, as well as my spouse, Ilona Smeets, and our wonderful daughters, Heleen and Floor.

Introduction

As the twenty-first century begins, jazz has finally managed to achieve a measure of respectability in the musical establishment. Large institutions such as the Smithsonian Institution, the Library of Congress, and the Lincoln Center of Performing Arts spend considerable budgets on researching, archiving, and performing the legacy of jazz. Universities and conservatories throughout the world are building distinguished educational programs and hire musicians and musicologists of name to add luster to their course offerings. Repertory orchestras seek to re-create the music and sounds of the past, reproducing historic recordings in painstaking detail. There are conferences, meetings, and conventions where researchers and fans, students and performers, historians and record collectors meet, while a seemingly endless stream of CD reissues and book publications finds its way to the specialized jazz sections of book and record stores.

Still, the position of jazz is far from rosy. The genre has neither the mass appeal of pop music (and its consequent economic pull) nor the social status of the sixteenth- to nineteenth-century western European genres, generally known as classical music. To date, classical music appears to be the dominant musical art form, generating considerable budgets for performance and education—with strong governmental support in the Western world—and steadily drawing dedicated audiences. Due to the relatively low status of their music, jazz musicians, educators, and researchers as well as university jazz faculty and orchestra boards often find themselves negotiating subtle antagonistic forces of social prejudice, commercialism, and even racism—elements that have shaped the creation of jazz since its origins roughly a century ago.

In the face of these contrary forces, the institutionalized jazz community has embraced, virtually unanimously, Edward Kennedy "Duke" Ellington (1899–1974) as its prime weapon in the continuous battle with the musical establishment, to win acknowledgment for jazz. Ellington, after all, is the epitome of jazz: a great innovator and original musician-composer-orchestrator, the creator of an impressive body of work in many genres, a true jazz dignitary who steered clear of controversy yet sought to express his personal voice and racial pride in an uncompromising way. In addition, he founded and led one of the most distinctive jazz orchestras for five straight decades, in the meantime negotiating and crossing many real and imaginary boundaries, the limiting confinements of his music's loaded epithet being one of these. One of the most honored and celebrated jazz figures, the recipient of numerous awards, prizes, and honorary doctorates, Duke Ellington, it is often maintained, is the greatest jazz composer, nay, the greatest American composer of the twentieth century, a musical genius who was "beyond category."

Inevitably, this view comes at the price of historic simplification. In all the understandable praise bestowed on Ellington, something seems to be missing: three important decades of his remarkable career are closely intertwined with the work of William Thomas "Billy" Strayhorn (1915–1967). A member of Ellington's team from 1939 until his untimely death at the age of fifty-one, Strayhorn created hundreds of compositions and arrangements for his musical partner—well over five hundred are known to be recorded—including some of the best-known and most played pieces in postwar Ellingtonia. Close to fifteen hundred surviving autograph scores in Strayhorn's hand—an estimated four-fifths of his total work for the orchestra—representing original compositions as well as arrangements of a wide array of works by other writers, document his tremendous contribution.

Not only was Strayhorn's contribution invaluable from a practical point of view—it significantly reduced Ellington's workload—but more important, Strayhorn brought a new musical approach to the already idiosyncratic sound of the orchestra, expanding the boundaries of the jazz genre in yet another direction. Working from a radically different musical and personal background, Strayhorn created a separate musical entity within the realm of Ellingtonia, employing an original and sophisticated musical vocabulary that drew from a different harmonic, rhythmic, and melodic source. His compositions opened new vistas, especially in terms of musical architecture, as he infused developmental techniques typically associated with European art music into an African-American idiom. Outside the Ellington organization, Strayhorn had an important, yet for the public eye largely hidden, musical life as a composer, arranger, and lyricist, writing for musical theater and in non-jazz genres.

In the popular imagination, heroes and role models are solitary figures, so it does not come as a surprise that Strayhorn's contributions to the repertory of Duke Ellington's Famous Orchestra to some form an unwelcome factor in the canonization of the orchestra's namesake. Part of the jazz community, sensitive to even the slightest trace of criticism after Collier's at times hostile and ill-researched Ellington biography (1987), sees any attempt to draw a historically more correct picture of the elusive Ellington-Strayhorn partnership as an attempt "to exaggerate the importance of his [Strayhorn's] splendid contribution—*at Duke Ellington's expense* [italics added]" (Dance, 1993b). Others believe that "only pedants can care where one pen left off and the other begun" (Giddins 1998, 257). Thus, discussing Strayhorn's role in the Ellington repertory has become controversial and tends to degenerate rapidly into a debate about the relative merits of both composers. To some, the issue is quite simple. In Gunther Schuller's view, for instance, Ellington was the "innovator" and Strayhorn merely a "follower" (Schuller 1998)—point-blank qualifications that do little justice to either composer.

Performers of the Ellington orchestra's repertory appear to be equally ill at ease with Strayhorn's role. Trumpeter and bandleader Wynton Marsalis, for instance, on tour with the Lincoln Center Jazz orchestra to celebrate Ellington's birthday centennial with a chain of concerts that included the Ellington-Strayhorn adaptation of the *Peer Gynt Suites 1 & 2*, told a Dutch newspaper reporter that he was "not convinced that Strayhorn arranged the *Peer Gynt* [Suites 1 & 2]" (Lagerwerf and Mantel 1999, 12). The autographs show, however, that Strayhorn scored a hefty 80 percent of the suite. Still, in Marsalis's view, even if Strayhorn was largely responsible for the orchestrations, that would be of minor importance: "The [musical] language Strayhorn employed in his work stems directly from Ellington; he was a Duke Jr. of sorts. So much so that hadn't they been collaborators, Duke might as well have sued him for plagiarism" (ibid.). Marsalis's stance is not exceptional and has been voiced in numerous variations from the beginnings of the Ellington-Strayhorn partnership. Yet, against this oft-repeated view that Strayhorn composed in an Ellingtonian vein, as an "alter ego for the Duke" as one headline had it (Wilson 1962), Strayhorn himself maintained on various occasions that his style was fundamentally different.

These two diametrical positions—Strayhorn as Ellington's apprentice and assistant versus Strayhorn as independent composer—stood at the outset of my research. The mere fact that indeed a book can be written that deals with Strayhorn's music solely, separate from Ellington's style and oeuvre, answers the question as to which view of Strayhorn's music is the more accurate.

So far, researchers have approached the oeuvre of Ellington's orchestra—and the Strayhorn legacy embedded therein—predominantly through the surviving studio recordings, preserved air checks, and (amateur) live recordings, and understandably so. Recording with his orchestra was one of the main tasks Ellington appears to have set for himself, and he took virtually every opportunity to record his work (at times at his own expense), even if there was no immediate need for the material. Indeed, years after his death, an impressive collection of never-released and hitherto unknown studio recordings surfaced, eventually donated in 1984 to the Danish Radio by Ellington's son, Mercer, and later partly issued on a series of ten compact discs as *The Private Collection* (Saja Records, CDs 91041-91045 and 91230-91234).

Still, even though the Ellington orchestra recorded an astonishing amount of music, issued on hundreds of LP records and CDs, these recordings document only part of the orchestra's history. Numerous works written for the orchestra, from originals and arrangements to complete theater shows (such as two versions of *Jump for Joy*, and *Beggar's Holiday*), were never recorded, for a variety of reasons, often practical. Even the charismatic Ellington was not fully autonomous in planning his records (see for instance Tucker 1999, 4), since producers always kept an eye on the marketability of the final product. Any picture that takes into account only the orchestra's recordings will necessarily be incomplete, as it ignores too many important works—not recorded, but certainly performed.

Until recently, recordings were the only musical source available to scholars. Jazz, as a performer-oriented art, is firmly rooted in an oral tradition and although written scores certainly are part of the creative process, publication of the music in printed form is most uncommon. In fact, Ellington appears to have been quite protective of his scores and tended to hide them, as well as Strayhorn's scores, from those who might be interested in the company secrets. Jimmy Jones, called on to direct the theater show *My People*, actually had to lead the orchestra without access to any of the show's scores:

> Some very funny things happened. He [Ellington] would never give me conductor's sheets. I would ask for conductor's sheets and he would walk away.... He's never lost for words, no matter what the situation is, so he eventually made a reply. He says: "Well James,... [you] have to know the score [by heart], in case someone is missing." (Nicholson 1999, 346–347)

Lacking written sources, most jazz scholars create their own scores—known as transcriptions (see for instance DeVeaux 1997 or Berliner 1994)—meticulously taking the actual notes from the record to represent them in writing. Generally, when it comes to taking down solos, or works by smaller outfits, the results are quite satisfactory, but the challenges in transcribing big band jazz are daunting. After all, while it may be romantic to think of the big bands as democratic collectives that spontaneously created music in rehearsal, the truth is that with the growth of their personnel, jazz orchestras from the 1930s on more and more became reading bands, largely relying on detailed written parts when performing ensemble passages. Contrary to popular belief, the majority of the musicians active in the dozens of top name bands and the hundreds of territory orchestras as a rule were excellent sight readers. Since their jobs required them often to play and record new music with little preparation, and since band books could hold hundreds of numbers, being a good sight reader was a prerogative for any jazz musician pursuing a career as a section player. The Ellingtonians were no exception: often, "the ink on the sheet music would still be wet when we were cutting the record," trombonist Buster Cooper recollected (Hajdu 1996, 234).

Consequently, attempts to transcribe Ellington's and Strayhorn's music, full of unorthodox voicings and unexpected instrumental combinations, all too often do not accurately render what was actually played, as some examples of published transcriptions over the past years have shown. For instance, a comparison of Schuller's transcription of *Sepia Panorama* (Schuller 1995) with the original autographs and the recording shows that only two of his transcribed chords in a particular six-part brass tutti section (measures 29–36) are correct, while the other twenty have up to five wrong notes per chord, with an average of three. Using such an erroneous score as the basis for musical analysis will yield questionable outcomes, as Rattenbury's study of Ellington compositions (1992), based on similarly flawed transcriptions, painfully displays.

Although transcriptions necessarily will remain a significant research tool, one of the most important developments in jazz research during the last two decades has been the establishment of dedicated jazz manuscript collections, such as the Smithsonian Institution's Duke Ellington Collection (housed in National Museum of American History, Washington, D.C.). This collection, containing an impressive number of autograph scores and band members' parts, has dramatically enhanced the possibilities for scholars to address certain hitherto elusive issues, such as Ellington's and Strayhorn's musical languages as well as their collaboration. Luckily, this sudden availability of written source material does not stand on its own. All over the country, jazz musicians' estates are opening up their vaults and seeking a safe haven for their paper documents. A handful of specialized jazz music manuscript archives, with dedicated archival staffs, have become the guardians of this invaluable source material that is rapidly increasing. Other collections still are housed in the repositories of their respective estates—as is the case with part of Strayhorn's music or Charles Mingus's—which often are willing to accommodate researchers. The written music sources preserved in these various archives can help to increase significantly the accuracy of transcriptions, to cast a light on material not recorded but apparently played—as band book numbers, penciled musicians' remarks, and other clues attest—and to provide answers to questions beyond the scope of existing recordings.

For the Strayhorn researcher, the implications of Strayhorn's autograph scores go considerably beyond such practical applications. Since the Ellingtonians were the main interpreters of Strayhorn's work, their recordings can be problematic when it comes to addressing Strayhorn's style. Ellington, in his role of orchestra leader and consequently interpreter of Strayhorn, often took liberties with his associate's scores. However, the degree to which he edited his associate's music varied. Thus the orchestra's readings could range from verbatim performances of Strayhorn's compositions—such as *Overture to a Jam Session*—to far-reaching reworkings, as occurred with *Orson*. No apparent system seems to underlie these adjustments, though in those cases when Ellington shortened a piece, possibly for practical reasons, possibly for aesthetic reasons, he tended to take out nonthematic material, such as introductions, transitions, modulations, and codas. If changes were made, they seldom involved the actual notes—melody, chords, orchestration, rhythmic placement, and so on—but rather dealt with the *order* of musical events. Consequently, with the obvious exception of ad-lib solos and the rhythm section—typically not incorporated in the score but communicated orally and further elaborated during rehearsals—the vast majority of Strayhorn's autographs in great detail represent the actual music played by the orchestra's sections, with one extremely important exception: musical form.

While it is impossible to know exactly how Strayhorn envisioned—and afterward evaluated—the orchestra's realization of his work, his detailed scores in my opinion nevertheless give the best possible and most intimate perspective on his compositions and arrangements. Strayhorn thoroughly knew the Ellington orchestra and he wrote with the performers in mind (as did Ellington). Therefore, the gap between notation in Strayhorn's scores and the interpretation of those scores is usually relatively small. Whenever this gap exists, it does not stem from any intrinsic inadequacy of his notational system as such. In jazz, as in other genres, notation is context-dependent and adequately functions within that context as a prescriptive tool, as long as composer and performers know and understand the underlying conventions (*de*scriptive notation, i.e., capturing what was actually played, is highly problematic in any genre). For Ellington, Strayhorn, and the members of orchestra, these conventions were part of their everyday professional lives. Played as written, a Strayhorn score can yield a first-rate jazz performance, as the Ellington orchestra proved numerous times. If one wishes to liberate Strayhorn from Ellington's shadow—an important step in understanding the musical symbiosis of the two composers—Strayhorn's autographs therefore give the primary text.

The autograph collections become all the more important since they contain hundreds of Strayhorn scores that remained unrecorded during his life, from sketches to arrangements, from musicians' parts to full-fledged compositions. The posthumous recording of twelve such pieces by the Dutch Jazz Orchestra (see Appendix C) received worldwide acclaim: the jazz press hailed these works as "stunningly modern" ("CD Reviews," 71) and "superior pieces" (Harrington 1996, B7).

The advantages of working with autograph scores—accuracy, immediate access to the composition per se, often a hitherto unknown work—come with a number of disadvantages as well. The manuscript collections are not complete, as an estimated 20 percent of Strayhorn's work has been lost, while of the surviving material at least another 20 percent is incomplete. In addition, written scores allow for different possible interpretations. Furthermore, when working with jazz scores (either autographs or transcriptions), one has to guard against some of the greatest fallacies in musicology: the confusion of the written source with audible music, the idea that a manuscript unequivocally reflects the composer's intentions and, finally, the notion that written music has a greater validity as a work of art than nonwritten music. Even with these possible pitfalls, the autograph scores provide the most powerful tool in understanding Strayhorn's music.

Crucial in defining Strayhorn's role in the Ellington repertory is the status of his autograph scores and, whenever they contain new and original compositions, the extent to which they are proof of authorship. After all, it is conceivable that Strayhorn's scores represent just orchestrations or expansions of material essentially written by Ellington (although one might just as well argue the reverse). If this were the case, the autograph score would provide no solid ground for establishing authorship. Yet, in general, both Ellington and Strayhorn conceived their original compositions as *orchestral* works, prohibiting any attempt to separate the arrangement from the composition. Moreover, many of their instrumental works are in a sense themeless, that is, they do not consist of a clearly rounded-out theme against an orchestral background. This absence of an apparent theme-orchestration dichotomy excludes a two-step process in which one was the composer and the other the arranger. From Ellington's *Harlem Airshaft* to *Track 360* to *After Bird Jungle*, and from Strayhorn's *Mid-Riff* to *Blues in Orbit* to *Ballet of the Flying Saucers*, it is virtually impossible to separate the thematic material from the orchestral setting (which may account for the relatively small number of Ellington and Strayhorn works that have found their way into the jazz musician's standard repertory). Asked whether he simultaneously conceived composition and arrangement, Strayhorn answered "I suppose.... I don't really know. I don't really think of it. You get your ideas and you define the form. You have to nail the ideas down first. Then you get the formula—how long, what key, the technical details" (Dance 1967, 18). In another instance he left no doubt about both his and Ellington's working habits: "We both naturally orchestrate as we write" (Coss 1962, 23).

The surviving manuscripts fully corroborate Strayhorn's claim. For instance, much as Strayhorn saved a large number of his own sketches (some three hundred are in the repository of his estate), his papers contain fewer than two dozen sketches by Ellington. Not a single composition later attributed to Strayhorn appears to draw on these sketches. If fleshing out each other's ideas would have been a structural part of the collaborators' working scheme, one would expect to find at least some Ellingtonian leadsheets in Strayhorn's possession. Yet, with the sole exception of *Blue Belles of Harlem* and *Blutopia*—Ellington works that could never be mistaken for Strayhorn originals—there are none. True, the dividing lines in the repertory become somewhat less evident for the multipart scores on which Ellington and Strayhorn collaborated, such as *Beggar's Holiday, A Drum Is a Woman, Anatomy of a Murder,* and *Saturday Laughter.* Yet even in these collaborative projects, they appear to have cleanly divided the work at hand between the two of them, each composer writing separate numbers.

While this division of work was certainly rooted in artistic considerations, it was mostly dictated by practical considerations. With the Ellington orchestra on the road for the larger part of the year, Strayhorn—who rarely traveled with the band—as a rule worked on his own. For instance, while preparing the material for the album with Rosemary Clooney (*Blue Rose,* CBS CD 466444-2), he stayed with the singer in Los Angeles, mailing the scores to Ellington. Consequently, while Ellington appears always to have had a copyist at his disposal, Strayhorn often extracted his own scores, as documented by some three hundred surviving sets of instrumental parts in Strayhorn's hand.

The ultimate proof of authorship lies in the respective and distinctive styles of the two collaborators, which is not only visible on paper but, first and foremost, audible. Both Strayhorn's and Ellington's oeuvres, though historically intertwined, nevertheless form coherent, separate musical entities, especially in terms of harmonic, melodic, and structural design. Their respective scores fully underwrite this individuality.

In sum, Strayhorn's autograph scores, together with his idiosyncratic style, provide proof of his authorship: a composition or arrangement in the handwriting of Strayhorn is a composition or arrangement by Strayhorn.

This study is not a biography of Billy Strayhorn. Readers who want to know more about his life and times should read David Hajdu's provocative *Lush Life: A Biography of Billy Strayhorn* (Hajdu 1995).[1] Neither does this study propose to compare Strayhorn with Ellington, but it seeks to inventory, analyze, and evaluate the music of Strayhorn on its own terms. It identifies in Strayhorn's compositions a number of salient features that are easily recognized on the surface—his musical fingerprints, so to speak—as well as characteristics that lie under the surface, such as harmonic language and his approach to musical form.

Chapter 1, Fantastic Rhythm, traces Strayhorn's development as a budding composer and arranger in Pittsburgh. The next chapter, The Renaissance of Arranging, looks into Strayhorn's earliest works with and for Ellington, while Chapter 3, The Strayhorn Effect, discusses his breakthrough works in 1941, such as *Take the "A" Train* and *Chelsea Bridge.* Chapter 4, Thinking with the Ear, points out which are the essential elements in Strayhorn's compositions and arrangements of the 1940s and how these elements set his scores apart from those of Ellington. In Chapter 5, Writing and Arranging Companion, the first collaborative suites of Ellington and Strayhorn are explored, while Chapter 6, "He Is He and I Am Me," dissects the myths that have surrounded the collaboration of both composers. The next chapter, Wounded Love, looks into the remarkable works Strayhorn wrote while away from the Ellington organization. Chapter 8, Masterpieces by Strayhorn, unravels Strayhorn's often hidden contributions to the successful LP albums recorded by the Ellington orchestra in the 1950s. The subsequent chapter, The Whodunit Game, returns to Strayhorn's musical style and plots the development in his later arranging and composing. Chapter 10, North by Southwest, discusses Strayhorn's final compositions, including *Blood Count* and *The North by Southwest Suite*.

Four appendices round out my research. Appendix A, Scores of Scores, reproduces two autograph scores, respectively by Strayhorn and Ellington. The reproductions will help researchers with the identification of Strayhorn's and Ellington's handwriting. Appendix A further points out the wealth of information these unique documents provide. Appendix B lists the more than five hundred Strayhorn autographs that were recorded during his life by the Ellington orchestra (and others). This appendix answers the intriguing "who-wrote-what" and leads listeners to the vast amount of uncredited Strayhorn works on recordings by the Ellington orchestra. Appendix C lists those Strayhorn works that have been posthumously premiered on record, while Appendix D lists the over four hundred Strayhorn compositions known to date.

In each chapter there is ample material for the general reader. While the discussion of the musical examples is geared to readers who can follow a jazz-theoretical discussion, my aim has been to accommodate those who do not have these skills. Especially Chapters 5 and 6, which deal with the Ellington-Strayhorn collaboration, and Chapter 8, which details Strayhorn's contributions to the later Ellington band, require no musical training whatsoever. Even the most technical chapters, 4 and 9, contain discussion that should be accessible to the lay reader.

Whenever relevant or enlightening, Ellington's approach to composing will be laid against Strayhorn's. These comparisons do not amount to an analysis and evaluation of Ellington's music; a study of his compositional style remains eagerly awaited.

Something to Live For

Chapter One

Fantastic Rhythm: The Pittsburgh Years

AT THE END of his life, Strayhorn looked back on his adolescent years in Pittsburgh as of minor importance. Acknowledging that he had "worked around, played gigs," he also said that at the time he didn't "consider [himself] good enough" (Dance 1967, 19). Reminiscing as Ellington's key collaborator, Strayhorn said that as a teenager he had only written "a couple of things" and "hardly knew what an arranger was" (ibid.). Nevertheless, these were his formative years, the unlikely beginnings of a truly amazing musical career that built on a thorough understanding of European classical music, American popular music, and jazz.

Strayhorn's embarrassment with his juvenile work may well be rooted in the disturbing recollections of a problematic childhood. Yet, growing up as a sensitive, intelligent, and exceptionally talented youngster under far from ideal conditions, Strayhorn coupled his musical knowledge with his personal experience. "All of his tunes have a deep feeling behind them," Ellington trombonist Lawrence Brown noted, "you hear him in his music, which to me is the mark of a real musician" (Nicholson 1999, 202). To understand his music, one needs to understand Strayhorn.

William Thomas Strayhorn was born on November 29, 1915, in Dayton, Ohio, the third of six Strayhorn children who would survive infancy.[1] Life was a struggle for his parents, Lillian Young and James Nathaniel Strayhorn. By the time William was six, his family had moved numerous times as his father pursued a number of low-paying jobs. The Strayhorns finally took up residence in Pittsburgh, where the rapidly growing electrical and steel industries provided opportunities for unschooled laborers. After various relocations in the suburbs of the Steel City, they settled in the Homewood district in 1926, a poor, mixed-race working-class area largely supported by the steel mills. Embittered by poverty and

Growing up in Pittsburgh's poor Homewood district, Billy Strayhorn made money running errands for a local drug store. From his earnings he bought a piano and sheet music and got himself piano lessons. Extremely talented, as both a performer and a composer, he was dedicated from the start.
(*Walter van de Leur Collection*)

disillusioned by the grim prospects for African Americans, James Strayhorn took more and more to drinking. When intoxicated, he would often vent his frustrations on his family with verbal abuse and physical violence, and on young William in particular. William's mother, who felt especially connected to her son (who at this point was known to most as Bill), tried to shield him from his father's rage. For several years, she sent him on long visits to her in-laws in Hillsborough, North Carolina, during school vacations. There, Strayhorn's grandmother, a church pianist, encouraged him to experiment at the keyboard. Before long, Strayhorn decided he wanted a piano of his own. Selling newspapers in the street and running errands for Pittsburgh's Pennfield Drugs—the neighborhood drugstore where he eventually became a clerk and soda jerk—Strayhorn managed to save some money. When he left grade school, he was able to buy himself an old upright player piano. Dedicated from the start, he took piano lessons through the local music store, from a teacher named Charlotte Catlin.

American music was quite diverse in the mid-twenties when Strayhorn turned his attention to music. Jazz, ragtime, Harlem stride, Dixieland, novelty piano, blues, vaudeville, Broadway theater music, popular song, European-American music (from Gershwin to waltzes and fox-trots), light classics, and traditional European classical music were all part of the musical landscape. Yet, as a freshman at Westinghouse High School, where a progressive music teacher named Carl McVicker led a number of musical outfits, including a swing band, Strayhorn chose to be involved in the school's classical orchestra. Eventually he would become Westinghouse High's number one pianist, performing classical piano concertos and playing with the school's Orchestra Club.

With his first music teacher, Ms. Catlin, or slightly later in his first or second year in high school, Strayhorn took counterpoint classes, traditionally the first step in classical music-theory initiation. A handful of his exercises survive, one in F, titled *Allegro ma non troppo, Opus 1/No. 2* (REC), and two untitled manuscripts, one in $A^{\flat}$ and one in C (both REC). Though ordinary counterpoint exercises, they reveal that Strayhorn's musical ambitions were serious and that his studies were in full gear. The tongue-in-cheek opus number and the classical tempo marking further suggest that Strayhorn had already begun to acquire a certain familiarity with the standard European repertory.

From roughly the same period dates an unfinished harmony exercise in Strayhorn's hand (untitled manuscript, REC), in all likelihood assigned by his high school piano and harmony teacher Jane Patton Alexander, "a middle-aged musical conservative" (Hajdu 1996, 14). The exercise calls for the harmonization of an A-minor melody with a prescribed set of chords, given as a figured bass. The student further has to "modulate by enharmonic change and also by common chords, include passing notes and embellishments, and [a] sequence of 6 secondary 7ths." Though he appears never to have finished the assignment, it bespeaks an advanced theoretical level at which Strayhorn apparently was supposed to be competent. From this type of exercises to independent composing must have been just a small step for the young Strayhorn.

The first documented independent composition by Billy Strayhorn is *Concerto for Piano and Percussion* ("Concerto," REC), premiered in the winter of 1934 at Westinghouse High (Hajdu 1996, 16). Written for his high school friend Michael Scrima, a percussionist, the work included parts for timpani and xylophone. Only nineteen bars of the manuscript fragment, marked "Allegro," have survived. There are a number of curious passages in this short manuscript. The four opening bars (written on two double piano staves, numbered I and II), seem to call for chords in both the piano *and the xylophone*. Similarly, on verso of the manuscript (mm. 7–18), where Strayhorn turns to a two-staff system with the xylophone part scribbled over the piano accompaniment, a two-bar passage of five-part chords is marked "xylophone." Yet, the xylophone traditionally is played with no more than two mallets, which excludes xylophone chords—it was not until the early 1960s that Gary Burton developed the four-mallet *Burton-grip*. Even with the Burton-grip it is technically impossible for a single player to execute what Strayhorn's score seems to suggest: four-part chords against a melody in octaves—a total of six voices. Further surprises may be found in measure 2, which calls for a xylophone glissando that starts two octaves beneath the instrument's range. Finally, the role of a crossed out four-bar introduction, marked "rhythmically," and calling for timpani in G and D (in octaves!), is uncertain as well.

Even though the existing manuscript for the *Concerto for Piano and Percussion* provides few clues as to the work's length, structure, or musical content, it does cast light on some of its central ideas. Especially the harmonic approach of the composition displays Strayhornisms that would return in much of his later work. For instance, the minor-major seventh chords of measures 1 and 2 would recur as one of the main harmonic ideas in *Chelsea Bridge* (1941), while the perfect fourths voice leading in the upper chord structures (mm. 7–10) are mirrored by the voicings that color the opening bars of *Rain Check* (1941). Further idiosyncrasies may be found in the so-called hemiolas in the xylophone—repeated rhythmic patterns incongruent with the underlying meter—foreshadowing the modulatory section at the end of the second chorus of *Take the "A" Train* (1941).

Inconsistencies in the instrumentation aside, the *Concerto for Piano and Percussion* shows Strayhorn adventurously pioneering with a then little-used instrumental combination, sparked by the mere availability of percussionist Scrima. Around 1934, hardly any literature for mallet instruments existed—Béla Bartók (1881–1945) had not yet composed his *Music for String Instruments, Percussion, and Celesta* (1936) nor the *Sonata for Two Pianos and Percussion* (1937), generally considered to rank among the highlights of the instrument's repertory. In the European-American music of composers such as Darius Milhaud (1882–1974) or George Gershwin (e.g., in his *An American in Paris*, 1928) xylophones did indeed play a role, but as "effect" instruments in an orchestral setting rather than as full-fledged solo voices. Similarly, the instrument's use in theater and vaudeville orchestras—and from the 1930s on in cinema—as a rule was restricted to Mickey-Mousing, humorously supporting onstage or on-screen slapstick action. Even in jazz, the use of the xylophone (later replaced by the more versatile vibraphone) was still a novelty, with Red Norvo's 1933 recording of *Hole in the Wall* (Brunswick 6562) as one of the first records to bring the instrument to the attention of a larger public. Especially Gershwin's *An American in Paris* may have been known to Strayhorn—as a budding composer he may have turned to this work for inspiration. Indeed, Strayhorn's borrowing apparently was such that decades later some of those present at the premiere of *Concerto for Piano and Percussion* "would swear they had heard Billy Strayhorn play [Gershwin's] *Rhapsody in Blue*" (Hajdu 1996, 17).

From roughly the same period as the *Concerto for Piano and Percussion* date two entirely classical waltzes. The first waltz, titled *Valse*[2] (BSC), marked "Lento sostenuto" and signed "Wm. Strayhorn" is a three-part through-composed Chopinesque piece for piano solo in B♭ minor. Strayhorn's charming waltz builds on a romantically flowing, eight-bar theme constructed along classical lines, with well-proportioned antecedent and consequent phrases (Ex. 1-1).

Valse is written in a full-blown nineteenth-century European Romantic idiom, which bespeaks Strayhorn's thorough understanding of the classical piano literature, undoubtedly acquired through extensive study of the repertoire. With smoothly integrated harmonic planes—B♭ minor, its relative major D♭ (over pedal point), as well as a more daring section in the remote key of A—Strayhorn articulates the well-balanced, through-composed three-part architecture of the piece. Further to enhance this articulation he uses thematic and harmonic variation, a refreshing touch of chromatic counterpoint in the reiteration of the theme and a small-scale developmental section which even leads to a "faux reprise"—a deceptive passage that suggests a thematic recapitulation but is harmonically off-center.

Ex. 1-1. *Valse*, mm. 1–8

The waltz ends with a delicate coda marked "perdendosi" (dying away)—a subtle ending to an eloquent piece.

Though stylistically outside his later work and juvenile in its imitative quality—the waltzes of Chopin are tangibly present—*Valse* displays some of the musical concepts that played a key role in much of Strayhorn's future compositional techniques: formal balance, an advanced harmonic language, and an economic use of musical material. In addition, like virtually all of Strayhorn's later work, *Valse* radiates a musical honesty and simple beauty that belies its composer's sophisticated theoretical approach.

In approximately five years time, from his first counterpoint exercises to this organically developing waltz, Strayhorn mastered the essentials of composition, successfully exploring one of its most complex aspects: the composition of musical form. Strayhorn possessed a very promising compositional talent indeed.

A second waltz, simply titled *#2* (BSC), consists of a single-line melody against piano chords. The work is in all likelihood intended for piano and clarinet, since Strayhorn's manuscript bears the name of Raymond Wood, a young reed player. The appearance of Wood's name on the manuscript indicates that this work dates from the winter of 1934, when Strayhorn had just graduated from high school—he and Wood met shortly after Strayhorn's graduation (Hajdu 1996, 20). The two-staff score does not provide absolute certainty regarding instrumentation—waltz *#2* could have been envisioned as a piano solo as well, although with some awkward technical points. Although Wood may have been involved in the composition of the piece (his name on the manuscript could be the composer's credit), the piano accompaniment seems to be Strayhorn's. Probably tailored to the abilities of the clarinetist, this straightforward da capo waltz in minor nowhere exceeds the level of a piano book etude: on all levels it is much simpler and far less sophisticated than *Valse*. In fact, the marked difference in compositional refinement and musical content between the two waltzes strongly suggests that Strayhorn may have reworked some of his friend's ideas into a fitting piece, a type of assignment he was to perform occasionally for a future friend of name and fame.

On October 12, 1934, Wood and Strayhorn filed copyrights for two songs, *I'm Still Begging You* and *You Lovely Little Devil* (unpublished, both LOC). Both piano-vocal leadsheets are vintage Tin Pan Alley tunes, each with a four-bar introduction, a verse and an AABA chorus. Though Strayhorn's text setting of Wood's somewhat amateurish lyrics certainly has its weak spots, the tasteful piano accompaniment is detailed and displays a clear professionalism—it easily measures up to the commercial sheet music of the time. Between the two classical waltzes and these pop tunes, Strayhorn now had tried his hand on at least two distinct musical genres. Though musically of little significance (again Strayhorn may have helped out his friend), *I'm Still Begging You* and *You Lovely Little Devil* primed Strayhorn for a far more important musical project he was soon to undertake.

In the winter of 1935, Strayhorn became involved with the preparations of a musical show for his alma mater's "Stunt Day"—a yearly event for which the graduation class organized a vaudeville program with music and comedy. Word of his musical proficiency was spreading in the Pittsburgh area—delivering goods for the Pennfield Drugs, Strayhorn often ended up on a piano bench: "when I would deliver packages, people would ask me to 'sit down and play us one of your songs'" (Coss 1962, 22), he later reminisced. In need of assistance, some of his former schoolmates asked him to help them out with their act. Before long, he found himself ambitiously writing the entire book, dialogue, and music for a twenty-minute musical show. A small musical outfit of three reeds, two trumpets, and a rhythm section accompanied the production. Strayhorn titled it *Fantastic Rhythm*. After a successful premiere at Westinghouse High in the spring of 1935, Oliver "Boggy" Fowler, one of the initiators who sought a career in show business, asked Strayhorn to rework *Fantastic Rhythm* into a full-scale music production. Strayhorn revised and expanded the work into a commercial version, which toured the greater Pittsburgh area in 1935 and thereafter went on the road in western Pennsylvania. As late as 1944, ten years after its creation, *Fantastic Rhythm*—which according to its creator was "put on [for] a grand two nights" (Strayhorn 1962)—was still running. Fowler spent three years producing the show at navy bases throughout the Pacific (Hajdu 1996, 100).

A total of fifteen manuscripts survive of at least thirteen different original songs and production numbers from *Fantastic Rhythm*. Though most scores are untitled, their lyrics enable identification, while the vivid memories of some of the show's participants provide further detail (Hajdu 1996, 25–28). *I'll Never Have to Dream Again* (untitled manuscript, REC), and *Let Nature Take Its Course* (untitled manuscript, REC) as well as the title tune *Fantastic Rhythm* (DH) have survived as piano-vocal leadsheets, similar in design to the earlier copyright scores for the two Strayhorn-Wood pieces.[3] Only part of the *Overture* (score untitled; parts titled "Ouverture," all REC) remains, as an arrangement for the small band that backed the initial high school edition. The remaining manuscripts are sketchy or incomplete. Of *Life Ain't Nothing but Rhythm*, also known as *The Rhythm Man* (untitled manuscript, REC and DH), and *The Sob-Sisters* (untitled manuscript, DH), only vocal parts with incidental background chords remain, while from *My Little Brown Book* (REC) only the verse survives. Of all the later arrangements for the twelve-piece Moonlight Harbor Band—a popular dance band in Pittsburgh's black ballrooms and the pit orchestra for the commercial edition of *Fantastic Rhythm*—only the first trumpet part for *Office Scene* (REC) still exists. For the other titles remembered by *Fantastic Rhythm*'s cast members, *It Must Be a Dream*, *The Silent Fight* (possibly the same as *Office Scene*), *We Are the Reporters*, *Don't Mess Around with the Women*, and *Harlem Rumba*, no musical material is known to exist.[4]

With the script as well as unknown portions of background music and production numbers lost, it is not possible to reconstruct and evaluate the show as a whole. Furthermore, it is uncertain whether two additional piano-vocal works written around the same time, *So This Is Love* (BSC) and *A Penthouse on Shady Avenue* ("Penthouse," REC), were intended for the production. None of the available sources mentions these titles, nor did any of the participants recall them—they may have been discarded (Hajdu 1997). Though incomplete, enough material survives of the show's essential compositions to gain a sense of the quality of the music and the lyrics.

The title tune, *Fantastic Rhythm*, is an arrestingly syncopated AABA song, with a ragtime piano accompaniment. Melodically the piece is somewhat reminiscent of the earlier *Concerto for Piano and Percussion*, as it similarly builds on a rhythmic melody. Again, Strayhorn's writing displays a predilection for using chromatic lines to create musical interest and surprise. The refreshing upper-chromatic $C^\flat$ in mm. 1 and 3 (Ex. 1-2)—alternated with a C in the intermediate measure—is a case in point. In keeping with its melody, the quite unexpected harmonization of *Fantastic Rhythm* derives from adventurous chromatic alterations as well. Though the piece is in major, Strayhorn deceptively starts the first bar on the tonic minor chord, delaying the major chord proper until the third measure. More chromatism may be found in his use of tonally alien, altered substitute dominants, such as the modern $F^\flat 9^{(\sharp 11)}$ in mm. 4 and 6, and a $C^\flat 7$ in m. 8 (Ex. 1-2). These chords, together with their propelling rhythm, give the song a crisp and rousing flavor.

In adapting this theme song for the show's overture—a common practice in theater music writing—Strayhorn dramatically changed the perspective: the

Ex. 1-2. *Fantastic Rhythm*, mm. 1–8

Overture is quite atypical for a curtain raiser.[5] The opening section remains entirely in minor—the sunny turn to major has disappeared, as well as the happy rhythmic drive. Melodically, the *Overture* may draw on *Fantastic Rhythm*, but Strayhorn has torn the theme to shreds, interspersed with full-bar rests for the entire band and reiterated, dissonant chords posing questions that are never resolved (Ex. 1-3). It sets an ominously dark atmosphere, more fitting for the title sequence of a Hitchcock motion picture than a Stunt Day show entitled *Fantastic Rhythm*. In the entire *Overture*—which further builds on two unidentified themes that in all likelihood recurred later in the show—this uneasiness remains, as minor harmonies and dissonant voicings prevail, accompanying false-happy melodic outbursts. It must have left the teenage audience at Westinghouse High baffled.

It is as if the composer with this *Overture* is distancing himself from some of the all too upbeat material in *Fantastic Rhythm*, prefacing the narrative with a commentary on what is to follow. Possibly, Strayhorn himself was not too convinced that life was "nothing but rhythm" as one of his own songs for the show had it—the worsening situation at home, caused by his father's excessive drinking, gave him sufficient reasons to dampen any optimism. In his later writing Strayhorn would incorporate his musical subtexts more subtly than he did in this minutes-long and quite sinister opener, placing angular lines against some of his most angelic themes, as if to counter their purity (e.g., in *Isfahan*).

At the heart of *Fantastic Rhythm* stand three ballads, two waltzes—*I'll Never Have to Dream Again* (untitled manuscript, REC) and *It Must Be a Dream* (lost)—and *My Little Brown Book* ("Brown Book," BSC). The latter appears to be the most successful effort, pairing fairly decent lyrics with some unconventional harmonic touches. From the original manuscript of *My Little Brown Book* only the verse survives (though incomplete), together with an earlier sketch for the chorus, melodically unrelated to the final version. Strayhorn would arrange the piece a number of times for the Ellington orchestra, which first recorded it on June 26, 1942, featuring singer Herb Jeffries in an otherwise unremarkable Strayhorn arrangement. The song remained in the book for singer Al Hibbler, who performed it many times in the 1940s, making *My Little Brown Book* the only work from *Fantastic Rhythm* to be truly saved from oblivion.

Ex. 1-3. *Overture*, mm. 1–9

The verse, never used for the later recordings of *My Little Brown Book* with the Ellington orchestra, adequately sets the mood:

> *I used to have your picture*
> *A ring that once was yours*
> *And other little fixtures*
> *That every girl adores to have*
> *To remind her of the boy she loves*
> *But since the day you went away*
> *And left me all alone*
> *The only thing that I can say you left to be my own is:*

> *My little brown book [etc.]*

Melodically, the gently flowing chorus of *My Little Brown Book* seems conventional, but with the bridge Strayhorn breaks away from the common AABA format. In most of the thirty-two-bar Tin Pan Alley songs of the period, the release generally provides a melodic (and often textual) climax with a denser rhythmic movement, usually over a string of secondary dominants. The bridges of Ellington's *It Don't Mean a Thing (If It Ain't Got That Swing)* (1932) or Gershwin's *I Got Rhythm* (1930) stand as two classical examples of this format. Strayhorn, however, lets the release of *My Little Brown Book* function as a couplet that stands between the repeated A-strains. Instead of building up to a climax, his bridge thus seems to step back as if in a temporary reflection, further articulated by the *parlando* melody as well as the modulation to a different key. Strayhorn uses this type of what one might call a modulatory release or mid-chorus modulation in other vocal works (*Let Nature Take Its Course* and *So This Is Love*) as well as in instrumental compositions such as *Chelsea Bridge*.

The lively theater song *Let Nature Take Its Course* is more upbeat in its music, despite the open cynicism about love in its lyrics.[6] The score shows Strayhorn closely following the text, with the most effective passages being the reiterated blue notes and sudden breaks at "Don't stop him!" which are followed by snappy piano commentaries (Ex. 1-4, mm. 25 and 28). An abrupt mid-chorus modulation toward the bridge provides sharp contrast—with a notable $D7^{(\sharp 9)}$ chord in the second bar. Similar to *My Little Brown Book*, this release withdraws in reflection when the singer—who has just advised her daughter simply to surrender to any male overtures—muses about the nature of the male sex: men, "they all have a one-track mind." Textually and musically, *Let Nature Take Its Course* is one of the more convincing songs of *Fantastic Rhythm*, and Strayhorn knew it: more than a decade after he composed the song, he still felt confident enough about it to integrate it into *Beggar's Holiday* (1946) and still later in *Rose-Colored Glasses* (1954).

To what extent *So This Is Love* and *A Penthouse on Shady Avenue* are related to

Ex. 1-4. *Let Nature Take Its Course*, mm. 21–28

Fantastic Rhythm is unknown, although especially the latter seems too topical to stand on its own. The general layout of the manuscripts, the handwriting as well as the musical and textual contents are consistent with the other known songs. The two works would have fitted in nicely. Strayhorn may have composed both songs for the show only to find that their complex chromatic melodies were over the heads of the amateur performers. As Hajdu reports (1996, 26), certain vocalists had such problems with their parts that Strayhorn had to simplify their songs. This may account for the atypical elementary diatonic melody of *I'll Never Have to Dream Again*.

The innocently romantic *A Penthouse on Shady Avenue*[7] expresses hopes for a better future:

> *I'm waiting for that distant day*
> *When I'll have dough enough to say:*
>
> *Let's build a little penthouse on Shady Avenue*
> *A cozy heaven-sent house especially for two*

This imagined prosperity will not only improve living conditions (Pittsburgh's Shady Avenue and some of its sidestreets were, then as now, elegant and expensive locations—especially from the perspective of Strayhorn's Homewood district) but it will also buy off any romantic competition:

> *I'll get rid of all your relations*
> *With hundred-dollar bills*

The central musical idea in *A Penthouse on Shady Avenue* is a chromatic line that moves down from the tonic to the flatted seventh, and up again to the major seventh (Ex. 1-5). Strayhorn underscores the flatted seventh with an A7 chord that is built on the raised fourth step and moves up to the dominant B♭, harmonic touches that lend the song its flavor. This formula (both the line and its harmonization) is repeated throughout the chorus, with alterations. The device may sound contrived, but the music flows naturally, though the song is not easy to sing.

With its inventive melodies and unconventional form, the lofty *So This Is Love*[8] is the most exquisite song written around the time of *Fantastic Rhythm*. A 1950s leadsheet (REC) by the Ellington orchestra's copyist Thomas Whaley suggests that Strayhorn later sought to copyright the work, possibly to interpolate it in one of his prospective theater shows.[9]

The lyrics of *So This Is Love* are more convincing than most of those for *Fantastic Rhythm*, though still marred by some dilettante rhymes:

> *I thought I knew the feeling when it started*
> *And when we parted I felt a pang;*

Ex. 1-5. A Penthouse on Shady Avenue, mm. 13–16

But this time something in me sang a plainsong
This is the same song it sang:

So this is love
This trembling of the heart
The pain when I'm apart from you
Well, I declare—I swear I would have never known

That this is love
The thrill in being near
The aching urge to hear you say:
"You'll be my own."

I thought that I had felt all emotion
I thought that I had seen ev'rything
It seemed my heart was through with devotion
But then you came along with spring

So this is love
This lightness in the head
The way my heart gets red
When someone mentions your name
Well I declare:
So this is love

If the failed attempts at inner rhyme ("plainsong" and "same song") and a number of flawed lines ("you came along with spring" and "the way my heart gets red") leave something to be desired, Strayhorn compensates for these shortcomings with his superb musical setting. His eloquent, through-composed score expresses the confusing emotions of newfound love, in which (Strayhorn's score suggests) uncertainty prevails. Where the lyric is affirmative, the music, both in its larger architecture as well as in its individual melodic and harmonic gestures, mainly asks questions. The harmony under the characteristic opening interval of the chorus (Ex. 1-6, m. 13), a dramatic major sixth drop against a half-diminished chord—on "love"—dwells on a secondary dominant B♭7 and its delay Fmi7$^{(♭5)}$,[10] postponing the tonic as if to counterbalance the all-too-positive "so this is love." This expert passage is but one of the many outstanding moments in this surprisingly full-grown song.

So This Is Love sums up the characteristics shared by most of Strayhorn's mid-1930s vocal compositions. A four-bar piano opening sets the tempo and mood, followed by a *parlando* verse over a barely moving chord progression that leads to the chorus in a new key. The verses tend to move in a rather limited harmonic

Ex. 1-6. *So This Is Love,* mm. 13–16

space that often modulates stepwise upward for the second half of the verse. Without exception, Strayhorn's choruses, loosely following the AABA format, are formally intricate and do not follow the patterns laid out in most popular songs. Unexpected mid-chorus modulations and irregular phrase lengths are coupled with the extensive use of chromatics (both melodic and harmonic). This gives these compositions their own unmistakable identity, yet at times threatens to make them somewhat artificial. The lyrics all describe pain, separation, and unrequited love, often observed from a cynical distance and garnished with a world-weary view of life.

Strayhorn's writing in the American popular song genre evidently drew on the idioms of the Broadway writers, including Cole Porter and George and Ira Gershwin. The Gershwins appear to have been looking over Strayhorn's shoulder while he wrote *Fantastic Rhythm*—the melody of the buoyant *Life Ain't Nothing but Rhythm* comes astonishingly close to *I Got Plenty of Nuthin'* from *Porgy and Bess* (premiered in the same year, and in all likelihood not known to Strayhorn at the time). On the other hand, the descending interval that gives *So This Is Love* its characteristic color is reminiscent of Cole Porter's *I Love You*, which, however, was written in 1943. Still, just out of Westinghouse High, Strayhorn set unlikely high standards: Porter graduated from Yale and the Gershwins attended City College of New York (then "the Harvard of the poor")—they were a generation older than Strayhorn too.

All these early vocal works culminated in Strayhorn's masterful song *Lush Life*. He reportedly started work around the time he was engaged with *Fantastic Rhythm*, though he apparently did not complete the song until about 1936 (Hajdu 1996, 34). Although *Lush Life* cannot be dated to 1936 with certainty, songs such as *So This Is Love* show that Strayhorn possessed the necessary musical and lyrical skills. It is also certain that Strayhorn finished *Lush Life* before he entered the Ellington organization late in 1938 (see Chapter 3).

Lush Life[11] stands as a mature and exceptionally well-wrought song or, rather, a Lied. Even the few flawed spots in the lyrics are this time counterbalanced with a number of exquisite textual finds. The lyric is set to a through-composed melodic line, underscored by chromatic harmonies that spiral around the work's main key of D♭. Strayhorn carefully matches the changing mood of his softly ironic and fatalistic poem with the music. First an ascending line underlies the cherished recollections of better times:

> *I used to visit all the very gay places*
> *Those come-what-may places*
> *Where one relaxes on the axis of the wheel of life*
> *To get the feel of life, from jazz and cocktails*

Then, the register changes and the chromatically altered chords voice the insight that now,

> *Life is lonely again*
> *And only last year*
> *Everything seemed so sure*

The text setting of *Lush Life* is profusely detailed and carefully follows the lyric with a free-flowing, irregular structure. For instance, the rhythmic flow picks up momentum to depict the motion of "the wheel of life," while the melody markedly drops out of key on the word *jazz*, suggesting a blue note (Ex. 1-7, mm.

Ex. 1-7. *Lush Life*, mm. 1–7

Ex. 1-8. Lush Life, mm. 29–32

3-6). Lush Life is full of this manner of secure word painting. Yet, as in some of the *Fantastic Rhythm* songs, the score at the same time seems to provide commentary, suggesting different readings of the poem. For instance, the absence of harmonic motion—established through the prolongation of the tonic in the opening bars, which oscillate between D^{b6} and C^{b7} (Ex. 1-7, mm. 1-3)—lends an extra dimension to the text: "the very gay places" and "those come-what-may places" may not be what they seem. One of the highlights is the unexpected F^b which underscores "sure" (Ex. 1-8, m. 32)—the harmonic shift places a towering question mark over the supposed sureness.

Decades later, after pianist-singer Nat "King" Cole recorded the song in 1949, *Lush Life* would become one of Strayhorn's best-known and most frequently performed songs.[12] Since then virtually every jazz performer of name has performed the song, including tenor saxophonist John Coltrane,[13] while countless pop singers (from Linda Ronstadt to Ricky Lee Jones) have it in their repertoires. A small musical setting, however, best suits the intimate atmosphere of *Lush Life*. Among the most rewarding renditions are those rare ones recorded by the pianist-composer himself, such as the January 14, 1964, version from Basin Street East.[14] Though his singing is slightly out of tune, Strayhorn delivers the song convincingly and with more irony than his contemporaries with their often too heavy torch-song readings.

Out of high school and still earning a living as a soda jerk and delivery boy for Pennfield Drugs, Strayhorn's hopes of pursuing a career in classical music seemed to assume a more definitive shape when he enrolled in a private conservatory in 1936. He studied piano and music theory: "I went to the Pittsburgh Musical Institute for about two months, and the man with whom I was studying, Charles Boyd was his name, was a very wonderful man" (Nicholson 1999, 201). Boyd's sudden death from a heart attack at the age of sixty-one stopped Strayhorn's studies cold: "he was so wonderful that I didn't think there was anyone else there who could teach me. So I didn't stay" (Strayhorn 1962). There may have been more to the preliminary end of Strayhorn's classical studies, as gradually his focus was shifting from classical music and theater songs to jazz.

With his friends Mickey Scrima and guitarist-arranger Bill Esch, he spent more and more time listening to jazz, to pianists such as Teddy Wilson and Art Tatum, as well as to the many "name bands," such as those of Fletcher Henderson, Jimmie Lunceford, and Duke Ellington. As Scrima observed: "What he realized, we talked about, was that everything he loved about classical music was there, in one form or another, in jazz—and here was a place he could apply himself" (Hajdu 1996, 32).

Yet even before that, Strayhorn had been fascinated by jazz. When the Ellington Orchestra, on its way up from the Southwest to New York, stopped in Pittsburgh for a one-week engagement in June 1934, he caught a show. Almost thirty years later, Strayhorn recalled what impressed him most—not the electrifying performance of the Ellingtonians in their sharp attire, but a *chord*: "[Ellington] played *The Rape of a Rhapsody*, that was the name of the number. Oh, it was wonderful, that's what started—that's what really got me. He had a chord which I have never discovered, I haven't heard it since, I couldn't figure this chord out. I went home after going to see this show at the Penn Theatre in Pittsburgh, and I couldn't figure out what was in that chord, it was just wonderful" (Worth 1962).

His growing fascination with jazz, combined with the racial segregation that virtually excluded African Americans from the concert stage, eventually changed the course of Strayhorn's career as a composer and as a pianist: from piano waltzes his focus shifted to music for jazz orchestra. The Moonlight Harbor Band—the twelve-piece outfit that accompanied the commercial edition of *Fantastic Rhythm*—was an obvious candidate for Strayhorn's first orchestral jazz works. Although his *Fantastic Rhythm* arrangements for this orchestra are lost, one manuscript remains that in all likelihood was written for the Moonlight Harbor Band: *Ugly Ducklin'* (REC), possibly for the orchestra's dance book.[15] It is not known whether Pittsburgh's jitterbugs ever got a chance to jive to *Ugly Ducklin'* (the manuscript is incomplete), but if they did, they would have heard a surprisingly hip and harmonically advanced piece, with a haunting, chromatic circling melody. To underscore the tune, Strayhorn turned to a harmonic concept that had been present in the verses of virtually all of his pre-1939 songs (including *Lush Life*): a two-chord ostinato in lieu of the expected traditional chord sequence (Ex. 1-9). The ostinato here consists of a tonic chord and its altered dominant over a two-bar bass line. Most striking is the anticipation of the dominant, which comes a beat and a half "too early": pure bebop language. Note how Strayhorn gives the bass the flatted fifth of the altered dominant (Ex. 1-9, m. 6, first beat), which causes the chord to sound as its tritone-related dominant. The ostinato stops only to yield to one-bar interjections at the end of each ten-bar phrase and finally to give way to a more regular bridge built on a rhythmically placed chord sequence: *Ugly Ducklin'* would have swung infectiously.

Even though the instrumentation called for a slightly smaller jazz outfit, *Ugly Ducklin'* could very well have been written for Duke Ellington and his Famous

Ex. 1-9. *Ugly Ducklin'*, mm. 5–8

Orchestra—a group Strayhorn was to join later. Indeed, after Strayhorn had written no fewer then three different arrangements of *Ugly Ducklin'* over the course of the 1940s—alternately titled *Don't Take My Love* (1939 and 1941, both REC) and *Jenny Lou Stomp* (1943, DEC [sketchbook 2:40–44], copyright registered in 1944 in the name of Billy Strayhorn)—Duke Ellington's orchestra finally recorded *Ugly Ducklin'* on August 7, 1951, under yet another title: *Smada* (the copyright now curiously registered in both Ellington's and Strayhorn's names).

It is remarkable how *Ugly Ducklin'* foreshadows certain techniques that played key roles in later developments in jazz. Apart from its bebop elements, such as the chromatic melody built on altered chord extensions and the anticipatory dominant, the work's harmonic ostinato points to the much later so-called modal jazz recordings of Miles Davis, Gil Evans, and John Coltrane, developed mainly in the late 1950s. However, much as modal jazz is often based on two-chord sequences (as under Coltrane's solo on *My Favorite Things*),[16] or ostinato bass lines (for instance in Miles Davis's *So What* and *Solea*),[17] the ostinati there appear on a much larger scale than in *Ugly Ducklin'*. Furthermore, though Strayhorn's harmonies do share the repeated harmonic patterns and the absence of frequent chord changes with modal jazz, his chromatic melodies are different: in modal jazz the melodic movement is loosely based on diatonic scales—the so-called modes, such as the Dorian or Phrygian mode that lent the style its name. In Dizzy Gillespie's *A Night in Tunisia* (circa 1942),[18] "grown out of his restless regimen of harmonic experimentation" (DeVeaux 1997, 418), one finds an earlier example of static harmony—similar to *Ugly Ducklin'*, *Tunisia* breaks into a more common harmonic pattern for the bridge. The harmonic ostinato remained an important tool in Strayhorn's musical language; examples can be found in the opening bars of *A Flower Is a Lovesome Thing*, *Passion Flower* (both 1939), *Flame Indigo* (1941), and *Le Sacre Supreme* (1944), among others.

In 1937, Strayhorn founded his own jazz combo, named the Mad Hatters. Modeled after the Benny Goodman trio, his group grew in the course of the year to five pieces (clarinet, vibraphone, piano, bass, and drums), just like its example.

The band played extensively in the larger Pittsburgh area, allowing Strayhorn to hone his skills as a jazz pianist. (Two test pressings made by the Mad Hatters in 1938 reveal that his piano style was largely modeled after Teddy Wilson's.) In addition, Strayhorn wrote all of the group's arrangements, mostly pop tunes and jazz standards, as well as a number of new compositions: the ballads *Something to Live For* and *Your Love Has Faded*, the more lively *If You Were There* and the rather uninspired *Strayhorn's Latest*.[19]

With the exquisite songs *Something to Live For* and *Your Love Has Faded* Strayhorn turned away from his previous vocal works whose baroque irregularity often posed insurmountable challenges to the abilities of the vocalist. Each ballad pairs a convincing and personal lyric to a singable yet original melody. It proves that Strayhorn had learned from his work on *Fantastic Rhythm*. His songwriting had matured while retaining all of its compositional characteristics, such as tritone-related substitute dominants, modified AABA structures (8-7-7-8 for *Something to Live For* and 4-4-8-4 for *Your Love Has Faded*), and chromatic melodies. He now dealt with his musical material more economically, and the quality of his lyrics especially shows dramatic improvement; neither song has a single flawed line. Together with *Lush Life* and *My Little Brown Book*, these Pittsburgh songs remained dear to Strayhorn, as he kept returning to them over the course of his career. *Your Love Has Faded* remained the lesser known of the two (Ivie Anderson's rendition, recorded in 1939, is arguably the best). Ella Fitzgerald recorded a captivating version of *Something to Live For* in 1965, in a poignant arrangement by its composer.

The relative success of *Fantastic Rhythm* and the respect Strayhorn earned from his peers with his piano playing and song writing did not change his position as an outsider. "He had a hard time making friends," Mickey Scrima recalled (Hajdu 1996, 18). His classmates characterized Strayhorn as "very unusual," someone who was a "genius" and "didn't socialize much" (ibid.). Nicknamed "Dictionary" for his "grand vocabulary," some even got so far as to call him a "sissy" (ibid.). Strayhorn must have known that with his talents and ambitions he was a social misfit, and his lyrics reflected this: *Something to Live For* "embodies the whole of his youthful frustration" (ibid.).

After the Mad Hatters folded in the summer of 1938, Strayhorn found new employment with various regional big bands: the Buddy Malone Orchestra, Honey Boy Minor and His Buzzing Bees, the Bill Ludwig Orchestra, and the Rex Edwards Orchestra (Hajdu 1996, 44). The latter, a dance band formed by nineteen-year-old drummer Anthony Edward D'Emilio in mid-1938, was a mixed-race band, unprecedented for the Pittsburgh area. Strayhorn worked as an arranger for all these outfits, yet for the Rex Edwards Orchestra he took on an even greater responsibility: in addition to filling the piano chair he also led the group's rehearsals. Later understating his output (and completely ignoring *Fantastic Rhythm*), Strayhorn told Leonard Feather (1943, 13) that he "had only written ten arrangements in his life [before December 1938], and those for an obscure rehearsing band." Among the tunes he arranged for these outfits were the Sam Coslow and Frederick Hollander song *True Confession* (REC), popularized in 1938 by Louis Armstrong and His Orchestra, his own *Something to Live For* (untitled manuscript, REC), and a driving version of Irving Berlin's *Remember* (REC),[20] which became the signature theme for the Rex Edwards Orchestra.

Strayhorn's adolescent years in Pittsburgh had laid the groundwork for his future career, both musically and personally. Having assiduously explored a variety of musical genres—classical music and Broadway-style theater music—he had abandoned his initial ambitions and had turned to a musical field that was socially acceptable for a young black pianist-composer: jazz. Out of the confrontation between his sensitive, intelligent personality and his often harsh surroundings Strayhorn had created a personal musical style in which he sought and found refuge. His music at the same time reflected beauty and conflict, and allowed for multiple readings. But he needed a larger canvas than the Pittsburgh musical scene could provide: Strayhorn was ready for a career move. The arrival of Duke Ellington with his Famous Orchestra in Pittsburgh, early December 1938, created an unexpected opportunity, one that Strayhorn was to grasp with both hands.

Chapter Two

The Renaissance of Arranging: First Works for and with Duke Ellington

BILLY STRAYHORN'S career prospects improved unexpectedly and dramatically when he met Duke Ellington.[1] Their first meeting took place on December 2, 1938, at the Stanley Theatre in downtown Pittsburgh, where the Ellington orchestra had settled for a week-long engagement. "I was more or less forced by my friends to go and see [Duke Ellington], in Pittsburgh," Strayhorn said. "I was a soda jerk and a delivery boy in a drug store. [I had written some things] but they were unheard, they were just heard by the customers of the drug store and they got after me to have someone else hear them. So he was the one" (Nicholson 1999, 201). As Strayhorn recollected, Ellington—impressed by the youngster's compositions—not only decided to have Strayhorn as his lyricist but gave him an assignment on the spot: "He had an idea for a lyric. He said: 'You go home and write a lyric for this,' and I did" (Strayhorn 1962).[2] Strayhorn modestly neglected to mention that he was also asked to write *music* for his future employer. According to Leonard Feather, the most candid and reliable contemporary source on Strayhorn's early work for the Ellington organization, Strayhorn

> ran over a few original tunes at the piano [at his first meeting with Ellington]. He couldn't leave them with Duke as they had never been written down. Duke was sufficiently impressed to invite Strayhorn to arrange one of them for the band. "I was so thrilled" he recalls, "I didn't know what to say. Duke was very nice to me and let me stay in the theatre all next day working on the number." (Feather 1943, 13)

There is no knowing which piece or pieces Strayhorn adapted for Ellington's orchestra, but two manuscript scores of original songs, *Something to Live For* (untitled, REC), incomplete, and *Lonely Again* (REC)—Strayhorn's original title

As soon as he arrived in New York (February 1939) to work with Duke Ellington, Strayhorn came into his own. Encouraged by Ellington, he blossomed as a composer, arranger, and pianist. Strayhorn now no longer hid his homosexuality, and soon shared dwellings with Aaron Bridgers.
(*Courtesy Rutgers Institute of Jazz Studies*)

for *Lush Life*—seem very likely candidates.³ Indeed, these manuscripts, found by the author in a stack of scores (REC) that all date back to 1938, bear all the traits typical of his 1938 pre-Ellington works, such as the six-stave layout found on *Remember*, the score for the Rex Edwards orchestra. Yet they now refer to Ellingtonians Johnny Hodges and Juan Tizol.⁴ Moreover, after poring over Ellington's scores in April and May, 1939, Strayhorn would swiftly adopt the more convenient four-staff short-score format his employer used, as exemplified by a sketchbook with music written between March and the end of June 1939 (sketchbook 3, DEC).⁵

Apparently within a day of seeing the Ellington orchestra perform live on stage, Strayhorn arranged two of his original works from Pittsburgh in a way that would have fitted the orchestra perfectly. In an almost instantaneous assimilation of Ellington's writing style, he scored both arrangements for specific voices in the orchestra, naming personnel (Bigard, Hodges, Tizol) on the manuscripts, and designing cross-section passages that were comparable to Ellington's, such as a four-part background for two altos, valve trombone, and baritone in *Lonely Again*. Furthermore, he created a variety of orchestral sonorities, from chalumeau-register clarinet over three-part trombones to lyrical trumpet over four-part reeds, and from densely scored six-part brass tutti passages to unison saxophone counterpoint. In keeping with his earlier works, Strayhorn closely followed the expressive force of the lyrics—for instance, matching "romance is mush, stifling those who strive" with a heightening of dissonance in the brass backgrounds.

Apparently, for Strayhorn, who had only "heard the band a few times on records and on the air" (Ulanov 1946, 221) as well as in a few concert performances, it was a small step from scoring for outfits like the Moonlight Harbor Band or the Rex Edwards Orchestra to writing for the Duke Ellington Orchestra. Even though their musical backgrounds were quite different, Ellington and Strayhorn shared a fascination for orchestral sonority, harmonic richness, and formal balance. In Strayhorn's words: "I'm sure the fact that we're both looking for a certain character, a certain way of presenting a composition, makes us write to the whole, towards the same feeling" (Coss 1962, 23). Still, their ways of expressing this "same feeling" differed greatly. While the scores for *Lonely Again* and *Something to Live For* may have used some trademark Ellingtonian devices—most notably cross-section voiced backgrounds and writing for individual musicians—they were unquestionably written by another composer whose personal voice resounded throughout. "[We] actually write very differently," Strayhorn explained; "he uses different approaches—the way he voices the brass section, the saxophone section. He does things differently than I do" (Coss 1962, 23). Indeed, Strayhorn's personal approach becomes apparent in the quartal trumpet chords in his arrangement of *Something to Live For*, a modernist intervallic structure (all chord tones are a perfect fourth apart instead of successive thirds) that he continued to use in the early forties.

In February 1939, a month after Strayhorn had joined the organization, Ellington took the first of his new associate's scores into the recording studio for a date with Johnny Hodges and His Orchestra. From the mid-1930s on, Ellington had occasionally offered his key musicians the opportunity to record under their own names, with smaller units drawn from the big band. The February 27 sessions for Vocalion were in that vein, featuring a group of seven Ellingtonians and additional vocalist Jean Eldridge. As with most of these so-called small-band sessions, the material consisted of popular tunes and blues-based originals written either by Ellington or by one of the soloists. The outfit cut four sides: two vocal works, *Like a Ship in the Night* and *Mississippi Dreamboat*, and two instrumentals, *Swinging on the Campus* and *Dooji Wooji*. Strayhorn was involved with *Mississippi Dreamboat*, which had some Ellington scoring as well, and *Swinging on the Campus*.[6] Both arrangements offered little more than some orchestral backgrounds and an occasional tutti passage, as was typical for these small-band recordings. It was the recognizable voices of the various soloists—Barney Bigard, Johnny Hodges, Cootie Williams, Rex Stewart, Lawrence Brown, Juan Tizol, and later Ben Webster and Ray Nance—not the orchestrations, that marked the small bands as an identifiable part of the Ellington realm. Consequently, it is impossible to detect Strayhorn's voice in these sides: the scoring is unobtrusively functional. Still, as Feather reported (1943, 13), Strayhorn's scores were successful: "[after] the first couple of sessions, [he] acquired a little more confidence....and before long he was in full charge of the writing for these small-band dates, writing more of the music than Duke himself."

A month later Ellington was back in the recording studio. First, Rex Stewart & His Fifty-Second Street Stompers recorded three sides for Vocalion and next the full band did four numbers for Brunswick. Though it went by unnoticed, on this March 20 session the full band recorded the first true, albeit unofficial, Ellington-Strayhorn collaboration: *Pussy Willow*. With its unison saxophone theme against brass answers, *Pussy Willow* could easily pass for an Ellington composition, although for a while he had not been using this type of antiphonal section writing usually associated with the swing arrangements played by Fletcher Henderson's orchestra.[7] Nevertheless, the first eight-bar riff theme of *Pussy Willow* stemmed from an untitled sketch Strayhorn drafted before or shortly after his arrival in New York, the handwriting dates this manuscript to no later than March 1939. The Henderson style still enjoyed Strayhorn's avid attention, as reportedly he had fashioned another new composition along similar lines: *Take the "A" Train* (Hajdu 1996, 55–56).[8] Ellington must have seen the potential of Strayhorn's partially finished riff theme and fleshed it out, though no other manuscripts for *Pussy Willow* survive.

The next day the band recorded the first work jointly credited to Ellington and Strayhorn, *Something to Live For*, which in truth was Strayhorn's Pittsburgh original in an Ellington arrangement.[9] Thus, at two consecutive recording sessions two types of inaccuracies slipped into the composer credits—inaccuracies that would recur in various forms in a large part of the credits concerning the Ellington-Strayhorn collaboration. Strayhorn's involvement with Ellington originals would customarily be left uncredited, as was the case with *Pussy Willow*, while both composers would often share credits where only one of them was the actual author, as had happened with *Something to Live For*. It should be noted that none of this was out of the ordinary in the music industry, where copyrights often accrued to whoever happened to be in charge of filing them. In combination with the omission of arranger's credits, customary to the present day, this practice rendered many of Strayhorn's contributions to the Ellington oeuvre invisible.

Before he went abroad with his entourage on their second transatlantic tour—from March 23 till May 10, 1939—he "parked [Strayhorn] in the house [on 409 Edgecombe Avenue, New York]" (Nicholson 1999, 201), which Ellington shared with his family. "This is Billy Strayhorn," Ellington matter-of-factly told his sister Ruth, "he's going to stay with us" (Nicholson 1999, 201). During this period Strayhorn (and Ellington's son, Mercer) had the opportunity to pore over Ellington's scores to improve his understanding of Ellington's orchestration and composition techniques. "So he looked at my things and decided, I suppose, that it all looked very simple, so when I came back he said, 'I've been looking at your things and I think I could do some of that.' I said, 'Yeah, all right, have a shot,'" Ellington recalled (Nicholson 1999, 209). The "things" Strayhorn must have been looking at ranged from Ellington's everyday idiosyncratic arrangements to some of the highlights in the pre-1939 period. The repository of the Duke Ellington Collection stores dozens of carefully written Ellington scores, including *Reminiscing in Tempo, Caravan, In a Sentimental Mood, Solitude,* and *Echoes of Harlem*, which Strayhorn may have studied, provided Ellington kept them in his apartment at the time.

This was an invaluable learning opportunity, and it must have deepened Strayhorn's understanding of how Ellington wrote for his orchestra (as his first arrangements for the orchestra had shown, he had already grasped some of this aurally). The most important elements Strayhorn absorbed during this period were Ellington's trademark writing for individual musicians, as well as his concept of "cross-section voicing," creating uncommon blends of instruments. Throughout his career, Strayhorn would apply these techniques in his own compositions, though in a personalized way. Nevertheless, it is clear that he derived these important concepts from Ellington's work, and, consequently, they stand as the most important influence of Ellington on Strayhorn.[10]

Apparently Strayhorn drew inspiration from his study of Ellingtonia for original compositions as well: "I stayed at home and wrote a few things like *Day Dream*" (Coss 1962, 22).[11] That same spring he also composed *Passion Flower* (incomplete, DEC), the first of a string of emotionally involved ballads he would write for altoist Johnny Hodges. Harmonically and melodically, both compositions are consistent with Strayhorn's earlier Pittsburgh works, and they are a far cry from the Ellington repertoire.

The use of chromaticism in Strayhorn's earlier work gained in sophistication and force in his gorgeous *Passion Flower*. Strayhorn abandoned the elaborate web of unexpected chords and twirling lines that crowded pieces such as *So This Is Love*, to adhere to a leaner, more conceptual approach: *Passion Flower* stands out by the economic use of musical material. Thus, the parallel moving whole-tone chords, F#9$^{(\flat5)}$ and F9$^{(\flat5)}$, that blur the original key of G, also give birth to the melody, which is built on the flatted fifths that determine the flavor of these chords (Ex. 2-1—the accompaniment is drawn from Strayhorn's 1941 small-band score).[12]

Simultaneously, a single rhythmic cell |♩♩ ♫♩♩.|, which roots in the one-bar harmonic rhythm, governs the architecture of the two eight-bar phrases. These phrases move in limited melodic spaces, while their keys are an augmented fourth apart.

The harmonization of these two phrases consists of a single effective idea: a chromatic descending line of altered dominants, substituted in the bridge by an incidental tritone-related chord. The bridge follows the rhythmic and harmonic design of the opening bars, moving to a new altered chord tone on every second eighth of the last beat, mirroring the initial descending gesture in contrary motion (Ex. 2-2).

The key plan of *Passion Flower*—at a tritone, or two minor thirds, distance—follows a pattern already existent in some of Strayhorn's earlier compositions, where harmonic planes tend to be one or more minor third intervals apart. Ernö Lendvai (1971) describes in detail how Béla Bartók tends to move the tonal centers in his works along an axis of minor third intervals, starting on the tonic, sub-

Ex. 2-1. *Passion Flower*, mm. 1–16

dominant, or dominant. Lendvai calls this the axis system. This axis system builds on the notion that chords or tonalities that are one or more consecutive minor thirds apart (their roots constitute a diminished-seventh chord) share the same pivotal diminished chord on the seventh scale degree. This diminished chord is the upper structure of the altered dominant and thus serves as the pivot between the four tonal centers reached along each axis. Hence, moving from C along the tonic axis, one can smoothly modulate to the tonally foreign keys of $E^\flat$, $G^\flat$ or $B^{\flat\flat}$, by means of different enharmonic spellings of the diminished seventh pivot B-D-F-$A^\flat$. Strayhorn repeatedly makes use of Lendvai's "axis theory." Lendvai's axis system functions as an organizing principle of tonal centers, and Strayhorn was aware of its musical ramifications, especially with respect to the enharmonic possibilities of dominants. Thus, in *Lush Life*, the altered $A^\flat 7$ (Ex. 1-8, m. 31, beat 4) becomes an altered $C^\flat 7$ (its root a minor third higher), which negotiates the transition to $F^\flat$, in turn a minor third above the original $D^\flat$. The key plans of *So This Is Love* and *Passion Flower* (both center around the keys of G and $D^\flat$, two minor thirds apart) similarly draw on the implications of the axis system.

The chromatic harmonies and the extensive use of altered chord tones for the melody give *Passion Flower* a floating, tonally detached character. Especially the whole-tone, autonomous dominant chords point up Strayhorn's admiration for the French "impressionist" composer Claude Debussy (1862–1918), who was one of the first composers to free chords from their functional-harmonic chains. Though it would take a couple of years before *Passion Flower* would find its place in the repertory of the Ellington orchestra (the first studio recordings stem from 1945), the composition became one of the major showcases for Johnny Hodges, who played it in dozens of unmatched, resplendent renditions.

Ex. 2-2. *Passion Flower*, mm. 17–24

Before October 1939, Strayhorn fashioned another ballad for Hodges along similar harmonic and melodic lines: *A Flower Is a Lovesome Thing* (first performed at an unissued air check on February 13, 1941). Like *Passion Flower*, the work makes extensive use of whole-tone chords in static harmonic fields rather than relying on functional-harmonic chord progressions (the first four bars are based on one chord only: $B9^{(\flat 5)}$).

The introspective *Day Dream* is less radical in its harmonic and melodic design, although chromatic chord relations again play an important role. The bridge, fashioned around a sequence, is harmonically advanced for its time, based on a device that would become central in postwar bebop compositions: the use of suspended ii-V chord progressions. The first bar of the sequence starts with a $B^{\flat maj7}$, the flat supertonic for the target chord A^{maj7} in the next bar (Ex. 2-3). On beat three this flat supertonic chord alters to the supertonic proper, which now functions as the delay for the dominant E7, for A. Turning this pattern into a sequence, Strayhorn again liberates the music from its tonal gravity. Years later Sonny Rollins used the same sequence in the B and D strains of his 1954 *Airegin*; even the melodic movement is virtually the same.[13] Although forward looking, this progression was not entirely new in American music. George Gershwin, for one, had harmonized a five-bar passage in *Bess, Oh Where's My Bess*, from his 1936 opera *Porgy and Bess*, along similar lines: in measures 33–39 of the song, Gershwin chromatically descends from $A^\flat$ to $G^\flat$ with the same suspended ii-V progression. This short passage, however, is embedded in a polyphonic texture and therefore does not stand out as clearly as in *Day Dream*. It was Miles Davis's recording of songs from *Porgy and Bess* (1958) that first gave jazz musicians widespread exposure to Gershwin's use of the sequence.[14]

Shortly after the Ellingtonians returned to the United States, Strayhorn earned stewardship over yet another branch of the Ellington enterprise, the vocal arrangements. "When he came back [from Europe], the band went to the Ritz Carlton Roof in Boston. Ivie Anderson [the orchestra's vocalist]...asked me to do some new material for her," Strayhorn said (Coss 1962, 22). Among the pieces she asked him to arrange was *The Jumpin' Jive* (untitled, sketchbook 3:37–41, DEC). A popular Cab Calloway jump number, *The Jumpin' Jive* was not an obvious choice for the Ellington band. The delivery of this rhythm-and-blues novelty

Ex. 2-3. *Day Dream*, mm. 17–20

depended largely on Calloway's showmanship and stage personality, while the role of his fifteen-piece band consisted mostly of hollering answers to the leader's jive-talk lyrics. The piece turned out to be another test case for Strayhorn's arranging skills, and for his adaptive capacities in particular: *The Jumpin' Jive* had to be *Ellingtonized*. Building choruses around interlocking riffs and massive six-part brass chords with pointed unison saxophone lines, Strayhorn turned *The Jumpin' Jive*—untypical fare for the orchestra—into genuine Ellingtonia. "It seemed to click," Feather writes (1943, 13), "and from then on [Strayhorn] took care of most of the vocal and pop song assignments."

Strayhorn's newly acquired task as arranger of non-Ellington material was important, yet easily overlooked. Hit songs came and went, and since an important part of his organization's income derived from the more commercial dance dates, Ellington needed new arrangements constantly. Every now and then he would try to cash in on a successful pop song by recording it, but most of the aesthetically rather limited material was intended for dance halls only.[15] Among the many unrecorded titles Strayhorn arranged in his first year with the orchestra were pieces like *Moon Love* (DEC), adapted from the second movement of Tchaikovsky's Fifth Symphony by Mack David and Andre Kostelanetz; *The Breeze and I* ("Breeze + me," BSC), a song by Al Stillman and Ernesto Lecuona that was popularized by Jimmy Dorsey's band; the Glenn Miller hit *I'm Stepping Out with a Memory Tonight* ("Stepping Out," sketchbook 1:8–10, REC), and Jack Yellen and Sammy Fain's *Good Night, My Beautiful* (untitled, sketchbook 3:13–15, DEC).

In the second half of 1939, more and more Strayhorn small-band arrangements and an occasional original appeared on record.[16] Most of these works were consistent with the earlier arrangements, although Strayhorn started to gravitate toward more elaborately orchestrated scores. The scores for *Blues a-Poppin', Skunk Hollow Blues*, or *I Know What You Know (I Know What You Do)*, recorded by groups led by Hodges and Cootie Williams, went a little further than the standard whole and half-note ensemble backgrounds used previously. Strayhorn scored each chorus differently, varying the orchestral backgrounds and alternating rhythmic ensemble passages with contrapuntal lines. The one work that stands out among these small-band recordings is *Your Love Has Faded*, an original Strayhorn had composed for his Pittsburgh jazz trio The Mad Hatters, premiered on record by Johnny Hodges and His Orchestra. The first Strayhorn ballad to be recorded by Hodges, *Your Love Has Faded* marked the birth of a composer-performer team that in later years arguably produced some of the most sophisticated ballads in jazz history. The alto features *Isfahan, Pretty Girl, Ballad for Very Tired and Very Sad Lotus Eaters, Rod La Roque*, and the final, wrenching *Blood Count* were all inspired by and written for Hodges's inimitable alto sound, whose plaintive readings of Strayhorn's themes opened up an intense emotional depth.

Two days after the session with Hodges, Ellington recorded *Your Love Has Faded* with the full orchestra as well. Half of the score, the instrumental chorus, was scored by Ellington while the remainder was by Strayhorn, who did the vocal chorus. It was one of the last times ever Ellington scored one of his associate's originals—with the exception of an instrumental chorus of *Strange Feeling* (1944) and eight bars of *Manhattan Murals* (the 1948 *Take the "A" Train* reworking). Now that Strayhorn was responsible for the vocal scores, Ellington tended to stick to instrumental choruses only, leaving the vocal sections to his collaborator. This instrumental-vocal division of work occurred more often in the next two years,[17] and was consistent with Ellington's own cut-and-paste composition technique, in which he combined blocks of music into an organic whole. Thus the renowned, and later mythologized, teaming up of Ellington and Strayhorn had become a reality. Despite romanticized accounts that both composers were "capable of interacting so seamlessly...that even the two of them had trouble pinpointing where one man's contribution ended and the other's began" (Palmer, 1967), this teaming up was taking place exactly at the seams of the collaborative works.

The full-band arrangement of *Your Love Has Faded* is not as convincing as the small-band version. Ellington's instrumental chorus seems incongruously brassy for the intimate composition, while Strayhorn's own background scoring for the vocal chorus, a dressed-up version of the effective earlier small-band score, does not employ the orchestra to its full sonic powers: Strayhorn seems to be struggling in his attempt to use the large ensemble for his more intimate work. In true Ellingtonian fashion, the coda was appended later, taken from an earlier Strayhorn score for *Your Love Has Faded*. This coda displays an important characteristic found in numerous Strayhorn scores, often in modulatory sections,

Ex. 2-4. *Your Love Has Faded*, mm. 53–58

introductions, or codas: the handing down of a melodic kernel through various voices of the orchestra (Ex. 2-4). As simple and straightforward the imitation of the song's last phrase may be here, a more complex imitation of thematic material would become an essential building block in the sophisticated textures of Strayhorn's later works, where fragments of phrases often enter on new scale steps or unexpected beats.

The October 16 sessions also featured the last Strayhorn originals the full Ellington Orchestra was to record for the next fourteen months: *I'm Checking Out, Goom-Bye* (first recorded as *Barney Goin' Easy*); *Killin' Myself*, a somewhat forgettable Strayhorn original in which the author exchanged some hip spoken lines with Ivie Anderson; and *Grievin'*. As with the earlier *A Lonely Co-Ed*, recorded June 1939, Strayhorn shared credits for *Grievin'* with Ellington, who wrote the larger part of the arrangement. *Killin' Myself* remained uncopyrighted during his life.

On November 22, Barney Bigard and His Orchestra recorded two new works, *Minuet in Blues* and *Lost in Two Flats*, written especially for this particular group. In the faux-classical *Minuet in Blues*, with some tongue-in-cheek etude-like piano playing by the composer, Strayhorn furnished the break preceding the trumpet solo with another scoring technique that was to become part of his orchestral palette: the thickening of a repeated melodic line by means of added voices.

Around this time, Strayhorn had moved out of the Ellington quarters to share a basement apartment with Aaron Bridgers. Strayhorn had met Bridgers in the fall of 1939, after Mercer Ellington introduced them to each other. Frank and open about their relationship, in a time when most homosexual women and men were forced to be secretive about their sexual orientation, the two would live together until Bridgers left for France in 1947.

By February 1940, almost exactly a year after Strayhorn's first work with the Ellington organization, some important changes had taken place in the orchestra, changes that ushered in one of its most rewarding periods, in both economic and artistic terms. In October of the preceding year, Ellington had hired bassist Jimmie Blanton, who virtually overnight redefined the role of the double bass in jazz. Four months later tenor saxophonist Ben Webster joined the orchestra, expanding the reeds to five voices. Their contributions turned out be so significant that the 1940–41 Ellington band became known as the Blanton-Webster band. In addition to hiring new personnel, Ellington had recently freed himself from the management of Irving Mills and had landed a new contract with the prestigious record label Victor, whose studios and engineers were superbly equipped to record the band. The immense popularity of "swing" music, even though Ellington only partially catered to the swing-crazed audience, boosted record sales and performance opportunities. For the first time in his career working with a full-time assistant who was in charge of all the pop arrangements, he could now devote all his energy to writing originals. In the first three months of

1940 the orchestra recorded widely acclaimed Ellington works, such as *Jack the Bear* ("Take It Away," DEC), *Harlem Air Shaft* ("Once Over Lightly," DEC), *Concerto for Cootie* (DEC), *Ko-Ko* (DEC), and *Cotton Tail* (DEC—of the last three DEC houses only parts).[18]

Strayhorn's later accounts of his contributions to this period of unequaled productivity in the band's history at times contradict the manuscripts that have survived. He named *Jack the Bear* as one of the works he fleshed out (Strayhorn 1962), but the entire manuscript ("Take It Away," DEC) is in Ellington's hand. The order of the musical events on the manuscript does not exactly match the final recording, but this is fully in keeping with Ellington's working methods and does not necessarily bespeak the hand of another party. Moreover, the piece sounds thoroughly Ellingtonian. However, Strayhorn's vivid description of a tune that he reworked by infusing solo spots for Blanton could point to one of the other bass features of that period, but no written evidence has survived.[19]

Another work that does raise questions about Strayhorn's co-authorship is *Concerto for Cootie*, trumpeter Cootie Williams's last glorious recording with the orchestra before he left in November 1940 to join Benny Goodman. Especially the eight-bar introduction, for which the original score is lost, is so full of Strayhornisms that it must be the work of Ellington's protégé.[20] The through-imitation of Williams's opening phrase (rhythmically displaced in the penultimate bar), the extreme chromatic voice leading, and the tonal rootlessness that causes the music to float all point in the direction of Strayhorn. In his discussion of the work, Hodeir (1956, 286) notes that the introduction of *Concerto for Cootie* is harmonically unrelated to the rest of the work: "The harmonic language of *Concerto for Cootie* is, on the whole, extremely simple. *Apart from the introduction*, the general climate of the piece is...resolutely consonant" (italics added).

Strayhorn continued to arrange pop tunes and standards, such as *Day In, Day Out*, for which he wrote an extensive arrangement with a notable modulation, and the rather run-of-the-mill *My Last Good-Bye* (both recorded January 9, 1940). He also tried his hand at the 1939 Erskine Hawkins hit tune, *Tuxedo Junction*, a riff theme soon to be popularized by Glenn Miller's orchestra. Not finishing the arrangement, Strayhorn used his favorite perfect fourth intervals to voice the upper structures of the six-part brass chords and spiced them up with some chromatic inner voice leading (Ex. 2-5).

The unfinished manuscript got an unexpected afterlife when Ellington appended it to an incomplete composition for which he had scored two contrasting sections with a total of twenty-eight bars. Ellington worked around *Tuxedo Junction*'s recognizable melody by simply omitting the theme Strayhorn had assigned to the saxophones. He replaced the resulting open spots with ad-lib fills, which were played somewhat uncomfortably by baritone saxophonist Harry Carney. Furnishing a solution to the abrupt key change, from his composition in F to Strayhorn's B♭ arrangement, Ellington played a connecting piano phrase before the transition. More minor adaptations occurred as the brass section slightly altered the rhythmic phrasing of its chords, playing most notes staccato. In need of more material, Ellington added two twelve-bar blues solo choruses, one for bassist Blanton and one for tenorist Webster, after which he simply recapitulated the three preceding sections in reversed order. The resulting work, which he titled *Sepia Panorama*, would be the orchestra's radio theme for the next six months until a full Strayhorn original, *Take the "A" Train*, replaced it in January 1941.

Sepia Panorama stands as a textbook example of Ellington's often streetwise composition techniques, infusing nonrelated material by another composer (Hawkins et al.), filling up the holes with blues choruses, and restating the same material in a different order. Moreover, the work illustrates how certain elements of Strayhorn's sound (in this case, quartal chords) had started to permeate that of his employer. In many Ellington compositions, such as *Harlem Air Shaft*, *Jack the Bear*, *Bojangles*, and *Sepia Panorama*, a kaleidoscopic contrast formed the structuring principle, and this made it fully acceptable to insert blocks of music from different origins. Feather (1943, 14) noted that "often [Strayhorn] would split a job with Duke, fill in eight bars here and voice a chorus there. Part of *Sepia Panorama*, the band's 1941 [actually 1940] radio theme was his." The splice work didn't go by unnoticed: Schuller (1989, 130) felt that *Sepia Panorama* "seems frag-

Ex. 2-5. *Tuxedo Junction*, mm. 1–8

mented in all its conflicting juxtapositions. Nothing quite leads logically to anything else."[21]

In the second half of 1940 the orchestra performed and recorded more and more Strayhorn arrangements. Most of these scores were effective but uneventful, such as the happily swinging *The Five O'Clock Whistle*, or *There Shall Be No Night*, written in the style of the sweet dance bands. Although these arrangements blended in unobtrusively with the Ellington repertoire, they all bore Strayhorn's musical imprint, most notably in their modulations and transitions. In *There Shall Be No Night*, for instance, Webster's last strain of the instrumental chorus flows smoothly into the transitional phrase, while in the penultimate bar Strayhorn underscored singer Herb Jeffries's sustained $E^\flat$ with two tonally foreign chords built upon (again) altered upper-chromatic chords, Emi7 and E7, before resolving to the tonic proper $E^\flat 6$.

The arrangement of *Chloë* (*Song of the Swamp*), atypically (but justly) credited to Strayhorn on the label of the original Victor issue, must have puzzled Ellington connoisseurs at the time. On first hearing, the piece sounds like a genuine Ellington arrangement, with Joe Nanton's "jungle style" talking trombone and Blanton's bass breaks mirroring the earlier *Jack the Bear*. On the microlevel, the clues may not have been apparent, but to the careful listener the overall structure of the score hints at its author: the smooth and almost unnoticeable modulation from F to $D^\flat$ by means of an imitated melody fragment, followed by another caesura-less modulation to $B^\flat$ after the tenor solo, and the short but integrated coda that rounded out the piece, were not Ellingtonian. Ellington would typically have written brisker modulations to forge sharper contrasts between the arrangement's segments, favoring marked two- or four-bar modulations over Strayhorn's through-composed key changes. Furthermore, rather than using thematic material in the modulation, the ever-resourceful Ellington would have come up with a new idea.

While Ellington preserved the new highlights of his oeuvre in shellac, Strayhorn's rapidly growing book of original scores for the full orchestra remained virtually untouched. Among these scores were the big band arrangements of *Day Dream* (BSC) and *My Little Brown Book* ("L.B.B.," DEC) as well as new originals such as *Sweet Duke* (DEC) and a piano feature named *Tonk* (BSC), all written between February 13, 1940, when Webster joined, and November 6, 1940, when Cootie Williams left. Among these unrecorded works, the eccentric *Tonk* is the most remarkable.[22] Conceived as a miniature "piano concerto," in all likelihood to be performed by Ellington, it joined a series of compositions in which the leader himself highlighted one specific soloist for an entire three-minute composition.[23] Ellington had first used this format in 1936, when he wrote *Echoes of Harlem* for Cootie Williams and *Clarinet Lament* for Barney Bigard. Analogous to the classical concerto, these works center around a single soloist accompanied by the orchestra, but their structure largely deviates from their European counterparts and was mainly built on idiomatic jazz formats.

Tonk uses elements from the Harlem stride piano idiom in which Ellington excelled, but Strayhorn modified and distorted this style into something wholly modernistic, evocative of the works of French piano composers Erik Satie and Francis Poulenc. True to the stride idiom, the left hand plays the characteristic leaping bass with the expected tonic chord on two and dominant chord on four, but Strayhorn altered the chords to G6$^{(\flat 5)}$ and D7$^{(\sharp 9)}$ (Ex. 2-6). Over these repeated chords hovers an angular melody that seems tonally disconnected, as it circles around the dissonant minor third and minor thirteenth of the scale. *Tonk*'s eight-bar theme travels through a variety of keys, orchestrations, and settings (Strayhorn even assigns a flute part to baritone saxophonist Harry Carney) and is framed with orchestral answers, through-imitated modulatory sections, and a tongue-in-cheek grandiose coda that calls for two short piano cadenzas.

If most of Strayhorn's arrangements and compositions for the Ellington orchestra so far could have been mistaken for Ellington imitations, which on closer inspection they weren't, then *Tonk* could have corrected such impressions instantaneously. Ironically, for a work evidently designed to showcase the orchestra's piano player, nothing in *Tonk* is Ellingtonian, as it displays a different and brighter orchestral sound and larger structural arches. To a certain extent—although it was much shorter—*Tonk* evokes the piano works of George Gershwin more than any piece associated with Ellington, with one important difference: Gershwin worked supposed jazz elements into an otherwise symphonic style, while Strayhorn wrote for a genuine jazz orchestra. According to Jablonski (1987, x), "Gershwin's Americanisms are rooted in popular song and dance, the music of the lyric theater, spiced with superficial borrowings from jazz: rhythmic syncopations, 'blue' notes and indigo harmonies." Gershwin himself asserted that "some people go so far as to affix the jazz label to my *Concerto in F* [composed in 1925], in which I have attempted to utilize certain jazz rhythms worked out along more or less symphonic lines" (Jablonski 1987, 104). The score for *Tonk* proves that

Ex. 2-6. *Tonk*, first strain

orchestrating for the Ellington orchestra now no longer held any secrets for Strayhorn. It also shows that he could transform elements associated with Ellington's writing and playing—in this case, the "jazz solo concerto" and the stride piano style, almost extinct by 1940—and turn them into a personal musical language.

As *Tonk* remained unrecorded, Strayhorn's newly found voice was still largely unheard in the Ellington orchestra. Though Ellington studied the score of *Tonk*, jotting down chord symbols on the finished manuscript, he apparently made no attempts to record or perform the work. Thus, for the larger part of 1940, most Strayhorn originals remained obscure, overshadowed by his employer's impressive creative output. Unexpectedly, three days before the end of the year—just before a broadcasting ban that would spark the public breakthrough of Strayhorn the composer—Strayhorn the arranger suddenly found a place in the limelight.

The orchestra was scheduled to record one instrumental and two vocal selections on December 28 in the Chicago studios of Victor. One of the vocal scores was a new piece composed by Ted Grouya and Edmund Anderson entitled *Flamingo*. The other vocal number was *The Girl in My Dreams Tries to Look Like You*, a tune attributed to Mercer Ellington but scored by his father and Strayhorn. *Flamingo* was an attractive, yet traditional, romantic thirty-two-bar pop song. Musically the song had some nice touches, such as a shift to parallel minor in the third measure (the reverse of the opening bars of Strayhorn's own *Fantastic Rhythm*), a refreshing move to a nontonal chord in the fifth bar ($^\flat$VI7, better known as the tritone-related double dominant)[24] as well as a bridge whose harmonies deviated from the conventional patterns.

Setting out with this material, Strayhorn composed an arrangement that is a triumph of form and orchestration. Where most of the vocal arrangements of the day were constructed with a string of choruses interspersed with short modulations (usually no more than four bars), some sort of opener, and a little tag, over a third of Strayhorn's arrangement contains new material in transitional and modulatory sections. While the accompaniment of the vocal chorus proper is already attractive and detailed (exemplified by the little wind motif that echoes the lyric in the first bar of the bridge), the success of the arrangement lies in its architecture, founded on the introduction, the complex modulations that separate the chorus and the final half-chorus, and the coda.

Flamingo's initial bars are an exposition rather than an introduction, as they present the song's characteristic opening interval ("flamingo," spelled out by the trombone and echoed by the trumpet) as well as the main rhythmic cell that is one of the arrangement's unifiers. On a subliminal level, the introduction exposes the tonal ambiguity Strayhorn explores in the arrangement, pointed up by the grating layers of saxophones and brass (Ex. 2-7, mm. 6-7) and a low-register repeated polytonal chord: Fmi over D (Ex. 2-7, m. 8). It creates a dissonant texture evocative of the modernist Russian composer Igor Stravinsky.

As the vocal chorus draws to an end, Strayhorn starts the first half of a complex thirty-bar transitory section that will modulate from D♭ to D via A♭ and F, and back to D♭. All modulations build on the song's original material: both the I-minor chord and the ♭VI7 chord that give the A-strains of *Flamingo* their distinctive flavor. Strayhorn first interpolates this ♭VI7 chord in the second half of bar 40 (Ex. 2-8, the B♭♭7 is for practical reasons enharmonically spelled as A7), where it starts a chain of chords that first serve to obscure the original tonal center D♭ and consequently lead to the modulation to A♭, by means of chromatic descending dominants. Weaving a texture of layered chords under the ending of the last strain, the orchestra's sections come in on different beats, to further the sense of tonal detachment. According to Jeffries, only during the recording did Strayhorn suggest that he do the vocalise that so beautifully tinges the first half of this transition but is absent in the original manuscript: "He came in and suggested that: 'Do that "Oh, oh" in there, and do that modulation down through it.' He really directed that whole record" (Hajdu 1992).[25]

Ex. 2-7. *Flamingo*, mm. 1–8

The next two modulations, from A♭ to F and from F to D (along Lendvai's dominant axis!) are varied but congruent as they follow the same modulatory path: the tonic is altered to a tonic-minor, the delay for, again, the tritone-related double-dominant (Ex. 2-8, mm. 49-50 and Ex. 2-9, mm. 59-60). A final modulation, under Hodges's hazy solo, signaled in the reeds by an echo of the wind motif (Ex. 2-9, mm. 69-70), and harmonically prepared through Emi11/E♭mi11/A♭13, takes the piece back from D to D♭.

The integrated eight-bar coda following the last vocal strain, represents the

Ex. 2-8. *Flamingo*, mm. 38–55

THE RENAISSANCE OF ARRANGING   41

Ex. 2-8. *Flamingo,* mm. 38–55 *(cont.)*

Ex. 2-9. *Flamingo,* mm. 55–70

Ex. 2-9. *Flamingo,* mm. 55–70 *(cont.)*

final nonthematic section. Rhythmically, it builds on the closing bar of the introduction, while harmonically it largely draws on the first transitory section (mm. 40-45), as it travels through tonally remote harmonies with ♭VI7 as pivotal chord. To complete the circularity of the arrangement, the trombone closes out the piece with a variation on the initial "flamingo call" (not in Strayhorn's score, but added to the trombonist's part during rehearsals).

The general liquidity of the caesura-less arrangement, its structuring elements, the sophisticated modulations and integrated introductory, transitory, and closing sections—all based on the economical use of harmonic and rhythmic material—make *Flamingo* unique in the jazz writing of its time. All musical means were geared to the articulation of a highly organized, well-balanced, and tight-knit form, and as theory-conscious as the piece may be, Strayhorn fully applied his harmonic knowledge to express the song's romantic lyrics, successfully communicated to the record-buying public: *Flamingo* became a hit for Duke Ellington and His Orchestra. Consequently, Herb Jeffries made it his signature piece and later founded a venue in Florida named "The Flamingo Club." "Flamingo? That's the bird that brought me. Most people come to this planet by stork; I came by flamingo," Jeffries later maintained (Haufman 1999, 7).

Strayhorn's contemporaries received the work with great admiration, as then budding pianist-composer John Lewis told Strayhorn-biographer Hajdu (1996, 86): "*Flamingo*...had nothing to do with what had gone on in jazz at all before. It sounded as if Stravinsky were a jazz musician." To Ellington (1973, 153), *Flamingo* was "a turning point in vocal background orchestration, a renaissance in elaborate ornamentation for the accompaniment of singers....Since then, other arrangers have become more and more daring, but Billy Strayhorn really started it all with *Flamingo*." The impact was such that twenty-one years after its composition, *Flamingo* was the only arrangement to be listed in a tally of all-time favorite Ellington recordings, polled for *Down Beat's* Silver Jubilee issue ("List of Favorites" 1952).

In the year and a half that he had been working for Ellington, Strayhorn had started to develop his own language for the orchestra both in originals (*Passion Flower, Day Dream, Your Love Has Faded, Tonk*) and arrangements (*Tuxedo Junction, Chloë, Flamingo*)—using quartal chords, through-imitation, repeated melodic and rhythmic gestures, extensive chromatic voice leading, tonally independent sound structures, polytonality, and large, through-composed modulatory sections—all geared toward the expression of compositional structure. At times he drew inspiration from his collaborator, not through mimicry, but by transforming and translating Ellingtonian devices (Harlem stride, cross-section voicing, and "on the man writing"), to incorporate them into his own vocabulary. When 1940 drew to a close, Billy Strayhorn was on the verge of a major breakthrough, a breakthrough that would make his music, if not his name, known to listeners throughout the world.

Chapter Three

The Strayhorn Effect:
A New Way of Writing for Jazz Orchestra

NEW YEAR'S DAY 1941 held an unpleasant surprise for the Ellington organization. A smoldering dispute between the radio industry and the nation's largest performing-rights organization, the American Society of Composers and Publishers (ASCAP), had exploded. From the early days of radio, the networks had paid ASCAP for the rights to broadcast the music it licensed, based on five-year contracts. With its current contract due for renewal in 1940, ASCAP demanded a 100 percent increase in royalties, which already had been more than quadrupled since 1931. By the end of 1939, the major radio networks foresaw a confrontation and started to work on an alternative music licensing organization: Broadcast Music Inc. (BMI). The networks' initiative was further fueled by the frustration that resulted from ASCAP's exclusive membership: in order to gain entry a writer had to have published at least five successful songs. This precluded a large contingent of young composers and favored established writers and publishers, who consequently controlled the majority of the music played on network radio. Within a year after opening its offices in early 1940, BMI had signed licenses with numerous publishers and with the majority of the broadcasters (including the largest, CBS, owned by Columbia), and the new licensing body was ready to take action. As of January 1, 1941, hundreds of radio stations refused to broadcast any music—old or new—by ASCAP members, virtually blacking out all ASCAP-controlled repertoire for much of 1941.

Ellington, an ASCAP member of six years, thus saw his compositions and recordings banned from the airwaves. This created a serious problem: on January 3, the band was scheduled to open a two-month engagement at the Casa Mañana in Culver City, California, with air time every night. Such broadcast engagements were important, since radio was the most effective way to reach millions of households across the nation. On the air, live performances still outnumbered recordings. In fact, radio had been instrumental in disseminating Ellington's music and gaining him fame and fortune (see Tucker 1993, 78; Hasse 1993, 111–112; Nicholson 1999, 77–78). All of a sudden, Ellington needed a new radio repertory that would be acceptable for the networks: a repertory that consisted of music not copyrighted in his name.

Ellington turned to his son Mercer and Strayhorn, both of whom fell short of the ASCAP registration requirements and thus could provide music that steered clear of the ban. As Mercer Ellington recalled, "Overnight, literally, we got a chance to write a whole new book for the band.... He [Ellington] needed us to write music and it had to be in our names" (Hajdu 1996, 83–84). Rather than replacing the orchestra's existing repertory with "a whole new book," Ellington proceeded carefully. From February 20 until June 5 he stayed away from recording studios and live radio broadcasts, keeping his band employed with the regular so-called one-nighters. Since such dance engagements did not include any radio involvement (see e.g., Timner 1996, 42–43; Stratemann 1992, 166–167; Massagli and Volonté 1999, 54–57), they were not affected by the broadcasting ban, and Ellington could use his own repertory without any restrictions. By June 1941, Ellington was back to recording works copyrighted in his own name (such as *Are You Sticking* and *The Giddybug Gallop*) even though the battle between the radio industry and ASCAP still continued for almost a year, and the ban remained effective.

But at two recording sessions (January 15 and February 15, 1941) and at a number of radio broadcasts in between, Strayhorn and Mercer indeed got their "big break" as the younger Ellington called it (Hajdu 1996, 83). Ellington's son contributed five works to his father's repertory[1] while Strayhorn offered seven compositions (not counting co-credited, uncredited, and unrecorded but possibly performed works). Strayhorn's first piece to be featured as a result of the broadcasting ban was *Take the "A" Train*, recorded twice in the winter of 1941.[2] In addition, *Chelsea Bridge, Clementine, A Flower Is a Lovesome Thing, After All,* and *Love Like This Can't Last* were tried out at air checks around the same time. Apart from *A Flower Is a Lovesome Thing*, which remained unrecorded till July 17, 1946, the full band made commercial recordings of these compositions at various sessions in the course of the year, together with another new original, *Rain Check*.

Three of these 1941 recordings, *Take the "A" Train, Chelsea Bridge,* and *Rain Check*, stand out for different reasons. *Take the "A" Train* became one of Strayhorn's best-known and most performed compositions. The "impressionistic" *Chelsea Bridge* was the first piece to draw wide attention to Ellington's new collaborator. *Rain Check*, the least-known of the three, stands out due to its uncommon structure and its reliance on motivic material. The latter two works furthermore earned Strayhorn a place on the band's piano bench.

It was exceptional that Strayhorn got a chance to work with Duke Ellington and His Famous Orchestra, and the timing was perfect. The band, seen here at its historic performance in Fargo, North Dakota (Jack Towers's recordings immortalized this dance date), was at its zenith. The three-inch stack of instrumental parts visible in front of tenorist Ben Webster contained many Strayhorn contributions.
(*Photograph by Jack Towers; Walter van de Leur Collection*)

Take the "A" Train was the first credited, full-fledged Strayhorn composition for the big band that was neither arranged by Ellington (unlike the earlier *Something to Live For* and *Your Love Has Faded*), nor co-composed to a certain extent (as *Grievin'* or *I'm Checking Out, Goom-Bye* had been). The song reportedly was composed late in 1938 or early in 1939 (Hajdu 1996, 55–56), shortly after Strayhorn had first met his future employer, but the famous *arrangement* of *Take the "A" Train* definitely stems from January 1941, though the four-part saxophone background in which Ben Webster rests might hint at its 1939 origins.[3] *Take the "A" Train* must have been the most performed work by the Ellington orchestra. After Ellington adopted it in the fall of 1941 as the band's signature theme (replacing *Sepia Panorama*, which was partly by Strayhorn), *"A" Train* opened and closed virtually every concert. The record also became one of Ellington's biggest commercial successes, "a leitmotif of the swing era" (Hajdu 1996, 85).

With his *"A" Train*, Strayhorn contributed his share to a tradition of descriptive train pieces in American music (see Schuller 1989, 61–62), a tradition of which Ellington's 1933 *Daybreak Express* arguably was the unrivaled exponent, a stunning train portrait in music, matched by a staggering performance of the orchestra.[4] *Daybreak Express*, "quite literal in its descriptive approach" (Schuller 1989, 62), captures the steam engine's wailing whistles and ringing bells, the thrumming of the tracks as the train picks up momentum for a hurtling trip through hilly landscapes and sleepy towns, and the final wheezing and hissing as the express pulls into the next station. Trains continued to return in Ellington's writing, though pieces such as *Track 360* and *Happy-Go-Lucky-Local* (the latter co-credited to Strayhorn) were less literal in their evocation of railroad sounds.

Although *"A" Train* is one of the most programmatic pieces in Strayhorn's oeuvre, it is still far less descriptive than the aforementioned train pieces. "The reason we gave it that title," Strayhorn explained, "was because they were building the Sixth Avenue subway at that time, and they added new trains, including the 'D' Train, which came up to Harlem, to 145th Street, and then turned off and went to the Bronx, but the 'A' Train kept straight on up to 200-and-something Street. People got confused. They'd take the 'D' Train, and it would go to Harlem and 145th Street, but the next stop would be in the Bronx. So I said I was writing directions—take the 'A' Train to Sugar Hill" (Dance 1967, 19). While it conjures the sounds and noises of a modern New York subway express train dashing through the tunnels, changing tracks with shrieking brakes, and vanishing in the underground darkness, *Take the "A" Train* is not so much about a subway ride as about *movement*.

From the moment the saxophones leap in with their now famous, catchy AABA theme—centered around the hallmark shift to the supertonic flatted-fifth chord in measures three and four—against interlocking brass figures, the tune lunges forward. Each of the three choruses brings new whirling section work, from the agile flowing saxophone chords under Ray Nance's trumpet solo to the off-beat plunger-muted brass interpolations in the final chorus. For contrast, Strayhorn shifts gears with a vigorous four-bar transition at the end of Nance's solo chorus, with fast-moving, metrically shifting diminished sax chords against a sustained unison G in the brass, to signal the modulation from C to E♭ (the next step on Lendvai's tonic axis). Later the forward motion comes to a temporary halt with again a rhythmically displaced cross-section bell-chord that builds to a majestic altered E7, aptly evoking the horn of a subway train, echoed from the hollow tunnels (Ex. 3-1).[5] This bell-chord displays both Strayhorn's modern harmonic taste and his aptitude for conceptual composition. The whole passage originates in two musical ideas: a descending major-seventh interval and the after-beat entries of the various instruments (the performance is at slight variance with Strayhorn's autograph: some voices were doubled and the final dotted quarter note was shortened—note durations were often subject to change).

With its chromatic eighth-note lines, "A" Train's bebop-flavored theme is surprisingly modern, though the chord changes seem to owe a debt to the 1930 Jimmy McHugh/Dorothy Fields composition *Exactly Like You*.[6] Yet, the work's merit lies not only in its attractive thirty-two-bar AABA theme, but also in the coherent underlying structure and the cleverly composed balance between the orchestral sections. Turning the piece into more than the sum of its parts, each of the three-and-a-half choruses plays a designated role in the archlike structure. Strayhorn composed a gradual buildup of tension, with a climax at each of the two pivoting points, the first at the modulation to E♭ where Nance changes from muted to open horn, and the second at the bell-chord that leads the piece to its out-chorus.

Adding another high point to their already impressive recordings, the musicians of the Blanton-Webster band found inspiration in Strayhorn's clever score and gave a superbly swinging performance. Ray Nance, who had replaced Cootie Williams a mere two-and-a-half months earlier, rose to the occasion and delivered a solo that became a classic. As an integral part of *Take the "A" Train*, it has been imitated numerous times since, even by Nance himself. About six months after

Ex. 3-1. *Take the "A" Train*, mm. 95–96

its first recording, Ellington adopted Strayhorn's tune as the band's signature theme, a surprising choice given that its predecessors, *East St. Louis Toodle-Oo* and *Sepia Panorama*, had been more representative of the Ellington orchestra's sound.

Stylistically, *Take the "A" Train* stands out in the Strayhorn repertory as a rather atypical work. With its string of choruses, ample solo space against background riffs, and unison saxophone lines with snappy brass answers, the piece was more true to the swing conventions laid down in numerous contemporary big band arrangements than to Strayhorn's own compositional style and musical vocabulary. Indeed, the piece's ending, with its diminuendo repetition that leads to a major-sixth chord in the saxophones, was a Swing Era cliché developed in bands like Benny Goodman's and Glenn Miller's. Straightforward swing was hardly ever a goal of Strayhorn's music, but for *"A" Train* he drew his inspiration from the swing arrangers. At first, he actually rejected the tune, fearing Ellington would consider it "too much like Fletcher Henderson" (Hajdu 1996, 84). Yet the score was more than an exercise in style mimicry, as Strayhorn transcended most of his predecessors by summarizing what had been the very essence of the swing style of the past decade, while alluding to the emerging bebop idiom. As DeVeaux (1997, passim) details, at the end of the 1930s musicians such as Coleman Hawkins and Lester Young were exploring harmonic and melodic avenues that proved seminal for the development of the new genre; *Take the "A" Train* and Ellington's *Cotton Tail* indicate that bebop indeed was "in the air."

The great success of *"A" Train*—to the general audience the piece became virtually synonymous with Duke Ellington—has raised questions with respect to Strayhorn's authorship. In his contribution to "The Billy Strayhorn Suite," a special commemorative section of *The Village Voice*, musicologist Andrew Homzy broke the news that Ellington wrote part of *Take the "A" Train*:

> On the first recording of [*"A" Train*], made January 15, 1941,...the final A section is a simple repetition of the initial statements. For the famous Victor recording, [exactly] one month later, this A section has been re-scored—the counter riffs of trumpets and trombones have been replaced with a harmonized mass-brass response to the unison saxophone melody. *Evidence in the Ellington archives* [actually Duke Ellington Collection] suggests that Ellington wrote the new passage, as well as two of the best-known episodes in that masterful score—the piano intro and the pyramid effect that follows Ray Nance's trumpet solo. He was still embellishing and improving Strayhorn's work. (Homzy 1992, 6; italics added)

The cited "evidence" is not conclusive, and none of these claims holds up against the surviving manuscripts. Piano introductions were hardly ever written out, and likewise no document has survived for the opening bars of *"A" Train*.

They may have been devised by either Strayhorn or Ellington (the latter being the pianist on the recordings), though the former seems to be the most likely candidate. Not only did Strayhorn generally preconceive his piano introductions (such as for *Chelsea Bridge*), but they typically reflected the musical material of the introduced composition. In *"A" Train*'s case, the introduction plays with the tune's central $D7^{(\flat 5)}$ and its related whole-tone scale—harmonic and melodic ideas that Strayhorn had been working with earlier as well (e.g., in *Passion Flower*). Ellington tended to state the mood and tempo in his piano introductions, and as a rule, he did not hint at the ensuing compositional material (hence his usage of the same gestures in the introductions to different compositions).

Material regarding the second point (the re-scored final eight bars of the first chorus) can indeed be found on Strayhorn's surviving handwritten parts ("A Train," DEC) for Stewart, Tizol, and Nance. To these parts, Tizol added the new section; he often copied any last-minute changes to his fellow-musicians' parts. Since he reportedly refused to extract Strayhorn's work when the latter had just joined the team in 1939, Tizol's handwriting might suggest that Ellington indeed was the author of the new background. Yet, after almost two years, Tizol's unwillingness to cooperate with Strayhorn appears to have vanished.[7] Furthermore, both the voicings of the new bars and the repeated rhythmic gesture are fully consistent with Strayhorn's previous work for the orchestra, which could just as well indicate that he was the author.

Finally, the original score in Strayhorn's hand, now in the repository of the Strayhorn Estate, refutes Homzy's claim that Ellington wrote "the pyramid effect that follows Ray Nance's trumpet solo." Strayhorn solely composed that section, as well as the rest of *Take the "A" Train*. Even if Ellington were the author of the introduction and the later re-scored eight bars, it is hard to maintain that he was "still embellishing and improving Strayhorn's work." The achievements of *"A" Train* by no means derive from these revisions.[8]

A month after the first recording of *Take the "A" Train*, Ellington tried out three more new Strayhorn compositions at a radio broadcast from the Casa Mañana, including *Chelsea Bridge*. As the unissued recording of this performance reveals, this was essentially a public rehearsal; apparently the piece was virtually new to the orchestra, and the band audibly struggles through the score. Strayhorn's absence at the piano was most notably felt, as Ellington appears unaware of the introduction and the essential piano interludes his associate had composed. Still, this air check is invaluable: it is the only known recording of the full, unabridged version of *Chelsea Bridge*.[9]

Although said to be inspired by one of James McNeill Whistler's hazy, dark-toned paintings of London's Chelsea Embankment,[10] *Chelsea Bridge* is in essence a nonprogrammatic work that explores the ambiguity of chromatic harmonies. It also bespeaks Strayhorn's fondness for the French composer Debussy (who is known to have favored Whistler's work as well, as Strayhorn may have been aware).¹¹ The main compositional idea of *Chelsea Bridge*—the parallel movement of tonally independent chords—as well as its subdued orchestral colors, allude to some of Debussy's orchestral works, such as his symphonic triptych for orchestra and female chorus *Nocturnes* (1897–1899). Debussy referred to "Nuages," the first movement of *Nocturnes*, as "an experiment in the different combinations that can be achieved with one color—what a study in gray would be in painting" (Vallas 1933, 274), a description that strikingly fits both Whistler's London paintings and Strayhorn's composition.

While Debussy is distantly present in *Chelsea Bridge*, one of his contemporaries comes through more clearly: the melodic and harmonic movement of the theme's first three bars echoes the second movement of Maurice Ravel's six-part piano work *Valses Nobles et Sentimentales* (1911, orchestrated by the composer in 1912). Ravel had used the same chords in the earlier "Oiseaux Tristes," the second movement of *Miroirs* (1905). Strayhorn later maintained, "Until I had written [*Chelsea Bridge*] I had not yet heard the *Valses Nobles et Sentimentales* of Ravel. Therefore, I don't think one could speak of an influence" (Binchet and Carles 1966, 49; see also Ulanov 1946, 225).¹² This striking yet unintentional resemblance between Ravel's movement (marked "Assez lent, avec une expression intense") and *Chelsea Bridge* illustrates that Strayhorn partly worked from a similar compositional perspective, stressing the individuality of chords while employing them for their specific colors. Still, much as Strayhorn may have applied some of the principles that ruled the works of these French impressionists, *Chelsea Bridge* is entirely original in its use of the sonoric capacities of the jazz orchestra. By blending these turn-of-the-century European elements into an otherwise African-American idiom, Strayhorn went beyond a mere imitation of his sources and created a "American Impressionism" instead.¹³

Chelsea Bridge opens with Strayhorn's four-bar piano introduction which sets the atmosphere while employing one of the aforementioned Debussy-like compositional concepts: the parallel movement of detached chordal structures (Ex. 3-2). Strayhorn's broken major-seventh nine piano chords, an utterly modern sound in the jazz vocabulary of the time, are not related to any tonality and do not stand in any functional harmonic relationship.¹⁴

Ex. 3-2. *Chelsea Bridge*, mm. 1–4

The resulting absence of a tonal center continues in the subsequent first theme, which is characterized by an ascending B♭ Aeolian minor scale that surprisingly leads to the major seventh, underscored by a third-inversion B♭mi6 (Ex. 3-3). This chord moves down a whole step in the next bar, further obscuring the tonality and affirming the independence of the harmonies. Only when the rhythmic placement of the melody shifts from the weak fourth beat to the more affirmative first beat (m. 9) the relative tonality of D♭ major becomes apparent, to be swiftly abandoned by an abrupt modulation to F♭ major for the release. A quasi-improvisando but carefully designed melody leads this bridge through an intricate harmonic plan that touches on remote keys (A major and G major), while modulating from F♭ back to B♭ minor. In the final bars of the release Strayhorn again veils the tonality by ending on a D♭9, which chromatically descends to B♭9 (instead of the expected F7 for B♭ minor).[15]

In the second chorus, Strayhorn changes the mood by infusing a faster moving line of descending, bird-song figures in the clarinet, underscored by high, dissonant voicings in the other reeds, partly in contrary motion. In this chorus, the first of the two piano interludes serves as a pickup of the reed theme, which provides a change in musical character.[16] When the original theme is presented against this reed theme—now a dissonant counterpoint—in the last eight bars of the second chorus, both take on a new musical meaning: the opening theme, which appeared tranquil and peaceful at its first statement, assumes a more dramatic character while the enigmatic and somewhat confusing secondary theme, which disrupted the pensive atmosphere, gains in clarity and musical objective, hence resolving the musical question posed by its initial exposition.

Ellington, however, skipped exactly these last eight bars of the second chorus for the famous commercial recording of December 2, 1941, replacing them with the final eight of the third and last chorus. Remarkably enough, Tizol still played

Ex. 3-3. *Chelsea Bridge*, mm. 5–12

the pickup to his theme, to be boldly pushed aside by the entry of the trumpets. It left the cut clearly audible. Now that the contrapuntal section was omitted, the role of the secondary theme remained fortuitous. On the lesser-known recording for Standard Radio (September 17, 1941) this concurrence of reeds and trombone indeed was recorded, but here the essential third chorus was cut.[17]

The third and final chorus, performed only at the February broadcast, gives *Chelsea Bridge* what the two issued recordings lack: a satisfactory completion and a sense of equilibrium. To achieve this, Strayhorn had designed fresh, denser orchestrations of the main theme, with the brass and reed sections alternating between fore- and background in a four-bar pattern. Thus, the final chorus offers a new dynamic level while casting another light on the theme's character. Though not up to par with many of Strayhorn's more complex arrangements of the period, *Chelsea Bridge* did have a thought-out structure, a miniature "crescendo" form built on variations of the theme and its counterpoint, creating a dynamic intensification with each new chorus.[18]

At the time of its release, *Chelsea Bridge* shared little in common with any of the contemporary jazz works. The composition even broke away from Ellington's oeuvre through its radical and consequent employment of a harmonic and melodic concept. Curiously, the jazz critics who had almost unanimously hailed Ellington's nonconformist music, likening his work to composers from the classical field such as Delius,[19] now accused Strayhorn of not writing jazz. The British critic Stanley Dance, for instance, noted that "Mr. Strayhorn is an example of today's youth in jazz. He throws tradition overboard. He will have originality at the expense of beauty....Listen to *Chelsea Bridge*, an example of an obsession for tone color and voicing which excludes everything else that matters" (cited in Homzy 1992, 6).[20] Schuller, who earlier compliments Ellington's "tone poem" *Dusk* as going "beyond the confining labels of jazz" (Schuller 1989, 122), judges *Chelsea Bridge* more favorably than Dance, but he too seems concerned about its jazz content, noting that although the piece "stands as a lovely musical vignette," it offers *"just enough* spontaneous variety to give this short tone poem its 'jazz' substance" (ibid., 1989, 135; italics added).

Strayhorn's contemporaries, nevertheless, were deeply impressed with *Chelsea Bridge*, as well as with other recordings of Strayhorn material that came about that year (Hajdu 1996, 86–87). Composer-arranger Gil Evans, who was writing for the Claude Thornhill Orchestra around the commercial release of *Chelsea Bridge* and whose work with Miles Davis's *Birth of the Cool* recordings (1949) became a landmark in jazz arranging, explained: "From the moment I first heard *Chelsea Bridge*, I set out to try to do that. That's all I did—that's all I ever did—try to do what Billy Strayhorn did" (Hajdu 1996, 87).[21] Nevertheless, during his work with Thornhill, Evans developed a style of his own. Though musically and technically quite distinct from Strayhorn's writing, in character many of Evans's "cool jazz" arrangements indeed resemble *Chelsea Bridge*; his work fits the label "American Impressionism" as well.

Another composer-arranger to be inspired by *Chelsea Bridge* was bassist Charles Mingus, although he primarily looked to Ellington's writing for inspiration. According to Mingus biographer Brian Priestley (1982, 27, 203–204), *Chelsea Bridge* stood as a model for a number of later Mingus compositions: *This Subdues My Passion* (1946), *Minor Intrusion* (1954), *Profile of Jackie* (1956), and *Duke Ellington's Sound of Love* (1974), the latter also deliberately citing *Lush Life* and *Take the "A" Train*.[22]

In addition to *Chelsea Bridge*, the Ellington orchestra featured more new work from the Casa Mañana, such as *Clementine*, and a new full-band version of *A Flower Is a Lovesome Thing*. Two days later, the Ellingtonians commercially recorded *After All*, which features a sing-song melody against a tasteful orchestration, its most notable event being the caesura-less modulation from C to D♭ at the end of the first chorus (mm. 32-33). For the first time a closing device shows up in *After All* that would become one of the few clichés that slipped into Strayhorn's vocabulary and was to be found predominantly in his ballads: a final brass chord on the tonic, often in cups, entering on the second half of the last bar.[23]

Together with *Clementine* and *After All*, *Love Like This Can't Last* entered the book. Judging from the existing recordings, the latter held repertory for part of 1941, and in all likelihood disappeared when singer Ivie Anderson (for whom the song was tailored) left the band in August 1942. Though decidedly more upbeat, *Love Like This Can't Last* is a direct descendant of its through-composed counterparts *So This Is Love* and *Lush Life*. The organic flow of the AABACCBA song conceals its irregular structure, which includes a seventeen-bar introduction, strains of uncommon lengths (fourteen and eighteen bars), and an extensive modulatory interlude followed by a variation on the eight-bar bridge (augmented to twelve bars).

The final recorded composition related to the recording ban and typically associated with Strayhorn's 1941 breakthrough was *Rain Check*. *Rain Check* dates from the Casa Mañana engagement, although it was not recorded until December 3, 1941. "That was about rain," Strayhorn said when asked about the piece, "about being in California in January, February, March.... It was raining and I was sitting at home in Los Angeles and writing" (Dance 1967, 19). As Mark Tucker has noted, "For Strayhorn, looking back, the piece was linked to no program or

Ex. 3-4. *Rain Check*, mm. 9–12

picture other than the compositional process itself and the specific circumstances under which the work was undertaken" (Tucker 1986). Though his titles were hardly ever programmatic, Strayhorn felt that "titles are very significant. They're kind of psychological…and they usually come out of the situation or from what you're working with" (Dance 1967, 19).

In musical terms, Strayhorn in *Rain Check* was "working with" two motifs that not only form the building blocks of the rhythmic trombone theme but also underlie much of the other material in the score: an ascending perfect fourth interval (a), and a syncopated, descending broken seventh chord (b) (Ex. 3-4).

Rain Check features a well thought-out harmonic plan that ensures a tight formal design, with as main structural pillars two contrasting eight-bar tutti passages (Ex. 3-5 and Ex. 3-6) that anchor the thirty-two-bar ABAC theme and its related solo sections. The first tutti, a fanfare-like section with a two-part texture of saxophones and brass (note the quartal chords in the trumpets), is firmly rooted in a pedal point on the dominant, but the second tutti is tonally insecure because of the polytonal chords in the brass against the shifting chords in the reeds. For further contrast, Strayhorn has reversed the roles in the call-and-

Ex. 3-5. *Rain Check*, "tutti 1," mm. 1–8

Ex. 3-6. *Rain Check*, "tutti 2," mm. 98–106

response patterns, with densely scored textures in reeds and brass in the second tutti, as opposed to the more transparent quartal chords and unison lines in the first tutti. Thus, the same motivic material yields related yet contrasting segments.

Between these two contrasting tutti passages—harmonically stable and unstable—stands the ABAC theme of *Rain Check*, delivered by Juan Tizol on valve trombone, over a chromatic counterpoint in the reeds. With the rhythm section more felt than heard, the whole theme is perceived as consisting of two contrapuntal lines rather than of a melody over chord changes. There are many other fine moments in *Rain Check*, such as Ben Webster's driving solo, the angular reed special headed by the clarinet and charged with dissonants in drop-two voice leading, and a sixteen-bar piano solo by Strayhorn. As Mark Tucker has noted, "*Rain Check* stands as a youthful, durable composition, overflowing with ideas that are kept closely reined by the composer's sure sense of structure...[where] each event seems both new and organically right" (Tucker 1986, 21–22).

Not only did the 1941 recordings provide a stage for Strayhorn's compositional style, they also featured the composer at the keyboard. Although he had played piano on a number of recordings with the Hodges and Bigard small bands, Strayhorn's recorded appearances with the Ellington band had been rare prior to the ban, with the recording of *Flamingo* as the only known instance with Strayhorn at the keyboard. If his piano playing in *Flamingo* was limited to background runs that could easily be missed by the casual listener, in *Chelsea Bridge* and *Rain Check* it was fully exposed, and the dissimilarity with the style of the orchestra's leader is immediately apparent.

Strayhorn's playing is distinguished by a light touch, and it excels in cascading single-line runs—often in sixteenth and thirty-second notes, with triplets or quintuplets. He displays a certain youthful eagerness in these first recordings with the orchestra and is more soloistic than Ellington. At times Strayhorn even gets in the way of the orchestral voices. In many respects, his playing most notably points to two contemporary piano giants who exerted an important influence on him: Teddy Wilson, who, according to Strayhorn, "very skillfully reconciled a classic touch and technique to the rigorous demands of jazz piano playing" ("Billy Strayhorn on Pianists," 29), and Art Tatum, whose "sheer harmonic and technical facility...is without peer among present-day pianists" (ibid.). Apart from these two players, Strayhorn was well acquainted with the styles of band-pianists Earl Hines, Count Basie, and (of course) Duke Ellington, ragtimers Willie "The Lion" Smith and Thomas "Fats" Waller, as well as the younger generation of pianists such as Mel Powell, Joe Bushkin, Frank Froeba, Nat "King" Cole, Mary Lou Williams, Cleo Brown, Hazel Scott, and Errol Garner. His discussion of their respective styles (ibid., passim) not only evidences careful study, but also displays the advanced descriptive musical vocabulary that Strayhorn had at his disposal to express stylistic differences.

His keyboard technique and playing, predominantly gleaned from Teddy Wilson and Art Tatum, certainly places Strayhorn within the contemporary jazz scene. However, what sets him apart from Wilson and Tatum, and indeed from all other contemporary jazz pianists, is his reliance on Debussy, Ravel, and Satie. In the choice of his chords, in their often high registration and their colorist weight, Strayhorn's keyboard technique was in keeping with his approach to composition, as seen, for instance, in *Chelsea Bridge*. His often florid fills hint at nineteenth-century European piano literature—composers who come to mind are Franz Liszt and Frédéric Chopin—and thus link his playing to piano techniques outside the jazz idiom.

Furthermore, the integrated piano interludes in *Chelsea Bridge* and *Rain Check* point up another (related) aspect in Strayhorn's piano style: the piano could be a means to articulate more sharply the form of his compositions. In order to achieve this, Strayhorn composed his piano breaks in advance rather than relying on improvisation (the almost identical closing runs on *Flamingo* and *After All* further illustrate this practice). Thus, his piano playing was in keeping with, and played a role in, his composition techniques.

BROADCAST BAN OR NO, at least fifteen Strayhorn compositions written or adapted for the Blanton-Webster band remained unrecorded, all of superior quality.[24] These unrecorded works were adventurous, each of them experimenting with either form, orchestration, or harmony. Even though they each bear their individual characteristics, these compositions share a marked departure from the general Ellington repertory, not only in their harmonic, melodic, and structural design, but also in emotional content.

The most surprising work in this group is the fully through-composed, twelve-minute *Pentonsilic*, a work of almost symphonic dimensions that travels through a number of keys, meters, tempo changes, and moods. The eighteen-page autograph of *Pentonsilic* provides few clues to the work's origins or intentions, while even the title (an acronym?) remains a mystery.[25] Two distinct themes of different lengths form the basic thematic material: a thirty-two-bar upbeat curtain raiser and an inspired twenty-eight-bar ballad, charged with continuous modulations. Between the expositions of these themes stand variational and developmental sections (including a faux-Baroque five-part counterpoint against the first theme and a section in 5/4 meter with Stravinsky-like orchestral hits) as well as structuring passages that signal tempo changes or modulations. In the final episode of the work (mm. 331-375), Strayhorn masterly layers both themes, furthering the dramatic force of the work. Even though he consciously designed his thematic material to make this final coupling possible, the music sounds entirely natural. In addition, Strayhorn proves that he was able to cast a lavish wealth of ideas in a composition that is a convincing synthesis of form and content. *Pentonsilic* demonstrates that Strayhorn's art was getting more and more expansive, overflowing the borders of the tried and true three-minute formats: his music required larger dimensions. As Strayhorn noted: "It used to be we got into a record session with new stuff, all too long. We'd just cut the material down to three minutes" ("Swee' Pea...Is Still Amazed," 1956).

Surprisingly, Schuller signals "two dangers in Strayhorn's writing and through his influence in the Ellington band's style. One is Strayhorn's inability, like Ellington's, to develop material compositionally beyond the vignette or cameo stage" (Schuller 1989, 135). Although he states elsewhere that "Strayhorn's role in the Ellington canon will perhaps never [be] completely or precisely defined" (ibid., 136), according to Schuller, "this lack of developmental technique was to have serious consequences for much of the extended work writing of Ellington and Strayhorn in the post-1945 period....Second, one hears in [works such as] *Chelsea Bridge* the hint of a certain effeteness which was to mar much of Strayhorn's work" (ibid., 135–136). In light of Strayhorn's homosexuality, Schuller's second criticism seems loaded. Unfortunately, others have also elected to apply similar homophobic terminology: Collier calls Strayhorn's music "overripe,...a tropical rainforest thick with patches of purple orchids," while he curiously blames Strayhorn for "encouraging [Ellington's]...tendency towards lushness [and] prettiness at the expense of the masculine leanness and strength of his [Ellington's] best work, the most 'jazzlike' pieces" (Collier 1987, 273–274).[26]

Nevertheless, not only *Chelsea Bridge, Rain Check*, or *Pentonsilic* but virtually all of Strayhorn's works for the Blanton-Webster band take the edge off Schuller's (and Collier's) critique: these were powerful, authoritative compositions and arrangements in which compositional development was one of the prime motives—no trace of this presumed "effeteness" can be found. (To this author, the aesthetic categories applied here by Schuller and Collier per se are invalid.) Time and again, Strayhorn shows himself to be in full command of structural complexity. Admittedly, neither Schuller nor Collier, nor others who vented similar criticism against Strayhorn's work (e.g., Lambert 1999, 108), had access to compositions such as *Tonk* or *Pentonsilic*, works that would have contributed to a more complete picture of Strayhorn's art. Yet, these critics might have taken into account the structural sophistication of well-known Strayhorn works, such as *Rain Check* or his arrangement of *Flamingo*. Still, since Schuller, Collier, and others were aware of the enigmas that surrounded the Ellington-Strayhorn collaboration, their remarks were premature, to say the least.

As argued above, part of Strayhorn's musical language drew on fin de siècle composers such as Debussy and Ravel, especially in terms of orchestral colors and the use of nonfunctional harmonies. But his command of musical architecture was rooted in older classical techniques. Most of his works are linear compositions, that is, they typically have some sense of thematic and harmonic development as well as a network of interrelationships between the various musical elements. This approach is related to what Charles Rosen (1971) has termed the "Classical Style," and it may be found in the works of Haydn, Mozart, and Beethoven, whose legacies loomed large in the repertories of their numerous musical heirs in European nineteenth-century music. The main principles that govern the architecture of these compositions—both low-level (thematic construction) and high-level (musical form)—must have been part of the curriculum at the Pittsburgh Musical Institute. In all likelihood Strayhorn had gained an understanding of classical composition techniques even earlier, through his piano studies: before developing an interest in jazz, Strayhorn said, he studied "the three B's—Bach, Beethoven and Brahms" (Dance 1967, 19).

European art music by no means has an exclusive claim to the phenomenon of linear development, as it can be achieved along many other paths than those chosen in classical music. Indian ragas, for instance, are strongly developmental, but they assume a wholly different perspective (the gradual unfolding of a melodic and rhythmic mode). Closer to home, Ellington had shown in masterpieces as diverse as *Old Man Blues, Dusk,* and *Ko-Ko* that formal balance could equally well be achieved through a rhythmic, dynamic, and orchestral unfolding (paired with contrast) rather than through harmonic and melodic development.

But Strayhorn drew predominantly on classical, developmental techniques and thus—ironically enough—he accomplished in his compositions exactly what Schuller later tried to achieve in his so-called Third Stream works, a term he coined in 1956 to describe a type of music that attempted a self-conscious fusion of "basic elements of jazz and Western art music" (Schuller 1988, 1199). As Schuller saw it, in Third Stream compositions "jazz musicians can find new avenues of development in the large-scale forms and complex tonal systems of classical music" (ibid.). If Strayhorn's writing can at all be said to have foreshadowed the Third Stream, it was because his compositions intrinsically dealt with issues of musical form and development. Unlike Third Stream, Strayhorn's work was never motivated by a premeditated attempt to mix "improvisational techniques and concepts with straight composition" (Schuller 1996, 19).

Not only did Strayhorn's compositions challenge the limitations of the 78 rpm format (most of them were too long ever to qualify for recording), they must also have stretched the perceptions of the Ellingtonians. The level of complexity of certain works (*Pentonsilic, Blue House, Blue Star,* and *Hipper-Bug*) would have required dramatic adaptation by the band members to a different style. *Blue Star,* for instance, called for a Ben Webster solo in the most uncomfortable key of concert E major—six sharps for the tenor—over uncommon, continuously modulating chord changes that abounded with altered chord tones and modernist harmonies (such as minor-major seventh chords). In similar vein, *Blue House* is riddled with chromatic harmonies while it also features a reed ensemble chorus of unorthodox nonresolving dissonant lines. Furthermore, most of these unrecorded works make extensive use of intricately textured sections with rapidly altering instrumentations, which bear only superficial similarity to Ellington's cross-section writing. Strayhorn used the various instrumental combinations not so much to mix colors but rather to express form (for instance, in the many abstract modulatory passages in *Pentonsilic*).

One can only guess the reasons for Ellington's reluctance to record or even perform these works. With two composers working full time for the orchestra, the steady stream of new music may have been more than the orchestra could possibly perform. On top of that, Ellington continuously had to negotiate between the desires of an audience mainly drawn to big-band music for dancing, and other goals he set for his orchestra. Most of Strayhorn's new contributions fully ignored the musical tastes of the larger audience, being too advanced and too different to secure them a place in the band's book. Finally, Strayhorn's writing may have been at odds with Ellington's own aesthetic sensibilities. While it would take years before certain compositions and arrangements finally got their premieres (such as *Allah Bye*, which was recorded in 1957, and *Lament for an Orchid*, recorded as *Absinthe* more than two decades after its date of composition), most of the material was simply put aside. Still, as surviving instrumental parts in the Duke Ellington Collection indicate, Strayhorn did not write these works as an academic endeavor. Since parts exist even for the lengthy *Pentonsilic*, at least some of them must have been tried out by the orchestra. As Mercer Ellington complained, "If I waited for the band to have a rehearsal, there would always be things by Billy they wanted to play, and when they had finished them they would be up and gone, and I would be left holding the music [I had written]" (Ellington and Dance 1979, 89).

IN THE FIRST HALF OF 1941, Ellington's partnership with his younger associate gradually reached a new phase. Their work on the theatrical revue *Jump for Joy* especially involved more and more true collaboration. The production started out as an initiative of Ellington and lyricists Paul Webster and Sid Kuller, but gradually more writers became involved, including Strayhorn. According to Patricia Willard (1988, 4), *Jump for Joy* was "a grand emancipation celebration in dance, sketch and song." As Hajdu (1996, 90–91) notes, Ellington "approached it as a musical vehicle for black pride,…a gutsy swipe at Uncle Tomism." Though reportedly a hit with the black West Coast audience, reviews were mostly negative, and the show folded after eleven weeks.

As dozens of surviving manuscripts illustrate, Strayhorn was deeply involved with *Jump for Joy*, though it is virtually impossible to ascertain to what extent his contributions were originals, arrangements, or collaborative works with Ellington, since the latter's hand is on a number of scores as well.[27] In addition to his compositions, Strayhorn arranged the majority of contributions by the other composers and lyricists involved with the production—Hal Borne, Paul Webster, Otis Rene, Mickey Rooney, and Sidney Miller.[28]

Of all his efforts for *Jump for Joy*, *Flame Indigo*[29] stands as the most remarkable Strayhorn contribution to the show. Though different in nature, the piece directly harks back to the harmonic design of his 1935 *Ugly Ducklin'*, which also centered around a static harmonic layer in a repeated rhythmic pattern. Harmonically, *Flame Indigo* is more sophisticated than its Pittsburgh counterpart, which drew on two chords only (built on I and $^\flat$II): here, Strayhorn designs a nonfunctional chord sequence that alternates the tonic with extended chords built on $^\flat$II and $^\flat$VI, with the resultant root progression of F-G$^\flat$-F-D$^\flat$. The lowered second degree is scored as a dominant-seventh chord throughout, but both major and minor chords appear over the lowered sixth degree, subtly altering the flavor of the progression, and further betraying a sense of functional harmonic movement. This ostinato, softly stated by two low-register trumpets and two trombones, underscores a wispy alto melody that exploits the chromatic possibilities of the shifting chords. As in *Ugly Ducklin'*, Strayhorn makes sure the ostinato doesn't grow weary, and replaces it in the bridge by a more propulsive and affirmative chord progression. The innovative piece did not go by unnoticed, and it received notable critical acclaim (see, e.g., Willard 1988, 27).[30]

The only work from *Jump for Joy* that survived the show and became known to a wider audience was Ellington's outstanding ballad *I Got It Bad (and That Ain't Good)*. It is uncertain to what extent Strayhorn was involved with the initial composition of the work, but the uncredited arrangement used for the Victor recording surely was his, culled from the more extensive versions of the song he had scored for the original revue. Though major sections were cut for the issued recording, Strayhorn's score perfectly complements Anderson's voice while delicately supporting her factual delivery of the bluesy lyrics. The record was an instant hit upon its first commercial release in the second half of 1941. In the next decades the arrangements for *I Got It Bad* remained Strayhorn's responsibility and he would write at least another fifteen different instrumental and vocal arrangements of the piece.[31]

Two recordings of *Rocks in My Bed*, also from *Jump for Joy*, illustrate how Strayhorn was capable of stretching an Ellington composition by transforming its harmonies. First recorded by Ellington (without the orchestra) and blues shouter Joe Turner as a string of straightforward, unaltered twelve-bar blues choruses, Strayhorn partly reharmonized *Rocks in My Bed* for the later full-band version with Ivie Anderson (Ellington scored the instrumental sections while Strayhorn did the vocal segment). In Anderson's second vocal chorus Strayhorn breaks away from the I-IV-V blues-changes, replacing them with a liquid string of dominants that are connected with chromatic passing chords. As a result of the substitute chords, he has to adapt the melody significantly, and consequently nothing of the original passage remains, apart from the lyrics. Strayhorn's role has changed from arranger to co-composer.

IN ADDITION TO his tremendous output—more than ninety surviving autographs for the big band can be linked with certainty to the period between November 1940 and June 1942 (about a third of those contain new compositions)—Strayhorn continued to contribute arrangements for the small-band sessions. By the end of 1941, the small-band activities of the Ellingtonians were less frequent, though they continued to be important testing grounds for new repertory. Out of these 1941 small-band sessions came *"C" Blues*, a minimalist composition consisting of a single-line, unaltered two-note riff over a twelve-bar blues progression in C. The first recording, by Barney Bigard and His Orchestra, showed both the strength and the weakness of the motif. Although surely an attractive and adequate opener for a loose jam session in which the Ellingtonians could show off their soloistic capacities, the riff was too meager to serve as a closing statement. The simple unison return to the theme on the small-band recording merely ends the piece, without concluding it. In its original setting, *"C" Blues* just fizzles out.

Strayhorn, the pianist at this session, must have realized that for a full-band version the piece needed a positive, strong conclusion, bringing the musicians back together after their soloistic escapades. For that purpose he composed two out-choruses. In the penultimate chorus Strayhorn starts teaming up the band behind the final soloist, and concludes in the last round with a full-blown brass-against-saxes tutti. These final choruses, full of chromatic voice leading and Strayhorn's trademark quartal chords, became an integral part of the *"C" Blues*. First recorded by the full band at the end of 1941 for a so-called Ellington Soundie[32] as *Jam Session*, the piece—rebaptized *C-Jam Blues*—became a stalwart in the orchestra's repertory, ranking among the twenty most played tunes (see, e.g., Massagli and Volonté 1999, 776–783, which lists over two hundred fifty performances that more or less follow Strayhorn's score).

Although bass player Jimmie Blanton had left the Ellington orchestra in September of the previous year, from an artistic perspective the so-called Blanton-Webster era came to a close just before the start of the first recording ban (August 1, 1942). Ellington's *Main Stem* and Strayhorn's *Johnny Come Lately* stand as the final products of arguably one of the most fruitful periods in the orchestra's history.[33] The Blanton-Webster band had seen Ellington at one of his highest artistic peaks, the culmination of a decade of visionary writing for an orchestra that among its many achievements could count its ability to keep up with Ellington's musical growth. Yet, behind the scenes, Strayhorn had become instrumental in helping Ellington realize his goals. First, he had lightened his employer's workload by shouldering gracefully virtually all the commercial assignments—an important part of the Ellington organization—as well as the majority of the small-band sessions and the larger part of the arrangements for *Jump for Joy*. Furthermore, he had contributed *Take the "A" Train* and fleshed out *I Got It Bad* and *C-Jam Blues*, musical cornerstones that helped to keep Ellington's music in the public eye during the following decades and produced a steady stream of income as well.

Strayhorn had started to use Ellington's orchestra in a new way. In works such as *Chelsea Bridge, Take the "A" Train,* and *Rain Check,* as well as in numerous unrecorded compositions and arrangements, his writing indicated new sonoric possibilities, while drawing on a compositional language unprecedented not only in Ellington's repertory but in the entire realm of jazz writing. Though he had certainly taken specific Ellington techniques as a point of departure (the famous cross-section writing and the reliance on the reed section), in works such as *Tonk, Flamingo,* and *Pentonsilic,* Strayhorn had stretched and transformed these techniques, fusing them with his own idiosyncrasies into a clearly recognizable and highly individual style.

With his work for the Blanton-Webster band, Strayhorn had added, silently and almost anonymously, an entirely new stylistic wing to the Ellington building—a building of which Ellington was still believed to be the sole architect.

Chapter Four

Thinking with the Ear: Strayhorn's Musical Fingerprints

AS THE REPORTER of the Chicago-based periodical *Music and Rhythm* noted in the magazine's "Hints" section, Strayhorn was "one of the most articulate arrangers" with whom he had discussed the intricacies of arranging ("Billy Strayhorn's Arranging Hints," 1942, 27). The article observed that Strayhorn had "given painstaking thought and study to the subject," and that therefore it was "little wonder" that he had been "Duke Ellington's protégé and understudy since January 1939" (ibid.).

Strayhorn told *Music and Rhythm* that for him the distinction between composing and arranging was marginal. Both drew on the same cognitive and intuitive elements and stemmed from the same musical source—in his case, a thorough understanding of harmony. "Since arranging and composing...are linked so closely together," Strayhorn said, "I highly recommend the study of harmony. The more thorough, the better and if intuitive feeling can be thrown in with hard study the combination can't be beat" (ibid.). Indeed, often Strayhorn's themes are so thoroughly woven into the musical background that the integrated thematic material virtually cannot be separated from its context. (The same can be said of numerous Ellington compositions.)[1]

Further explaining his approach to music writing, Strayhorn said that "arrangers and composers must see the piece on which they are working as a complete entity. They ought to use four or five dimensions and see all around the material—over, above, and under it, and on the sides too. Then the job becomes one of transposing the physical picture into an integral and complete mental picture. That's a challenge for any arranger" (ibid.). He continued to warn budding arrangers not to depend on the piano as an arranging tool: "I say a piano is not necessary [when arranging]. It helps when you're studying, but it can never give you the timbre of the orchestra, only the actual notes which you strike. Rather

Strayhorn was an accomplished pianist who was equally at home in the classical repertory and in jazz. For recordings with the orchestra he often replaced Ellington at the keyboard. Strayhorn tended to compose and arrange away from his instrument. (*Courtesy Rutgers Institute of Jazz Studies*)

than relying on the piano, I endorse what I might term thinking with the ear—the intuitive feeling again, but I can't overstress its importance" (ibid.).

Indeed, Strayhorn fashioned his scores, both the arrangements and the originals, along the lines he explained, if somewhat cryptically, in *Music and Rhythm*. While the 1940s saw some run-of-the-mill arrangements (e.g., *Amor, Don't Take Your Love from Me, That's for Me,* or *I Can't Begin to Tell You*), usually based on pop songs and typically paralleled by bland sounding performances of the orchestra, the larger part of his scores were identifiable as Strayhorn music, in which musical coherence is the main focus. In the majority of his works, the aim to create a "complete entity" was paramount, achieved by techniques that were, as he indicated in his arranging hints, in the first place compositional and which drew on his harmonic vocabulary as well as on his understanding of musical form. Much as Strayhorn's writing was rooted in his firm musical knowledge—his scores typically included elements that played with purely music-theoretical issues—his approach was foremost a "thinking with the ear," as he so aptly put it, an approach that expressed emotions rather than theory. To that goal, Strayhorn combined a wide array of individual musical techniques—musical fingerprints—that in most cases leave little doubt as to the author of a given piece.

For most swing band arrangers, the obvious plan for an arrangement was the da capo form, which in the majority of the charts boiled down to variations on the introduction-theme-solos-tutti-theme-coda format. Structuring elements—introductions, codas, modulations, and transitory sections—were typically short and of scant musical significance. By contrast, Strayhorn's pop tune arrangements have carefully worked out introductions, transitions, and codas, which he uses as structuring elements to secure the internal logic of an orchestration. Most notably, he often left out the obligatory solo and tutti passages that traditionally form the middle part of many swing band arrangements and replaced them with a short developmental section, as he had done in his breakthrough *Flamingo* arrangement.

The majority of Strayhorn's scores start with a fully worked-out introduction, ranging from a short four- or eight-bar introductory statement[2] to fully developed, more complex passages of uncommon lengths such as the introductions to *Tonight I Shall Sleep* (seven bars), *I'll Remember April* (ten bars), *Hear Say* (fourteen bars), *The Eighth Veil* (twenty-four bars and modulating), or *Overture to a Jam Session* (thirty-one bars). It should be noted, however, that it is not the (irregular) length of the introduction that identifies Strayhorn as the author (Ellington similarly used unorthodox lengths in some of his orchestral openers), but always the musical content.

The most outstanding of Strayhorn's introductions are written as complex contrapuntal textures, with lines that draw on thematic material. *The Man I Love*, for instance, builds on the first two bars of the song, while in *Night and Day* (1940 version), the introduction simultaneously cites material from the verse and from the chorus.[3] Often, in these introductions, instrumental solo voices or instrumental groups alternately emerge from and submerge into an orchestral background (e.g., in *Where or When*). In other instances, the introduction presents musical elements that play a role later in the score, such as the opening bars of *Flamingo*, which hint at the tonal ambiguity further explored in the arrangement.

In most cases, Strayhorn complemented the introductory section with a coda that—compared to the more common "tag"—again is relatively extended and of irregular length. As he did in his introductions, Strayhorn often used thematically, rhythmically, or harmonically related material for his codas.[4] Keeping an eye on the overall balance, he would typically write a more elaborate final section to complement an extensive introduction, such as the harmonically active thirteen-bar coda for *The Eighth Veil*.

At times, the coda is an exact reiteration of the introduction, with a short, added closing passage (ranging from not more than a chord to a two-bar phrase), a simple and effective way to create a sense of circularity within the arrangement.[5] More intricate is the plan in *It's Monday Every Day* (1947 version) and *There's a Man in My Life*, in which the recapitulation of the introduction is followed by a full, new closing section. Strayhorn often repeated structuring material, rather than thematic material, in order to bring out the internal logic of a piece.

After the thematic exposition (i.e., the delivery of the tune proper) many of Strayhorn's pop arrangements move into a distinctive section where he develops melodic, harmonic, or rhythmic elements from the theme, rather than simply continuing with the obvious tutti and solo passages over repeated changes.[6] Significantly, while he often would not write out the song's main theme in his score—generally known to the featured singer or instrumentalist, or readily available to the copyist on a professional leadsheet—many of his middle sections include a written-out soloist's or singer's part, since the melody there significantly deviates from the original theme. In *The Wonder of You* and *I'll Buy That Dream* the developmental sections play with thematic and harmonic material from the main theme, but in a number of other scores the development takes on the form of what might be called a "temporary modulation": a modulation to a preferably remote key for the duration of a single strain or a half-chorus, that then modulates back to the original key.[7] Such temporary modulations create a ternary form within the rather limited confines of these popular songs: the middle section constitutes a miniature development of the work's musical material.

One of the earliest instances of such a temporary modulation occurs in Strayhorn's 1943–44 vocal arrangement of Rodgers and Hart's *Where or When*, recorded more than a decade later as an instrumental for the *Ellington Indigos* LP (October 10, 1957).[8] To enhance the element of surprise, Strayhorn makes a fast but aurally logical transition to the temporary key, in this case through an enharmonic change: the melody's final D♭ becomes a C♯, the sixth scale degree in the new temporary key of E (one step up along Lendvai's tonic axis), underscored by the brass who play the first phrase of the theme (Ex. 4-1, m. 49). For an entire A-strain, Strayhorn sticks to the new key, which modulates back in measure 59, by means of D♯mi7$^{(♭5)}$-G♯7-F7$^{(alt)}$.[9]

While the return to the initial key in *Where or When* takes place swiftly, with a two-bar modulation, in a number of later scores the modulations back are more elaborate and become especially demanding on the singers. In *Can't Help Lovin' Dat Man*, Strayhorn modulates back from the temporary key E♭ to the original key of C halfway through the A-strain—singer Kay Davis was supposed to enter on a G, following the dissonant D9$^{(♭13)}$ chord (Ex. 4-2, m. 55). Her note is not given by

Ex. 4-1. *Where or When*, mm. 47–60

Ex. 4-1. *Where or When,* mm. 47–60 *(cont.)*

any of the other voices, though hinted at by the preceding dominant. The temporary modulation was cut and replaced with a repeat from the first chorus, possibly because Davis was unable to deliver the passage convincingly—even after the cut she sounds insecure in her performance.[10] While not altering the overall length of the song, the cut eliminated one of the key passages from the arrangement.[11]

An equally interesting passage in *He Makes Me Believe He's Mine* landed on the cutting room floor as well. Here, the temporary modulation moves to the parallel minor of the initial key and back. In this case, the cut cannot be explained by any presumed incapacity of one of the vocalists: the passage was entirely instrumental. Similar modulations may be found in *There's No You,* which temporarily modulates from F to D♭; in *Now I Know,* with a complex modulation from G minor to C minor; in *This Is Always,* which moves from G to G♭ and back; and in the arrangement of *Love Letters,* whose temporary modulation from F to A♭ is less of a departure and comes close to the more common tutti passage.

As Strayhorn indicated in his arranging hints for *Music and Rhythm,* composing and arranging were for him two sides of the same coin. While as an arranger he was often working with existent material written by others (whether Broadway composers or Ellington), his approach to the popular repertory was nevertheless essentially *compositional.* Instead of simply dressing up the tune with orchestral colors, he emphasized form, building elaborate introductions, codas, and developmental sections around the song (all based on the work's original musical material) to form the cornerstones of the arrangement's architecture. As may be expected, he applied a comparable approach to his own compositions of the period.

Ex. 4-2. *Can't Help Lovin' Dat Man*, mm. 47–57

In his original works of the mid-1940s, unrestrained by any pop format, Strayhorn similarly used various developmental techniques to achieve a ternary, fully through-composed form. In compositions such as *Hear Say* (from the *Deep South Suite*), *Overture to a Jam Session*, *Blue Heart*, and *Portrait of a Silk Thread* (the latter two unrecorded at the time), Strayhorn arrived at a ternary form through middle sections that stand in rhythmic and dynamic rather than harmonic contrast with the exposition, while developing thematic material.[12] In *Portrait of a Silk Thread*, for instance, Strayhorn breaks open the block-chord texture of the exposition and turns to a more contrapuntal section, where various voices phrase motivic material (Ex. 4-3). The closing line for the bass (m. 28) and the absence in

Ex. 4-3. *Portrait of a Silk Thread*, mm. 25–36

Ex. 4-3. *Portrait of a Silk Thread*, mm. 25–36 *(cont.)*

the autograph of a bass part for the remainder of the passage (Ex. 4-3, mm. 29-36) strongly suggest that Strayhorn envisioned the entire rhythm section to rest here, giving *Silk Thread*'s restrained middle section far less forward movement than its liquid chromatic exposition.

To a similar effect, the middle section of *Hear Say* consists of an irregular, forty-seven-bar passage that is mostly in 3/4 time, as opposed to the 4/4 of the surrounding sections, while it also contains a temporary modulation from A^b to G. The baritone theme in this section develops the trumpet's opening theme, over a texture that is largely contrapuntal (certain orchestral passages in *Hear Say* are reminiscent of *Pentonsilic*, especially the orchestral hits that precede the return to the theme). The middle section of *Blue Heart* stays closer to the exposition—its theme is a subtle deviation from the bridge—but here Strayhorn halts the harmonic movement and replaces it with a pedal point.

The lavishly detailed and Gershwinesque *Overture to a Jam Session*[13] is one of Strayhorn's more complex compositions of the period in general, as it welds large transitory and developmental sections into a tightly designed structure. Though little known, the work is one of the high points in Strayhorn's orchestral oeuvre, and it is more elaborate and expansive (a little over five minutes) than most of its contemporaries. *Overture to a Jam Session* is more elastic in its ternary architecture than the earlier da capo compositions. After an extensive middle episode that is largely shaped around pizzicato and bowed violin fragments (for trumpeter-violinist Ray Nance), the music almost comes to a halt. Strayhorn only in passing touches on the initial theme, expanding a gesture introduced in the development into a secondary theme. The secondary theme leads the piece to its final segment. In both the introduction and coda, a metrically displaced and rhythmically dense descending line forms the main building block. As ever, Strayhorn has secured the thematic relations: the line consists of inverted segments from the first theme.

A work that makes more straightforward uses of a bi-thematic design is *Lana Turner*, another example of the three-part architecture.[14] With its full secondary theme in a new key, the work resembles Ellington's earlier *Concerto for Cootie*, whose characteristics it largely follows: a "trumpet concerto" with a clearly marked, thematically and harmonically different middle section. Typically, where *Concerto for Cootie* has short modulatory transitions between its two harmonic levels (F and D$^\flat$) and marked caesuras, the transitory sections in *Lana Turner* are larger, more complex, and fully integrated. Again Strayhorn turns to a temporary modulation (from E$^\flat$ to G), with an extensive and fully through-composed return to the original key. As in *Overture to a Jam Session*, the reprise of the first theme is only partial: after three bars the recapitulation slides into a fourteen-bar closing section. The ternary form Strayhorn employs in these works serves a similar goal as the bridges in earlier works such as *My Little Brown Book, Let Nature Take Its Course, So This Is Love*, and *Chelsea Bridge*. The bridges in these pieces offered a temporary reflection. Now, Strayhorn makes the entire developmental section more detached, as he thins out the orchestration, slows down the harmonic rhythm, and often moves to new tonal planes.

The carefully designed architectures in Strayhorn's orchestrations were not academic exercises in complexity, but served an entirely musical goal: to entice and seduce the listener. The magnificent arrangement of *Where or When*, for instance, begins with individually unfolding lines that swiftly obscure meter and pulse, as if clouding a clear sky. As in virtually all of his scores, Strayhorn begins by introducing conflict, a classic narrative technique. The listener is drawn into a gradually unraveling musical adventure that places him or her in a different time and space. The ensuing sections tell a story, introduce new perspectives on the song's melody, and start subplots that are resolved along the way. In all of his pieces, he uses musical form as a means of expression, to create and communicate to the listener an "integral and complete mental picture," as he had explained in *Music and Rhythm*. Strayhorn's audience is taken by the hand and led through a fascinating musical landscape—enthralling, but never without danger.[15]

TECHNICALLY, COMPOSITIONAL FORM (whether in arrangements or originals) is one of the main elements that distinguishes Ellington and Strayhorn scores. Strayhorn's approach to form was strongly developmental, where Ellington tends to rely on contrast. The almost caesura-less flow encountered in most of Strayhorn's scores, is virtually absent in Ellington's writings. Though he left most of the vocal arrangements to Strayhorn, an incidental vocal score such as *I Never Felt This Way Before* ("Never Felt," DEC)—a 1939 Ellington original, re-scored by its author a year later—exemplifies this difference in form. Ellington's attractive arrangement (a showcase of his orchestration techniques) consists of two choruses, an instrumental chorus in B♭ and a vocal chorus in G, linked by a short transitory segment. A four-bar piano introduction opens the song, while an orchestral repeat of the final eight bars of the vocal segment serves as coda.

Though Strayhorn probably would have opted for an orchestral introduction (as in the majority of his scores) as well as for a different coda, it is the four-bar transitory passage between the instrumental and vocal choruses that bears Ellington's unmistakable signature and virtually rules out the possibility that his collaborator wrote the arrangement. This transitory passage (mm. 37-40) introduces a new and unexpected key: A♭. Here the autograph score is revealing. Ellington originally started this arrangement out in A♭ and later wrote a new instrumental chorus in B♭. For this new chorus he still used the B section of the earlier score, which he simply transposed a major second up. At the end of the instrumental section, however, Ellington returned to the transitory strain from his original A♭ score without any further adaptations. An unexpected and abrupt key change is the result, not only visible in the autograph, but also clearly audible on the recording.[16] In similar instances, Strayhorn used more integrated transitions. In all likelihood, he would have connected the two different keys, B♭ and G, with a pivotal passage (possibly in keeping with the axis-system). While *I Never Felt This Way Before* by no means represents Ellington's work, it is nevertheless exemplary of his predilection for hard cuts between segments.

IN ORDER TO MAKE all sections relate to each other, Strayhorn further used a variety of elements—harmonic, melodic, and rhythmic figures and passages—that not only guarantee the internal cohesion of a given piece, but also strongly unify his body of work (both the compositions and the arrangements) as a whole, clearly distinguishing it from Ellington's. Many of Strayhorn's musical fingerprints became more complex over the years, creating an even more recognizable sound in his later work. Although some of these elements at times may be encountered in Ellington's writing as well, there they appear mostly as isolated instances, as Ellington tended to move between a variety of contrasting ideas, while Strayhorn chose to adhere in each score to small, yet different sets of musical concepts.

One of those concepts in Strayhorn's writing is the specific type of dissonance that colors many of his pieces. This dissonance (one of the most readily audible fingerprints) stems from his harmonizations, while his voicing (i.e., the order of the chord tones and their distribution over the various registers) and instrumentation (i.e., the distribution of chord tones over the various instruments) further give the chords their distinctive Strayhorn quality.

Strayhorn often voiced the melody to move at a dissonant interval with one or more of the inner voices of the accompaniment. Usually, he placed the melody a minor or major ninth or a major seventh above either the first or the second voice in the background. This background may contain further internal dissonance between its own respective voices. In the opening bars of *Portrait of a Silk Thread*, for instance, the lead alto repeatedly clashes with the second trombone, which moves at sharp dissonance with the melody for the entire phrase (Ex. 4-4).

The instrumentation in this passage further adds to the Strayhorn sound: a high-register reed solo voice over a closely scored three-part trombone background. This is one of Strayhorn's favored instrumental combinations, and it can be found in many of his other scores.[17] In the later middle section of *Portrait of a Silk Thread* (see Ex. 4-3, p. 72), Strayhorn turns to a clarinet lead over muted trumpets, another of his preferred instrumental combinations, while adhering to the dissonant voice leading initiated in the exposition.[18]

The type of dissonant voicing that abounds in *Portrait of a Silk Thread* appears in the five-part reed backgrounds of numerous other scores, with the clarinet in its highest register hovering above the ensemble, often in partial contrary motion—a technique Strayhorn had started to employ in *Chelsea Bridge* and *Rain Check*. In the introduction of *The Eighth Veil*, for instance, Strayhorn assigns the clarinet a dominant and independent role as it breaks in on the second bar to move contrary to the rest of the reed ensemble in the following measures, sharply dissonant with the lower voices (Ex. 4-5, p. 78, mm. 2-6).[19]

In the harmony of these and similar passages, there is a striking absence of minor seventh chords, as well as half-diminished and diminished chords. In har-

Ex. 4-4. *Portrait of a Silk Thread*, mm. 1–4

monized lines (i.e., a line underscored by simultaneous moving voices) Strayhorn favored major over minor harmonies. In addition, he made extensive use of chord extensions (often altered). In the second bar of *Portrait of a Silk Thread*, for instance, Strayhorn underscored the lead alto's low G♭ with a dissonant F7$^{(\sharp 9 \sharp 11)}$ that takes over the consonant A♭ chord held by the trombones. Similar passages can be found in other scores.[20] Together with his abundant chromatic voice leading and the often applied contrary motion or partial contrary motion in his lines, this type of harmonization is one of the hallmarks of Strayhorn's ensemble sound. Especially the colors of Strayhorn's chords differ markedly from Ellington's section writing: Ellington in general tended to use more minor and diminished chords when voicing ensemble passages than Strayhorn (Van de Leur 1993, 65). Often, when writing minor chords, Strayhorn would still color them with a major seventh (as in the background ensemble of *Take the "A" Train* [1957 version] and in the theme of *Chelsea Bridge*).

In addition to their different choices in chords, Ellington more often would use so-called close-position voicing in his backgrounds and ensemble passages, where Strayhorn preferred open-position voicing.[21] In addition, Ellington preferred to use the lower register of the instruments, and consequently often wrote low-register dissonance. His treatment of the baritone is illustrative. The baritone is often given an individual line with chord tones that lie outside the basic harmony: sevenths, ninths, and thirteenths. Strayhorn, by contrast, wrote more middle- and upper-register dissonance, as exemplified by the reed solo over brass passages. Consequently, instruments play in their lower register less often. The Ellingtonian baritone treatment is largely absent from Strayhorn's orchestrations. While he treated it individually, the baritone part in a Strayhorn arrangement tends to be more consonant, as the dissonance is confined to the upper voices of the ensemble.

The examples from *The Eighth Veil* and *Portrait of a Silk Thread* show that an economy of means not only governed Strayhorn's construction of themes (as demonstrated earlier with *Passion Flower*) but indeed informed all other aspects in a score. Strayhorn developed the musical material in nonthematic passages from similar clear-cut ideas. Thus, the first bar of *The Eighth Veil* builds on planing triads in all sections (here leading to the repeated polytonal orchestral hits in measures 2 and 3, another Strayhorn technique). The consequent measures are derived from a single rhythmic-thematic motif with the descending minor third in the lead (Ex. 4-5; the motif is marked with a bracket). Similarly, the transitory passage in *Portrait of a Silk Thread* (Ex. 4-3, p. 72) uses sequentially repeated motifs, first in the trombones (mm. 25-28) and next in the clarinet with trumpets (mm. 29-32) and finally in the alto with trombones (mm. 33-36). Once a pattern is set, Strayhorn tends to stick to it, both on a microlevel (for instance, in the way he voices his chords) as well as on a macrolevel, where a given concept, such as the rhythmically displaced sequence model found in *Portrait of a Silk Thread*, may carry an entire passage, or even an entire composition.

Ex. 4-5. *The Eighth Veil*, mm. 1–8

Where concepts tended to govern Strayhorn's writing, Ellington seems to have worked case by case, proceeding from chord to chord, from passage to passage, as if designing each sound and phrase separately, without necessarily adhering to a chosen musical technique. As a rule, Ellington kept infusing new and musically unrelated ideas into the musical fabric of a given piece. Numerous Ellington recordings illustrate this practice, including the aforementioned *Sepia Panorama*, *Harlem Airshaft*, and *I Never Felt This Way Before*.[22]

Much as Strayhorn's harmonies in the passages examined so far derive their colors from dissonant voices that largely originate in homorhythmic movement (i.e., the melody and accompaniment move simultaneously), Strayhorn in other works uses a more polyphonic texture as individual instruments, rather than ensembles, create a canonic configuration. Layering independently moving voices, Strayhorn lets the music gradually alter its timbre as instruments drop in and out of the orchestral texture, which is essentially melodyless. This approach comes close to an early twentieth-century technique that Arnold Schoenberg in 1911 termed "Klangfarbenmelodie" (timbre melody). Strayhorn had begun to employ his own version of timbre melody—less rigid than in Schoenberg's conception, where each voice had to stick to one pitch—in the waltz-time introduction of an unrecorded arrangement of *Bli-Blip*, arranged for the theatrical revue *Jump for Joy*.[23] He used it more consistently later in *Hear Say* and *Strange Feeling*. The final bars of *Strange Feeling* exemplify how Strayhorn matches different orchestral voices, weaving a texture with altering colors. The episode concludes with a densely scored three-part cross-section passage in which the clarinet, first alto, and second trumpet grate over a dissonant chord in two reeds, two trumpets, and two trombones, while the bass clarinet and the third trombone state the whole-tone bass line that has been central in the entire composition (Ex. 4-6).

Ex. 4-6. *Strange Feeling*, mm. 53–59

More radical instances of timbre melody appear in his work (partly unused) for the 1959 film score *Anatomy of a Murder*, especially in the many versions of *Polly's Theme*, one of the central themes of the score. Example 4-7 gives a reduction of one of his many settings of the theme, this one partly used in *Low Key Lightly*, where it functions as a barely audible backdrop for Ray Nance's violin (mm. 33-40 in the original score or the second A-strain of the first violin chorus on the recording; the bridge is Strayhorn's as well).[24] Similar passages can be found both in the recorded and in an unrecorded alternate version of *Come Sunday* for Mahalia Jackson ("Come Sun," DEC) and in the first chorus of the arrangement of *Poor Butterfly*, though in these instances the orchestral texture serves as an accompaniment to a clearly melodic passage.

While Strayhorn's textures can be full and dense (as in the opening bars of *The Eighth Veil*), the more polyphonic passages shown above exemplify the lighter textures in his work. The most open and transparent background is the often occurring unison saxophone line under the melody. At times, this counterpoint forms a mostly consonant half-note accompaniment to the tune while unobtrusively traveling through the harmonic progression, connected by scale steps and chromatic passing notes.[25] Although the unison saxophone ensemble is an obvious and simple technique encountered in numerous swing arrangements (however, as a background it is strikingly absent in Ellington's writing), Strayhorn's single-line backgrounds often deviate from the standard paths, since his choice of altered chord tones, their chromatic connections, and their rhythmic placement give them a characteristic angular and dissonant quality. Measures 1-8 from *A Garden in the Rain* (Ex. 4-8) display the general appearance of this type of half-note movement (with some incidental connecting lines in Strayhorn's favorite sixteenth-note and sixteenth-note triplet figures).

Ex. 4-7. *Polly's Theme*, mm. 33–40

Even in this straightforward pop song Strayhorn displays a tendency toward a more dissonant counterpoint. In the bridge the line incorporates an increasing number of alterations and takes on a true bebop quality. While the counterpoint in *A Garden in the Rain* is simple and mostly consonant, in *Lover Man* the heightened dissonance of the saxophone line significantly colors the trombone's basic harmonic progression as Strayhorn leads the reeds through altered and extended chord tones, while diverging in measures 5 and 6 to his trademark dissonant chords (Ex. 4-9).[26]

Ex. 4-8. *A Garden in the Rain*, mm. 1–8

Ex. 4-9. *Lover Man*, mm. 7–12

Although he often gives the longer unison background lines to the reed section (or part of the reed section), at times Strayhorn condenses them to a more clipped single-line solo trumpet answer, typically at the end of phrases (e.g., in *He Makes Me Believe He's Mine* and *Lana Turner*), in codas (e.g., in *There's No You*), or at turn-around passages, such as in *Out of This World* and *As Long as I Live* (where incidentally the trombone answers). Over the course of the 1950s, Strayhorn further developed these unison backgrounds into a more chromatic and angular counterpoint that became another hallmark of his compositions, culminating in his 1956 arrangements of *Take the "A" Train* and *Day Dream* (see Chapter 8), and the scores of *Isfahan* and *Blood Count* (see Chapter 10).

Characteristic of Strayhorn's background writing are the specific rhythmic figures that appear in new and different guises in virtually every arrangement, and consequently form another easily recognizable element in his work. In its most common form, the figure consists of repeated staccato brass chords built with a combination of mostly sixteenth and eighth notes—with an incidental triplet or quarter note. Measures 5 and 6 of Strayhorn's 1943 *Where or When* arrangement (Ex. 4-10) show a typical instance of such a figure (on the 1956 recording the band played the repeated chords as a single sforzando chord).[27]

These rhythmic figures do not necessarily consist of strict repeats: the brass chords can move up or down after a while, as exemplified by a passage in the middle section of *Blue Heart* (Ex. 4-11). In measure 35, the trombones are freed from the locked chord structures and start to move independently under the trumpets. Similar passages can be found in the codas of *Blue Heart* and *Where or When*, where Strayhorn has given the independently moving line to the saxophones.

Comparison of Strayhorn and the bebop composers and arrangers active around the same time (Dizzy Gillespie, Charlie Parker, Thelonious Monk, Tadd

Ex. 4-10. *Where or When*, mm. 5–6

Ex. 4-11. *Blue Heart*, mm. 33–35

Dameron, Bud Powell) yields few similarities.[28] With few exceptions, the bop pieces were more frenetic in their musical movement, with much more emphasis on the brass and a lesser role for the reeds. Extensive introductions, spun-out modulations, transitions, and codas are typically absent, and while some arrangers at times used orchestral colors similar to Strayhorn's (Claude Thornhill in *Snowfall*, Tadd Dameron in *Our Delight* for Dizzy Gillespie and His Orchestra, and Gil Evans in *Donna Lee* and *Robbins' Nest* for Claude Thornhill and His Orchestra),[29] these works make a different impression: Strayhorn's writing is more subdued.

In an era that put increasing strain on the big bands (wartime measures, the draft, broadcasting and recording bans), most orchestrators and composers wisely kept an eye on the musical tastes of the public. Apart from Ellington's, most of the "name bands" (those led by the likes of Jimmie Lunceford, Count Basie, Cab Calloway, Lionel Hampton, Glenn Miller, Tommy Dorsey, Harry James, Benny Goodman) and their hundreds of regional counterparts largely shunned experimentation. Nevertheless, in some of the swing orchestras, bandleaders and arrangers allowed for more adventurous scores. The orchestras of Boyd Raeburn, Woody Herman, Artie Shaw, and Claude Thornhill all employed visionary writers, who, like Ellington and Strayhorn, sought to stretch the boundaries of the genre. In fact, the experimentation in orchestras such as Raeburn's and Thornhill's was more conscious and went further than Strayhorn and Ellington allowed themselves, as these bands also added instruments atypical for mainstream big bands, such as harp, flute, bass saxophone, French horn, bassoon, oboe, and English horn (cor anglais).

One suspects that some of these arrangers closely studied the Strayhorn arrangements that were part of the regular broadcasts of the Ellington orchestra (see Van de Leur 2001). George Williams, active for the adventurous Boyd Raeburn orchestra, was one of those who apparently keenly listened to Strayhorn. His arrangement of *Street of Dreams* cites the secondary theme of *Chelsea Bridge* virtually verbatim, while his arrangement of *Some Peaceful Evening* is so much in the vein of Strayhorn's vocal arrangements that it leaves one to wonder whether Strayhorn by some miraculous scheme wasn't indeed the arranger.[30]

In the arrangements of George Handy, one of Williams's fellow arrangers for the Boyd Raeburn orchestra, Strayhorn's influences are even more conspicuous. In his 1945-46 arrangements of *Temptation, Body and Soul, I Only Have Eyes for You*, and *More Than You Know* as well as in his originals such as *Dalvatore Sally*, Handy ably imitates some of Strayhorn's techniques, as well as his overall sound.[31] With titles such as *Boyd Meets the Duke* (by Eddie Finckel) and *Concerto for Duke* (a medley of Ellington titles arranged by George Williams),[32] the Raeburn arrangers acknowledged where their ears were, but Handy, for one, appears to have more readily picked out Strayhorn traits than Ellingtonian devices. Still, Handy's work in general is structurally far more fragmented than Strayhorn's and follows more an Ellingtonian vein, built on contrast.[33] Sadly, these virtuoso orchestras with their innovative arrangers led short, stressful lives and disbanded before the end of the decade.

In the 1940s, Strayhorn created an individual musical world, both in his originals and arrangements. The combination of his approach to form, harmony, counterpoint, voicing, and instrumentation created the unmistakable Strayhorn sound, laid down in forward-looking scores, which were repeatedly performed by the Ellington orchestra. Some contemporary arranger-composers, such as George Handy and George Williams, appear to have been working at times along the same lines as Strayhorn. Their work for Boyd Raeburn's orchestra, however, received far less exposure, as the orchestra was lesser known and less popular than Ellington's band. Clearly, the artistic freedom Ellington granted Strayhorn gave him an unparalleled position in the increasingly competitive and difficult world the swing bands were facing. Not having to negotiate the complex dance-music market—still largely affected by racism and commercialism—had irrefutable advantages for Strayhorn, who could write uncompromising music, regardless of its mass appeal.

Chapter Five

Writing and Arranging Companion: Credited and Uncredited Collaborations

HALFWAY THROUGH 1942 new troubles befell the Ellington organization. During the early 1940s, more and more public entertainment venues were closing down their stages, and the American Federation of Musicians (AFM), the musicians' union, blamed the popularity of radio for this decline in opportunities for live performance. It was the Federation's belief that the increasingly popular radio broadcasts replaced live music at hotels, dances, and the like, and thus the AFM demanded a compensatory royalty payment from the recording companies for each disc sold. In truth, the decline in the entertainment business resulted largely from the grim international political situation. With young men at war and women filling in for them in the workplace, the focus of young people had shifted to activities considered more virtuous than swing dancing. Furthermore, wartime measures, such as a cabaret tax and limitations on driving (to save gas), created serious problems both for the ever-traveling swing bands and for their audiences. As the record industry refused to fulfill the AFM's demands, the union called for a ban on all instrumental recordings, beginning August 1, 1942. For more than two years, the Ellington orchestra could not make any records, with the exception of so-called V-discs, produced exclusively for the U.S. Armed Services.[1] When in November 1944 the majority of the record companies gave in and the AFM lifted its ban, the musical landscape had changed for good. The popularity of big-band music had seriously declined, bebop had emerged, and wartime audiences, in search of reassurance, had embraced the romantic songs performed by a handful of idolized star singers, such as Frank Sinatra, Jo Stafford, and Dinah Shore.

For Strayhorn, the war years were nevertheless exciting. He traveled out to the West Coast with the orchestra, had the opportunity to meet many celebrities (including Orson Welles and Lana Turner) as well as important musicians

Strayhorn was the only individual whom Ellington truly allowed into his private musical sphere. On the surface the two men were opposites. The charismatic Ellington naturally gravitated to center stage, while the shy Strayhorn shunned the limelight. What they had in common was an immense passion and talent for music. (*Photograph by Frank Driggs*)

(among others, Lester Young), and befriended singer Lena Horne, who became his lifelong soul mate. Where once he had dreamt of a penthouse on Pittsburgh's Shady Avenue, he now frequented many of those come-what-may-places, including fine restaurants, famous night clubs, and Hollywood parties. At home in Manhattan, he and Aaron Bridgers entertained guests at their modest apartment, cooking lavish meals.

Professionally, Strayhorn continued to add to the orchestra's everyday repertoire. Furthermore, he got to work behind the scenes in Hollywood, arranging music for films that included the Ellington orchestra, such as the Soundies (three minute film-shorts), and the films *Cabin in the Sky* and *An RKO Jamboree*. Most significantly, Ellington would involve his associate in some of his more personal endeavors, such as the orchestra's Carnegie Hall debut, his first suites, and a theater show called *Beggar's Holiday*. It displayed Ellington's tremendous trust in Strayhorn and honed the two composers' methods when working on the same project. On the other hand, it showed that Strayhorn had to pay a price for being on Ellington's team: his contributions often remained unknown to the larger audience.

As the recording ban suspended most of Ellington's studio activities, new challenges lay ahead: the orchestra was scheduled to give its first concert at Carnegie Hall, on January 23, 1943. The concert celebrated the importance of Ellington as a composer and bandleader, ending a week baptized "National Ellington Week." Less overtly, the event also celebrated the collaboration between Ellington and Strayhorn. Not only had Ellington dedicated a special segment in the evening's program to three Strayhorn compositions, but he also had allowed his protégé to collaborate on some of his most personal works—an expression of Ellington's fathomless trust in Strayhorn.

In addition to programming a selection from his best-known and most favorably reviewed works of the past (such as *Ko-Ko, Cotton Tail,* and *Black and Tan Fantasy*) interspersed with hit tunes (*Don't Get Around Much Anymore, Rose of the Rio Grande*), Ellington set out to compose an original jazz work of unequaled proportions: *Black, Brown and Beige: A Tone Parallel to the History of the Negro in America*. From the early 1930s he had talked about a large-scale work in progress, an opera called *Boola*, which was to parallel African-American history (Tucker 1993b, passim). Over the course of twelve years, Ellington had largely laid out the programmatic contours of the work (alternately said to be in three, four, or five movements), yet by December 1942, roughly six weeks prior to its world premiere, the entire multimovement work still had to be written. Used to composing fast and under hectic conditions, Ellington started to work on what was arguably his most ambitious project ever, while still subject to the usual overloaded performance schedule. As the date of the widely advertised premiere loomed dangerously near, and rehearsals were well under way, he was still struggling with the third and final movement, *Beige*. Facing a deadline he couldn't possibly meet, Ellington brought in Strayhorn.

Almost a third of the thirteen-and-a-half-minute *Beige* consists of Strayhorn music, starting with a twenty-nine-bar background under Lawrence Brown's rendition of Ellington's masterly waltz-theme. The movement thereafter returns to Ellington's score for a transitional section in 4/4, led by trumpeter Harold Baker, but Strayhorn takes over for a partly stated tenor cadenza by Webster. *Beige* continues with Ellington's score for a thirty-six-bar saxophone special, again in waltz-time, to return to a full reading of Strayhorn's earlier cadenza. Overlooking Strayhorn's hand on the manuscript, Maurice Peress (who later scored the work for symphony orchestra) notes that this cadenza quotes the central themes from *Black, Brown and Beige*,

> Eleven chords are held by the orchestra. On the first and third, the tenor quotes *Work Song*. On the second we hear the tune from *Sugar Hill Penthouse*. On the final chord the solo begins with the jungle theme and unwinds by introducing the theme labeled [in the published score (Ellington 1963)] *Last of Penthouse*. Here we see Ellington [actually Strayhorn] doing what Beethoven did for his piano concertos: composing cadenzas." (Peress 1993, 158)

A piano transition by Ellington leads to a section known as *Sugar Hill Penthouse*, in truth a boldly inserted, full Strayhorn composition: *Symphonette-Rhythmique*, a three-minute piece written between November 1940 and June 1942, at least half a year before Ellington started to work on *Black, Brown and Beige*.[2] Whether the orchestra performed Strayhorn's composition separately during the Blanton-Webster era is not known, but it could cast new light on a statement by John Lewis (Knauer, 1990, 21–22, 37n3), who maintains that he heard portions of *Black, Brown and Beige* as early as 1939 or 1940. Tucker argues that as far as Ellington's work for *Black, Brown and Beige* is concerned, "signs point to most of the composing taking place in the six weeks before the Carnegie premiere" (Tucker 1993b, 80n13).[3]

Ellington and Strayhorn may have decided in consultation to infuse this earlier work. As Priestley and Cohen have noted (1993, 201), *Symphonette-Rhythmique* shares thematic material with other sections in the movement: *Beige* opens with a two-bar melodic gesture that stems from the head of Strayhorn's piece, while the transitional passage preceding Brown's solo cites the two-bar descending arpeggio from the *Symphonette* theme. Furthermore, as pointed out above, Strayhorn's tenor cadenza quotes the opening bars of the theme as well. In spite of this—rather superficial—motivic kinship of some sections, the episodic structure of the last movement of *Black, Brown and Beige* is generally conceived as "less balanced...than the other parts of the work" (ibid., 202) or even as "discordant, inchoate,...[and] thrown together" (Schuller 1989, 148).

Strayhorn later denied any direct involvement with *Black, Brown and Beige*: "[the] larger things like *Harlem* [1951] or *Black, Brown and Beige* I had very little to do with any of them other than maybe discussing them with him" (Coss 1962, 23). From his perspective as a composer this claim seems justified: even though he did help out with the composition of both extended works, they were clearly conceived by Ellington. As Strayhorn further noted, "because [these] larger works are such a personal expression for him...[it] wouldn't make any sense for me to be involved there" (Coss 1962, 23).

Though he downplayed his contributions to these works, Strayhorn pointed up another, and surely the most important aspect of the Ellington-Strayhorn collaboration. Their musical partnership consisted of *discussion*, an exchange of musical ideas, and a quest for solutions to compositional problems, which led to mutual inspiration, but not necessarily to joint compositions. Of the roughly three thousand scores surviving from their collaboration of almost thirty years, only fifty-two carry the handwriting of both composers, less than 2 percent. Especially in later years, when Strayhorn rarely toured with the band, the collaboration boiled down to conversation: "We do very well over the phone, because you're only confronted with essentials, really" (Strayhorn 1962). As Strayhorn explained, these telephone calls generally made it impossible to "play something on the piano or on a record" and in order to work around this problem they either had to "sing it or talk it, and singing doesn't really mean anything because we both sing equally bad" (ibid.). Ellington gave further corroboration of the nature of their collaboration in his autobiography. "In music," he wrote, "as you develop a theme or a musical idea, there are many points at which direction must be decided, and any time I was in the throes of debate with myself, harmonically or melodically, I would turn to Billy Strayhorn. We would talk, and then the whole world would come into focus" (Ellington 1973, 156).

At the time he started working on *Black, Brown and Beige*, Ellington indeed must have been "in the throes of debate" with himself, as he was tackling the complex task of designing a structure for the movements of his work. In his narrative script (Ellington n.d.) he had sketched the main building blocks of his first movement *Black: Work Song*, a "percussive leitmotif" (Tucker 1993b, 78), and a *Spiritual Theme* (known as *Come Sunday*). Yet, the actual structure of this movement could very well have been the outcome of a discussion with his associate: there is a striking structural congruence between *Black* and Strayhorn's *Pentonsilic*, which was written between November 1940 and June 1942. Though works of different character, dimensions, and implications, both are organized along analogous musical lines. *Pentonsilic* and *Black* both feature two distinct themes, the first an up-tempo, strong, and affirmative "curtain raiser," and the second a contrasting, emotionally intense ballad. In both works, too, the two themes conjoin in the final episode—a technique that requires the thematic material to be deliberately designed toward that goal.[4] As Ellington explained at the Carnegie premiere of *Black*, "These two [the *Work Song* and the *Spiritual Theme*] are very closely related and so that naturally necessitates developing the two and showing their close relationship" (Ellington 1943).

Using more than one theme for a large scale work seems inevitable—even many of Ellington's earlier short works featured more than one theme (*Concerto for Cootie, Harlem Airshaft*, and others)—but never before had Ellington or Strayhorn written two contrasting themes that function as each other's counterpoint in a separate section. It is conceivable that the two composers discussed the structural implications of a large-scale work and came up with this format as a possible solution. That the execution of the bi-thematic design led to such distinct results (Strayhorn's *Pentonsilic* and Ellington's *Black*) provides a clear illustration of the independent working habits of the two composers, as well as their different musical goals and aesthetics.

At Carnegie Hall, Ellington took the opportunity openly to acknowledge his collaborator: "The next section we get to Strayhorn, a young man who has really contributed so much to our recently acquired music" (Ellington 1943). Assigning ample space to Strayhorn, Ellington allowed three of his associate's works, according to the program (Kolodin 1943, 161): *Dirge, Nocturne*, and *Stomp*. Yet only two were performed, since *Nocturne* was dropped for unknown reasons.

According to Ulanov (1946, 253), *Dirge* left the audience baffled by "music that sounded more like Milhaud and the latter-day Stravinsky than Ellington, with only a bent note here and a slow syncopation there to remind them whose concert it was." Largely ignoring the customary parameters in jazz with its total absence of a rhythmic pulse or improvisation, *Dirge* indeed must have puzzled the audience. Even in Ellington's most introspective "mood pieces" (such as *Mood Indigo* or *Dusk*), the rhythm section still provides a forward drive, "keeping time." In *Dirge*, the rhythm section accompaniment is limited to bass-drum first-beat accents only, while the piano, guitar, and bass rest. (Strayhorn's score, however, indicates the customary down-beat bass notes on one and three; he must have taken the rhythm section out during rehearsals.) Against the free-flowing trombone melody of *Dirge*, that draws on the blues scale, stand orchestral interludes and a twelve-bar *pianissimo* coda of barely moving, dissonant chords by just a trumpet, trombone, and chalumeau clarinet.

Especially this final "*Mood Indigo* trio" may have sparked Ulanov's criticism, who felt that the work was "jazz only in its colors," and that its "out of tempo [scoring] implements its dry acrid figures: it really is a dirge." (In this segment Joe Nanton misread his part and was two bars behind, which led to some unintended dissonance.) At the same time Ulanov noted that "most *musicians* at the concert listened attentively and were deeply moved by Billy's somber chant for jazz instruments" (Ulanov 1946, 253; italics added). Homzy (1992, 6) felt that *Dirge* displayed Strayhorn's musical "immaturity, a lapse of taste, or simply the lack of connection Billy had with jazz and popular music in his youth." In Feather (1977) the piece found one of its few defenders: "The dirge, which proved a little too heavy for some of the more dedicated of Ellingtonians, was nevertheless very beautiful."

The concert continued with the third piece in the "Strayhorn group, *Johnny Come Lately*, already recorded and here titled *Stomp*.⁵ In an effort to rescue *Dirge*, Ellington (undoubtedly aware of the audience's bewilderment) stated somewhat uncomfortably,

> We feel that these two numbers [*Dirge* and *Stomp*] selected in the Strayhorn group are somewhat related. As we find it in the picture of the early jazz days, when a jazz band, or rather a small band, was picked to play at a funeral, they played the dirge—something like *that*—and then on their way back from the funeral we find the dirge resembling something like Strayhorn's *Stomp*, his *Little Light Stomp*. (Ellington 1943)⁶

It was nevertheless a telling gesture that Ellington included an inaccessible work such as *Dirge* to spotlight Strayhorn, as it spoke of his confidence in his collaborator.

But there was more Strayhorn to be heard at the Carnegie concert. In 1938, bandleader Paul Whiteman had invited Ellington to be one of six composers (the others being Roy Bargy, Walter Gross, Morton Gould, Bert Shefter, and Fred Van Eps) to contribute to a six-part "bell suite," entitled *Those Bells*.⁷ Whiteman's orchestra premiered *Those Bells* at its first Carnegie Hall appearance on December 24, 1938, billed both as his "Eighth Experiment in Modern American Music," and a "Christmas Night Jazz Concert." To fulfill his assignment, Ellington wrote a piano leadsheet entitled *Blue Belles of Harlem*, adapted for the sixty-three-piece orchestra by Van Eps, who was one of Whiteman's staff arrangers at the time. The reviewer of the *New York Sun* called the event

> a curious hodgepodge of a concert, in which the shades of Delius, Stravinsky, Debussy and various other estimable ghosts evicted virtually all traces of straightforward, vigorous jazz. On the whole, the "experiment" produced the best results in a six-section suite entitled *Those Bells* (each piece by a different composer), for it brought from the gifted Duke Ellington a charming fantasy entitled *Blue Belles of Harlem*, which was easily the finest music of the evening. (Kolodin 1938, 16)⁸

For the orchestra's own premiere of *Blue Belles of Harlem* at Carnegie Hall, Strayhorn extensively reworked the piano leadsheet which Ellington had kept in his files ("Blue Belles," DEC), turning it into a six-minute concerto for piano and orchestra. He added a harmonically stagnant introduction that evokes the sound of distant bells, charged Ellington's melodic lines with chromatic counterpoint, and extended the piece with a secondary theme for Hodges and Ellington. As he had done in his earlier arrangement of *Frankie and Johnny*, Strayhorn largely maintained the structure of Ellington's initial rhapsodic format, which exploited the alternation between 6/4 and 2/4 meters. Not surprisingly, Ulanov (1944, 8), unaware of the uncredited adaptation, heard "overtones suggestive of Ravel" in the piece.[9]

ALTHOUGH ELLINGTON'S 1943 Carnegie Hall debut as a whole received predominantly positive reviews, the critiques of *Black, Brown and Beige* were mostly negative. Most commentators looked merely at the technical merits of the work, largely ignoring or misunderstanding the extra-musical social and racial agendas that Ellington addressed. Disappointed, Ellington decided to stop performing the integral work.[10] Instead, he continued to use portions of *Black, Brown and Beige* over the course of his career (Hoefsmit 1993, 161–173), as well as adaptations and transformations.

It was probably due to this unfavorable reception of his first attempt at a large-scale, through-composed work, apart from more practical reasons, that Ellington abandoned the idea of a work of symphonic dimensions—with the exception of the thirteen-minute, single movement *Harlem* (1951). Instead, he turned to a format that could satisfy his ambitions and at the same time would silence his critics: the suite. The suite format dates from the European early Baroque period (seventeenth century), when it denoted a work consisting of a group of dances in various stylized dance rhythms with different moods, meters, and tempos. In nineteenth- and twentieth-century music, the term more and more came to refer to any assembly of pieces, often short. Ellington adopted the concept in this meaning.

The advantages of the suite format for Ellington were several. Since the movements of a suite could be relatively short and thus required less development, the format avoided the compositional difficulties inherent in a more extensive work. Most critics had found fault with the formal "inadequacy" of *Black, Brown and Beige* (DeVeaux 1993, 128) because they measured the merits of the work against the standards of the European symphonic tradition. By definition, a suite was less likely to be criticized for such reasons. In the meantime, a multimovement work comprising a number of shorter compositions and connected by a literary program could advance Ellington's extra-musical agenda equally well. As Ellington felt, "social protest and pride in the history of the Negro have been the most significant themes in what we've done" (Henthoff 1965, 366). Discussing the earlier *Jump for Joy*, he explained how he liked to deliver these themes: "[Jump for Joy] was well done because we included everything we wanted without saying it. Which is the way I think these social significance things should be handled, if it's going to be done on stage. Just to come out on the stage and take a soap box and stand in the spotlight and say ugly things is not entertainment" (Nicholson 1999, 234).

In practical terms, a suite better fit Ellington's working schedule, which generally allowed little time for the deliberate writing of large-scale compositions. Furthermore, Ellington could easily infuse music that had been composed earlier, a technique that saved valuable time. (As Strayhorn dryly observed, "Even the unscheduled work...is behind schedule" [Henthoff 1965, 367].) The recycling of existing music in *Black, Brown and Beige* had come at a price: one reviewer felt the work was a "series of brief, air-tight compositions, all prettily tied together by modulatory bridges—well, bridges of some kind or other" (Bagar 1943, 9). Indeed, in his May 1965 recordings of *Black, Brown and Beige*, Ellington split up the work in those separate "air-tight compositions," leaving out many of the connecting passages. In a suite, separate compositions (old and new, by Ellington and by Strayhorn) could be strung together directly, without bothering with connecting material.

Now that Ellington increasingly allowed Strayhorn to be involved with his most personal musical outings, the suite brought another significant advantage: it accommodated the division of work between the two composers. The larger part of the future "extended works" (a term that apart from the suites encompasses film scores, theater works, concept LPs, and others) consisted of a number of separate, self-contained movements, written independently by the two composers. Apart from its practical convenience, this type of collaboration had musical advantages. In their artistically more successful efforts, Ellington and Strayhorn covered a far wider musical gamut in these suites than each of them separately would have. This did not necessarily endanger the coherence of the suites, since the unique blend of the Ellington orchestra's voices usually secured the continuity within a suite (see also Chapter 6). On the contrary, the contrasting moods of the various movements in the more successful Ellington-Strayhorn suites often (not always) strengthen the coherence. As in many Ellington compositions, in the suites contrast functions as the main structuring principle.

The suite format made its debut at the orchestra's third Carnegie Hall concert, on December 19, 1944, and with some success. Though the *Perfume Suite*, as their first suite was titled, was musically much less coherent than *Black, Brown and Beige*, it received none of the dismissive criticism that Ellington's magnum opus had received. In 1943, Ellington had introduced *Black, Brown and Beige* with an exposition on musical development—the work's "closely related" themes required "developing the two and showing their close relationship" (Ellington 1943)—but his description of the *Perfume Suite* drew on a purely extra-musical register. Ellington's introduction united the four movements largely by *contrast*: "In the *Perfume Suite* our aim was not so much to try to interpret the mood...implied by the label on the commercial products, but more so to try to capture the character usually taken on by a woman who wears different brands of—or rather different blends of perfume.... We divided them into four categories: *Love, Violence, Naiveté* and *Sophistication*" (Ellington 1944).

The four movements of the *Perfume Suite* stem from such distinct and unrelated sources that the program rather than the music provided the continuity, if any. Movement one, the lush ballad *Love*, is taken directly from Strayhorn's score for *Pentonsilic* (mm. 291-381), expanded with an introductory section that is based on yet another Strayhorn score, an unrecorded arrangement of Mack Gordon and Harry Warren's 1941 ballad *Where You Are* ("Where U R," BSC). For the second movement, a vocal selection titled *Violence*, Ellington and Strayhorn rearranged a dramatic and somber Strayhorn work from mid-1943, called *Strange Feeling*, which in turn used material from an earlier unrecorded composition, *Leticia* (BSC). That work dated back to the orchestra's stint at the Hurricane, where from May till September 1943 the Ellingtonians accompanied a floor show called *Strange Feeling*, featuring dancer Letitia Hill. Strayhorn wrote the show's signature theme, and over the course of the year developed it into *Strange Feeling*, writing two more arrangements of the piece ("Strange B$^\flat$ Feeling," BSC, and "X-Strange," DEC) prior to its 1944 Carnegie Hall performance.[11] For the version of *Strange Feeling* used in the *Perfume Suite*, Ellington arranged the instrumental chorus, while Strayhorn scored the remaining vocal chorus and closing section.

The suite continued with an Ellington piano solo called *Dancers in Love*, for the occasion retitled as *Naiveté*. The fourth and final movement was Ellington's unfinished *Sophistication*, completed by Strayhorn. The original title of this work, *Coloratura*, referred to the stratosphere blowing of trumpeter Cat Anderson—the latest addition to the band—and again bore little resemblance to the "character taken on by a woman who wears different blends of perfume."

For Ellington and Strayhorn, the suite became the designated format for collaborative extended works in the following decades. Generally, their suites continued to be compiled along similar lines as the *Perfume Suite*, consisting of a mix of (retitled) old and new compositions by Ellington and Strayhorn, unified by a programmatic title and explanatory remarks. Cooperative suites of the 1940s included the *Magazine Suite*, for which Strayhorn wrote the Hodges-feature *Esquire Swank* (although the altoist shares the credits with Ellington), the socially aware, four-part *Deep South Suite*,[12] and *The Symphomaniac*.

The Symphomaniac and *The Tattooed Bride* (the latter by Ellington), both premiered at the last Carnegie Hall concert that was to be dedicated solely to the Ellington orchestra (November 1948),[13] were the last multimovement works for years to come. The two-part *Symphomaniac* showed (as had, to a certain extent, the earlier *Perfume Suite*) that without a clear-cut, preconceived program that laid out the general ideas, simply stringing unrelated movements into a suite was unsatisfactory. For instance, the first movement, *Symphonic or Bust*, is a curious collage by Ellington, comprising segments taken from Strayhorn's introductions to *The Eighth Veil* and *Blue Belles of Harlem*, set against some new portions of orchestral material, that seem to draw on Strayhorn's *Overture to a Jam-Session*. Unrelated Ellington piano solos are scattered between the sections. More becoming is the suite's second movement, *How You Sound* (no manuscript known), which seems to have no Strayhorn involvement. While unremarkable, this movement does not suffer from the first movement's hasty cutting and pasting. Without any programmatic explanations, the *Symphomaniac* lacks all coherence and stands as one of the weakest suites in the orchestra's repertory.

The two composers returned to the suite format in the latter half of the 1950s. From then on, they wrote numerous suites. Especially those suites with more concrete themes (notably *Such Sweet Thunder*, based on Shakespeare characters, and the *Far East Suite*, inspired by the orchestra's tour through the Near and Middle East) rank among their best collaborative efforts.

As the recording ban kept his Famous Orchestra out of the commercial studios, Ellington's income more than ever depended on live performances. Shortly after its 1943 Carnegie Hall debut, the band landed a regular nightclub engagement at The Hurricane in New York City, which lasted six months. The stint included nightly fifteen-minute local broadcasts on weekdays—the band was off on Mondays—and a half-hour show aired on Sunday nights, called *Pastel Period*. The music for the latter program centered around the more subdued "mood pieces" of the band. Instead of opening with a snippet from *Take the "A" Train*, the orchestra now played the atmospheric *Moon Mist*. Inevitably, the extended Hurricane residency with its daily broadcasts had a marked impact on the orchestra's repertory: the book included more and more pop tunes and standards, interspersed with some "old timers" and a handful of newer and quite successful Ellington songs in a popular vein, such as *Do Nothing Till You Hear from Me*, *I'm Beginning to See the Light* and *Don't Get Around Much Anymore*.[14]

As Strayhorn contributed a growing number of arrangements, his style slowly permeated the orchestra's sound. Over the course of the war years his arrangements came to dominate the numerous radio appearances. Other arrangers provided material as well, most notably pianist-composer Mary Lou Williams (who, like Strayhorn, was from Pittsburgh). According to Kuebler (1997b), Williams wrote at least seventeen arrangements for Ellington during her stint with the orchestra (1942–43), including a take on Irving Berlin's *Blue Skies* (her most famous score, also known as *Trumpet-No-End*) as well as standards and pop tunes such as *Star Dust*, *I Love Coffee*, *Ogeechee River Lullaby*, and *Sweet Georgia Brown*.[15] Other incidental contributions—arrangements and originals—came from clarinetist-tenorist Jimmy Hamilton, who had succeeded to Barney Bigard's chair in the reed section by mid-1943, previously filled by Chauncy Haughton and Sax Mallard.[16]

As Ellington increasingly relied on arrangers other than himself—in the meantime toning down his own frantic musical work—he quietly abandoned what had been one of the trademarks of his early orchestra: the larger part of its repertory had always been "Ellington music." In the 1930s, even the many arrangements in the band's book were generally conceived by its leader, which had put Ellington in a league of his own. While there were other orchestra leaders in the late 1930s and early 1940s who to a certain extent had invented their own sound, such as Count Basie, Cab Calloway, Chick Webb, Jimmie Lunceford, Benny Goodman, Harry James, or Glenn Miller, they did not lead "a *composer's* orchestra like Duke Ellington, but an *arranger's*" (Schuller 1989, 202). Apparently, Ellington's interest in arranging for his orchestra diminished over the course of the early 1940s.

Since the nightly broadcasts from the Cotton Club during the late twenties, Ellington had not had a regular slot on the radio networks, but this changed when the American Broadcasting Company (ABC) offered him a weekly one-hour show sponsored by the U.S. Treasury Department, beginning April 1945. Ellington's was the first black orchestra to get its own network program. In addition, the Armed Forces Radio Service (AFRS) hooked up to ABC's broadcasts, in order to produce a series of half-hour programs for the overseas forces, called *Your Saturday Date with the Duke* (in parts of Europe and the Pacific the war had not yet ended). Since these public service programs were also a means to sell war bonds, Ellington chose a repertory aimed at a broader audience, much like the earlier broadcasts from The Hurricane, even though ABC had given him "a free rein in the choice of material" (Valburn 1981). This meant more arranging for Ellington's associate. At least sixty different Strayhorn arrangements were aired during the four dozen Saturday afternoon shows the orchestra played between April 1945 and October 1946 at various New York City locations (with a five-month intermission that started in November 1945). While listening to Duke Ellington and His Famous Orchestra, millions at home and abroad unknowingly listened to the music of Billy Strayhorn.

During the *Saturday Date* period, Ellington and Strayhorn collaborated on a piece in a manner that resembled their earlier work for *Sepia Panorama*. In 1945, Strayhorn had scored an arrangement of *Out of This World* (by Johnny Mercer and Harold Arlen), originally sung by Bing Crosby in the Paramount motion picture of the same name. According to Alec Wilder (1972, 280), *Out of This World* "is one of Arlen's most direct and deliberately unrhythmic melodies, and unlike any of his other lyric ballads." The modal feeling of *Out of This World*, the irregular length of the work's sections, and the strong melodic and rhythmic analogies with Strayhorn's own *Ugly Ducklin'* must have appealed to him. He wrote an elaborate vocal arrangement of the song, with extensive counterpoint for Cat Anderson's trumpet. The orchestra gave three documented performances of the arrangement (without the introduction) at broadcasts between August and October, 1945. The performances sounded unconvincing: the orchestra was underrehearsed, Cat Anderson missed virtually all of his lines, and singer Kay Davis was out of tune. Always happy to recycle a good idea, Ellington discarded Arlen's original melody to rework Strayhorn's trumpet counterpoint, as well as several of his reed backgrounds, into a full solo statement for Anderson. Joining in with the revisions, Strayhorn added a new twenty-three-bar modulating introduction to replace his original eleven-bar opener. The piece still relied heavily on Out of This World, however, and as if to hint at the cover-up, the composers baptized their effort The Eighth Veil. Copyright was filed in both their names.[17]

But their collaborative effort on The Eighth Veil was not exemplary for the production of new material. In general, both composers wrote independently. Hence, between the two recording bans—a second ban halted all recording activity in 1948—Strayhorn individually wrote originals such as Portrait of a Silk Thread (DEC), Blue Heart (DEC), Le Sacre Supreme (BSC and DEC), Lana Turner (DEC), The Merry Ha! Ha! (DEC), Shadow Shuffle (BSC), and Jasmine (DEC, for small band), none of which were recorded or are known to have been performed.[18] This continued exclusion from recordings and concerts must have been disheartening, and the rate at which Strayhorn composed originals decreased markedly.

Recorded Strayhorn originals of the period (not counting the handful of pieces that went into the suites) are Mid-Riff, Air-Conditioned Jungle (co-written with Jimmy Hamilton, credited to Ellington and Hamilton), The Kissing Bug (with Rex Stewart and Joya Sherrill as co-composers), Double Ruff, Flippant Flurry, the imaginative Overture to a Jam-Session (curiously credited to Ellington), a first instrumental version of Violet Blue (with a secondary vocal theme this would become Multi-Colored Blue), as well as a small-band version of Charlotte Russe, which became one of Ellington's favorite solo piano works in later years as Lotus Blossom. In the late 1940s followed Brown Betty, Snibor, and Entrance of Youth (a concerto grosso for flute, French horn, piano, and jazz orchestra),[19] as well as the lesser-known Progressive Gavotte and Triple Play.

Yet, on average fewer than four new Strayhorn works a year (including the joint works with others) were added to the repertory between the bans, and thus Strayhorn's role for the orchestra was largely limited to that of staff arranger, a role which he nevertheless assumed with serious dedication. Consequently, his recorded arrangements for the Ellington organization in the 1940s greatly outnumbered the few recorded originals. Of some two hundred arrangements, more than half are known to have found their way into the band's book, but the orchestra undoubtedly performed a large part of the remainder at undocumented concerts and dance dates.

Ellington's confidence in his associate reached a new level when they became involved with a racially daring theater production, Beggar's Holiday (1946), a reworking of John Gay's The Beggar's Opera (London, 1729), to be performed by a mixed-race cast (Hajdu 1996, 101–102). Unlike the earlier *Jump for Joy*, the production featured a pit band rather than Ellington's own orchestra. In the months preceding the premiere of the theater show—scheduled to open on Broadway late 1946—Ellington was on tour with the Belgian-Gypsy guitarist Django Reinhardt. Unable to attend the rehearsals and try-outs, Ellington dispatched Strayhorn, who wrote and arranged large portions of the show, occasionally conferring with Ellington over the telephone.[20]

Most of the compositions for *Beggar's Holiday* seem rather conventional (possibly to better the show's chances for commercial success) and with few exceptions display few characteristics identified with either Strayhorn or Ellington. Nevertheless, in a number of works Strayhorn's musical identity comes through clearly. His most outstanding contributions are the rocking and steaming arrangement of Ellington's and John LaTouche's *On the Wrong Side of the Railroad Tracks* (Strayhorn wrote the verse) and the languidly moving *Brown Penny*. Further interesting material can be found in the (unfinished?) ballad *Cream for Supper*, the attractive clarinet feature *Fol-De-Rol-Rol*, and the ominously dark and angular *Boll Weevil Ballet*.[21] Much like *Jump for Joy*, *Beggar's Holiday* was in trouble from the very first rehearsals. The directors made extensive revisions, discarding numbers and requesting replacements. Despite all reworking, the show received mixed reviews at best, and folded after sixteen weeks, early in 1947. Most of the music remained unused. As Caine (1987, 99) notes, "Although that year [1947, following the creation of *Beggar's Holiday*] is relatively well represented in the Ellington discography by non-commercial recordings (radio airshots, concert performances, broadcast transcriptions and the like), only two examples are known of the band promoting this music in live appearance."

Ironically, Ellington's confidence in Strayhorn—in *Beggar's Holiday* Strayhorn had not so much represented his collaborator as replaced him—was nullified by an embittering incident. "Orchestrations under personal supervision of Billy Strayhorn," the Broadway Theatre's program read (reprinted in Stratemann 1992, 279), "music by Duke Ellington." For the first time showing his irritation about this lack of public recognition, Strayhorn reportedly walked out of the gala party thrown in honor of Ellington, on the night of the show's Broadway opening (Hajdu 1996, 104).

The trouble surrounding *Beggar's Holiday* coincided with a number of setbacks in Strayhorn's personal life. After having shared an apartment with Strayhorn for more than seven years, Aaron Bridgers was leaving their Convent Avenue dwellings for Paris, France, where he had been offered a position as a cocktail pianist. "This was a good time for me to go away," Bridgers told Hajdu (1996, 108). "Strayhorn needed some time alone. He was going through some things of his own."

As a result of Bridgers's departure, Strayhorn drew closer to Lena Horne, who had just married Lennie Hayton, an arranger and conductor. Hayton, who at the time considered a career in music publishing, at one point discussed the commercial and legal implications of Strayhorn's collaboration with Ellington. To his astonishment, Hayton found that there was no written agreement whatsoever. In addition, Strayhorn reportedly confessed that he had no idea of the commercial value of his work. According to Hajdu (1996, 109), "Hayton urged Strayhorn to be more attentive to the business side of his career with Ellington." Hayton's warnings had an immediate effect: "That was the beginning of problems with Strayhorn," Mercer Ellington told Hajdu (ibid.); "we didn't see very much of Strayhorn for a while."

Over the course of the 1940s, the actual collaboration on single pieces, which had occurred a number of times during the first years of the Ellington and Strayhorn partnership, tapered off. It is possible that this was partly fueled by Strayhorn's uneasiness with the aspects of the collaboration that *Beggar's Holiday* brought to the surface. But it appears that Ellington and Strayhorn had settled into a working habit in which each took care of his own music for the orchestra. In addition, Strayhorn's tasks were largely confined to writing arrangements, and after the Blanton-Webster era, Ellington and Strayhorn abandoned the practice of dividing the work on single arrangements. *Manhattan Murals*, a joint, rhapsodic reworking of *Take the "A" Train* for the orchestra's 1948 Carnegie Hall appearance, was one of the few exceptions. Strayhorn's score, which carries a short passage in Ellington's hand, weaves around Ellington's piano choruses.

Whenever the two composers actually worked together, they did so almost exclusively within the suite format, which integrated parts that were written separately. Those few cases in which they actually co-composed or co-arranged a single work were usually preceded by a two-step process. In *The Eighth Veil*, for instance, Ellington added a new melodic line to a complete and independently conceived Strayhorn arrangement, while in *Blutopia* Strayhorn reworked and expanded an unfinished Ellington composition. In *Black, Brown and Beige*, Ellington infused an earlier Strayhorn composition, while Strayhorn filled in a few open spots.

Nevertheless, for the larger part of the 1940s, Strayhorn mainly functioned as the Ellington orchestra's staff arranger, writing imaginative scores for dozens upon dozens of popular songs. Many of his original compositions remained unused and obscure, which was the price Strayhorn paid for working for Duke Ellington's orchestra, an orchestra headed by another composer. Yet it was to have serious consequences, consequences that cut right through the heart of Strayhorn's compositions and arrangements.

Chapter Six

"He Is He and I Am Me":
The Ellington-Strayhorn Collaboration

THE ELLINGTON-STRAYHORN team consisted of two different composers, who not so much co-wrote music but rather functioned as each other's soundboard and source of inspiration. As detailed earlier, the distinctions between their oeuvres can be found in a number of characteristics, such as in the musical "fingerprints." The most distinctive facet is the two composers' individual approach to musical form. In the absence of sources, this assessment of the Ellington-Strayhorn partnership could not be made during their lifetime, and consequently, critics, fans, and researchers sought to provide an answer to the question of how the two collaborated.

The orchestra's Carnegie Hall debut in 1943 not only placed Strayhorn in the limelight, but it also raised the curtain on a perennial myth about the Ellington-Strayhorn collaboration. Irvin Kolodin (1943) wrote in his program notes that Strayhorn's "assimilation of Ellington's mannerisms and the expression of them in ideas of his own has progressed to the point where members of the band can't be sure themselves whether a certain new creation is the work of Ellington or Strayhorn." Virtually all subsequent publications that address the collaboration between the two composers echo this assertion, and over the years a generally accepted lore developed according to which the compositions of Ellington and Strayhorn were indistinguishable. Thus, the composers were "alter egos" (Nielsen, n.d., 382) who "forged an almost telepathically close musical relationship" (Hasse 1995, 232)—where Strayhorn was "the female side of an artistically joint persona" (Jewell 1977, 63)—while their "talents and style did merge in a truly indistinguishable manner" (Schuller 1989, 138) and subsequently "even their music manuscripts began to look similar" (Homzy 1992, 6). Leonard Feather, whose discussions of the issue tend to be better informed, extended the band members' reported puzzlement to include the composers themselves: "[the]

musical vibrations between Strayhorn and Ellington were so sympathetic that sometimes neither they themselves nor members of the band could recollect at what point the work of the one had left off and the other had begun" (Feather 1960, 433; see also Feather 1965).

Although Strayhorn continued to work largely in the shadows, the number of people aware of his existence gradually increased over the course of the fifties, and consequently the Ellington-Strayhorn collaboration received more attention in articles, on LP jackets, and in radio interviews, even though certain forces within the Ellington organization deliberately deemphasized Strayhorn's contributions (Hajdu 1996, 169–170, 206, 259–260). But defining Strayhorn's role turned out to be problematic. Despite Strayhorn's growing reputation, the true scope of the collaboration remained a mystery to audiences, critics, and record buyers (if they thought about it at all), and understandably so, since Strayhorn's contributions to many of the LP projects went uncredited. The shared credits for works such as *A Drum Is a Woman* and *Such Sweet Thunder*, for instance, did not reveal what *exactly* he had contributed.[1] Hence, it was impossible to develop a clear sense of his style or an insight into the dynamics of his musical partnership with Ellington. An attentive listener may have been aware of the similarities between, for instance, the *Mood Indigo* score from the *Masterpieces* album and the vocal version of *Day Dream* for Ella Fitzgerald, but how was he or she to know that they were authored by the same person? If one accepted the first arrangement as a genuine Ellington score, as suggested by the album's title (*Masterpieces by Ellington*) as well as by Ellington's frequent revisions of his music, and assumed that Strayhorn had written the second score—most Ellington-aficionados by now knew that Strayhorn was responsible for the majority of the vocal arrangements—the obvious conclusion was that Strayhorn had fully mastered the Ellington style.

Those who probed the available sources for clues about the elusive workings of the partnership, all unquestioningly accepted one given: the hierarchical nature of the collaboration. Strayhorn, it was assumed, composed within a framework that was completely Ellingtonian, a style invented, developed, and intellectually owned by the orchestra's leader. As producer Granz explained, struggling in his preface to the deluxe 4-LP boxed edition of *Ella Fitzgerald Sings the Duke Ellington Songbook* to justify the anomalous inclusion of the Strayhorn originals *Day Dream, Take the "A" Train, Clementine, Lush Life, Chelsea Bridge*, and the jointly credited *Just A-Settin' and A-Rockin'* and *A Portrait of Ella Fitzgerald*: "Duke Ellington and his side-kick Billy Strayhorn are virtually interchangeable" (Granz 1957). According to Granz, Strayhorn's pieces could be characterized as "Ellington-influenced writing and, in a sense, examples of Ellington-type compositions" (ibid.), which for him justified the inclusion of Strayhorn works on an album bearing Ellington's name, even though it deviated from the initial songbook concept. Obviously, from a producer's point of view this solution was more elegant

The Ellington-Strayhorn collaboration has been the subject of speculation and mystification. Strayhorn and Ellington were quite different composers, who worked from different personal and musical backgrounds. They hid the true dynamics of their musical partnership and tended to give cryptic answers whenever the "who-did-what" was asked. (*Photograph © Gordon Parks*)

than matching the title of the album with its contents (there were also works by Hodges and Tizol) which would have made it awkwardly long.

The trademark sound of the Ellington orchestra further blurred the view on Strayhorn's style. Ellington's writing was so tightly intertwined with the specific sound quality of his orchestra that whoever heard the band could not help but in the first place hear Ellington. Ellington's music was barely thinkable without the orchestra, and vice versa. Strayhorn's orchestral works too were filtered through the interpretations of the band and thus inevitably took on an Ellingtonian quality. It was the orchestra rather than the alleged interchangeability of the two composers that succeeded in passing off the movements of the more successful suites (most notably *Such Sweet Thunder* [see Chapter 8] and *The Far East Suite* [see Chapter 10]) as works that transcended the individual constituents. Though in retrospect it is not difficult to single out the three Strayhorn movements in *Such Sweet Thunder*, or his contributions to the *Far East Suite*, they do blend in perfectly with the other movements, representing different shades from the same set of colors.

Thus it was easily concluded that Strayhorn's writing had to be based largely on that of his employer and therefore lacked any specific individuality. After all, the main differences between the two composers have to be sought in the deeper layers of their work: specific use of harmony, form, melodic construction, and others—characteristics that are more difficult to detect. The similarities between their styles, by contrast, are readily accessible and become apparent on first hearing: both scored with the reed section as point of departure, preferred dense five-part harmonies that included ample dissonance, prominently featured the trombones in middle-register three-part harmony, and often used the trumpets as an extension of the lower brass, with barely any doubling in the voices. From Strayhorn's very first work for the band it had been clear that he shared with Ellington a passion for orchestral colors, for rich harmonies as well as honest music without compromise.

Still, Kolodin and Granz were wrong. Other than adapting (not adopting) certain techniques (Ellington's cross-section orchestration and the personalized "on the man" writing), Strayhorn absorbed but few of "Ellington's mannerisms." Rather, he had independently worked out techniques for the orchestra that might have been Ellington's, but were not. In *Chelsea Bridge*, for instance, the *conceptualization* of certain voicings drew on Ellington, such as the saxophone ensemble with clarinet lead, but the harmonies used, the melodic lines, the rhythmic placement, and the inner voice leading were all uniquely Strayhorn's.

Although Strayhorn with some amusement observed the "whodunit game indulged in by the band" (Strayhorn 1952, 2), he could be outspoken about his artistic autonomy: "I write entirely differently [and] I function independently....He is he and I am me....It works, because he doesn't tell me what to write or how to write. He just says 'Write something.' He knows it is going to be me"

(Wilson 1965, 13). As he told another reporter: "I've always written what I wanted how I wanted for Duke. Sometimes I turn things in; other times we have a conference" ("Swee' Pea...Is Still Amazed," 1956, 15). At another occasion he detailed how in his writing for the orchestra's individuals he deliberately sought to preserve his individuality:

> You have someone like Clark Terry, whom you know. You know his sound, and you know how he plays, so you write something that fits him, but that's not *you*. You really need to write something that fits his sound and is *your* sound too—a combination of what you do and what he does. That's what he also wants, because he can sit and play all night what *he* plays. He's an artist, and like all artists he wants to do new things. (Dance 1967, 18)

Ellington lent more credence to the mythical notion that the differences were marginal: "We discuss things, but I find that if I'm going to do the arrangement, it is about the same as if he'd done it. That happens even when we may not agree on things" ("Swee' Pea...Is Still Amazed," 1956, 15). In his autobiography, Ellington described their musical rapport in psychological terms: "He was not, as he was often referred to by many, my alter ego. Billy Strayhorn was my right arm, my left arm, all the eyes in the back of my head, my brainwaves in his head, and his in mine" (Ellington 1973, 156). On other occasions he hinted that their mutual understanding verged on the telepathic:

> I may be somewhere like in Los Angeles—he is in New York—and I get to the seventeenth bar of a number, and I decide, well, rather than sit here and struggle with this, I call Strays. I will call him and I say: "Look, I'm in E-flat or someplace, and the mood is this—and you know, this lad is supposed to be walking up the road and he reaches a certain intersection and I can't decide whether he should turn left, right, go straight ahead or a make a U-turn." And he [Strayhorn] says, "oh yes, I know what you mean...and very often, without anymore than that, we come up with practically the same thing. ("A Duke Named Ellington")

As Feather (1965) found out: "Confront either of them with the question concerning who scored which tracks, and you will be met with a typical Ellington-Strayhorn evasion; they have been dodging answers along these lines for some 25 years." Yet in one widely cited instance, Strayhorn more or less detailed one of his contributions to an Ellington suite, a contribution which to him included telepathy:

> I can give you a good example of something we did over the phone. We were supposed to be playing the Great South Bay Jazz Festival [August 3, 1958, East

Islip, Long Island] about three years ago. Duke had promised a new composition to the people who ran it. He was on the road someplace. So he called me up and told me he had written some parts of a suite. This was maybe two or three days before he was due back in New York, and that very day he was supposed to be at the festival. He told me some of the things he was thinking of. We discussed the keys and the relationships of the parts, things like that. And he said write this and that. The day of the festival, I brought my part of the suite out to the festival grounds. There was no place and no time to rehearse it, but I told Duke that it shouldn't be hard for the guys to sight-read. So they stood around backstage and read their parts, without playing, you understand.

Then they played it. My part was inserted in the middle. You remember I had not heard any of it. I was sitting in the audience with some other people who knew what had happened, and when they [the orchestra] got to my part, [and] then went into Ellington's part, we burst out laughing. I looked up on the stage and Ellington was laughing too. Without really knowing, I had written a theme that was a kind of development of a similar theme he had written. So when he played my portion and went into his, it was as though we had really worked together—or one person had done it. It was an uncanny feeling, like witchcraft, like looking into someone else's mind. (Coss 1962, 23)

The suite in question was the five-part *Jazz Festival Suite*, performed once at the festival and recorded in February of the next year as *Toot Suite*. Strayhorn's vivid description notwithstanding, his account is supported neither by the recording nor by the surviving manuscripts. Ellington's autograph scores for four of the six movements survive: *Red Garter, Red Shoes, Red Carpet (Part 1)* and *Red Carpet (Part 3)*. The autograph scores for the final movement, *Ready, Go!* (mainly a head chart) and the middle section of *Red Carpet* are missing. Only the latter fits Strayhorn's exposé: it is indeed nested between Ellington's sections. Yet, apart from its two twelve-bar blues choruses in the key of F, *Red Carpet (Part 2)* bears no musical relationship whatsoever to any other part of the suite, whether in melodic contours, harmonizations, rhythmic figures, or even orchestration: the middle part is the only section scored for reeds only. If Strayhorn's emergency movement fitted in nicely, it was because the movements of *Toot Suite* were not bound by any musical relationship whatever, and not due to any "kind of development" or "witchcraft": Strayhorn laid a smoke screen.[2]

What both Ellington and Strayhorn expressed with their anecdotes about their collaboration was the close musical rapport they felt. Even though they tended to write quite differently, at times they struck on the same solutions, as Ellington found out when he asked Strayhorn to set the first four words of the Bible—"In the beginning God"—to music: "His theme started on the same note as mine, it started on F, and ended a tenth above, on A-flat, and out of the six notes only two of them differed" (Nicholson 1999, 365).

Those more intimately familiar with the Ellington organization—band members, copyists, and certain publicists and producers—must have been keenly aware how the lines ran through the repertory. Apart from the composers themselves, who undoubtedly (as opposed to Feather's claims) must have known who had authored what, the long-time band members must have had little difficulty identifying the many musical and extra-musical clues that identified the composer of a given work. Not only did Strayhorn's distinct handwritten parts provide an obvious hint (he extracted no fewer than three hundred of his own scores), but the French word play in his titles, his occasional conducting of the band in recordings of his own pieces (Feather 1943, 14; Granz 1957) as well as the discussions of his compositions with Ellington and individual band members (Hajdu 1996, 148) left little doubt about his contributions. Most important, the differences in musical content must have been clear to those steeped in the Ellington style. Yet, all loyally adhered to the unwritten company policy that in the end *it did not matter* who had written what: "As they [Ellington and Strayhorn] will tell you," Feather dutifully noted, "it is unimportant how the charts were assembled; all that counts is the typical Ellingtonian end" (Feather 1965).

Still, no matter how distinct their styles, after more than a decade of collaboration, the music of Ellington and Strayhorn at times indeed showed traces of cross-fertilization. While Strayhorn's writing was perceived by most critics as largely derived from his employer's style (as detailed earlier, he had adopted certain concepts), they both acknowledged that the influences, if any, were *mutual*. Their musical relationship was nonhierarchical. Strayhorn told *Down Beat*: "I'm certain Duke influenced me. He says I've influenced him, but I don't know....I'm not even sure he knows." According to Ellington that was "inevitable...we been together so long." ("Swee' Pea...Is Still Amazed," 1956, 15). Although Ellington wrote the larger part of the recorded score of *Anatomy of a Murder*, there is a striking Strayhornesque quality to pieces such as *Hero to Zero, Sunswept Sunday*, and *Midnight Indigo*. In *Hero to Zero*, for instance, the orchestral background to Paul Gonsalves's solo consists of consecutive entries by various instruments, an orchestral texture that resembles Strayhorn's technique of timbre melody (Strayhorn applied it in his own arrangement of *Low Key Lightly* from *Anatomy of a Murder*, where it appears in a more radical and dissonant fashion).

For Ellington, who spent most of his time touring, performing, and recording with his band, there were few opportunities to listen to composers other than himself and Strayhorn, and so, performing his associate's music night after night for two decades, Ellington's writing began to bear audible traces of the Strayhorn Effect. To confound matters further, Strayhorn's two bluesy riff tune movements for the *Newport Jazz Festival Suite* could easily pass for Ellington compositions, as could his "jungle-style" introduction to Ella Fitzgerald's *Take the "A" Train* (a conclusion indeed drawn by Sturm [1995, 153], who suggests that the "remarkable five-part train whistle effect...for clarinet and four plunger-muted trumpets" was "probably Ellington's," and throughout his book credits the arrangement to both; it is nevertheless entirely Strayhorn's).

FOR ELLINGTON AND STRAYHORN, the nature and function of their scores differed. The perennial anecdotes about music written on shirtsleeves notwithstanding,[3] Ellington (like Strayhorn), for the larger part of his career, relied on written scores and parts, a practice he started somewhere in the early thirties as a result of the increasing complexity of his music and the growing number of voices in his band. The hundreds of detailed scores and literally thousands of written instrumental parts in the repository of the Duke Ellington Collection belie any claims that the Ellingtonians were poor sight readers. The repertory changed so quickly that they simply had to rely on written parts, especially since the book included many works played only once or a couple of times (such as most music for *A Drum Is a Woman* or *Such Sweet Thunder*).

Ellington's scores range from detailed written manuscripts, recorded virtually without changes (e.g., *Reminiscing in Tempo*, DEC) to mere sketches largely worked out on the bandstand with his orchestra (e.g., large sections of *The River*, DEC), an approach he used increasingly as time progressed. Strayhorn's manuscripts, by contrast, continue to display unmatched detail, carefully spelling out all musical events from the introduction to the coda. Strayhorn's oeuvre shows a corresponding internal coherence—that is, his compositional methods did not change significantly during the three decades of his collaboration with Ellington.

Still, although Ellington often wrote with careful detail, for him the manuscript score was a point of departure only, an intermediate step in a complex compositional process in which even a performance or recording was often temporary. His written scores were hardly ever a finished product, nor did they serve a goal in themselves: they constituted no more than a phase in the creation of a piece of music. Especially with respect to the order of musical events Ellington took a flexible approach. "Don't you know that?" copyist Thomas Whaley asked members of the Duke Ellington Society; "Duke will give me a score, and I extract it. We go into the record session and Duke will tear that score all apart....I have it marked A, B, C, and D. And the first thing you know, Duke says: 'We start at E. And we'll go back to B'" (Whaley 1965). In producer Irving Townsend's words,

> the final polishing of any Ellington arrangement is done as the band plays it, and Duke, to the bewilderment of people who have watched him record, writes and rehearses music in segments, usually of eight measures and almost always without a written conclusion....Duke's final instructions for a performance might go as follows: "Start at letter C. Then go to A and play it twice, only the

second time leave off the last two bars. These bars are at the beginning of a sheet you have marked X. After X I'll play until I bring you in at C again and you go out with letter D. Any questions?" (Townsend 1960, 321–322)

Ellington's technique confused the newcomers in the band. "It's like nothing else!" tenorist Al Sears said, after joining the orchestra in 1944:

Really, you've got no idea what it's like till you've actually tried playing in the band. You start at the letter A and go to B and suddenly, for no reason at all, when you go to C, the rest of the band is playing something else, which you find out later on isn't what is written at C but what's written at J instead. And then the next number, instead of starting at the top, the entire band starts at H—that is, everybody except me. See, I'm the newest man in the band and I haven't caught on to the system yet! (Nicholson 1999, 260)

Indeed, an Ellington score may contain all musical events but not necessarily in the final order, as he often drastically rearranged a work's architecture in rehearsals and at recording sessions, such as in *Jack the Bear* ("Take It Away," DEC) or in *Bakiff* (DEC). More than once he culled a version from different arrangements of the same work, instructing his copyist to transpose and infuse a specific section from elsewhere. In I *Never Felt This Way Before* ("Never Felt," DEC), for example, Ellington directs copyist Tizol to an earlier instrumental score of the piece: "First 6 [bars] of $A^\flat$ Cho[ru]s [and] Transpose to $B^\flat$." Similarly, in one of his scores for *I'm Beginning to See the Light* (DEC) he wrote "to old sheet[,] then over." In addition, Ellington often collated works from different, unrelated manuscripts as in *Sepia Panorama* and *Black, Brown and Beige*, exemplified earlier. Furthermore, he typically deleted large sections from his own scores, sometimes because they carried more choruses than fit a 78 rpm record, as was the case with *I'm Slapping 7th Avenue with the Sole of My Shoe* ("Slapping 7th Ave," DEC; see also Schoenberg 1997), sometimes because the trimmed scores apparently better met his aesthetic criteria.

Revising music formed an integral and essential element in Ellington's writing. He knew he was going to edit his scores extensively at rehearsals and recording sessions, take things out, change blocks of music around, infuse material written earlier, or adopt an idea from any of his band members, honing the final form of the piece through a process of trial and error. As a result, the transitions in many Ellington compositions are relatively abrupt, the key changes often sudden, and the caesuras between sections usually sharp and clearly audible (Van de Leur 1993, Chapters 3–5).[4] This juxtaposition of contrasting sections governed the structural design of ragtime and stride, genres that had dominated Ellington's musical upbringing. Yet, the resultant music was usually far from fragmented, as Ellington masterly sculpted his disjunctive building blocks into a convincing continuity—a balancing act of contrast and variation, linked by a chain of hard cuts rather than through a smooth melodic and harmonic development. As Priestley and Cohen (1993, 202) noted in their discussion of *Black, Brown and Beige*: "When one comes to ask what are the distinguishing qualities of the work as a whole, one of them is very definitely the use of contrast and surprise, balanced as it is by an unshakable sense of forward movement." And: "As to the developmental techniques which were new to Ellington at the time, their use remains rare in his work (the *Tattooed Bride*, though on a smaller scale, is possibly more thorough-going)" (ibid., 203).

The paths Ellington followed in his creative process differ markedly from Strayhorn's composition techniques. As detailed in the previous chapters, Strayhorn's writing was characterized by an archlike, tightly knit architecture, with integrated transitions, smooth modulations, and composed introductions and codas as important pillars of structure. His autograph scores clearly reflect this: unlike Ellington, Strayhorn generally wrote his scores linearly and allowed for little reorganization. Even longer works, such as *Overture to a Jam Session* (recorded under his supervision exactly as written) and *Pentonsilic*, Strayhorn wrote in one single, secure gesture, with virtually no reordering or erasures in the manuscript: prior to writing his scores down Strayhorn invariably had planned how all segments would fit in the musical narrative.[5] Thus, all segments followed a necessary order that left no room for structural rearrangement.

Yet, the final realization and interpretation of Strayhorn's music depended largely on the performances of the Ellington orchestra, mostly supervised by its leader. Since editing scores was a natural and indispensable part of his own compositional techniques, Ellington approached his associate's scores with a similar editorial strategy. Many times he chose to take out sections or to change the order of musical events in a Strayhorn manuscript. As he told a Los Angeles radio station with typical Ellingtonian flair:

> There is nothing like taking a Billy Strayhorn orchestration in a recording studio....This is the first time it is to be played and you start to record it, and then take it and turn it all around...have it come off, [and] just destroy the whole orchestration-pattern. It doesn't destroy it, but twist it around, turn it upside down, and this and that....This is an interesting analysis and diagnosis. This is prescribing not the cure but to keep it down..., because...maybe Billy Strayhorn's orchestrations might sound *too good*....And we don't want Strayhorn to sound too good *too young*. (Worth 1962)

For once, Strayhorn's response gave a glimpse of how he must have felt about Ellington's all-too-true account of how he approached his associate's work. "You wanted to know about collaboration, and now you know," Strayhorn replied, "*This* is the *real* story" (ibid.).

The short exchange between the two collaborators for the radio microphone indeed gave more of the "real story" than the many romanticized musings about telepathic collaboration. Not informed by any fear that Strayhorn might "sound too good," Ellington's editing of Strayhorn's scores was the inevitable consequence of the two composers' distinctly different approaches to both the compositional process and the written score as well as their different aesthetic sense and artistic goals. "When it sounds good, it is good," Ellington famously remarked (Nicholson 1999, 313),[6] but what sounded good to Strayhorn apparently not always sounded good to Ellington, for *structural* reasons. At the heart of the interference with his associate's music stood a radically different assessment of compositional form. Ellington's sense of musical form, rooted in a background of ragtime and early jazz, and developed over the course of his career into an idiosyncratic approach to musical structure, differed importantly from Strayhorn's, which drew mainly on melodic and harmonic development. As a result, Ellington's editing—such a strong and effective tool in getting the most out of his own music—at times yielded curious results when applied to Strayhorn's work.

The 1943 version of *Tonight I Shall Sleep* is one of many examples of a Strayhorn arrangement that underwent serious editing. Strayhorn had written an attractive arrangement of this titular Ellington novelty, which included two modulations: one from $E^\flat$ to $D^\flat$ at the end of the first chorus and one from $D^\flat$ to E for the final half-chorus and coda. For the uncommonly short radio performance (under two minutes) of June 6, 1943, these two modulations were fully cut. Soloist Webster plunges right after the first $E^\flat$ chorus into the coda which, without any connection to the preceding music, is audibly in the "wrong" key of E. Moreover, the remaining single chorus by no means justifies or counterbalances the extensive introduction and coda, which now seem too weighty. Other edits are equally striking. In both *Can't Help Lovin' Dat Man* and *He Makes Me Believe He's Mine*, Ellington discarded Strayhorn's temporary modulations—the climaxes of the arrangements—while in many other works important structuring elements such as introductions, codas, tuttis, backgrounds, or even entire choruses were cut.[7]

Although deleting sections did not necessarily alter the order of events, it did generally affect a work's coherence and often undermined its framework. More important, the reorganization of pieces cut deep into a work's composed structure. In arrangements such as *All of a Sudden My Heart Sings, The Cowboy Rumba, The Wildest Gal in Town, I Fell and Broke My Heart, Don't Be So Mean to Baby, It Is Mad, Mad, Mad!*, and *Take Love Easy* as well as in a long list of other scores, Ellington reorganized the music.[8] While the final version was in most cases satisfactory, the edits did definitely weaken the original arrangement as they interrupted the flow of chosen instrumentations, cut off ensemble lines before their conclusion, and interfered with the compositional structures of these works. Moreover, in many cases earlier material from the arrangement replaced blocks of deleted music, making the resultant performance less varied. In *Don't Be So Mean*, for instance, the first eight bars of section D are played four times, replacing the omitted sections B and C, which have different orchestrations—the break is covered up by four bars of piano. While Ellington's adaptations of Strayhorn's arrangements still result in acceptable music, the damage caused by cut or reshuffled sections in more personal Strayhorn originals is definitely greater.

In 1950 Orson Welles approached Ellington to write the score for a theatrical version of *Faust* (Welles retitled the play *Le Temps Court* and premiered it in Paris with another play in a program under the heading *The Blessed and the Damned*). Ellington, as usual busy touring with his orchestra, offered Welles his collaborator as replacement, and thus Strayhorn traveled to Paris to prepare the score on location. The entire production suffered from the erratic and unfocused behavior of Welles, who kept changing the script. In the end all of Strayhorn's (and Ellington's) music for the six-piece ensemble fell between the cracks, including the beautiful *Helen's Theme* (untitled, BSC), the signature song for Helen of Troy, the female protagonist. Seeking to use his canceled music, Strayhorn composed a new work for the Ellingtonians that was built on *Helen's Theme* and, hinting at the work's origins, retitled it *Orson* (BSC).

On the orchestra's only known commercial recording of *Orson* (see Chapter 9 for analysis), "the whole orchestration-pattern" indeed is "twisted around, and turned upside down": Ellington skipped the introduction as well as four bars of the theme, and took out the five-bar modulation and the subsequent second chorus. Incomprehensibly, he deleted Strayhorn's majestic coda, to replace it with the introduction—now an irrelevant afterthought—and ended with a tenor repeat of part of the theme. In the process almost half of the music was discarded, while the form of the original was annihilated, and its strong internal necessity and sense of purpose evaporated. Moreover, none of these edits seem to make any musical sense. In its original form *Orson* is a self-contained, through-composed work that addresses multiple musical and emotional levels, but in its recorded version it does not go beyond the single statement of a theme, however inspired.

The very nature of these edits makes it highly unlikely that they were made by Strayhorn himself. Clearly, a composer who so carefully designed his scores would not afterward take out sections or alter their order, a process that led repeatedly to weak or illogical transitions. If Strayhorn had intended his scores to function like Ellington's manuscripts—that is, as a step in a compositional process—he, too, would have written them in a less linear way, facilitating the reordering of material. But Strayhorn's integrated transitory and modulatory sections could not be edited out without serious consequences.

True, there were all kinds of practical reasons that could stand in the way of an integral recording of a score, such as the limited length of the 78 rpm record; insufficient rehearsal time, which made the more difficult passages treacherous;

or the unexpected absence of a musician, which could call for impromptu solutions. Still, most of Strayhorn's arrangements were not excessively long, and even during the 1940s there were ways to work around the 78 rpm time limit, since V-Discs and Standard Radio Transcriptions allowed for recordings that exceeded the three-and-a-half-minute straitjacket. Moreover, the extensive radio time the orchestra obtained during the 1940s, as well as the prestigious performance venues such as Carnegie Hall, challenged Ellington to write longer works. And even before that, the duration limits of records had not stopped Ellington from writing and recording longer works, as documented by multiside recordings of compositions such as his six-and-a-half-minute 1931 *Creole Rhapsody* or the twelve-minute *Reminiscing in Tempo* (1935), and it would not stop him during the rest of his career (e.g., the 1951 thirteen-minute *Harlem*). Even with the emergence of microgroove records, which caused the average length of Ellington's own recorded works to expand, he continued to cut extensively in Strayhorn's scores.

Neither does the difficulty of Strayhorn's scores provide sufficient explanation for these edits. True, many of his complex arrangements and originals required an orchestra capable of performing at the highest level, but so did Ellington's scores. Numerous recordings prove that if they applied themselves (and had sufficient preparation time), virtually no work was beyond the capacities of the Ellingtonians, from the 1933 virtuoso train evocation *Daybreak Express* to the 1938 *Braggin' in Brass*—which called for a breakneck hocket section for the trombones—and from the string of top-shelf recordings for the Blanton-Webster band to virtuoso albums such as *Anatomy of a Murder, Afro Bossa*, and the *Nutcracker Suite*. None of the sections cut from Strayhorn's scores are significantly harder to perform than passages that were retained, with the possible exception of an incidental vocal score that may have been too hard for the orchestra's often weaker vocal wing.

Significantly, Ellington nowhere seems to have rewritten Strayhorn's actual notes. If Ellington had felt that a section by Strayhorn fell short of his standards, he easily could have made the necessary changes. In fact, one would expect Ellingtonian inserts to replace discarded segments, but there are none. If Ellington made changes other than cuts, they typically concerned the assignment of soloists. For instance, if Strayhorn called for a Paul Gonsalves ad-lib solo, Ellington might hand the part to trumpet player Harold Baker. In only a handful of instances does he appear to have changed the instrumentation, partly for practical reasons, such as the absence of a key instrumentalist.

In sum, Ellington's edits were not necessitated by any apparent shortcomings or problems in the musical material of his associate's scores. His reordering must have been inspired by reasons entirely aesthetic. Ellington's neglect or perhaps rejection of original Strayhorn works, such as *Portrait of a Silk Thread, Le Sacre Supreme, Cashmere Cutie*, and *Pentonsilic*, further suggests a different aesthetic assessment of compositions. Strayhorn did not write these works as intellectual exercises. In most cases instrumental parts were extracted for the Ellington orchestra either by Strayhorn himself or by one of the orchestra's copyists. The wear on those parts indicates that they were at some point tried out by the band (unused sets of parts are easily identified as they are not scattered through the various individual band members' books, but sit in one stack). Yet, the absence of book numbers on those parts—titles on the working repertory of the orchestra carried numbers, written or stamped on the parts—indicates that they were not "in the book" and in all likelihood were never performed in public.

The mere fact that Strayhorn's shelved compositions were undoubtedly less accessible works again provides no sufficient explanation for Ellington's decision to keep them out of the book: he himself incessantly wrote and performed works that were, like these Strayhorn compositions, fully outside the mainstream of big-band music, such as *New World A-Comin'*, *The Clothed Woman*, and *The Tattooed Bride*.

To what extent should one be concerned about the structural integrity of Strayhorn's work, which suffered most from Ellington's edits? One could maintain that there is much more to Strayhorn's music than structural coherence, and that structural coherence is not the prime criterion for the aesthetic success of his music. After all, the Ellington orchestra as a rule performed Strayhorn's melodies, harmonies, and orchestrations as written, and often sans pareil. One could further maintain that Ellington's editing was an essential part of the performer's tradition that is jazz, and that the reification of compositions (especially written scores) bespeaks a Eurocentric approach and perpetuates one of the textbook fallacies of musicology. In fact, one could argue that the entire concern with composed form belongs to an altogether different musical environment and is alien to jazz. But neither Ellington nor Strayhorn were average jazz composers (they often vented their uneasiness with the term "jazz"[9]) and scholars have repeatedly singled out Ellington's command of musical form as one of the aspects that set him apart from his peers. Form did matter greatly to Ellington, as evidenced by his continuous tinkering with the order of musical events, both in his own and in Strayhorn's material. Form mattered to Strayhorn too, as he evidently put great effort into creating intricate structures in his compositions. The importance that both composers assigned to composed form is one of the reasons they themselves stressed repeatedly that "jazz" was too restrictive a term for their music, as it caused critics to apply an inappropriate and excessively limited set of criteria to their works. Form mattered greatly to Ellington and Strayhorn, but Ellington composed form on the bandstand and Strayhorn on paper.

One could maintain that Ellington's editing was part of what Strayhorn (1952, 2), in an article by the same title for *Down Beat*, approvingly had termed "the Ellington Effect." "Ellington plays the piano," Strayhorn wrote, "but his real instrument is his band. Each member of his band is to him a distinctive tone color and set of emotions, which he mixes with others equally distinctive to produce a third thing, which I like to call the Ellington Effect." As he further explained: "Sometimes this mixing happens on paper and frequently right on the bandstand. I have often seen him exchange parts in the middle of a piece because the man and the part weren't the same character" (ibid.). Clearly, for Strayhorn, the Ellington Effect revolved around his employer's famous "on the man writing," as well as the trademark sound of his carefully assembled orchestra. Over the years, the term has been used to encompass other aspects of Ellington, from his persona to his harmonic and melodic language.

Yet, Strayhorn's *Down Beat* tribute did more than graciously celebrate the achievements of Ellington. After dismissing the negative critical reception that tended to surround any change in the orchestra's lineup, Strayhorn took the opportunity to pry his own musical style loose from his partner's, in unequivocal terms. "I think my playing and writing style is totally different from Ellington's" (ibid.), Strayhorn boldly stated.

THE *DOWN BEAT* ARTICLE was published at a time when Strayhorn was growing increasingly uncomfortable with certain aspects of his collaboration with Ellington. As Mercer Ellington told David Hajdu, around 1953 "Strayhorn had looked into his royalties and such, and he was upset. They had a talk about it, but Strayhorn wasn't satisfied, and he pulled away. There was some distance between them there" (1996, 121). As it turned out, Tempo Music Company Inc.—the publishing firm Ellington had founded in 1941—had been negligent in executing its tasks. Tempo's title catalogues, copyright registrations, credits on incidental published sheet music, credits on record labels, and even the firm's own files formed a virtually impenetrable web of omissions, inaccuracies, and contradictions. The publisher failed to file copyrights for works that were actually recorded or listed in its catalogues (Tempo Music, Inc. n.d.; 1967a; 1967b), credited authors who had no part in the creation of given works, and repeatedly re-registered one composition under different titles—often changing the composer's credits (see Appendix D). To be sure, it wasn't Ellington personally who was arrogating composer credits that fully accrued to Strayhorn. Tempo was run by his sister Ruth and Danny James, then married to Ruth Ellington (later Mercer Ellington became part of the firm as well).

Numerous Strayhorn originals, including *Air-Conditioned Jungle*, *Overture to a Jam Session*, *Esquire Swank*, and *Flippant Flurry* had been registered in the name of Duke Ellington, even though the record labels in most cases correctly credited Strayhorn. (The earlier inaccuracies surrounding *Pussy Willow*, *Your Love Has Faded*, *Something to Live For*, and *Sepia Panorama* were made by Robbins Music Corporation.) In some cases, Tempo bluntly re-registered works initially copyrighted in Strayhorn's name alone under new titles and with Ellington's name added to the credits. *Jennie Lou Stomp*, for instance, was re-copyrighted in both composers' names as *Smada* (even though Tom Whaley's copyright leadsheet carries Strayhorn's name only), similarly, *Hominy* was re-registered in both their names as *All Roads Lead Back to You*, and two more copyrights were filed for *Hominy: Charlotte Russe* (1946) and *Lotus Blossom* (1959), the title under which the work is generally known. This miscrediting carried on well after Strayhorn's death: virtually none of his works issued on the ten-volume Private Collection (such as *Rod La Roque, Blousons Noirs, Frère Monk*, and *Cordon Blue*) were credited properly, even though the original scores were readily accessible to Mercer Ellington and Stanley Dance, the producers of the CDs.

As stated above, it was not Ellington who sought to take credit for Strayhorn's work (on the contrary, he often gave Strayhorn credit during his concerts) and it is also unlikely that there was any willing attempt on the part of Tempo Music to belittle Strayhorn, or to deemphasize his role. Tempo's modus operandi when it came to copyright registrations was quite typical in the music industry, where copyright registrations served to make money, rather than to establish intellectual ownership.

Consequently, Tempo Music never attempted to copyright any of the hundreds of arrangements by Strayhorn—though it did file his adaptation of the folk-traditional *Frankie and Johnny* under Ellington's name—while Ellington's name was added to originals composed solely by Strayhorn, including *Hear Say, Brown Betty, Orson*, and *Smada*, a practice Tempo also applied to works such as *All Heart* (originally known as *Entrance of Youth*), *Tymperturbably Blue*, and *BDB*. Conversely, Strayhorn's contributions to works such as *C-Jam Blues* and *Rocks in My Bed*, and his work for *Jump for Joy, The Perfume Suite, Beggar's Holiday, Blutopia, Black, Brown and Beige*, and *Harlem* remained uncredited. Finally, due to the apparent administrative chaos at the publisher's offices, Tempo failed to register numerous Strayhorn compositions that were nevertheless listed in its catalogues: *I Can Dream, Let Nature Take Its Course, Life Ain't Nothing but Rhythm, I Remember, Never Meet, Upside Looking, Can It Be* (with lyrics by Leonard Feather), and *Penthouse* (i.e., *A Penthouse on Shady Avenue*). Tempo kept most of the relevant leadsheets for these works in its files; they simply were never sent out to the Library of Congress for proper copyright registration.[10] (A further indication for the working standards of Ellington's publisher may be found in the various issued catalogues: Tempo alternately listed *Take the "A" Train* as a Strayhorn and an Ellington-Strayhorn composition, while *Hayfoot, Strawfoot*, by Lenk, Drake, and McGrane was wrongly listed as an Ellington composition.)

Yet, Strayhorn's growing unhappiness did not altogether stem from matters financial; as Feather explained, "The actual source of his frustration was artistic" (Hajdu 1996, 122). Indeed, there was more to Strayhorn's artistic frustration than the inconsistencies in the copyright registrations and the absence of public recognition. The extensive interference with his originals must have revealed to him that apparently even Ellington at times did not fully recognize and understand him as a composer. One wonders to what extent the recordings of April 1953, for Capitol, hastened Strayhorn's decision in the course of that year to give serious thought to other professional and artistic options. Ellington vigorously went to work with Strayhorn's scores, taking out sections and incidentally reshuffling the order of pieces, the most blatant example being the aforementioned *Orson*. Strayhorn felt strongly about correct readings of his compositions. Nat "King" Cole's 1949 recording of *Lush Life*, for example, which deviates in places from the original, reportedly infuriated Strayhorn (Hajdu 1996, 111). Though Strayhorn's response to the Ellington orchestra's Capitol sessions is not known, these very sessions mark the beginning of an unprecedented two-and-a-half year period during which he contributed virtually no new material to the orchestra's repertory. At the time, he had already finished *All Day Long*, *Coffee and Kisses*, *Gonna Tan Your Hide*, *Night Time*, and *September Song*, the only known scores from his hand the band was to record in 1954 and 1955.[11]

It is hard to assess whether the fate that befell some of Strayhorn's works in the Ellington organization affected the friendship and collaboration of the two composers. Strayhorn mostly spoke glowingly and loyally about his collaboration with Ellington, and he may have felt that working with this remarkable artist and his unsurpassed orchestra sufficiently compensated for the occasional, less felicitous interpretations of his compositions and arrangements. Furthermore, there were the glorious readings of pieces such as *Overture to a Jam Session*, *Mid-Riff*, and, later, *Snibor*, *Smada*, and *All Day Long*, to name just a few.

Though he tried to become more independent from the Ellington organization in the 1950s, Strayhorn's attempts to break away in the end were half-hearted, and he found out, as would Johnny Hodges, that a musical life outside the Ellington organization was complicated and not necessarily more rewarding. When Strayhorn returned to the Ellington fold by the end of 1955, Ellington sought better ways to accommodate him. Not only would they share the credits to all the future suites (resulting, ironically, in credit for works to which Strayhorn had not contributed [see Appendix D]) but, more important, Ellington encouraged Strayhorn to initiate his own projects. Thus, their remarkable association continued in the years that followed—at times flourishing in some of the most rewarding music created for the Ellington orchestra, and at other times stalling in missed chances and lost opportunities.

Chapter Seven

Wounded Love:
Away from the Ellington Organization

THE TEN-INCH 33-1/3 rpm "long-playing" record was introduced commercially in 1948 by Columbia and at the time allowed approximately fifteen minutes per side—eventually duration increased to around twenty-five minutes per side with the introduction of twelve-inchers and microgroove pressing. This new technology liberated Ellington and Strayhorn from the time limitations that the 78 rpm record had imposed on their recorded compositions. But the record companies were slow in offering the orchestra studio time. Postwar audiences had come to embrace different genres of popular music. The popularity of ballroom dancing—the prime reason for the existence of the swing bands—had seriously declined, while bebop had become an important competitive force within the jazz arena.

In December 1950, the Ellington orchestra finally recorded its first LP, called *Masterpieces by Ellington*. The album included four compositions: *The Tattooed Bride*, a relatively recent Ellington composition written for the 1948 Carnegie Hall concert, and three extended arrangements of works that all dated back to the 1930s: *Solitude, Mood Indigo*, and *Sophisticated Lady*. These last three selections would have warranted an expansion of the album's title to *Masterpieces by Ellington, Arranged by Strayhorn*. With the contribution of these new and interesting versions of Ellington classics, Strayhorn was now partaking in yet another branch of his associate's activities: the rejuvenation and updating of earlier work, to present it in new, modern, surprising settings. Revision was an important aspect in Ellington's writing, dating back to the earliest phases of his career. As altoist Russell Procope, who for decades played the solo clarinet in *Mood Indigo*, observed: "A new arrangement would freshen it [*Mood Indigo*] up, like you pour water on a flower, to keep it blooming. They'd all bloom—fresh, fresh arrangements" (Keys 1980).

In 1947, Strayhorn's lover Aaron Bridgers (right) relocated to France, which factually ended their seven-year relationship. Strayhorn's musical relationship with Ellington ran into problems as well, fueled by chaotic copyright registrations and artistic differences. In the first half of the 1950s, Strayhorn sought to carve out a career of his own. (*David Hajdu Collection*)

The fresh arrangements recorded for the *Masterpieces* sessions marked one of the occasions when Ellington and Strayhorn worked in almost perfect symbiosis. While Strayhorn reworked three of the highlights of Ellington's repertory, he allowed for an Ellingtonian approach by keeping the order of the choruses open and avoiding integrated transitions.

In *Mood Indigo*, for instance, Ellington sought and found the best order of the various segments, connected them with piano bridges (such as between the four-beat and waltz-time sections). He assigned solos to the obvious soloists (Russell Procope and Johnny Hodges), the less-obvious soloists (trombonist Quentin "Butter" Jackson and Strayhorn), and a newcomer: Paul Gonsalves. Ellington contributed the settings for the first, third, and final choruses, and let the "Strayhorn Effect" take over from the sixth chorus on. Strayhorn reshaped the theme of *Mood Indigo* with extensive contrapuntal lines and chromatic chord substitutions. In the deceptive modulatory eighth chorus, the tune's opening figure sets out on a chromatic journey. After a vocal rendition of the song by Yvonne Lanauze (a pseudonym for the little-known singer Eve Smith) and Quentin Jackson's virtuoso plunger-work, Strayhorn presents four double-time waltz choruses (chorus fourteen to seventeen), orchestrated with his trademark dissonant clarinet-over-saxophones lines and followed by a string of faux-reprises on "wrong" scale steps. Ellington's final piano transition brings the piece back home to one of his own settings of the theme. This daring *Mood Indigo* spans over fifteen minutes but through the shrewd confrontation between old and new—Ellington's 1930 setting versus Strayhorn's sections, or Jackson's jungle-style talking trombone versus Paul Gonsalves's bebop-bred idiom—the piece continues to intrigue.

The more concise remake of *Sophisticated Lady* again contrasts and blends Ellington and Strayhorn. In six choruses, with a full piano solo chorus by the arranger, *Sophisticated Lady* is taken to a new, modernist level. The first four choruses offer the obligatory theme and variations (based on an older Ellington score), but Strayhorn's densely scored, modulating fifth chorus moves into a transitional section that leads to a restatement of the theme: again he has wrought a ternary form. The arrangement derives its interest from the careful detail in the many intricately textured background passages and presages some of Strayhorn's later work: at the ending of the fifth chorus and in the imitations in the coda one hears hints of his 1960 arrangements for the *Nutcracker Suite*.

It is not hard to detect Strayhorn's hand in the orchestral settings of *Solitude*, the third revamped Ellington classic on the *Masterpieces* album. In this case his score is lost, but the voice leading in the first chorus, especially the independently moving baritone line, as well as the orchestrations that back up Harold Baker's trumpet solo in the fourth chorus and Hamilton's clarinet solo in the fifth, unmistakably identify Strayhorn as the arranger. Still, *Solitude* is the least rewarding of the three scores, as it offers too little variation and no surprises.

Although the artistic opportunities created by the new LP format may have been promising, the general fading interest in big-band music severely counteracted any momentum Ellington and Strayhorn might have derived from the liberation from the 78 rpm time limits. As recording and performing opportunities diminished, the first years of the 1950s brought commercial problems for the Ellington organization, and its leader fought a continuous battle to keep his band going. Furthermore, there were problems with some of the orchestra's personnel: old hands Johnny Hodges, Sonny Greer, and Lawrence Brown defected to form their own group, led by Hodges.

In the spring of 1950, while visiting Paris to work on Orson Welles's ill-fated *Faust* production, Strayhorn found out that Aaron Bridgers, his partner for almost a decade, would not be returning to New York. Back in Manhattan later that year, Strayhorn found solace in new social circles. He frequented the so-called Neal Salon, an informal gathering of mainly black, gay artists, who met at least once a week at the home of dancer Frank Neal and his spouse Dorcas. The group's members discussed their position as artists in segregated, postwar American society, and the difficulties and challenges they met. Strayhorn was strengthened by these meetings and felt encouraged to undertake projects outside the Ellington realm. "There are some things I want to do for myself for a change," he told Dorcas Neal at one of the Salon sessions. "I think I'm going to do them" (Hajdu 1996, 117). This personal reorientation coincided with a crisis in Strayhorn's collaboration with Ellington, caused by an accumulation of grievances, from copyright issues to artistic conflicts (see Chapter 6). "He wasn't on the scene a lot like he was before," Jimmy Hamilton told Hajdu (1996, 131). The change in Strayhorn's commitment was such that at one point Ellington even sought permanent replacement for his long-time collaborator, asking composer Frank Fields to take on Strayhorn's duties (ibid.). The prospective full-time replacement of Strayhorn gracefully declined the offer. But Ellington, who for more than a decade had been used to sharing arranging and composing tasks with a collaborator, consequently hired others, such as Luther Henderson, Dick Vance (briefly in the Ellington band in 1951–52 on trumpet), former Basie band trumpeter Buck Clayton, and ex-Lunceford composer-arranger Gerald Wilson. In addition, he drew more on the compositional skills of other band members, performing and recording works by, among others, Jimmy Hamilton (*Clarinet Melodrama, Theme for Trambean*) and Hodges replacement Rick Henderson (*Commercial Time, Frivolous Banta*).[1]

Since 1939, Strayhorn had devoted most of his professional time to writing and arranging for the Ellington orchestra, but from mid-1953 on (after the Capitol sessions which included the recording of *Orson*) he embarked on a series of serious independent projects—projects that, unlike the small-band recordings of the previous period, were not conducted under the wing of Ellington. Most of his new undertakings concerned small-scale, low-visibility productions. Evidently, Strayhorn did not seek to replace his hectic work for the Ellington orchestra with similar jobs, but instead tried to get involved in endeavors whose rewards would be primarily artistic. In addition, most of these personal projects included musical genres that his work with the Ellingtonians had not been able to provide. The first production in which he became involved as a composer was a play based on Federico García Lorca's surrealist *The Love of Don Perlimplín for Belisa in Their Garden*,[2] initiated by a group that called themselves the Artists Theatre, an experimental Off-Broadway company *avant la lettre* which Strayhorn had joined in 1953.

García Lorca (1898–1936), a widely acclaimed Spanish poet, dramatist, musician, and graphic artist, wrote a dozen innovative theater works including three well-known tragedies: *Blood Wedding* (*Bodas de sangre*, 1933), *Yerma* (1934), and *The House of Bernarda Alba* (*La casa de Bernarda Alba*, 1936). The last had been staged in New York in 1951, roughly two years before Strayhorn got involved with *Don Perlimplín*.

Like virtually all of García Lorca's writings, *Don Perlimplín* centers on frustrated love, boundless passion, and violent death. The play tells the story of the fifty-year-old nobleman and intellectual Don Perlimplín, who on instigation of his servant Marcolfa, marries the young and beautiful Belisa. During their wedding night, Perlimplín fails to consummate the marriage. But while he is sound asleep, the wedding night takes a different turn for Belisa: by dawn she has slept with "five representatives of the five races of the earth." In the weeks that follow, the adventurous Belisa falls passionately in love with an unknown adolescent, who, dressed in a red cape that hides his face, throws letters, weighted by stones, through her window. "It is not your soul I desire," he writes her, "but your white and soft trembling body." One night Perlimplín catches Belisa in their garden, waiting for her secret lover. She confesses to her husband that she has fallen desperately in love with the anonymous youngster, though she still has not seen his face. Enraged, Perlimplín tells Belisa that "in order that he should be completely yours, it has come to me that the best thing would be to stick this dagger in his gallant heart." Belisa anxiously follows her husband into the park to find she's come too late: the stranger in the red cape stumbles, fatally wounded, toward her, Perlimplín's knife in his heart. As he lowers his cape, the stranger turns out to be Don Perlimplín himself. While he dies in Belisa's arms she whispers, "But where is the young man in the red cape?"—Perlimplín's human sacrifice has been in vain.

In its day, *Don Perlimplín* created a great stir, partly because of its daring erotic nature and partly because the Spanish government saw the sexual betrayal of army officer Don Perlimplín as a dangerous disgrace for the military. Started in 1925 but not completed until 1929, the play was immediately banned by the Spanish censor and not published until 1931.

In the Artists Theatre's version, *Don Perlimplín* at once celebrated black and gay pride—a radical idea for its time, reportedly largely conceptualized by Strayhorn (Hajdu 1996, 126). (However, it is not clear how the play served as a vehicle for black and gay pride; it must have been modified somehow.) Four compositions remain of Strayhorn's piano-vocal score: one instrumental work, *Sprite Music* (in all likelihood to underscore the dialogue between the two Sprites, who veil the wedding night scene with a misty gray curtain), and three songs based on poems in the play: *Wounded Love*, *The Flowers Die of Love*, and *Love, Love* (the latter two are originally untitled works, titled and registered posthumously [see Appendix D]).[3] Incidentally, Strayhorn was not the only composer to set García Lorca's play to music: in 1961 the Italian composer Bruno Maderna (1920–1973) wrote an *opera radiofonica* based on *Don Perlimplín*.

Departing from his many harmonically and rhythmically intricate scores, Strayhorn here used simplicity as an expressive tool. In the majestic and at times almost Schubertian *The Flowers Die of Love*, for instance, he designed a simple, largely triadic melody over a one-bar ostinato in the left hand (Ex. 7-1). Over this figure, Strayhorn harmonized the melody using I, IV, and V triads with an alternation between major and minor as the only chromatic play.

Love, Love—in which García Lorca uses water as a metaphor for erotic passion ("within Belisa's thighs/the sun swims like a fish")—is similarly fashioned around an ostinato accompaniment: a two-bar left-hand figure on the tonic B and altered dominant F♯mi7 underscores a melody that drifts from and to the fifth of the tonality (Ex. 7-2). Like the poem, Strayhorn's music is full of aquatic metaphors, the waltz-time itself providing a quiet surge underneath the free-

Ex. 7-1. *The Flowers Die of Love*, mm. 1–10

Ex. 7-2. *Love, Love*, mm. 1–16

flowing lines and rapid descending runs, interrupted only by a short declamatory passage. Throughout, his piano accompaniment is strongly suggestive of the piano works of Francis Poulenc, whose spirit also hovers over *Sprite Music*.

The third and arguably most rewarding song is the torn *Wounded Love*, set to the most famous passage in García Lorca's play, and sung by the fatally wounded Don Perlimplín:

> *Love, love*
> *That here lies wounded*
> *So wounded by love's going*
> *So wounded*
> *Dying of love*

> *Tell everyone that it was just*
> *The nightingale*
> *A surgeon's knife with four sharp edges*
> *The bleeding heart, forgetfulness*
>
> *Take me by the hand, my love*
> *For I come badly wounded*
> *So wounded by love's going*
> *So wounded*
> *Dying of love*[4]

As opposed to the two other songs, *Wounded Love* has a harmonic progression more conventional for Strayhorn, including chromatic passing chords and a middle section in the parallel minor. In its emotional depth and theatrical expression, the song—or better, the lament—is extremely forceful. All of Don Perlimplín's conflicting emotions, his worshipful longing for Belisa's body and his inability (or unwillingness?) to consummate the marriage, are encompassed by the dramatic minor seventh descending from $B^\flat$ to C that opens the song (Ex. 7-3, m. 3). Strayhorn uses this figure—first presented in the two-bar piano-introduction—as a "love motif," and lets it reappear to underscore the key recurrences of "love." In opposition to this love motif, Strayhorn gives a "death motif" in the vocal part, consisting of a note repetition on the fifth ($A^\flat$) and first heard on "dying of love," to recur at "bleeding heart" and "take me by the hand." At each occurrence of the singer's death motif, Strayhorn's piano accompaniment gives the love motif, thus musically securing the connection between the two. In the meantime, this connection articulates one of the main subtexts of García Lorca's poem (love and death are related), and sums up the central theme of the play. Love and death further converge in García Lorca's repeated use of "wounded," a word that receives special treatment in Strayhorn's score: at each occurrence its setting creates an increasing tension against the underlying harmony. The stepwise expansion of the line further enhances the dramatic intensification.

Ex. 7-3. Wounded Love, mm. 1–4

The musical-dramatic techniques Strayhorn applies in *Wounded Love* bring to mind some of the greatest laments in operatic literature. In works such as *Lamento d'Arianna*, early baroque composer Claudio Monteverdi (1567–1643) similarly dealt with abandonment, unrequited love, and, above all, the multifaceted and contrasting emotions of the distressed human psyche. In fact, the approaches of the two composers are so similar that the musical content and dramatic functions of *Wounded Love* can be adequately described in the terminology generally applied to Monteverdi's so-called Venetian laments (written in Venice between 1608 and 1642), a terminology partly developed by Monteverdi himself.[5] For instance, all of Monteverdi's known laments start with a motto-opening, which serves to paint the protagonist's afflictions and simultaneously gives structure to the piece. In Strayhorn's setting, the love motif, first heard in the piano introduction, functions in the same way. Elsewhere in his score for *Don Perlimplín*, Strayhorn inserts text repeats not called for by the original lyrics (for instance in *Love, Love*) in order to fortify the emotive power of the song, a technique abundantly used by Monteverdi as well. But the most important aspect Strayhorn shares with Monteverdi's dramatic writing is that the harmonic and melodic movement is subservient to the expression of a state of feeling that arises out of the dramatic situation. None of this proves that Strayhorn willingly paralleled Monteverdi or was even aware of his music. But it shows that in these first compositions in a dramatic style, not bound to popular theater conventions, Strayhorn sought to express the textual content and its psychological implications through musical movement, and it is this that Monteverdi, too, strove to achieve in his dramatic works.

Even in translation, the quality of García Lorca's poems for *Don Perlimplín* easily surpasses in breadth and depth virtually every other lyric Strayhorn had set to music before. Working from this great dramatic poetry with its free-flowing meter and its irregular free verse, Strayhorn readily discarded the conventions he may have felt bound to in his earlier theater works (although even in his juvenile Pittsburgh works he displays a tendency toward text expression, as in the dramatic descending interval in *So This Is Love*). While he cast each song for *Don Perlimplín* in an individual structure, he achieved a secure coherence in the entire score, not only in his application of a handful of compositional techniques, such as the ostinatos and the sparse, open piano accompaniment, but also in the general atmosphere these works convey, which is restrained and honest, yet personal and emotionally expressive. Possibly the most surprising aspect in the score for *Don Perlimplín* is that it bears no reference to jazz whatsoever. Away from his regular orchestra, Strayhorn returned to idioms explored in his earliest works.

Not all of Strayhorn's new activity took place in the barely visible environment of vanguard experimentation, where it could be appreciated by only relatively small numbers of connoisseurs and supportive friends (some twelve hundred people attended the staging of *Don Perlimplín*). Among the first venues that held a promise for an independent commercial career was an invitation to provide arrangements for a Verve recording of an album titled *Music for Loving*, featuring former Ellingtonian Ben Webster. Producer Norman Granz's concept for the recording was to project Webster's sensuous tenor against a backdrop of strings. The ensemble consisted of a string quintet, expanded with a clarinetist (Strayhorn's long-time friend Tony Scott) and with rhythm section accompaniment (Strayhorn, piano; George Duvivier, bass; and Louie Bellson, drums). Strayhorn had previously done some string writing for Granz's concept album *The Jazz Scene*, for which he arranged *Sono* and *Frustration* (recorded 1949) for a similar lineup, with baritone saxophonist Harry Carney as soloist, and without the clarinet. But even as early as 1940, the arrival of trumpeter-violinist Ray Nance (who joined the Ellington band in 1940) had provided Strayhorn with a reason to familiarize himself with the violin, leading to an idiomatic use of the instrument in Strayhorn's *Overture to a Jam Session*. Strayhorn arranged two standards for the Webster sessions, *It Happens to Be Me* (Arthur Kent, Sammy Gallop) and the Gershwins' *Love Is Here to Stay*, as well as his own *Chelsea Bridge* and Ellington's *All Too Soon*. Webster had once performed the latter two works in their original version, when he was part of the Ellington reed section.

Although Strayhorn kept a keen eye on the idiomatic possibilities of the small string ensemble—alternating, for instance, between pizzicato and arco in *Chelsea Bridge*—these arrangements did not require any significant accommodations: he wrote them as if for the Ellington saxophones.[6] Consequently, *Love Is Here to Stay* is replete with his typical five-part reed section harmonies, with occasional interpolations of the clarinet, as an extra voice between the first and second violin. Other recognizable traits from his big-band work may be found in his setting of *Chelsea Bridge*, where Strayhorn's characteristic single-line clarinet commentary provides color, and the instrument is used to a similar effect in the introduction of *All Too Soon*. Still, Strayhorn's arrangements for *Music for Loving* bear few surprises, although they are effective in providing the romantic mood Granz must have had in mind in order to attract prospective buyers. In fact, the other arrangements on the album, written by former Woody Herman orchestrator Ralph Burns (a friend and admirer of Strayhorn), seem more daring and definitely are more through-composed.[7]

Not long after his work for *Don Perlimplín*, Strayhorn embarked on another theater project, this time with his friend Luther Henderson, the composer-arranger. Henderson previously had provided valuable assistance with projects such as *Beggar's Holiday*, but now he and Strayhorn struck out on their own with a Broadway show titled *Rose-Colored Glasses* (described in detail by Hajdu [1996, 127–130]). But the work never got beyond a rough sketch of the plot, a few scenes, and a couple of numbers. While their plans certainly had potential, Henderson and his new partner never completed the show. Strayhorn wrote some compelling songs, such as the beautiful ballad *Love Has Passed Me By, Again*, the catchy *Still in Love with You*, and the playful *Oo, You Make Me Tingle* (he also infused a handful of numbers written earlier: *Let Nature Take Its Course* and a song from the early 1940s, *If I Can't Have You*).[8]

The lightest works in Strayhorn's entire output are undoubtedly the shows he wrote as president and music director of the Copasetics, a group founded in December 1949 by a handful of tap-dance professionals in commemoration of Bill "Bojangles" Robinson. The Copasetics—named after Bojangles's catch-phrase "Everything is copasetic!"—consisted of about a dozen dancers who gathered weekly to eat and drink at one of the members' homes. Strayhorn, the only "non-hoofer" in the group, was introduced by his friend Charles "Cookie" Cook around 1950, and before long was elected president. Within a year or two, he started to contribute music, as the group annually produced a one-night show to raise money for charity. Between 1951 and 1963 Strayhorn wrote at least six short revues, but in all likelihood more (up to thirteen). These shows, advertised in Harlem's press as the "Annual Copasetics Dance," were important events in New York's black community. Press previews were filled with anticipation, and the publicity each time secured a sold-out house, in halls seating from 1,100 up to 2,000 patrons. The Copasetics could boast many famous names in their audiences, mostly professionals from the music and show business industry. Most Copasetics productions centered around light-hearted comical sketches, interspersed with songs written by Strayhorn and arranged for a slightly smaller than usual big band, under the stewardship of Milton Larkin (1910–1996), a Houston-born trumpeter-bandleader of some fame to those familiar with the band scene. Strayhorn's scores indicate that Larkin's band for the Copasetics had four reed players, three trumpets, a two-man trombone section, and rhythm.

The Copasetics Dances created new challenges for Strayhorn. The mood of the score had to be festive, the music readily playable by an orchestra that, no matter how competent, could never be expected to operate on the same level of musicianship as the Ellington orchestra, also writing and rehearsal time was limited for these one-time events. In addition, the music had to accommodate the "hoofers" who made up the larger part of the Copasetics. For the first time in his life, Strayhorn allowed himself to let infectious swing prevail over composed form, melodic beauty, and harmonic complexity. Still, the more than two dozen surviving Copasetics scores are varied and full of surprising melodic and harmonic turns, even if put together with the simplest of means. Between the obvious production numbers,[9] there are a number of genuine Strayhorn songs, such as *Feet on the Beat, Everything Is Copasetic, Everybody,* and *Swing Dance* (all BSC), some with forgettable lyrics, some fully instrumental.[10] A number of works defy evaluation, since only incomplete sets of parts survive. Titles of these pieces mostly refer to the dancers who made up the Copasetics, such as *Coles and Atkins* (BSC, for Honi Coles and Cholly Atkins), *Cookie* (BSC, for Charles "Cookie" Cook), and *Phace* (BSC, for Henry "Phace" Roberts), suggesting that these works were mainly dance routines.

Swing Dance, written for the 1962 show *Anchors Aweigh*, stands as an exemplary work of the types of instrumentals Strayhorn wrote for the Copasetics. As main material, he designed three complementary four-bar riffs against a repeated dominant chord (Ex. 7-4), somewhat in the vein of *Mid-Riff*. In the expository section Strayhorn calls for a staggered entry of the riffs, beginning in the trombones and followed by the trumpets and saxophones, weaving an increasingly dense texture. Next, he exchanges the various riffs between the orchestra's sections, varying the color of the resultant sound with the same basic material. In addition, he starts a chain of unprepared modulations, moving the tonality up in half-tone increments at an increasingly faster rate, while the ensembles keep exchanging their short themes. Finally, Strayhorn moves up the tonality in the faster stride of whole-tone steps, leading to a thundering episode of brass chords. This segment signals the entry of new material: a thirty-two-bar unison blues (the bridge is a mere chain of dominants, without thematic movement), stated by the entire orchestra (Ex. 7-5). The off-beat patterns of this secondary theme provide a forceful rhythmic counterpoint to a swirling tap-dance routine.

Although made up of the skimpiest material, *Swing Dance* is a hard-swinging, attractive piece that provides ample contrast. Like most of Strayhorn's Copasetics compositions, this production number might have been suitable for the Ellington orchestra as well: a section of towering brass chords that signals the modulated reprise of the unison theme seems especially tailor-made for Strayhorn's regular

Ex. 7-4. *Swing Dance*, mm. 9–20

Ex. 7-5. *Swing Dance*, mm. 73–88

musical forum. Strikingly absent, however, are the cross-section instrumentations, as Strayhorn mostly avoided the use of individual voices in the Milton Larkin orchestra. Consequently, the orchestra's sections, rather than singular instruments, form the smallest musical entities. Clearly, Strayhorn kept the arrangements simple from a practical point of view (limited rehearsal time) as well as for musical reasons. Not being sufficiently familiar with Larkin's instrumentalists, Strayhorn abstained from his usual complex orchestral textures. When in later years Ellington lost some of his orchestra's most distinctive voices (such as Hodges, who died in 1970), the focus in Ellington's writing also shifted from the individual to the collective.

ONE COULD GET THE IMPRESSION that an essentially different composer emerges from these works written outside the Ellington organization, a composer who felt liberated from the task to write "Ellington-type compositions" as Norman Granz (1957) had characterized Strayhorn's music for the band. True, in his independent work Strayhorn explored genres and idioms that had no place in the Ellington repertory. Yet, their topicality notwithstanding—piano music for a García Lorca play inevitably differs from big-band work that underscores a tap-dance show—his independent compositions nevertheless belonged to the same musical world as his work for the Ellington orchestra.[11]

Indeed, Strayhorn himself didn't see any rigid boundaries between the various repertories, and there was even some traffic between his strictly personal initiatives and the orchestra's band book. For instance, he arranged both *Love Has Passed Me By, Again*, from *Rose-Colored Glasses*, and *Wounded Love*, from *Don Perlimplín*, for the Ellington orchestra (though they remained unrecorded), while for his *Feet on the Beat* he used a vamp that strongly resembles a figure he had used a year earlier as the opener for his arrangement of *Dance of the Floreadores* from the *Nutcracker Suite*.[12] In adjusting *Wounded Love* and *Love Has Passed Me By, Again* for the orchestra, Strayhorn fully preserved the original intimate atmospheres, without any apparent transposition to a different voice. If recorded by the Ellington orchestra, these works would not have stood out as essentially different from the other works in the repertory.[13]

While his temporary absence from the Ellington band caused no structural stylistic break in his work, it allowed Strayhorn to free himself from the orchestra's restrictions and limitations, however few, such as its specific and virtually unaltered instrumental lineup. Moreover, working on these independent projects allowed Strayhorn to supervise every step in the process, from the initial conception to the eventual public performance, a kind of artistic freedom that his work with Ellington did not allow.

After the two composers reestablished their musical collaboration later in the 1950s, Strayhorn continued to work outside the Ellington organization. His submergence in the relative anonymity of the Copasetics (the group was well known in African-American circles but received little exposure elsewhere) must have provided a welcome counterpoint to his frantic work for the Ellingtonians, of which a large amount was coming his way.

Chapter Eight

Masterpieces by Strayhorn: Writing for Albums

ALWAYS IN HIS ELEMENT when challenged, Ellington managed to survive the early 1950s, a period of unparalleled difficulty in the orchestra's history. Turning the departures of key personnel (Hodges, Brown, and Greer) into an advantage, Ellington recruited younger players and in the following years further rejuvenated his orchestra. Musicians such as trumpeter-flugelhornist Clark Terry, trumpet player Willie Cook, tenorist Paul Gonsalves, and drummer Louie Bellson were all raised on bebop and thus brought a modern way of playing to the orchestra. Rather than disbanding (as virtually all his contemporaries were forced to do), Ellington chose to wait for better times, paying his band from the steady flow of royalties that its earlier successes still generated, and at times accepting demeaning gigs such as those at the *Aquacade*, where he had to provide background music for a family show that included a color-fountain display and ice skaters.

In hindsight Ellington made the right decision in keeping his band together, and things really started to look up when Johnny Hodges returned to the flock in August 1955. Around the same time, Ellington managed to convince Strayhorn to become more involved again, most notably in the realm of joint projects. Terminating an uneventful three-year contract with Capitol Records late in 1955, Ellington first signed with the independent Bethlehem label for two LPs, then entered into a contract with the more prestigious Columbia Records later in 1956. Under the new contract, Strayhorn was promised more artistic freedom, as well as full credit for his work. Having resumed work late in 1955 with a new arrangement of *I Got It Bad (and That Ain't Good)* for Hodges (commercially recorded in June 1957),[1] Strayhorn's first real project in the renewed partnership was the LP *Blue Rose*, featuring singer Rosemary Clooney in a number of predominantly older Ellington and Strayhorn songs, all arranged by Strayhorn. The recordings took

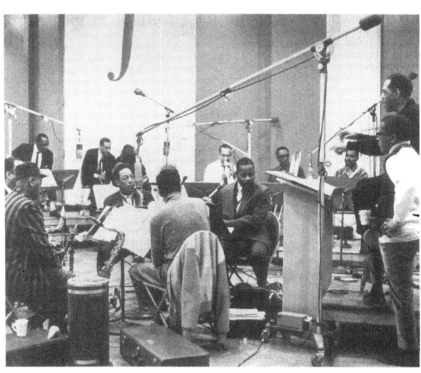
Strayhorn returned to the Ellington fold in the second half of the 1950s. Now that Duke Ellington had survived the demise of the big band era, he and Strayhorn engaged in some of their most rewarding recording projects.
(*Photograph by Chuck Stewart*)

place early in 1956 (Clooney's voice was dubbed in later). Especially the beautiful arrangements of *Sophisticated Lady* and *Passion Flower*—the latter as if to celebrate the return of Hodges[2] but in truth written in 1949, long before he left the band—demonstrate how much the orchestra's sound owed Strayhorn.

Shortly after the Clooney sessions, the band went back to the studio for recordings that would find a place on two LPs for the Bethlehem label: *Historically Speaking—The Duke* and *Duke Ellington Presents*....Although Ellington had promised Strayhorn that he would be given full credit— "From now on your name is up there, right next to mine" (Hajdu 1996, 154)—this new agreement had not fully dawned on Ellington's associates. For *Duke Ellington Presents*...Strayhorn arranged at least five of the ten orchestral pieces and contributed an original, but the latter went uncredited and Strayhorn's name was remarkably absent from the liner notes. The text on the record sleeve maintains that the orchestra "primarily plays the arrangements of Duke" and credits vintage inspired Strayhorn arrangements to Ellington, citing "Duke's lush chords" in Strayhorn's setting of *Laura*, identifying his arrangement of *My Funny Valentine* as "a colorful bit of Ellingtonia," noting the "Ellington mood" in *Day Dream*, and finding "Duke's rich and colorful orchestral chords" in *Deep Purple* (Muranyi 1956). Furthermore, consistent with its habitual negligence, Tempo Music failed to copyright the final track of the album, Strayhorn's original *Blues I + II*, retitled *Blues*. The jacket credits Ellington as the author of *Blues*; according to the liner this piece was "a fitting close to Duke's album" (ibid.).

These sessions early in 1956 marked the beginning of a commercially and artistically productive period that was to put Ellington fully back on the map as composer and bandleader. It coincided with a creative peak in both his and Strayhorn's writing, and was furthered by inspired performances of the band. The orchestra's legendary July 7 performance at the Newport Jazz Festival was followed by a cover article on Ellington in *Time* magazine a few weeks later. Though the two events were initially unrelated (Ellington had been under consideration as a cover subject before Newport), the article focused prominently on the concert, establishing the performance as a turning point in Ellington's career, at least in terms of public appreciation.

Strayhorn's contribution to the key performance at Newport, though musically of minor importance, was nevertheless significant. He wrote two-thirds of the jointly credited *Newport Jazz Festival Suite*, an invaluable publicity stunt cooked up by festival organizer George Wein and Columbia's A & R (for artists and repertory) executive George Avakian. *Ellington at Newport* was the orchestra's best-selling record ever, in itself a remarkable feat in the post-Swing Era.

The rejuvenated Ellington-Strayhorn team embarked on other prestigious projects that same year. One was a suite that centered around the works of Shakespeare, to be premiered in 1957 at the Stratford Music Festival, and another was an allegorical television special, entitled *A Drum Is a Woman*, to be produced for the *U.S. Steel Hour*. *A Drum Is a Woman* seems to have been mainly masterminded by Ellington, but the larger part of the orchestral score is recognizably Strayhorn's.[3] Apart from an incidental orchestral piece, such as *Rhumbop*, co-written with Jimmy Hamilton, Ellington mainly created the looser small-group backgrounds, relying on his capacities to work out head charts with his musicians on the stand, and aided among others by Clark Terry, who provided the solo parts for *Hey, Buddy Bolden*. Still, as Strayhorn maintained, the collaboration was their "closest ever" (Worth 1962), though it is unknown what exactly set this collaboration apart from other episodes. Remarkably, while Ellington's story line of *A Drum Is a Woman* continuously refers to jazz, most of Strayhorn's orchestral pieces do not. The score is a mixed bag of quasi-Caribbean numbers and showy theater music. Even if they collaborated more closely than ever on *A Drum Is a Woman*, Ellington and Strayhorn failed to convincingly marry music and lyrics. With its rather naive narrative and the uneven music (nevertheless performed glowingly by the orchestra), *A Drum Is a Woman* is a dated and somewhat flawed work.

While still engaged in the production of *A Drum Is a Woman*, Ellington and Strayhorn set out to sketch the contours of the tentatively titled *Shakespearean Suite*. For Strayhorn this preparation consisted mainly of rereading the complete works of Shakespeare (Hajdu 1996, 156). He first focused on *A Midsummer Night's Dream*—from which he also drew the suite's final title *Such Sweet Thunder*[4]—one of Shakespeare's plays traditionally dressed up with ample music. (The most distinguished score for *A Midsummer Night's Dream* is undoubtedly by Felix Mendelssohn-Bartholdy, with the famous wedding march at the beginning of Act Five.) As a first step, Strayhorn distributed a number of the play's main characters over the instrumentalists: "Clark [Terry, flugelhorn] = Puck; alto [Johnny Hodges?] is Hermia; John [Sanders, trombone] = Lysander; violin [Ray Nance] = Tatania [sic]; clarinet [Jimmy Hamilton] = Oberon."[5]

In the midst of these preparations, Ellington unexpectedly agreed to premier the work months before its initial deadline. As a result, Strayhorn suddenly was faced with a greatly shortened schedule, and instead of composing new sections, he ended up infusing two earlier compositions, apparently at the instigation of Ellington (Hajdu 1996, 160). His *Pretty Girl* (recorded by Hodges in 1956), retitled *The Star-Crossed Lovers*, now served to portray Romeo and Juliet, while his slightly more recent *Lately*, also from 1956, became the eleventh movement of the suite, as *Half the Fun*. The only new movement Strayhorn delivered was the intricate *Up and Down, Up and Down*, a virtuoso display of contrapuntal writing, in which a number of cross-section instrumental groups brilliantly evoke the mischievous fairy Puck. The work's title is from one of Puck's lines: "Up and down, up and down/I will lead them up and down" (*A Midsummer Night's Dream*, III.2.396–97). Other than scoring a small section for Ellington's forceful opener of *Such Sweet Thunder*,[6] Strayhorn apparently had little to do with the other nine movements. Yet, true to their new understanding, this time he did share the credits with Ellington for all twelve movements. Although Strayhorn's *Star-Crossed Lovers* is typically singled out as one of the highlights of the suite—at any rate it became its most performed selection—the larger part is genuine Ellington, and it ranks among his best writing.

More work that called for the services of Strayhorn was under way. In 1955 Norman Granz had initiated a multi-album project with singer Ella Fitzgerald for his Verve label, to record the highlights from the repertories of the great American songwriters. As the third production in this series, Granz envisioned *Ella Fitzgerald Sings the Duke Ellington Songbook* to fill four ten-inch LPs, twice the size of the earlier double albums that were dedicated to songwriter Cole Porter and the writer-lyricist team Richard Rodgers and Lorenz Hart. To fill these discs, the production required some sixty-odd songs from the Ellington library. "It was done under the worst conditions," Granz recalled. "We planned far in advance, but in the end Duke failed to do a single arrangement" (Nicholson 1999, 315). While Strayhorn brought thirteen new arrangements to the sessions, Ellington had finished only one: a rocking remake of Tizol's *Caravan*. Even with the addition of orchestral scores already in the band's book, *Rockin' in Rhythm* and *Perdido*, and a last-minute head arrangement of *I'm Beginning to See the Light*, the material fell seriously short of what Granz needed. To save the project, it was decided that Fitzgerald would do nineteen tracks with a small combo featuring former Ellingtonian Ben Webster. The poor preparations of the sessions notwithstanding, Strayhorn turned out some of his most rewarding vocal arrangements, including a rhythmically intricate version of *Take the "A" Train*, as well as an unsurpassed version of *Day Dream* (see Chapter 9 for detailed analysis of this arrangement).

In order to fill the remaining tracks, Ellington came up with the idea of a four-movement suite, entitled *A Portrait of Ella Fitzgerald*. For the occasion, Strayhorn rearranged his 1948 *Entrance of Youth*, recorded as the second movement and retitled *All Heart* (possibly the work's original title), while adding two more compositions for which Ellington furnished the titles *Royal Ancestry* and *Beyond Category*. Ellington's own contribution formed the fourth part, a blues, mainly improvised, called *Total Jazz*. On the recording, Ellington delivers spoken introductions to the first three movements over Strayhorn's piano extemporizations, to change roles with his associate for the final movement. As Ellington states after the third movement: "I think it is only fitting that Billy should have the responsibility of the concluding statement" (Ellington 1957).

Although Ellington acknowledged Strayhorn's importance, here and elsewhere, other forces counteracted any public recognition that Strayhorn might receive from it. One of those forces was publicist Joe Morgen, who had worked his way into the Ellington organization. Responsible for numerous press releases that accompanied the now steady stream of Ellington orchestra LPs and projects, Morgen held a professional and personal grudge against Strayhorn's role in the orchestra. Consequently, even when album jackets tended to dedicate increasing space to the musical collaboration between Ellington and Strayhorn, Morgen successfully kept Strayhorn's name out of the printed press (Hajdu 1996, 166–171).

In his private life, Strayhorn gravitated more and more to Francis "Goldie" Goldberg, a cook by profession. (Strayhorn himself held a reputation among friends as a fine amateur cook.) Strayhorn's friends described Goldie as a good-looking, dominant, and possessive man who drank heavily. By 1958, Goldberg had moved in with Strayhorn.

Shortly after the Fitzgerald sessions, the band was back in the Columbia studios for yet another project, the recording of the *Ellington Indigos* album. The album contained six arrangements from Strayhorn's hand, which, as was by then typical, accounted for more than half of the orchestral material for a session. The recordings included a number of imaginative pieces, such as Strayhorn's 1943–44 arrangement of *Where or When*, as well as new arrangements of *Night and Day*, *Dancing in the Dark*, *Prelude to a Kiss*, *Willow Weep for Me*, and *Solitude*. In the next year, more commercial work followed for an album titled *At the Bal Masque* (*Poor Butterfly*, *Indian Love Call*, *Lady in Red*, *Alice Blue Gown*, *Donkey Serenade*, and *Gypsy Love Song*). Strayhorn also contributed to a so-called stockpile session—recordings Ellington made at his own expense—in the RCA studios in March 1959 (a number of stockpile sessions were issued after Ellington's death; some have remained on the shelf). At this particular session, singer Lil Greenwood worked her way through the usual mix of standards and Ellington and Strayhorn originals (a total of eleven songs) in skillful yet somewhat average Strayhorn arrangements. There was one highlight: a rare version of *I Got It Bad* including an orchestration of the seldom-heard verse—Strayhorn's sixteenth documented version of this song since he first arranged it for *Jump for Joy* in 1941.

Strayhorn's arrangement of *I Got It Bad*, from this never-released stockpile session with Greenwood, was the only score that survived in some form the unsuccessful attempt earlier that year to revive *Jump for Joy*. Teaming up with the show's original lyricist Sid Kuller in Miami Beach, where Ellington had landed a four-week contract at a dining theater called the Copa City, Strayhorn had revised most of the show, rewritten the entire score, and added production numbers and new songs, partly in collaboration with Ellington,[7] and partly in collaboration with Thomas Whaley, who directed the choir. For clarity, Strayhorn had numbered his arrangements and new songs, occasionally adding letters ("Natives Dance 3a," "Natives Dance 3b") to indicate reprises and alternate versions. Greenwood's *I Got It Bad* carried number 20.

In addition to fresh versions of songs that stemmed from the original "revusical" there was a host of new tunes, virtually all written and arranged by Strayhorn.[8] According to the program (reproduced in Stratemann 1992, 398) the show was "produced, written and directed by Sid Kuller" and "composed by Duke Ellington." Strayhorn was listed as orchestrator, together with Ellington.

Unfortunately, the new *Jump for Joy* had shared more with its predecessor than a number of dusted-off songs. Again being the wrong show at the wrong time and the wrong place, it folded within three weeks after its opening. Thus ended Strayhorn's final commercial involvement with the musical theater. An earlier attempt, the 1958 *Saturday Laughter* for which he and Ellington wrote some twenty-two songs, never even got beyond its initial drafts for lack of commercial backing (Hajdu 1996, 184–185).[9]

Around the time the band was in the studio for the stockpile session with singer Greenwood, Strayhorn departed for the film set of Otto Preminger's *Anatomy of a Murder* in Michigan, followed later by Ellington, who had accepted the engagement to write his first full-length film score. As a variety of sketches and scores indicate, Ellington and Strayhorn as usual divided the work between them. Ellington wrote the earthy *Flirtibird* as well as the driving opening theme, while Strayhorn was responsible for the creation of the sensuous *Polly's Theme*. Despite its title, the theme became a leitmotif for the main male protagonist Paul Biegler. It is possible that Strayhorn first envisioned the song to underscore the female protagonist, given its sensuous melody. At any rate, *Polly's Theme* was the working title for a number of segments in the underscore that all drew on the same melody, and eventually it was recorded under various titles: *Low Key Lightly, Grace Valse, Haupê*, and *Midnight Indigo* (some in Ellington arrangements). Still, only a small portion of Strayhorn's contributions were used for the movie's barely audible sound track (large portions of the film were without music altogether), and the consequent album for CBS. Numerous Ellington compositions remained unused as well.[10]

Under its new contract with Columbia, the Ellington orchestra was producing an incessant stream of albums. Rewarding albums such as *Ellington Jazz Party* and *Blues in Orbit* were alternated with albums of less artistic importance. Apparently, the various producers and A & R executives who helped to plot the orchestra's recording strategies (as well as Ellington himself) felt that an album's marketability called for the inclusion of arrangements rather than originals. In fact, the majority of late-1950s to mid-1960s recordings evolved around preexistent material and, as before, the task of creating the larger part of those arrangements fell to Strayhorn. Thus, the orchestra recorded Tchaikovsky's *Nutcracker Suite* (Strayhorn wrote the arrangements of at least six of nine movements), Edvard Grieg's *Peer Gynt Suite* (four out of five movements by Strayhorn), *Recollections of the Big Band Era*, and *Will the Big Bands Ever Come Back* (eight out of twenty-two arrangements by Strayhorn, most other tracks by guest-arrangers, though the CD reissue wrongly credits Ellington), music from the Charles Strouse Broadway show *All American* (eight out of ten arrangements by Strayhorn), an album with mainly French pop classics called *A Midnight in Paris* (at least nine out of thirteen), a collection of tunes from Walt Disney's *Mary Poppins* (at least seven out of twelve), and a variety of hits of the day, issued on *Ellington '65* (at least five out of eleven) and *Ellington '66* (at least seven out of twelve).

In his diplomatic way, Strayhorn maintained that he tackled every arrangement with the same level of dedication:

> You should say, "I wouldn't treat *this* any less carefully than I would *that*." You treat them [originals and pop songs] equally. I put the same effort into whatever I do. I try to do the best I can....I feel it is not right for an artist to turn his back on a simple melody just because it's not a great suite or something or other. After all, [pianist Vladimir] Horowitz plays *Träumerei* beautifully, and why shouldn't he? Why shouldn't you play a simple melody? It's a matter of being humble. All artists are humble. All *great* artists are humble. The ones who're not are not great artists....That does not mean you have to play it [a simple song] the way thousands of other people have played it. You can give it your own individuality. But you don't look *down* on these things, because if you look down, that's the end of you, your integrity, and everything. It's snobbery. (Dance 1967, 18)

Despite his fiery defense of their contents, some of the more commercial albums show signs of Strayhorn's waning interest. In somewhat more straightforward terms, Strayhorn confessed: "If I'm working on a tune, I don't want to think it's bad. It's just a tune, and I have to work with it" (ibid.). Apparently, repertoire that stemmed from Disney movies or the Beatles (*All My Loving*) was less inspiring for Strayhorn than themes historically associated with jazz (*Artistry in Rhythm, Good-Bye*), which Strayhorn turned into more imaginative scores.[11] At times it seems as if he provides ironic commentary on the all too meager material. *La Petite Valse*, for instance, a rather trivial and wholly tonal song, ends in mayhem as Strayhorn irreverently answers each antecedent two-bar phrase in C with consequent phrases in remote keys such as E major and A♭ minor.

Arguably, the most impressive arrangements from the period are those he wrote for the *Nutcracker Suite*, a lucid adaptation of Peter Ilyitch Tchaikovsky's orchestral score, fashioned after the ballet. Rather than turning to jazzed-up renditions of the movements—known as ragging the classics—Strayhorn (and Ellington) virtually recomposed the ballet, using a wide array of techniques to render the original into a new and strikingly personal work. In the *Overture*, for instance, Strayhorn not only calls for a much slower tempo than Tchaikovsky, but he reorganizes the movement altogether. He deletes sections, such as the entire da capo repetition, and focuses on minute details in the original to enlarge them in his arrangement, as if with a magnifying glass. In Strayhorn's hands, Tchaikovsky's four-bar transition from the first to the second theme turns into a melancholic wah-wah trombone feature, while he takes a scalar descending background line, of minor importance in the original movement, to carry the entire coda. All his other movements show the same high level of musical detail, a firm balance between wit, irony, and tribute. Strayhorn caricatured neither his own nor Tchaikovsky's music.[12]

Strayhorn and Ellington tried a similar route with the adaptation of Grieg's *Peer Gynt Suites Nos. 1 and 2* (1888, opera 46 and 55, a condensed orchestral version of Grieg's original twenty-three short piano pieces), but this time the music sounds less convincing. Part of the problem seems to lie in the material itself. Where Tchaikovsky's light ballet music offered multiple themes, tempos, and meters, Grieg's often somber and languid underscore to Henrik Ibsen's epic play, with movements such as *Morning Mood* and *Åse's Death*, left little room for irony or humorous re-composition. Furthermore, while Strayhorn had invested considerable time in doing the *Nutcracker*, he had far less preparation time for *Peer Gynt*, as the whole idea developed when the band unexpectedly had three extra recording days at the Columbia studios. The hasty preparations are reflected in the absence of movements five to eight of the original *Peer Gynt Suites* (*Ingrid's Lament, The Arabian Dance,* and *Peer Gynt's Homecoming*), pieces that seem more complicated to adapt for jazz orchestra. Furthermore, Strayhorn's settings of ;an *Ase's Death* and *Solvejg's Song* follow with suspicious closeness the widely available *Edition Peters* piano transcription of the *Peer Gynt*, a copy of which is indeed present in the Duke Ellington Collection. The pressure on both composers (Ellington scored the second movement, a gutsy remake of *In the Hall of the Mountain King*) possibly rubbed off on the Ellingtonians, who on the recording sound uninspired and at times are strikingly out of tune.

Nevertheless, Strayhorn dealt most seriously with his adaptations of both Grieg and Tchaikovsky. "In both cases," he said, "we had to consider the composers. They're not dead. They're alive, and that's *their* music and we didn't want to offend them" (Dance 1967, 18).

ANOTHER MULTIMOVEMENT WORK, *Suite Thursday*, was issued on the same album as the *Peer Gynt Suites*. This work, in four movements, was inspired by John Steinbeck's novel *Sweet Thursday*. On the original release it was credited to Ellington and Strayhorn, though Tempo's copyright registrations for the individual movements exclude Strayhorn. His role in writing the music remains unclear, as none of his scores (if any) survive. Two of Ellington's scores, *Lay By* and *Zweet Zurzday* are in DEC, which makes Strayhorn the candidate for *Schwiphtiey* and *Misfit Blues*, but both movements bear too little audible traces to warrant positive identification of his contribution. One suspects the hand of Jimmy Hamilton in part of *Schwiphtiey*, while *Misfit Blues* seems largely Ellingtonian. If not in an ostensible musical way, Strayhorn still played a role in the work's creation, by providing a typewritten, witty synopsis of the book (DEC, both the style and handwritten additions identify him as the author). Trying "to keep it short, and still catch the parts you [Ellington] might have the most empathy with" (Strayhorn 1960), he sketches the main characters: "Doc, a high IQ type from

[the] University of Chicago who makes a shaky living in his pad catching and selling specimens of marine life for college and research laboratories; and Suzy, a crude but proud gal down on her luck who briefly inhabits The Bear Flag, but is too frank and hot-tempered to make a successful prostitute" (ibid.).

According to Strayhorn's summary,

> Doc is beloved by all the folks of Cannery Row because of his natural, instinctive kindness and helpfulness, and the slight plot centers on their efforts to "help" him when they sense that his depression is not really caused by his inability to write a research paper on emotional manifestations in octopi, but by the fact that nothing so big can be accomplished by a man so obviously in need of a woman as he is. And of course the woman turns out to be Suzy. They can't get together on Page 1 because both are proud, defensive, and seemingly incompatible by reason of wildly different backgrounds, mental capacities and aspirations[,] if any. But, they can't stay apart either, because—well—You dig? So on Page 273 they drive off to LaJolla in Doc's old car to catch the morning tide to catch some special specimens, and everybody's ecstatic, especially Doc and Suzy. (ibid.)

In Strayhorn's words, "the mood evoked [by Steinbeck] in the sympathetic reader is akin to the mood of Duke's *Black, Brown and Beige* (or possibly *Harlem Airshaft*)—gay and funny, sad and tragic, but conveying through simple people and incidents the essence of human nobility[,] touched with the ridiculous[,] which gives it reality" (ibid.).

As before, the relationship between the suite's program, the titles of the movements, and the music is highly elusive, although this time the composer(s?) warded off any foreseeable criticism by building most movements around a motif derived from a broken half-diminished chord. The characteristic interval of the motif is a minor sixth drop from the flatted fifth to the minor seventh. It serves as the main thematic thread in *Suite Thursday*—a thin thread indeed, but sufficiently impressive to some of Ellington's critics: according to Stanley Crouch (1988, 442), it points up "how sophisticated the composing for the organization had become."

After the orchestra's triumphant performance at Newport in 1956, Ellington was almost unanimously regarded as one of the most constant and crucial factors in jazz. In the following years, a steady stream of prizes, awards, and eventually honorary doctorates would come his way, to underscore his growing stature. Yet, much as Ellington had been largely responsible for creating his orchestra's style prior to 1940, the sound of the 1950s Ellington band (quite removed from that of the earlier Ellington orchestras) relied on the work of two composer-arrangers. The responsibility for a significant part of the band's repertory fell entirely to Strayhorn. In addition to prominent contributions to most of the suites and to some of the stockpile sessions, he provided the larger share for the more visible commercial projects. As a result, the sound of the Ellington band in the 1950s was equally indebted to Ellington and Strayhorn, even though it was understood by its audiences as purely Ellingtonian. Despite his invisibility, Strayhorn had become the most significant creative force behind the Duke Ellington Orchestra, next to the orchestra's leader. Ellington himself was fully aware of this fact. He correctly identified Strayhorn as "one of the most important people in our group [the Ellington organization]—very seldom seen in public appearances, but always heard" (Ellington 1964).

Chapter Nine

The Whodunit Game:
The Mature Style of Billy Strayhorn

AFTER HIS CREATIVE OUTBURST for the Blanton-Webster band, Strayhorn's writing for the Ellington orchestra went into a phase of perpetuation rather than innovation, and early in 1950 he was mostly elaborating concepts that harked back to earlier works. This led to well-conceived but less surprising pieces such as the hard-swinging *All Day Long* (1951) and the more relaxed *Boo-Dah* (1953). Around the same time, however, Strayhorn wrote the arrangements for the *Masterpieces by Ellington* album, discussed earlier, which pointed toward the style he would develop in the years that followed. Writing for a renewed and modernized Ellington band, Strayhorn changed his sound. This new sound is reminiscent of bebop and cool jazz, newly developed jazz idioms of the time. His compositions and arrangements gained in melodic, harmonic, and structural complexity, while at the same time his use of musical material grew still more economic. The extensive and at times over-ornate orchestral scores from the 1940s (*Pentonsilic, The Eighth Veil*) made way for leaner orchestrations that nevertheless gained notably in expressiveness.

Among the first originals in the 1950s to come out of a different mold was the harmonically tricky and rhythmically agile *Upper Manhattan Medical Group* (commonly referred to as *U.M.M.G.*), a tribute to Strayhorn's friend and personal physician, Dr. Arthur Logan. In a way, the piece also salutes the Copasetics: "listen to some of the figures in Strayhorn's pieces, like *U.M.M.G.*, those are dances—tap dances maybe—and you can't mistake what they essentially are," Ellington wrote in his autobiography (Ellington 1973, 100). "You can dance with a lot of things besides your feet. Billy Strayhorn was...[a] dancer—in his mind. He was a dance-writer" (ibid.). Indeed, while many of Strayhorn's earlier pieces emphasized other musical parameters, rhythm became increasingly prominent in his later work. Where many earlier pieces often used a limited rhythmic vocabulary (e.g., in *Chelsea Bridge* or *Rain Check*), the theme of *U.M.M.G.* was rhythmically more varied. The Ellington orchestra made a number of excellent recordings of the piece.

Though seemingly another standard AABA song, *U.M.M.G.* is harmonically far more radical than most such songs. Strayhorn has harmonized each note of the theme as an altered or extended chord tone (Ex. 9-1), a technique prevalent in bebop. The most notable harmonic turn occurs in the fifth bar of *U.M.M.G.*, where the melody dives to its lowest point through a tritone interval, underscored by an A7$^{(\#9)}$ in its first inversion.[1] It is in fact a double-diminished seventh chord in its second inversion, built on the raised fourth step G—a chord that achieves its power from its multiple chromatic leading tones.[2]

From his earliest days as a composer, Strayhorn had used upper-chromatic dominants and double-dominants (e.g., in *Fantastic Rhythm* and *Ugly Ducklin'*, and especially in *Flamingo* where he used the tritone relationship to initiate a number of sophisticated modulations). However, his usage of the chord in *U.M.M.G.* is fresh and unexpected, as the anticipated V never comes: the chord functions as a delay for I rather than as an upper-chromatic dominant for V.[3] For maximum effect, the A7$^{(\#9)}$ comes on the downbeat, where it coincides with the first occurrence of a downbeat melody note since the opening of the song.

As the larger part of the melody travels through chordal upper structures, *U.M.M.G.* refuses to become rooted. The only truly consonant passage can be found in the arpeggiated ascending B♭mi11 over its major parallel D♭ in bars five and six. But this passage is barely perceived as a tonic, since it has so much forward drive and since the root of the tonic is not doubled in a significant way in the melody.[4] Only in the final measures of the theme is the home-chord truly reached, with the same progression as in bar 5 (Ex. 9-2). The melody's jump from the tonic to the sixth and the repeat of the phrase combine to produce a sense of unresolvedness in the final bars. This kind of openness played an increasing role in Strayhorn's later work.

The tonal ambiguity that Strayhorn explored in many of his earlier works is taken to a new level in *U.M.M.G.* Virtually every ii7-V7 progression stems from minor keys, and consequently most temporary supertonic chords are half-diminished, which further obscures the tonality of the piece. The use of half-dimin-

Ex. 9-1. U.M.M.G., mm. 1–8

Baritone saxophonist Harry Carney plays, while Strayhorn reads along. The musicians in the Ellington band had great respect for Strayhorn. He always sought to write music that fitted the individual musicians.
(*Courtesy Rutgers Institute of Jazz Studies*)

ished chords as part of ii7-V7-delaying ii7-V7 progressions as well as the harmonization of U.M.M.G.'s melody and the rhythmic placement of the notes shows that Strayhorn's harmonic thinking had developed parallel to bebop. In fact, the half-diminished harmonies in U.M.M.G. call to mind typical bebop compositions such as Dizzy Gillespie's *Woody'n You* (see, e.g., DeVeaux 1997, 311–312), written around 1942. Since much of Strayhorn's earlier work had pointed in the same harmonic direction (as early as 1933 he had used similar progressions in *So This Is Love*), the bop language for Strayhorn was close to home and fitted his own idiom perfectly. To the extent that U.M.M.G. may have owed something to Dizzy Gillespie and his peers, it was only fitting that this trumpeter appeared as a guest soloist on one of the song's recordings.[5]

Strayhorn was to apply the characteristic harmonic turn seen in bar 5 of U.M.M.G. in a number of other works of the period, such as in the second bar of the little-known but eloquent and soft-spoken *Ballad for Very Tired and Very Sad Lotus Eaters*. Composed for Johnny Hodges and a small ensemble, the song was recorded with the composer at the piano for an LP called *Duke's in Bed* (Verve 2304383). In *Lotus Eaters* Strayhorn uses virtually the same progression as in U.M.M.G., against a large descending interval (a major seventh) that moves out of key (Ex. 9-3) and lands on a downbeat.

Although based on the same idea as the opening bars of U.M.M.G., this passage is more conventional, as Strayhorn scores the chord as a full diminished chord on I (rather than as an inverted dominant: the expected E is missing from the chord), a more commonly used delay of the tonic (see, e.g., *Spring Is Here* from Richard Rodgers [1939]). *Lotus Eaters* and U.M.M.G. also resemble each

Ex. 9-2. *U.M.M.G.*, mm. 29–31

Ex. 9-3. *Ballad for Very Tired and Very Sad Lotus Eaters*, mm 1–2

other in the rare occurrence of the tonic chord. When it does appear in *Lotus Eaters* (mm. 2, 6, 10, 14), Strayhorn puts it in its second inversion, turning it into a dynamic rather than a static harmony. By contrast, he repeatedly confirms the subdominant in each A strain by means of ii7-V7 (in measures 5 and 13), and later in the bridge he similarly establishes IV and ♭VI, both functioning as temporary harmonic planes (Ex. 9-4). In earlier works such as *Passion Flower* and *Chelsea Bridge*, Strayhorn had always steered at the end of tonally uncertain passages to harmonically clearer grounds with an affirmative V-I. *U.M.M.G.* and *Lotus Eaters* thus importantly expanded his tonal detachment: Strayhorn here overtly postpones the tonal confirmation to the final bars of the chorus, while emphasizing transient harmonic planes.

Where the occurrence of the ♭VI7/I-I connection mainly colored and intensified the melodic and harmonic movement in *U.M.M.G.* and *Ballad for Very Tired and Very Sad Lotus Eaters*, with the cunningly refined *Cashmere Cutie* Strayhorn finally based an entire composition on this progression.[6] Not known to be performed or recorded during his life, *Cashmere Cutie* is one of those Strayhorn masterpieces that combine an enthralling melody with rich harmonies and an exquisite orchestration.

Similar to works like *Boo-Dah*, *Cashmere Cutie*—cast in extended forty-eight-bar ABAC form—is built on a simple four-bar reiterated gesture, which in this case starts with a diatonically ascending line (each time at a higher step in the scale). But Strayhorn alters the direction of the line at each second half of the phrase (Ex. 9-5, measures 3–4, 7–8) with increasingly nonharmonic quarter-note triplets. Strayhorn harmonizes this four-bar thematic cell with two chords only: the tonic chord and again a ♭VI7 (this time in first inversion), harmonically similar to the double-diminished seventh chord in *U.M.M.G.* and *Lotus Eaters*. The alternation of the fully tonal, consonant antecedent bars with the harmonically enigmatic consequent bars lends the piece a brooding atmosphere, heightened in the orchestral score by the dense brass structures that are pitted against the saxophone ensemble lead.

Apart from Strayhorn's more radical application of the ♭VI7-I connection in this composition, the sophistication of *Cashmere Cutie* derives from its through-

Ex. 9-4. Ballad for Very Tired and Very Sad Lotus Eaters, mm. 17–24

Ex. 9-5. *Cashmere Cutie*, mm. 1–12

composed form. Instead of writing variations on the theme, Strayhorn keeps unfolding and developing the four-bar thematic building block. Where his piano leadsheet carries a theme that is in itself unconventional enough, the orchestral score consists of so many thematic transfigurations—including rhythmic displacement—that it is impossible to say where exactly the theme ends and the development starts.

Strayhorn continued to compose ballads, "harmonically and structurally among the most sophisticated in jazz" (Hossiason 1988, 1165). His ballads share certain musical characteristics, such as intricate harmonic progressions and strong expressive melodies that tend to center around distinctive intervals (e.g., *So This Is Love*), around melodic gestures (e.g., *Ballad for Very Tired and Very Sad Lotus Eaters, Isfahan, Pretty Girl*), or around specific chords (e.g., *Passion Flower, Chelsea Bridge*). Nevertheless, as a group, Strayhorn's ballads are quite diverse. Strayhorn wove his most significant ballads for the Ellingtonians around the expressive voice of Johnny Hodges, arguably the finest Strayhorn interpreter.

Both Ellington and Strayhorn had a very close musical rapport with Johnny Hodges. He was featured in many ballads, tailored to his stellar command of the alto saxophone. Hodges paired his creamy tone, impeccable diction, and stunning glissandi with a deep understanding of the music he played. He was never sentimental and never lost himself in effects. In fact, when performing those great ballads written especially for him, Hodges virtually remained motionless and seemingly unaffected, keeping a safe distance from too teary renditions. This made him an excellent spokesman for Strayhorn's music.

Tellingly, during Hodges's absence from the Ellington band (from March 1951 till August 1955), Strayhorn turned to other voices in the orchestra rather than to the new alto saxophonists who took over the second chair (among others Willie Smith and Hilton Jefferson). One of the few ballads Strayhorn adapted for the orchestra during Hodges's absence was the medium-slow *Theme for Helen*, another deeply emotional composition, composed earlier for the Orson Welles production of *Faust* and retitled *Orson*.

In order to articulate the thematic overlaps that are the cornerstones of the cleverly modified AABA format of *Orson*, Strayhorn divided the theme between the recently returned valve-trombonist Juan Tizol and trumpeter Harold Baker. This idea is lost on the only known commercial recording for Capitol (see Appendix B), since the first trumpet answer was cut. Highlighting the structural breaks, the trumpet takes over exactly where the exposition deviates from the expected format, namely at the end of the first A (Ex. 9-6, mm. 8-11, cut at the original recording), where a faux reprise of the antecedent on a new harmonic plane extends the strain to thirteen bars, and at the end of the truncated bridge—the consequent is clipped short to three bars—which coincides with the restatement of the first phrase (Ex. 9-6, m. 26). Like the later *Cashmere Cutie*, *Orson*'s theme

Ex. 9-6. *Orson*, mm. 1–33

is based on transfigurations of a motif, and in its organic thematic unfolding moves away from the thirty-two-bar standard song format. *Orson* also abounds with Strayhorn's favorite harmonic shadings, chords (often altered) whose roots connect chromatically (Ex. 9-6, measures 2, 6-7, 9-11, 13, 16, 20-25).

Yet *Orson* stretches farther than its beautifully epic theme. Strayhorn crafted an orchestral setting that cannot be separated from the song. Especially the breathtaking epilogue is sorely missed from the heavily edited 1953 recording by the Ellington band. In this final episode, the theme's opening gesture climaxes in two trumpets and two trombones, soaring over the orchestra, which audaciously hammers out low-scored chords in one of Strayhorn's favored fingerprint sixteenth-note rhythms. The coda concludes with scalar shifting harmonies over a pedal point on the dominant (reminiscent of similar passages in *Rain Check* and later *Blood Count*), connected by an incidental chromatic transitory chord, and leading to a final ritardando phrase in the third trombone (Ex. 9-7).

Ex. 9-7. *Orson*, mm. 73–84

The return of Hodges in the fall of 1955 seems to have renewed Strayhorn's inspiration for ballads since in this period he composed one of his most outstanding ones: the sumptuous *Pretty Girl*, later incorporated in *Such Sweet Thunder* as *Star-Crossed Lovers*. Again, Strayhorn crafted a showcase for Hodges, a naturally flowing melody that is nevertheless nowhere predictable, set against a warm orchestral background. Hodges never failed to give his best on *Pretty Girl/Star-Crossed Lovers*, and the piece was repeatedly singled out as one of the highlights of *Such Sweet Thunder*.

The expressiveness of the piece springs from Strayhorn's secure harmonizations and the strong yet delicate melodic movement. The melody derives from a repeatedly altered small fragment, cast in a truncated ABA form (8-8-6) and subdivided in four-bar segments. The harmony of *Pretty Girl* revolves around the ♯IV or ♭V scale degree, which serves as the root for chromatic dominants that either move up to I/V or down to IV, each time underscoring the melody's pivotal high alteration of the fifth. Again, Strayhorn obscures the tonality across long stretches as the melody comes in on the subdominant, which serves as the transient harmonic plane. In the bridge he turns to an extensive use of the dominant pedal point in sharp contrast with the strong chromatic relationships in the first eight bars: IV/V and I/V, lending the piece a gospel-like quality. Strayhorn cleverly reverses the harmonic progression from the opening (IV-♯IV-I/V) to a more conclusive I-I7-IV in the recapitulation, a simple yet extremely effective find.

Unfortunately, Strayhorn later took out *Pretty Girl*'s original majestic modulation and coda, to replace it with a trombone-and-reeds statement of the theme.[7] This was possibly done to accommodate Hodges, as the move from D♭ to D is definitely uncomfortable for the alto. As Strayhorn explained, discussing his collaboration with Hodges,

> there may be some awkward technical aspect that he [Hodges] will point out to you, as concerning his performance. You don't want *that*. It's like a suit of clothes. You want it to fit. You don't want it to be baggy anywhere. I'm not a saxophone player. If he says, "this is awkward here. This is an awkward position of notes," then you say "Is it really? Is it impossible?" If he keeps trying it, and it is impossible, you say, "Well, all right, I'll change it." (Dance 1967, 18)

Still, the cut in *Pretty Girl* is remarkable: there are barely any other documented instances where Strayhorn decided to alter a score.[8]

Not all of Strayhorn's music was as intricate as these ballads. At the other end of his compositional spectrum stands a group of blues-based pieces which, in terms of thematic and harmonic invention as well as formal construction, are far less complex.[9] In general, Strayhorn's blues seem to have a lighter touch than the rest of his work. He often provided Ellington with blues- and riff-theme-based compositions that consisted of just a handful of orchestral choruses and background riffs, and that mainly served as a backdrop for improvisations. Since the blues provided maximum flexibility in choice of soloists and duration, they formed convenient material for concerts and recording sessions. Like Ellington, Strayhorn could write this type of piece swiftly, and both composers often wrote twelve-bar frameworks on the spot to fill out an album.

Furthermore, the swinging blues undoubtedly enjoyed considerable popularity among the Ellington orchestra's audience and among many of the band members as well. Johnny Hodges, for one, recorded many straightforward blues pieces while he worked away from the band, and reportedly his 1950 departure from Ellington was partly fueled by the orchestra's more ambitious repertory: "We didn't like the tone poems much," Hodges said (Hasse 1993, 297). Lacking structuring elements, the blues compositions deviated importantly from Strayhorn's more idiomatic, through-composed scores. Still, many of these blues-derived works often display his characteristic melodic and harmonic turns and, most notably, his recognizable orchestrations.

In *Blues in Orbit*, for instance, Strayhorn adds Clark Terry's trumpet to the reeds to lead three different blues choruses in six-part linear harmony (i.e., the reeds do not move parallel to the trumpet lead), an instrumentation he had applied earlier in *All Too Soon* for Ella Fitzgerald and in the opening section of his arrangement of *Sophisticated Lady* for Rosemary Clooney. The relative lack of thematic movement in *Blues in Orbit* creates a sense of immobility (complemented by Ellington's static piano fills), a quality found in other works of the period as well, such as *Lately* (incorporated into *Such Sweet Thunder* as *Half the Fun*) and *So Easy* (also known as *Frou-Frou*). By consequence, in *Blues in Orbit* the music seems almost frozen in time, and without a clear introduction or a coda, there are more questions than answers.

The forceful *Northern Lights* (1959), the fourth movement from the *Queen's Suite*, is not a blues, but like *Blues in Orbit* it lacks a definite melody and has a similar open ending. Strayhorn reportedly wrote the movement for Ellington after the latter described the aurora borealis to him (Ellington 1973, 112–113). *Northern Lights* consists of motivic fragments in clarinets and trumpets, sprinkled over orchestral chords, without any specific sense of direction. Consistent with the openness of the piece, Strayhorn ends *Northern Lights* with a subtle twist of his standard second-half-of-the-bar tonic chord. Almost as if to parody his own

Ex. 9-8. *Northern Lights*, final bar

formulaic muted trumpet ending, the trumpets come in on the third beat with an A♭maj7, forming a bitonal chord with the underlying Fmaj7 in the trombones, baritone, and bass: the final chord does not truly close the piece and hangs in the air like a question mark (Ex. 9-8).

Since the orchestra's output in the second half of the 1950s included a number of albums that contained mostly Strayhorn rearrangements of preexistent material (see Chapter 8), his contribution to the ever-changing yet always recognizable "Ellington sound" predominantly took the form of orchestrations. Though Strayhorn's innovations became less comprehensive than they had been in some of his earlier works, he continued to explore new techniques while taking advantage of the growing contingent of modern players in the band. Apart from the increase of harmonic and melodic complexity that was apparent in all of his writing, Strayhorn's work from this period displays his growing preference for more open orchestral textures, largely the outgrowth of his increased emphasis on individual contrapuntal lines. Where vertical relationships tend to dominate the larger part of big band jazz—due to a common strict adherence to a rigid harmonic rhythm—Strayhorn sought to give more room to horizontal lines in background formations, granting the individual voices freer movement. By the mid-1950s, multilinear writing had become one of his most expressive tools, and it would govern a number of his later originals, including *Up and Down, Isfahan, Bluebird of Delhi, Carribee Joe*, all of his work for *Anatomy of a Murder*, and *Blood Count*. As a result of this emphasis on polyphonic writing, Strayhorn's orchestral textures opened up. Even in concerted passages he tended to include only part of the section's voices, rather than using all voices available to him.

The breathtaking 1957 score of *Day Dream*, for Ella Fitzgerald, exemplifies the main traits in Strayhorn's still maturing orchestral style for the Ellington band.[10] As if to mirror the experience of dreaming while being awake with a similar duality in music, the arrangement of *Day Dream* parallels the airy and sensual atmosphere of John LaTouche's lyrics with the use of so-called polychords. Polychords relate to two different tonal centers simultaneously. The score opens with a succession of such polychords, here in the shape of major triads in all three possible inversions in the highest reeds—clarinet and two altos—against tritone-related triads in three muted trumpets (Ex. 9-9). An ethereal passage with sharply dissonant, hazy tone clusters results, further deepened by the tritone line in the bass, which appears unrelated to the chords, and Strayhorn's dense piano runs. (Due to imbalance of the original recording, the orchestral background is hard to distinguish.) Only with the last chord, $G13^{(\sharp 11)}$ (the dominant for C), the passage takes on a more secure tonal direction, and retrospectively (or, rather, "retro-auditively"), sounds as if partly built on the dominant and its chromatic substitutes.[11]

Against Ella Fitzgerald's crystalline voice, Strayhorn scored a warmly breathing background that suggests regular inhalation and exhalation. Orchestral voices move from dissonant to consonant chord tones, continuously altering the color and weight of the harmonies and providing a steady pulse of tension and relaxation. The trombones, for instance, come in on the second bar of the vocal chorus with a low-register line that travels through major and minor thirteenth chord tones (Ex. 9-10, m. 8), greatly enhancing the forward motion of the chromatic planing in the reeds. By contrast, the downbeat of bar 9 is resolutely consonant and releases all tension: the trombone line has not so much resolved as evaporated, to start a new and more dissonant line in the next half of the bar, again leading to a fully consonant chord in measure 11. At the turnaround (mm. 13-14) the texture becomes increasingly polyphonic and dissonant as voices move in and out of chord structures, leading to a sharply dissonant, altered dominant chord. With the return to bar 7, the tension is released again, as if releasing its breath.

The baritone and the clarinet receive special treatment in the arrangement. While the baritone plays the chord root most of the time, it abandons its low register at pivotal points in the arrangement to provide structure and direction. In bar 21 (Ex. 9-10), the baritone starts an eighth-note line that partly echoes the melody and foreshadows the pickup to the instrumental middle section of the score. This developmental section starts at the end of the vocal chorus where the eighth-note line returns, as the baritone takes the lead in a pyramidal orchestral send-off (Ex. 9-11, p. 156, bars 37-38). By means of a-synchronously entering voices Strayhorn effectively controls the dynamic expansion of the passage, which in bar 39 explodes into an orchestral tutti against Hodges's lyric alto.

Ex. 9-9. *Day Dream*, mm. 1–6

The previously unrecorded introduction of *Pretty Girl*,[12] a remarkably polyphonic segment with canonic entering voices, resembles *Day Dream* in its dynamic balancing of voices (Ex. 9-12, p. 157, mm. 1-4). This passage further brings to mind the introduction to *Concerto for Cootie*, though *Pretty Girl*'s discarded opening bars are harmonically more radical, as they are in the key of C, while the piece itself is in the adjacent key of D♭. At the end of bar 2 of the introduction, a mid-phrase hesitation is followed by a fully affirmative line in the second half of the passage. In *Day Dream* Strayhorn creates a similar effect, but with different means. There, the trumpets (joined by the orchestra) restate the baritone's line in measures 37–38 (Ex. 9-11), which gives the initial baritone line a sense of insecurity.

Ex. 9-10. *Day Dream*, mm. 7–22

Ex. 9-10. *Day Dream*, mm. 7–22 (cont.)

In *Day Dream*, Strayhorn prominently contrasts the silken sound of Jimmy Hamilton's clarinet with Harry Carney's deep anchoring baritone. Apart from assigning the often dissonant lead to the clarinet, much like he did in *Chelsea Bridge* and *Rain Check*, in his later work, Strayhorn progressively separates the clarinet from the other voices. After leading the clusters in the introduction of *Day Dream* and adding color to an incidental chord (Ex. 9-13, p. 158, m. 22), the clarinet is called on to answer the lyrics. At "I'm in a daze" (Example 9-13, m. 26), it first leads in one of Strayhorn's favored cross-section instrumentations—clarinet with trumpets—with interval structures that are tonally detached from the underlying harmony, while at "I moon around feeling hazy" (m. 30), the clarinet provides dissonant "bird calls" (the first being an arpeggiated quartal chord). Although Jimmy Hamilton was capable of improvising virtuoso fills, Strayhorn carefully designed these phrases, a stylized recollection of the New Orleans ad-lib high-riding clarinet. He had applied similar, though more conventional, clarinet lines in some of his arrangements in the mid-1940s (*Prisoner of Love*, *We'll Be Together Again*, and *Come to Baby, Do*) to reemploy them prominently in *Day Dream*, as well as in the delicate orchestrations of *Wounded Love* [13] and in his superb arrangement of Gordon Jenkins's *Good-Bye*, the sign-off theme of the Benny Goodman Orchestra (recorded by the Ellingtonians for the album *Will Big Bands Ever Come Back?*). Strayhorn's writing for clarinet culminated in the witty yet intricately written *Bluebird of Delhi*, which he fully developed from similar fragmentary bird calls (see Chapter 10).

A final clarinet bird call in *Day Dream* (Ex. 9-14, p. 158, m. 53), based on the baritone line from measures 17 and 34, signals the close of the arrangement with a return to polychords. Strayhorn's orchestration here is as simple as it is

Ex. 9-11. *Day Dream,* mm. 37–41

effective. While Ella Fitzgerald, the reeds, and the fourth trumpet have reached their final C^{maj13} (in its second inversion: both the baritone and the bass have the fifth, leaving the piece unresolved), the trombones oscillate chromatically around the tonic triad, again in second inversion (mm. 54-56). Above this growling layer, the trumpets move diatonically from G to F and back, but in half-time, repeatedly clashing with the other voices and striking a sharply dissonant F♯ chord over the tonic C chord in the penultimate bar. For four wrenching beats this extremely dissonant polychord hangs over the orchestra like a thick fog, to clear up in the final

Ex. 9-12. *Pretty Girl,* mm. 1–4

bar with the trumpet section's move up to G, now perceived as upper structure of the tonic.

A similar passage with a partially delayed resolution occurs at the end of *Cashmere Cutie*, where Strayhorn postpones the final chord in the trombones. The reeds (in octaves) have comfortably landed on the sixth in the penultimate bar (Ex. 9-15, m. 103), but the trombones enter an eighth note later with D major, a half step above the target chord D♭, which they finally reach in the last bar. In both cases Strayhorn achieves and resolves the dense vertical relationships between the sections by means of strong linear movement and polyphonic writing.

Through this more polyphonic writing, Strayhorn created multiple musical layers and importantly strengthened the expressive force of his music. It opened up even more emotional subtexts than before, as if he allowed the tension and conflict that had always been present in his music to come to the surface. Close

Ex. 9-13. Clarinet "bird calls," mm. 22 and 26

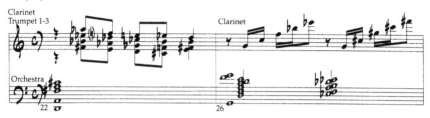

Ex. 9-14. *Day Dream*, mm. 53–57

Ex. 9-15. *Cashmere Cutie*, mm. 101–104

listening to his music reveals that virtually all his compositions, from his early *Fantastic Rhythm* scores on, share similar multiple layers. Strayhorn's music radiates a sense of honesty and integrity, and many who knew him have described his personality in just these terms. But while Strayhorn's themes may seem merely beautiful and delicate, their musical underscore often reveals a more complex and decidedly less peaceful side. This seems also in keeping with Strayhorn's character. Despite the seclusiveness of his personal life— "Strayhorn is a funny guy, he won't tell you a whole lot," said Whaley (1965)—many who knew him more intimately became aware of his darker sides. To some, Strayhorn seemed "a tortured genius" with an "enormous sadness" beneath his gentle and friendly exterior (Hajdu 1996, 211).

Around the time he scored his arrangements for the Ella Fitzgerald sessions, Strayhorn also composed what is undoubtedly his most polyphonic piece: *Up and Down, Up and Down (I Will Lead Them Up and Down)* for *Such Sweet Thunder*. The title (like the title of the entire suite) stems from Shakespeare's *A Midsummer Night's Dream*.[14] In the play, a fairy named Puck fools the other protagonists so that they repeatedly fall in love with each other, which leads to all kinds of awkward situations. Transposing some concepts of the play to music, Strayhorn divided the orchestra in no fewer than nine different cross-section instrumental combinations, each with its own color. In all likelihood, these paired instruments portray the various couples in *A Midsummer Night's Dream*, the victims of Puck's machinations.[15] Clark Terry, whimsically portraying Puck, freely moves through the complex textures these combinations weave. The high point of Terry's performance comes at the ending when his trumpet "speaks" one of Puck's lines: "Lord, what fools these mortals be" (*A Midsummer Night's Dream*: III.2.115).[16]

Largely by means of melodic inversion, condensation, and dissection, as well as through rhythmic transformations, Strayhorn generates *Up and Down* from simple diatonic material, presented in the exposition (Ex. 9-16). The majority of the instrumental groups consist of two voices—clarinet and violin, clarinet and alto, clarinet and tenor, alto and tenor, alto and trombone, tenor and trombone—while the one group that consists of three instruments (clarinet, alto, and tenor) appears at the exposition only. Apart from a tutti passage (at the beginning of Clark Terry's solo, mm. 34-62), the largest cross-section combination covers five

Ex. 9-16. *Up and Down*, main material

voices: baritone, two trumpets, and two trombones.[17] These instrumental groups state the various motifs and their derived contrapuntal lines, either in contrary motion or in parallel motion. The parallel passages run almost invariably in thirds (or a third and an octave apart).

Example 9-17 reproduces a passage exemplary of Strayhorn's "Bach-with-a-beat" writing for *Up and Down*. Four of the nine instrumental groups state different overlapping motifs and their derived counterpoint. The consequent of the exposition appears here in the first clarinet and violin (mm. 10-14) while the tenor and first alto enter a bar later with the antecedent (mm. 11-14). Additional counterpoint in the second alto and third trombone, an imitation of the antecedent's tail in contrary motion, thickens the texture. The pleasantly flowing diatonic lines, however, provide too little musical conflict to develop the piece, and, to stir the waters, Strayhorn inserts a new gesture (mm. 9-10) that breaks

Ex. 9-17. *Up and Down*, mm. 9–15

through the diatonic environment as the voices appear temporarily to move outside the tonality. With the return of the new gesture in measures 14-15, now resolving to a B major chord over C♯ (truly outside the tonality), the piece moves to a more fragmentary section with denser and more chromatic movement.

Due to the contrapuntal nature of the work, large parts of *Up and Down* lack a harmonic progression. Instead, the emphasis lies on the melodic and rhythmic linear movement. The bass has large sections with pedal point on tonic and dominant planes, with the exception of mm. 34-50 and 91-102, where Strayhorn counterbalances the static layers of the intermittent passages with a refreshing forward motion. Strayhorn first breaks through the polyphonic texture with a conventional orchestral riff-theme against a written-out solo for Clark Terry at mm. 34-50. The repeated eight-bar section might suggest the beginning of an AABA form, but the expected bridge never comes: the piece returns to its original polyphony with new, and now fully chromatic counterpoint. This time, Strayhorn sets various instrumental groups against one another in contrary motion (Ex. 9-18), while Terry fills the gaps with more trumpet answers. Toward the end of the passage, shreds of the initial counterpoint reappear, and the harmony starts to progress more decisively, creating a buildup that signals the return to the exposition, although the recapitulation is cut off by a full-band five-part descent that concludes the piece, while Terry recites his Shakespeare.

Ex. 9-18. *Up and Down*, mm. 51–61

Strayhorn turned to a simpler use of polyphony in his 1957 arrangement of *Take the "A" Train* for the *Duke Ellington Songbook*. After the forceful introduction with its convincing train whistle of clarinet over plunger-muted wah-wah trumpets,[18] the arrangement turns to a powerful off-center full-band counterpoint against the vocals. It is at the same time melodically strong and surprising (Ex. 9-19). Due to the rhythmic asynchrony between the vocal and the instrumental line (in octaves) and the continuous use of harmonic anticipation, the background at times seems to run ahead of the original melody while at other times it seems to lag behind. Where the rhythmic placement of the original melody of *"A" Train* follows a pattern of four-bar legato phrases with down-beat entries and off-beat endings on one and three (in the bridge), the fragmented counterpoint follows an entirely different logic.[19] Its entries and off-beat endings come at unexpected points, virtually ignoring the bar lines. For contrast, Strayhorn turns in the bridge to a catchy background with bluesy minor sevenths, but again it is rhythmically deceptive: each second entry is two beats early, further destabilizing the meter.

Ex. 9-19. *Take the "A" Train* (1956), mm. 25–56

Strayhorn has spiced up the harmonies abundantly with altered chord tones and extensions. Most notably, he has allowed for anticipatory harmonic shifts, a D7$^{(\flat 5)}$ against C in bar 34, a D7 against C in bar 42, G7$^{(\flat 13)}$ against Dmi in bar 45, and G7$^{(\flat 9\sharp 11)}$ against Dmi in bar 61. In its strong use of harmonic anticipation, the entire treatment of the background line is boppish.

THE REACTIVATED COLLABORATION with Ellington at the end of 1955 sparked a highly creative period that lasted until Strayhorn's deteriorating health began to take its toll in the mid-1960s. The reawakened public interest in the Duke Ellington Orchestra and the resulting improvement of recording possibilities, as well as the worldwide emergence of jazz festivals, combined to spur the compositional activities of both men. As if to acknowledge that Ellington's editing of Strayhorn's music had been partly responsible for the latter's temporary estrangement, alterations as drastic and fundamental as in *Orson* no longer occurred in the post-1955 Strayhorn repertory. In many cases, the orchestra stuck to "the ink" without any serious edits.

In his writing for the orchestra, Strayhorn continued to rely on linear harmonic and melodic development and on large structural arches, the same compositional techniques he had used in his earliest pieces. But at the same time he enlarged the technical and emotional scope of his style. He pursued more fully the concept of widened tonality (explored previously in *Flamingo*), postponing tonic chords in *U.M.M.G.* and tonicalizing temporary harmonic planes, while treating melodies entirely as upper-structure lines. A similar radicalization of earlier techniques may be found in his use of polytonality. In the opening and closing sections of *Day Dream*, for instance, he applied the concept of polytonality more radically than he had in the introduction to *Flamingo*.

The technical expansion in Strayhorn's writing paralleled one of the main developments in postwar jazz: bebop. A piece such as *U.M.M.G.*, for instance, used a language similar to that of bebop, especially in its melodic conception, rhythmic placement, and harmonization. Yet, the bop elements in *U.M.M.G.*— the emphasis on upper chord structures and the use of substitute progressions— had been part of Strayhorn's compositional palette all along, even in early works such as *Ugly Ducklin'*, and thus did not mark a departure from his earlier style.

His rhythmic language, however, increasingly deviated from his earlier work. While he still used some of his favorite figures (such as the dotted half-note followed by two eighths, the last eighth note tied across the bar), his approach was more flexible and he tended to let the melodic movement float more freely over the underlying chords (as in *U.M.M.G.*).

In its atmosphere, Strayhorn's composing was more reminiscent of the relatively short-lived "cool-jazz" wave that at the end of the 1940s followed the emergence of bop. As did Strayhorn's writing, the genre bore more relation to swing than to bebop: it was largely based on tenorist Lester Young's playing with Basie (late in 1930), as well as on the work of arrangers such as Claude Thornhill, Gerry Mulligan, and, not surprisingly, Gil Evans. In addition, the cool-jazz writers deliberately turned to western European music for inspiration, and groups such as The Modern Jazz Quartet determinedly worked more polyphonic textures into their playing. (The Modern Jazz Quartet, headed by composer-pianist John Lewis, also became one of the main performing units for so-called Third Stream compositions.)

It is impossible to determine whether Strayhorn deliberately sought to incorporate these newer idioms, but if he did, he managed to do so without altering his compositional approach or straining his own voice. Still, his writing showed important differences from bebop and cool jazz, most notably in its absence of bop's typical focus on extrovert virtuosity (exemplified by the often very fast tempos and rhythmically dense themes). In addition, the bop writers typically based the core of their repertory on existing pieces, writing new lines over harmonically altered progressions. By contrast, Strayhorn's compositions invariably consisted of new material.

If the influence of bebop and cool jazz on Strayhorn's compositional techniques remains difficult to prove, it is certain that European art music continued to inform his writing. His focus shifted, however, from intricate modulations and quasi-symphonic works (*Tonk, Pentonsilic, Overture to a Jam Session*) to a more melodic unfolding of his music. While his arrangement of *Flamingo*, for instance, was largely inspired by the multiple harmonic functions of the upper-chromatic dominant, he developed works such as *Orson* and *Cashmere Cutie* or the arrangement of *Day Dream* largely along horizontal lines. This interest in melodic development led to a significant growth in his use of polyphony, prioritizing the horizontal over the vertical. To keep these more complex textures clear, Strayhorn wrote leaner orchestrations and thus diminished the role of the orchestra as a whole. It resulted in a more intimate writing style.

Strayhorn's increased use of melodic development allowed him to create more flexible structures. Less constrained by the implications of a chord progression, and consequently less bound to a rigid harmonic rhythm, Strayhorn further blurred the dividing lines between structural units in a composition. Where in *Flamingo* the underlying AABA structure still remains visible underneath the arrangement, in compositions such as *Cashmere Cutie* and *Up and Down*, the architecture is so flexible that it is unclear where the thematic exposition ends and the development begins.

The complex character of Strayhorn's work makes it almost autobiographical. He combined honesty, integrity, and beauty with an internal conflict that had its roots in his troubled youth. As his life took an unexpected, grim turn, this autobiographical aspect would increasingly dominate his writing, resulting in some of his darkest works.

Chapter Ten

North by Southwest: The Final Years

LATE IN THE FALL of 1959, Francis Goldberg moved out of Strayhorn's apartment on West 106th Street. The incompatibility of their characters had set off a string of conflicts that could no longer be reconciled. In need of more pleasant company, Strayhorn began to spend more and more time at the home of Marian and Arthur Logan, the latter being the physician of Strayhorn, Ellington, and most of the Copasetics. The Logans, and especially Marian, shared many of Strayhorn's passions, including music, the fine arts, food, literature, and flowers. The couple socialized with many well-to-do African Americans, and through these circles Strayhorn became involved with the civil rights movement. Eventually he became acquainted with Dr. Martin Luther King Jr. Strayhorn provided silent support for Dr. King's activities, and escorted Lena Horne when she sang at one of the movement's rallies. He also participated in the famous March on Washington (August 1963), as a member of the inner circle of Dr. Martin Luther King.[1]

Early in 1964, Strayhorn was diagnosed with cancer of the esophagus. "He discussed it matter-of-factly, in very measured tones," Strayhorn's friend Bill Coleman told Hajdu (1996, 233). "He was resigned, and obviously had been resigned about important matters before" (ibid.). Later that year, Strayhorn started to gravitate toward Bill Grove, whom he knew through friends from the Neal Salon. Grove was a graphic designer and art director, a quiet and serious man. His character answered to Strayhorn's needs in this phase of his life. "Billy became more serious after his diagnosis for cancer—more serious for music, more serious in general," Bill Coleman reflected (Hajdu 1996, 234).

Strayhorn tried to maintain his habitual pace in writing for the Ellington orchestra. In the spring of 1964, the band recorded material that was issued on *Ellington '65* and *Ellington '66*, while late that summer the *Mary Poppins* LP was cut, all with contributions by Strayhorn. Nevertheless, his condition was so

A snapshot taken at a recording session in 1959 with the Ellington band and Dizzy Gillespie (left), seems to show early signs of Strayhorn's health problems. According to many, Strayhorn, a heavy smoker, drank too much as well. Four years later, he was diagnosed with cancer, to which he succumbed in 1967.
(*Courtesy Rutgers Institute of Jazz Studies*)

severe that for the first time since he had begun to write music, Strayhorn's creative output decreased dramatically. For more than a year he did not write a single original work, although he did fulfill his arranging obligations. In January 1965, Strayhorn scored another round of pop tunes, to fill out *Ellington '66*, and later he contributed two movements (*Island Virgin* and *Fiddle on the Diddle*) to the forgettable *Virgin Island Suite*. That suite would be the final multimovement work he co-wrote with Ellington.

Recorded after the *Virgin Island Suite* (but written earlier), the far more profound *Far East Suite* was the musical outcome of the orchestra's 1963 tour through the Near and Middle East. At the behest of the State Department the Ellington band paid visits to Syria, Jordan, India, Sri Lanka (then Ceylon), Pakistan, Iran (then Persia), Lebanon, and Turkey. Strayhorn traveled with the orchestra. A suite inspired by these travels premiered in England early in 1964 as *Impressions of the Far East*. Originally in four movements, the suite consisted of Ellington's *Amad* and *Depk*, and Strayhorn's *Agra* and *Bluebird of Delhi*. When the orchestra recorded the work in the studio two years later as the *Far East Suite*, new movements were added. Strayhorn's earlier composition *Elf*, retitled *Isfahan*, became the third movement, while Ellington contributed *Tourist Point of View*, *Mount Harissa*, and *Blue Pepper*.[2] A final movement, *Ad Lib on Nippon*, was conceived by Jimmy Hamilton and Ellington on the occasion of the orchestra's visit to Japan in the summer of 1964.

The *Far East Suite* is generally seen as one of the highlights of the Ellington-Strayhorn collaboration, and rightfully so. Part of the work's success seems to stem from its uncommonly long period of gestation. While most other multimovement works were written under heavy time pressure, the *Far East Suite* resulted from a process that allowed the composers to design the individual movements with greater care. More important, different from earlier suites, the work's program drew on musical materials instead of nonmusical themes such as perfumes, a book, or a jazz festival. Rather, Ellington and Strayhorn found inspiration in the impressions made on them by the vibrant musical cultures in the Asian and Arab countries through which they had traveled. They intelligently transformed perceived musical idioms into idiosyncratic works, not unlike their approach to Tchaikovsky's classical ballet music. Thus, the two composers avoided any all too obvious Orientalisms.

Where most descriptive jazz music tends to portray the urban sounds of the industrial age, from trains to apartment buildings, Strayhorn's *Bluebird of Delhi* portrays a mynah bird that "used to sing a pretty lick in Stray's hotel room [in New Delhi]. He was always talking to it— 'How are you today?', 'Good Morning!', 'Do you want something to eat?'—but the bird never answered him until he was leaving the room and Delhi. Then it sounded off the low raspberry you hear at the end of the number" (Ellington 1973, 199).[3]

Bluebird of Delhi consists of three large sections that each are made up of smaller segments. A two-part opening section for solo clarinet (in C and A♭) is followed by a section in B♭. This section has a secondary theme, first played by the clarinet and subsequently by an orchestral tutti. The third section returns to material from the opening passage.

In the opening section, Jimmy Hamilton's clarinet portrays the bird's capricious phrases over big city traffic noises that rumble underneath, evoked by two trombones and bass (Ex. 10-1). Strayhorn has chosen the unequivocal use of bi-tonality as a musical metaphor to draw the scene: while the melody circles around a broken C9, the background builds on a dominant A♭ scale, with an ascending flatted fifth for "Oriental" flavor. Strayhorn dissolves the bi-tonality in the next segment, which starts out unambiguously in A♭ (the bird phrase transposed a major third down), but becomes increasingly chromatic as the clarinet moves into broken diminished chords.

The ensuing section, in a new key (B♭), introduces the secondary theme that plays with melismatic figures over a pedaled tonic, typically associated with "Asian" idioms (Ex. 10-2). In fact, this segment strongly resembles the traditional configuration of classical Indian music, where a melody moves against a drone—an unchanging tone or group of tones, usually consisting of a root and perfect fifth, and often doubled in octaves. Indian melodies are generally based on

Ex. 10-1. *Bluebird of Delhi*, mm. 13–16

Ex. 10-2. *Bluebird of Delhi*, mm. 31–40

modes, that is, scales that contain the basic pitch material for a given piece. Characteristic in these scales is the asymmetric distribution of tone material: groups of smaller intervals are separated by groups of larger intervals. From this material the piece, or *raga*, is built, with abundant ornamentation and variations in intonation. The three opening bars of Strayhorn's secondary theme indeed do imply this idiom, but he gives it a distinct jazz flavor in the subsequent bars (Ex. 10-2, mm. 34-35), where the phrase moves into bebop territory with a chromatically altered, descending line.

Next, unison saxophones repeat the clarinet statement, now over three-part trombones that play a transformation of the Indian drone, while at the same time echoing the mynah's grace-notes (an earlier mutation of the drone occurs in the opening bars, where the trombones and bass play planing perfect fourths, the inversion of the typical drone interval). The trombones furthermore point ahead to the modulatory section, which builds on a rhythmically altered, dense brass setting of the bird call, temporarily leading the piece to $E^\flat$ for a full-band rendition of the secondary theme. A da capo repeat of the mynah's trills rounds out the piece.

Agra is the only genuine baritone piece Strayhorn is known to have written (his 1948 baritone feature *Paradise* was originally composed for alto under the title *Blue Heart*). The Indian city of Agra was once the capital of the Mughal Empire, until the emperors moved their capital to Delhi in 1637. The city is known for the Taj Mahal, an impressive marble tomb built by the fifth Mughal emperor, Shah Jahan. The Shah erected the edifice as a "symbol of eternal love" in memory of his second wife, Mumtaz Mahal, a Muslim Persian princess. The Taj rises on a high red sandstone base, topped by a huge white marble terrace on which rests the famous dome, flanked by four tapering minarets.[4] Inspired by the scene, Strayhorn captured the serene presence of the marble mausoleum in forceful baritone lines, convincingly played by Harry Carney.

Like *Bluebird of Delhi*, *Agra* uses transformations of Indian idioms, though more obviously so. A drone bass (F-C), stated at each measure's first downbeat underlies the entire movement. Against this drone, the baritone has a chromatic melody that mainly circles around F minor and its major parallel $A^\flat$, while hazy brass chords add dissonance and tonal ambiguity. In its structure, the piece employs techniques Strayhorn had used in *Cashmere Cutie*; the theme of *Agra* develops organically from a melodic gesture and a rhythmic cell.

Strayhorn's third and most famous contribution to the *Far East Suite* is the cunning composition *Elf*. For the recording, the piece was retitled *Isfahan*, after Persia's former capital, but Strayhorn had composed it months before he had set foot in the Middle East. Another showcase for Johnny Hodges, *Isfahan* is a high point of the suite. Hodges's handling of the enchanting theme and especially his timing of the a capella alto pickup phrases are unsurpassed. Ellington remembered Isfahan as "a city of poetic beauty" (Ellington 1973, 325), and Johnny Hodges's performance is a perfect match.[5]

The central melodic idea of *Isfahan* is the downward unfolding major seventh chord in the alto (Ex. 10-3). Strayhorn intelligently exploits the enharmonic duality of the line. Starting an interval lower in measure 4, the a♭'-f'-d♭' retrospectively sounds as the upper part of the B♭♭maj7 that appears in bar 5. This B♭♭maj7 serves as an upper-chromatic delay for the dominant (in a chain of dominants that started in bar 2 with the B♭7(#5)). The bass of the major seventh chord moves a minor second down, yielding a suspended dominant on A♭ in bar six, establishing the return to the tonic. Note how the unison saxophone counterpoint not only adds color but also assumes harmonic functionality—for instance, in bar 2, where the saxophone line carries the seventh, absent from the trombones.[6]

The works he wrote for *Impressions of the Far East* belong to Strayhorn's final compositions for the Ellington orchestra. Strayhorn's condition swiftly worsened over the course of 1966, necessitating two operations and radiation therapy. Although his creativity was thereby greatly diminished, in the early months of 1967 he did contribute two new works to the orchestra's repertory. One was a medium swinger called *The Intimacy of the Blues* first recorded on March 15, 1967, and the other was the grimly titled *Blood Count*, a harrowing ballad for Hodges. Ellington added three sections to the originally untitled manuscript for *The Intimacy of the Blues* (the title may not be Strayhorn's). Together with his collaborator's

Ex. 10-3. *Isfahan*, mm. 1–8

original section, which he marked *High*, Ellington titled his additions *Figh, Fo* and *Fumm*.[7] However, he discarded his own sections and stuck to Strayhorn's blues only, a single-line theme over straightforward changes, while adding some background ensembles.[8]

Blood Count is generally assumed to be the last original that Strayhorn composed for the Ellington orchestra, but the evidence is elusive. Two scores survive, one titled *Blood Count*, and another titled *Blue Cloud*. Both scores provide only rough clues as to their earliest possible production dates, since they both refer to the orchestra's first bass trombonist Chuck Connors, who joined in July 1961.[9] For his tribute album to Strayhorn recorded in August 1967 (*...And His Mother Called Him Bill*), Ellington used the version titled *Blood Count*.[10]

Although in music-technical terms *Blood Count* is largely consistent with Strayhorn's previous writing, the piece explores emotions not heard in his work before. Much as all his earlier compositions seemed to resound a deeper biographical layer, in *Blood Count* Strayhorn uses musical metaphors to express openly his feelings of sadness, frustration, and failure.

Blood Count is in D minor, a remarkable key since Strayhorn hardly ever used minor tonalities in his work. He confirms this minor key decisively in the second half of the first eight-bar strain, where a desperately repeated gesture spells out the interval between the minor third and the tonic (Ex. 10-4). At the end of this first strain, Strayhorn uncharacteristically cuts off the alto's line to jump back to the initial melody, without any harmonic or melodic connection. With this hard cut he deviates sharply from his compositional habits. *Blood Count* grows increasingly unnerving in the bridge, with its anguished repeated descending gesture e"-f'-e', and the ending is utterly unsettling: over a pedaled bass, the trombones and trumpets alternately play a line of desolate descending major triads that keep falling back to a D minor chord, suggesting that there is no escape (Ex. 10-5). With its dramatic melody and interrupted thoughts, and the fatalism of its the final bars, *Blood Count* conjures the devastating consequences of Strayhorn's progressing cancer.

Ex. 10-4. *Blood Count*, mm. 5–8

As his musical partner for more than 25 years fell virtually silent, Ellington turned to others for assistance. For the first time since 1939, Strayhorn was not able to take charge of a vocal session. Consequently, Jimmy Jones, in striking emulation of his predecessor's style, arranged *Something to Live For* and *A Flower Is a Lovesome Thing*, two of Strayhorn's songs, for a new Verve record with Ella Fitzgerald (1965).[11] Occasionally, the orchestra still premiered earlier Strayhorn material, such as a little-known and initially untitled ballad for Hodges, recorded for the stockpile in 1965 and issued posthumously as *Rod La Roque*.

When the Ellington entourage left New York for another transatlantic trip early in 1967, Strayhorn, gravely ill, started to work on what would be his ultimate musical statement. Befitting a life led in the wings, he wrote the piece for an ensemble that, compared to the Ellington orchestra, was virtually invisible: the duo of Willie Ruff (French horn and bass) and Dwike Mitchell (piano). Thus, like one of his earliest works (the 1934 *Concerto for Piano and Percussion*), his final composition drew inspiration from a specific instrumental combination.[12]

Ruff had been a member of the Riverside Drive Five, a group that Strayhorn put together for a performance of some of his own music late in the spring of 1965 at the New York chapter of the Duke Ellington Society.[13] Dwike Mitchell's strong sound and Ruff's stunning command of the highest register of the French horn (at least a major third above the instrument's usual range c-f") gave Strayhorn a wide array of moods to work with. Little used as solo voice in jazz, the French horn sounds dark and somber in its lower register, full and sonorous in its middle register; in the upper and extreme registers the instrument produces a penetrating sound that borders on the aggressive. Through Willie Ruff's horn, Strayhorn expressed the whole gamut of sentiments that asserted themselves in the final stages of his life, from anguished frustration to resigned acquiescence.

A year after Strayhorn's death, the Mitchell-Ruff Duo recorded this final composition as *Suite for the Duo*, although the composer's own title was *The North by*

Ex. 10-5. *Blood Count*, mm. 53–60

Southwest Suite.¹⁴ As the copyright leadsheets (prepared by John Sanders) and Tempo Music's registrations (1967b) reveal, Strayhorn repeatedly altered the titles of the three movements before settling on the final titles: *Up There* (previously *Skippy*), *Boo Loose*, and *Pavane Bleu No. 2* (to be pronounced in French as *Pavane Bleu, Numéro Deux*; a pavane is a sixteenth-century stately dance in duple meter). Mysteriously, Tempo's catalogue (1967b) lists *Blue Cloud* as the alternate title for *Boo Loose*, though this title does not appear on any of the surviving manuscripts for the *North by Southwest Suite*. To further confound matters, Tempo's catalogue creates the misleading impression that the *North by Southwest Suite* is an independent work, as the catalogue fails to connect the suite with its separately listed movements. Since the Mitchell-Ruff recording of *Suite for the Duo* bore no reference to the work's original title, the *North by Southwest Suite* was erroneously believed to be a different and lost work of which only one movement remained: *Blue Cloud*, better known as *Blood Count*.¹⁵

In a departure from his usual working habits, Strayhorn invited the duo over to his apartment, to tailor the suite to their skills. Ruff recounts how Strayhorn went over the piano part with Dwike Mitchell:

> "What I've written here," he [Strayhorn] said to Mitchell, "is quite complete in the compositional sense. But I want this first meeting to feel to you like a fitting, as in 'fit' a custom-made suit. The compositional elements should fit *your* hands, which are so much larger and more powerful than mine....You know how to make sections like these on this page as big and as rich in sonority as you can. But here in this interlude, let the horn ring through....Let Willie's sound kind of hover over it all right there. And pause here, but only slightly....Over in this middle part, your line and the horn line are of equal importance. Balance is the key word; but that's the kind of thing you two do naturally anyway. I have left you space and, at the same time, given indications of essential details...." By now Mitchell was alive with excitement. His large fingers trembled as he carefully shaped them to fit the powerful, two-fisted chords Stray had written to underscore the horn theme. And wham! Stray was up off the piano bench at the huge sound Mitchell made. He stomped the floor and beamed at Mitchell. "Hell yes!" he hollered. "That's what I had in mind; I just don't have the hands and strength to make it sound that way." (Ruff 1991, 7)

In the words of Ruff, the resulting *North by Southwest Suite* "thunders with highly autobiographical overtones; the moods of a vibrant musical career, shutting down" (ibid., 10). The *North by Southwest Suite* is the only multimovement work Strayhorn wrote under his own steam. Its three movements are harmonically and thematically closely connected, even though Strayhorn worked from partly existent material (*Boo Loose* was written a few years earlier and recorded as

Pretty Little One in February 1963, by Duke Ellington's Jazz Violins). Interestingly, unlike all the suites on which he cooperated with Ellington, the *North by Southwest Suite* is truly nonprogrammatic, though the title has many overtones. A direction that does not exist on the wind rose, north by southwest leads to an imaginary place, a utopia. Indeed, the title may be understood in a Romantic manner, as in the final line of *Der Wanderer*—best known in Franz Schubert's lied setting—which summarizes one of the leitmotifs of nineteenth-century Romanticism: "There, where you are not, there is your happiness."[16] As a youngster, Strayhorn had expressed a similar Romantic notion in words and music. The verse of *Something to Live For*, composed in his early adolescence in Pittsburgh, already reverberates with Romantic overtones:

> *I have almost everything a human could desire,*
> *Cars and houses, bearskin rugs to lie before my fire.*
> *But there's something missing, something isn't there.*

The lyric painfully stands as a metaphor for Strayhorn's final years. As Willie Ruff observed, "He looked back at his own life and he couldn't find himself" (Hajdu 1996, 251).

The *North by Southwest Suite* combines all elements of Strayhorn's compositional universe, with its synergistic merging of African-American and European idioms. The work is written in the vein of a classical horn sonata, though in three movements only, as opposed to four for a typical sonata. The tempo markings of the three movements are fast-slow-fast. This macro-level tempo division is mirrored on a micro-level in the first movement, also marked fast-slow-fast. The expressiveness of the suite lies in its austere melodic movement, predominantly based on triadic gestures, in a harmonic space that is largely frozen. But the characteristic warmth of Strayhorn's music is strikingly absent: the *North by Southwest Suite* exudes a disturbing, merciless coldness.

The first part, *Up There*, opens with the solo horn bellowing angered, bitter cries in free-flowing meter (Ex. 10-6). Each time, the line rises more than an octave, to major and minor thirds and sevenths. Yet the menacingly dark, forceful piano chords that underscore the repeats of the horn theme contain no thirds or sevenths: they are quintal chords, superpositions of perfect and altered fifths. Thus, the genus of the tonality remains undetermined, which opens the door to the melodic exploitation of a blues-inflected major-minor duality. Still, most of Strayhorn's blue notes in *Up There* are blue notes by implication: the characteristic minor against major is absent.

The middle section of *Up There* (Ex. 10-7, p. 176) breaks away from the roaring piano accompaniment and turns to a more gentle waltz time in F♯. Here the horn and the piano have complementary melodies, in marked contrast with the opening section, where both instruments seemed captivated in separate musical worlds. But what starts out as a friendly consonant waltz becomes progressively macabre as both horn and piano seem incapable of breaking through their respective repeated notes C♯ and A♯. The segment appears to aim for melodic and harmonic development, but fails. In the final bars the failure is complete as the piano accompaniment loses grip and slips away in an increasingly dark and dissonant line, establishing the return to the recapitulation of the openly angry exposition.

Ex. 10-6. *Up There*, mm. 1–16

The second movement, *Boo Loose*, similarly expresses frustration. It is revealing to see how Strayhorn has transformed an earlier version of this movement, the tranquil and gently drifting *Pretty Little One*, into this dramatic, aggressive statement. *Boo Loose* starts out with two forceful piano blues choruses in B♭. Strayhorn has contracted *Pretty Little One*'s original twenty-four-bar blues theme to twenty bars, while replacing the graciously moving violin background with subdued, restrained piano chords. Though the triadic melody (Ex. 10-8) has a simple sing-song quality, the harmonic progression is based on more complex jazz-blues conventions. In the final bars, as the melody at last manages to break out of its repeated triadic formula and locked two-bar rhythm, *Boo Loose* moves to the parallel minor (B♭ minor) with a repeated plagal cadenza (IV-i), giving way to extemporized plaintive horn lines. Though *Boo Loose*, wedged between the harmonically barely moving outer parts of the suite, pairs a more definable melody with a functional-harmonic chord progression, the movement ends unresolved.

The final movement, with the enigmatic title *Pavane Bleu No. 2*, brings together the two preceding parts of the suite. *Pavane Bleu* shares its melodic

Ex. 10-7. *Up There*, mm. 33–48

Ex. 10-8. *Boo Loose*, mm. 25–30

material with *Boo Loose* as it is similarly derived from major triads (Ex. 10-9), while it shares its harmonic stagnancy with *Up There*. Like the final bars of *Blood Count*, the suite's closure is disturbing. *Pavane Bleu* doesn't end; it dies. With a repeated tonic-under-fourth figure, the horn sinks deeper and deeper into a dense morass of sustained piano chords (Ex. 10-10). There is no closure, no conclusive statement, just a final exhalation.

In keeping with his personality, Strayhorn's final work was not a monumental public statement but a highly personal expression. At the time of the creation of the *North by Southwest Suite*, the composer had little reason to expect that the work would ever be recorded.[17]

The autobiographical overtones of the *North by Southwest Suite* once more bring to mind the poem Strayhorn wrote while he was still a teenager in Pittsburgh. The poem, known as *Something to Live For*, "embodies the whole of his youthful frustration in a masterstroke of yearning" (Hajdu 1996, 38):

> *I want something to live for*
> *Someone to make my life*
> *an adventurous dream*
> *Oh, what wouldn't I give for*
> *Someone who'd take my life, and make it seem*
> *Gay as they say it ought to be*
> *Why can't I have love like that brought to me?*

Coming from an adolescent who didn't quite fit in with his surroundings and who in all likelihood at the time of the poem's creation was coming to terms with his homosexuality, the lyric may seem to bear few surprises. Yet, what does make

Ex. 10-9. *Pavane Bleu No. 2*, mm. 1–4

Ex. 10-10. *Pavane Bleu No. 2*, mm. 16–30

Something to Live For highly unconventional for a youngster from one of Pittsburgh's poorest areas, is that Strayhorn chose to set his poem to music—music that bears all those enchanting hallmarks of his best expressive work. Hence, the answer to the question young Billy Strayhorn raised in the lyrics of *Something to Live For* lies in the song itself. With its delicate harmonies, its expressive melody, and idiosyncratic form, *Something to Live For* attests that Billy Strayhorn indeed had something to live for: his music.

Chapter Eleven

Conclusion

IN THE PRESENCE of Bill Grove, Billy Strayhorn died from cancer at the age of fifty-one, on May 31, 1967. His passing left a lasting impression on those close to him. According to one of the mourners, gathered at Bill Grove's house, some two dozen people "had just lost their best friend" (Hajdu 1996, 256). Ellington, who heard the news while on the road with his orchestra, returned to Manhattan and read an impressive eulogy at the public memorial service that was held at St. Peter's Church. "Virtually paralyzed with despair" (ibid.), Ellington attested his deep-felt love and respect for Strayhorn.[1]

A few months after Strayhorn's passing, Ellington recorded... *And His Mother Called Him Bill*, a widely acclaimed tribute album in honor of his collaborator of twenty-eight years. On its original release, the LP contained thirteen Strayhorn works in impressive interpretations by the Ellington orchestra. With this album, Ellington and his musicians expressed their sorrow over Strayhorn's death, as well as their feelings of gratitude toward him. As Ellington wrote in his autobiography,

> Billy Strayhorn was always the most unselfish, the most patient, and the most imperturbable, no matter how dark the day. I am indebted to him for so much of my courage since 1939. He was my listener, my most dependable appraiser, and as a critic he would be the most clinical, but his background—both classical and modern—was an accessory to his own good taste and understanding, so what came back to me was in perfect balance. (Ellington 1973, 156)

Duke Ellington survived Strayhorn by almost seven years, years during which he continued to compose prolifically. Strayhorn had been a source of inspiration for his employer since 1939, and after his partner's death Ellington found solace

Billy Strayhorn (*David Hajdu Collection*)

in music. "I'm writing more than ever now," Ellington told a reporter upon the release of...*And His Mother Called Him Bill*, "I have to. Billy Strayhorn left that big yawning void" (Hajdu 1996, 261). In the years that followed, Ellington wrote ambitious works, including two more *Concerts of Sacred Music*, a work of operatic dimensions titled *Queenie Pie*, and a number of suites, including the *Degas Suite*, *The Afro-Eurasian Eclipse*, and the *Goutelas Suite*. As Mercer Ellington observed,

> When Strayhorn passed, [Ellington] was in the midst of various projects [such as the preparation of *The Second Sacred Concert*], and, realizing he did not have Strayhorn at his side, found out that in order to cover the same ground he had been covering, he had to work harder. If anything, Strayhorn's passing stimulated Ellington's ability to write and to write more music than he had to do before. (Nicholson 1999, 378)

According to trombonist Lawrence Brown, Ellington silently used shelved Strayhorn compositions in the years after his collaborator's death. "[Strayhorn] was the genius, the power behind the throne all of those latter years. There were so many things left unfinished that Strayhorn did—many of the things you think were new, were things Strayhorn left unfinished," Brown said (ibid.). However, neither the surviving manuscripts nor the music of Ellington's post-Strayhorn repertory support Brown's claim. As he had done while Strayhorn was alive, Ellington continued to write "Ellington music," rather than build on his collaborator's compositions and arrangements.[2]

In the final years of his life, Ellington paid increasing homage to Strayhorn. From 1971 on, he often closed his concerts with a contemplative solo piano performance of *Lotus Blossom*, similar to the closure of...*And His Mother Called Him Bill*.

Duke Ellington passed away on May 24, 1974.

HISTORICALLY, STRAYHORN'S IMPORTANCE lies first and foremost in his hundreds of contributions to the repertory of the Ellington orchestra. From the moment Strayhorn joined the Ellington organization in 1939 until his untimely death, virtually every performance and almost every studio session of Duke Ellington and His Orchestra included arrangements and original compositions by Strayhorn. Appendix B, which lists over five hundred confirmed first recordings of scores by Strayhorn (an estimated 80 percent of his total contribution to the orchestra's repertory), reveals his tremendous achievement. The quality of these scores inspired some of the Ellington Orchestra's most outstanding recordings. While one cannot know how the Ellington Orchestra would have fared without Strayhorn, and whether Ellington would have achieved similar glories (and speculations to that respect are irrelevant), it is certain that the Strayhorn Effect did play an important role in the orchestra's repertory. Strayhorn provided Ellington with new compositional concepts that led to a different musical world, a world that enriched and strengthened that of his musical partner. Strayhorn's advice, comradeship, and even competition were a continuous source of inspiration to Ellington's creativity.

Many other composer-orchestrators (knowingly or unknowingly) partly based their work on Strayhorn's music. Among those whose music owes a debt to Strayhorn are the composer-arrangers who worked for the orchestras of Claude Thornhill and Boyd Raeburn, including George Handy and Gil Evans. Even those composers who primarily looked at Ellington, such as Charles Mingus, inevitably absorbed Strayhorn's music as well.

Strayhorn's musical significance transcends the already impressive role he played in the realm of Ellingtonia, where his often anonymous work reached the broader jazz-loving audience. But Strayhorn had already been active in Pittsburgh, long before he met Ellington. There he wrote some of his best songs: *So This Is Love*, *Lush Life*, and *Something to Live For*. During the years that the two composers collaborated, Strayhorn occasionally engaged himself in independent projects, such as his theater music for García Lorca's *The Love of Don Perlimplín for Belisa in Their Garden*, and his *Copasetic Dances*. These projects were even more anonymous, though they reached a small group of nevertheless dedicated listeners. Strayhorn's legacy furthermore encompasses a significant number of innovative orchestral compositions and arrangements, apparently written for Ellington's orchestra but never recorded during Strayhorn's lifetime. These obscure works, in conjunction with the already known Strayhorn repertory, reveal the true magnitude of his musical talent.

Strayhorn's invisibility during his long connection with the Ellington orchestra stands in marked contrast with his significance as a jazz composer. He possessed an advanced harmonic knowledge and paired his unfaltering talent for creating original melodies with a great rhythmic sensitivity. In addition, Strayhorn's understanding of musical form and internal balance was staggering. But Strayhorn's true forte lies in his capacity to weld all this knowledge and talent into naturally sounding, individual works, expressing the whole gamut of conflicting human emotions. With these means, Strayhorn composed some of the most sophisticated and meaningful works in the entire history of jazz.

IN THE TWO DECADES following Strayhorn's death, his music virtually sank into oblivion, with the exception of a handful of his most famous compositions, such as *Lush Life* and *Take the "A" Train*. But after a period of neglect, his legacy gradually came out of the shadows, for various reasons. In the late 1980s, the compact disc became the new standard for commercial audio-recordings, which brought a flood of reissues. Consequently, a large number of the Ellington orchestra's recordings, including many that had long been out of print, became available on CD and found their way to audiences old and new. Second, jazz performers increasingly sought and found inspiration in the past, which further led audiences and musicians to rediscover the legacy of the Ellington orchestra and its composers.

Furthermore, so-called repertory orchestras, dedicated to the musical legacy of the swing era, such as the Lincoln Center Jazz Orchestra (first under the baton of David Berger and later led by Wynton Marsalis) and the Smithsonian Institution's Jazz Masterworks Orchestra (alternately led by Gunther Schuller and David Baker) included an increasing number of compositions by Ellington and Strayhorn in their repertories.

In addition, certain musicians became advocates of the music of Billy Strayhorn. Among the early devotees of his work were saxophonists Michael Hashim and Joe Henderson, as well as pianist Fred Hersch, all of whom dedicated entire albums to Strayhorn's music.[3]

Jazz scholars and publicists, too, showed increasing interest in the orchestras of the past. Scholarly works on aspects of Ellington's music appeared (e.g., Dietrich 1995, Rattenbury 1992, Sturm 1995, and Tucker 1991 and 1993a), as well as more general overviews of his life and work (e.g., Collier 1987 and Hasse 1993). All these works addressed to a certain extent Strayhorn's role in the Ellington orchestra. Still, the topic remained elusive, in the absence of reliable sources.

The supplement to the *Village Voice* (a New York based weekly) of June 1992 marked a radical break from the perceived Strayhorn critique. Issued twenty-five years after his death, the supplement is dedicated in its entirety to Strayhorn. On the cover appears a king-size picture of the composer, alone at his piano keyboard. Entitled "The Billy Strayhorn Suite," this publication paints a new picture of the composer and his music, as most of the articles steer clear of the generally accepted lore of the Ellington-Strayhorn collaboration. As such, the *Village Voice* supplement provided a first correction to the usual views of Strayhorn as a composer.

David Hajdu's Strayhorn biography (1996) truly changed the perception of its subject. Hajdu's book reconstructs Strayhorn's life in compelling detail, based in large part on some five hundred interviews the author held across a period of ten years of arduous, path-breaking research. David Hajdu's careful research should set a standard in jazz biography.

In the same year that Hajdu's biography saw the light, the Dutch Jazz Orchestra issued *Portrait of a Silk Thread: Newly Discovered Works of Billy Strayhorn*, a CD with previously unknown Strayhorn music, rediscovered in the holdings of the Billy Strayhorn Collection and the Duke Ellington Collection. Both the biography and the CD received prominent coverage in the press. Thus, in recent years, Strayhorn's work has gained more critical acclaim than it did during the composer's secluded life.

Still, the larger part of the work remains to be done. To date, there are dozens and dozens of so far unrecorded compositions and arrangements (mostly orchestral scores) by Strayhorn. Furthermore, much of the music that has been recorded and performed by the Ellington orchestra is currently barely accessible, since it lives on out-of-print 78 rpm and LP records, or collectors' tapes of live radio broadcasts. In order to preserve and disclose this historically and musically important legacy, this material needs to be integrally recorded, in its full glory. Thus, even with all the beautiful music that is already available, Strayhorn's legacy still holds a tremendous promise for the future.

To use Billy Strayhorn's favorite catch-phrase: Ever up and onward!

Appendix A

Scores of Scores: Manuscripts at the Billy Strayhorn and Duke Ellington Collections

Shortly after Strayhorn's death, his nephew Gregory A. Morris, whom Strayhorn had named as the executor of his estate, vacated the Riverside apartment. Among Strayhorn's personal belongings were the tangible remnants of a remarkably productive career in music: some seven hundred scores in Strayhorn's hand, close to five dozen autographs by Ellington, original music by the likes of Luther Henderson, (Ellington band trumpeter) Freddie Jenkins, and others, published sheet music, and numerous copyist's scores and parts in the hands of Juan Tizol, Thomas Whaley, John Sanders, Herbie Jones, and various unidentified extractors. As Morris pursued a career in education, the scores (placed in plain brown envelopes in one-inch stacks) lay dormant in four banker's boxes. Every now and then Morris invited researchers and musicians to pore over the music, but apparently none of these incidental visitors could invest the time necessary to order and interpret the intimidating stacks of unsorted autographs.

The materials taken from Strayhorn's apartment, now known as the Billy Strayhorn Collection, presented only part of his surviving manuscripts. The other portion, over five hundred autograph scores and more than three hundred sets of instrumental parts, was stored in the library of the Ellington orchestra. These materials were in the custody of Mercer Ellington, the son of Duke Ellington, who was the executor of his father's estate after Ellington's death in 1974. The music was kept in various locations in Manhattan. Part was kept at some rented storage rooms at the Century/Franklin Warehouse on the Lower East Side, which housed most memorabilia from Ellington's apartment and the larger share of his music library. Eventually, materials that were stored in a garage owned by Mercer were taken to this location also, as was Thomas Whaley's private collection of compositions. Mercer kept another part of the music at his New York apartment, where it functioned as the working library for his own band, which still operated under the billing of The Duke Ellington Orchestra. The so-called Presentation Albums—blue, leather-bound volumes that contained both printed and autograph scores, compiled as a gift for Ellington's sixtieth birthday—resided at the offices of one of the estate's lawyers, while another, smaller (though not less significant) portion remained at Ruth Ellington-Boatwright's private Manhattan address, from which she ran Tempo Music. Here, another forty Strayhorn manuscripts would surface, including some of his oldest compositions dating back to his Pittsburgh years. There was busy traffic between all locations, as bits and pieces of manuscripts were taken out of the storage facility for reference or for use by Mercer Ellington's orchestra, while discontinued pieces were put back. Gradually, the careful organization implemented by Thomas Whaley got lost, as the 200,000 sheets of music were shuffled and reshuffled, like a deck of cards.

It was by coincidence that the late John Kinard, director of the Smithsonian Institution's Anacostia Museum, learned from Mercer Ellington that he still owned a considerable amount of the Ellington band's library. Although Mercer had donated Ellington's tapes to the Danish Radio in Copenhagen, the remainder of his legacy had not found a definitive destination. Kinard informed the director of the National Museum of American History, Roger Kennedy, who then asked John Hasse, curator in the Division of Musical History, to pursue the matter. The Smithsonian Institution already possessed outstanding collections in the history of music, including collections in African-American culture and a program of performance, compilation, and publication of recordings of American jazz. The emphasis in the Museum's research, public programming, collections, and exhibitions was increasingly shifting toward popular culture and cultural diversity, and the Ellington materials would strengthen the Museum's mission to preserve and interpret the national heritage of the United States.

After various inspections of the materials by staff members from the Archives Center and the Musical History Department—both divisions of the National Museum of American History—and after lengthy negotiations, the Ellington estate and the Smithsonian set a price for which the collection would be purchased. The Smithsonian drew up an additional working budget to cover the costs of acquisition, preservation, and cataloguing of the materials. In 1986, Congress passed a bill that gave the Institution a hefty one million dollars to be used for that goal. Due to various federal tax liens against the Ellington estate, the purchase could not be completed until March 1988, when the collection finally came to Washington, partly as a donation from Mercer Ellington. However, the deal did not include the music from Tempo's offices, which the Smithsonian acquired separately from Ruth Ellington-Boatwright in 1991.

On entering the three unheated and non-air-conditioned rooms in the Manhattan warehouse that housed most of the music, the Smithsonian staffers found a situation that defied all description. The wooden shelves, filing cabinets, and floors were packed with an overwhelming amount of materials: more than 600 cubic feet (21.5 cubic meters) of music manuscripts (scores and parts), published sheet music, photographs, correspondence, financial records, scrapbooks with press clippings, posters, and programs. There were audiotape recordings of concerts, radio broadcasts, and rehearsals and three-dimensional objects that ranged from band stands, the prizes and awards Ellington gathered throughout his life, clothing, some books, to even his electric piano. With the help of numerous interns, volunteers, and research associates, the Smithsonian's Duke Ellington Collection staff would spend nearly a decade in fully opening up the collection.

One of the persistent myths that has surrounded the Ellington orchestra is that it relied little on written music. According to Collier (1987, 253), all that Ellington left was "a trunk full...of bits and pieces that simply defied being put in order." He recounts how "baritone saxophonist Bill Perkins once had a chance to play with Ellington with a band put together for a television show. He [Perkins] reported, 'I thought, boy, I'm going to get to play those marvelous Harry Carney parts. Well, the fact is, there were no Harry Carney parts—they were all kept in Harry's head'" (ibid.). Collier's reliance on Perkins as a source is curious. The tenorist indeed once sat in with the orchestra, at the recordings for the television show *We Love You Madly* (January 10, 1973, for CBS). However, the music played did not come from the Ellington library, since Quincy Jones was the arranger and musical director for the program. If Collier had taken notice of the pictures reprinted in his own book, which show band stands loaded with instrumental parts (i.e., photo 14, following p. 182), he might have come to a more accurate assessment of the role of written music in the Ellington orchestra. (Collier's description of an Ellington arrangement, as "nothing but 'goose eggs,'" that is, rows of whole notes as vague reminders to the original player what he was supposed to play" [ibid., 253], holds little water either.) Apart from hundreds of detailed scores by Ellington and Strayhorn (and a host of other composers and arrangers), there are thousands and thousands of equally detailed and legible instrumental parts by dozens of different professional copyists, most of them registered members of the American Federation of Musicians.

Indeed, Collier's sources could not have been farther from the truth: the collections in Pittsburgh and Washington represent, either in instrumental parts or autograph scores, the majority of the Ellington Orchestra's repertory as well as an impressive amount of music written for other orchestras and occasions. The collections somewhat weakly document the first decade of Ellington's professional life, which started in 1923 (the oldest manuscripts date back to approximately 1930). During this period the Ellington orchestra was known to rely more on so-called head arrangements, that is, arrangements worked out during rehearsals. From the late 1930s on there is a more complete representation (although some major compositions seem to be missing) extending well into the final months of Ellington's life.

Similarly, not all of Strayhorn's early works have survived; especially his scores pertaining to various Pittsburgh orchestras are sorely missed. Luckily, his fellow Mad Hatters safeguarded their band books full of Strayhorn's arrangements for a good sixty years; some of that music is currently in the hands of biographer Hajdu. The larger part of Strayhorn's work for the Ellington orchestra does survive. Most of the music he wrote for endeavors outside the Ellington realm survive with varying degrees of completeness: while the score for his 1962 Copasetics Dance, *Welcome Aboard*, seems almost complete, the 1963 *Down There* is largely lost.

The manuscript scores (as a rule, in pencil), copied scores, and extracted instrumental parts come in a wide variety of sizes and materials: music sketch books, onionskin masters, photostats, photocopies, and dozens of brands of music paper, carrying the names of film companies, publishing houses, and music stores throughout the world. Ellington himself had his own manuscript paper manufactured, with his name printed in one of the bottom corners and his signature overleaf.

In addition to the actual music, the manuscripts carry a wealth of other information. Names, addresses, and phone numbers turn up on the pages, from all sorts of celebrities to forgotten, mostly female, admirers. Then there are the countless pages with calculations scribbled on the back (often on Johnny Hodges's parts), apparently to settle the endless financial discussions Ellington had with his band members. Itineraries, play lists for concerts, appointments, shirt sizes for the band's wardrobe, sketches, and lyrics—they were all written down on any sheet of music paper that happened to be at hand.

The dizzying complexity of the various manuscript collections reflects the special conditions under which these autographs were created. Since they were intended for use by the Duke Ellington orchestra only, hundreds of scores carry no titles at all or mysterious titles that defy identification. Furthermore, scores were hardly ever dated or signed. Numerous manuscripts seem incomplete as loose, usually untitled and unnumbered pages got separated from their mother manuscripts. Consequently, some scores ended up in different locations: the outer sections of Strayhorn's arrangement of *Flamingo*, for instance, are currently at the Smithsonian while the middle part is in Pittsburgh.

The never-ending revisions of the orchestra's repertory further add to the opacity of the surviving collections (for *I Got It Bad* alone, twenty-seven different and mostly incomplete sets of parts exist).

As the Ellingtonians carried their band books with them during the orchestra's constant travels, instrumental parts got misplaced or lost (bassist John Lamb reports that his band book was stolen from the band stand one night), while departing musicians—Ellington worked with no fewer than nine hundred different instrumentalists during his career—at times seem to have taken their parts with them. As Clark Terry once recounted, the parts could even be used as leverage to settle disputes: after an argument during a trip across the Atlantic, Ellington fired trumpeter Cat Anderson—in the middle of the ocean. Infuriated, Anderson told Terry "he'd show Duke," got his band book and threw it over the side of the ocean liner, straight into the water. "Now, he can't get rid of me," Anderson said to his section mate; "I'm the only one who knows the parts" (Kuebler, 1997). Apparently the trick worked, as Anderson was welcomed back into the fold before they got off the boat. As far as the Duke Ellington Collection is concerned, there might be some truth in this anecdote: indeed, many of Cat Anderson's parts are missing.

The manuscripts produced for the Ellington orchestra are distinctively different from regular, "legitimate" scores, since they were not intended for the uninitiated. The autograph scores in the Ellington organization mainly served as a means of communication between the composer (Strayhorn or Ellington) and his orchestra, with the copyist as an intermediary. Many composers typically seek the printed publication of their work, or at least try to make sure that the work will be accessible to future orchestras. Therefore they tend to prepare their scores in concordance with generally accepted notation conventions. However, neither Ellington nor Strayhorn took that aspect into consideration. Even though the jazz community (orchestras, educators, and scholars) craved the "actual notes," few attempts were made to publish the music, be it for performance or posterity.[1] For Ellington and Strayhorn, the goal of the autographs was the performance of music. Consequently, the Ellington band scores were interoffice mail, which allowed for an idiosyncratic approach to music manuscript writing, where speed and economy were the key parameters, as exemplified by many virtually stenographic music documents. For instance, since Strayhorn for all practical purposes often extracted his own scores, they could be strikingly sketchy: in his original setting of *Chelsea Bridge* he has omitted the work's theme, saving time by putting it directly into the instrumental parts.

The heart of the manuscript collections is made up of hundreds of these condensed or short scores written by Ellington and Strayhorn. Example A-1 reproduces the first page from the previously unrecorded *Blue House*, a typical sample of a Strayhorn short score. Closely following the layout and notational idiosyncrasies Ellington tended to use, Strayhorn has written the manuscript in concert pitch and has assigned each instrumental group of the orchestra (reeds, trumpets, and trombones) a separate staff. Indicative of its prominent role in the orchestra, the baritone has its own staff, scored in octave transposition (with a treble clef) and positioned between the saxophone and trumpet staves. At times, the score will carry a separate staff for a soloist's part, though not necessarily. Often the solo is scored in its legitimate staff, as is the case with Lawrence Brown's solo part in the fourth staff. If an instrumental group rests, its staff may be left out

Ex. A-1. *Blue House*, first page of autograph score.
(Courtesy Smithsonian Institution)

altogether, while at other times that staff will be used for a new instrumental combination. Remarkably, the larger part of the rhythm section—piano, guitar (until 1949 when Freddy Guy left), and drums—is entirely absent from the score. The only rhythm section instrument that appears in most scores is the bass. The bass may have its own staff, but in general it is written in the trombone staff, with the note stems pointing down. Yet, the bass part is largely generic, as it lacks detail and tends to roughly indicate the harmony (by means of the root and fifth) on down beats only, with some incidental exceptions. For instance, the second and third bars of system three (Ex. A-1) carry a more articulate bass part. Since the manuscripts as a rule do not carry chord symbols either, the orchestra's rhythm section members had little information as to what to play: they figured out their parts during rehearsals.

A further important deviation in the scores for the Ellington band from general manuscript writing practice is the striking absence of tempo indications, as well as the absence of expression and articulation marks. Even though there was a general understanding among big-band players on how to phrase a particular passage and how to balance the dynamics within a section, there were many possible ways of performing a piece. Again, Ellington and Strayhorn mostly relied on rehearsals to convey these matters, rather than putting them in the score. At times, however, Strayhorn could be more articulate with dynamics. Certain scores, such as *All Day Long* and *Lana Turner*, carry detailed expression markings.

Although not dated, the scores usually provide important information about their production dates. In Example A-1, at letter A, Strayhorn has indicated "Barney Rest," instructing his copyist to leave clarinet and tenor player Barney Bigard out of the ensemble—he is to join on clarinet under the first repeat. Similarly, the third page of the manuscript (not reproduced) calls for "Ben [Webster] Solo," and these two musicians allow for the affirmation of an initial time frame. Barney Bigard was already in the orchestra when Strayhorn came aboard, but the clarinetist left in June 1942, while Ben Webster joined in February 1940, to leave in August 1943 (Webster rejoined at the end of 1948 for a brief stay). Hence, the score for *Blue House* must have been written between February 1940 and June 1942.

The surviving instrumental parts for *Blue House* yield an even more accurate date of composition. Although the score may have been extracted into individual parts at any time after its creation, Ellington band copyists in general were put to work shortly after the completion of a given piece. The instrumental parts include a page for Ray Nance, which suggests a manuscript date between November 1940 (when Nance replaced Cootie Williams) and June 1942. The provenance of *Blue House*'s autograph makes for yet an even smaller time interval, since Strayhorn's handwriting shares many traits with most of his early 1941 work, such as *Take the "A" Train*: it is safe to date this score no earlier than January 1941 and no later than the summer of 1942.

Ex. A-2. *Manhattan Murals*, first page of autograph score
(*Courtesy Smithsonian Institution*)

Example A-2, the first page of *Manhattan Murals*, gives a typical instance of Ellington's handwriting (the title and measure numbers are by Thomas Whaley—also note the printed Ellington autograph in the right-hand corner). The layout of the score is similar to that of *Blue House*. Again the autograph provides clues for a date, as there are references to tenorist Al Sears in bars two, four, and six and (barely visible) altoist Russell Procope in bar four, which dates the manuscript between June 1946 and April 1949. Further clues can be found on the next pages, which refer to "kill" for trumpeter Al Killian, who was with the orchestra from December 1947 until June 1950. Since this manuscript was first used for a performance in November 1948 at Carnegie Hall, its creation date falls in the eleven-month period between December 1947 and November of the following year.

On close inspection, it turns out that Ellington is not the only author who worked on *Manhattan Murals*: in bar nine of Example A-2, Strayhorn takes over to finish the eight-page manuscript, making the score one of the few that both authors truly wrote as a collaborative effort.

Appendix B

Billy Strayhorn's Works on Record

The following is an inventory of Strayhorn's compositions and arrangements that are known to have been recorded during his life. Each entry builds on the surviving autograph score, which firmly establishes Strayhorn as the author of the recorded material.

I have compiled this appendix for a number of reasons. First, the recordings in this list provide an important aural insight into the characteristics of Strayhorn's style and the development of his art. As such, the list provides a practical solution for those readers who are not able to perform research on his autographs. At the time of this writing, part of Strayhorn's written legacy is still in private hands and not publicly accessible. Until such public access is permitted, the recordings give the closest possible representation of those autographs still under cover.

Second, since record sleeves and CD inlays generally provide no insight into issues of authorship, this appendix may answer those questions. For instance, while Ellington and Strayhorn share the arranger's credits for *The Nutcracker Suite*, neither the LP nor the CD reissue indicates the exact movements with which Strayhorn was involved. This appendix therefore gives the precise breakdown for this and other joint works.

Third, the sheer length of this list underwrites my argument (and Ellington's!) that while Strayhorn was "very seldom seen in public," his music was "always heard" (Ellington 1964).

This appendix does not give the full discography of each work, but rather a reference-recording for a given autograph. Each entry lists *only the first* recording (where possible, the first commercially issued recording) of a given Strayhorn score. Thus, even though the Ellington orchestra played Strayhorn's original version of *Take the "A" Train* virtually every day for decades, it is listed in this appendix only once. (Massagli and Volonté [1999, 1173–1194] list over eleven hundred recorded performances of "A" Train alone, all based on the original autograph.)

The recordings listed in this appendix cover an estimated 80 percent of Strayhorn's total contribution to the Ellington orchestra's repertory. Since I decided to list only those recordings I could aurally compare with the autographs, I have left all others out. During my research, I have come across a significant number of recordings (mostly arrangements) that bear all of Strayhorn's musical fingerprints but for which the score is apparently lost (or mistitled, or misplaced). In addition, some hundred scores written by Strayhorn for the Ellington orchestra could not be matched with an existent recording, even though the discographies list them as apparently being recorded. All too often, I have not been able to dig out these obscure recordings.

Matching Strayhorn's arrangements of the stable horses in the orchestra's repertory (such as *Solitude, Perdido, Caravan,* or *It Don't Mean a Thing*) with recordings was a daunting task. At times the quest for a matching recording remained unsuccessful, as dozens and dozens of different recordings exist for these titles, many out of print. The absence of a work in this list therefore does not necessarily mean that it was written by another composer. In sum, this list cannot be exhaustive and inevitably omits works that were in fact written by Strayhorn.

In a limited number of cases (indicated by "no manuscript known") this appendix lists works for which the original manuscript is lost or inaccessible. These selections have been included after extensive aural confirmation and are further corroborated by copyright status, other related manuscripts (such as sketches), interviews, articles, or other circumstantial evidence.

Each entry is built up as follows:

Full (copyrighted) title. "Manuscript title," Collection. First (issued) recording: Month, Day, Year. Performers. Matrix number. Title of the CD or LP (re)issue (record label and number). Relevant manuscripts. Remarks.

1. Full (copyrighted) title. Lists the title by which the piece is generally known. The order of the listing is strictly alphabetical by this title. Individual movements of multimovement works are listed under the title of the multimovement work, in the final movement order (or tracks, if no movement order is known), for example, *Perfume Suite: Love* (movement 1 of 4).

2. Manuscript title. Lists the title proper as found on the autograph manuscript. Many manuscripts carry more than one title, since compositions were often retitled after being recorded. Typically, this new title was added to the manuscript afterward, usually by those responsible for filing the scores in the Ellington library (such as copyists Thomas Whaley and John Sanders). In those instances where there are multiple titles on a score, the initial or apparently oldest original title is listed.

3. Collection. Lists the current location of the relevant manuscript or manuscripts for the convenience of future researchers. Abbreviations used for the different manuscript collections are listed in the Preface.

4. First (issued) recording. The listed recording date takes the current availability of the recording into consideration. If a slightly later recording is more readily available, this recording will be listed rather than an unavailable actual first recording. If a recording of a concert or broadcast performance was not originally issued but is currently available on CD, this recording is listed rather than a later, unissued, or currently discontinued studio recording. Discographers do not always agree on recording dates. For consistency, this appendix follows the dates as listed in Massagli and Volonté (1999).

In a limited number of cases, a re-recording has resulted in multiple entries for the same score. A score that has been re-recorded under a different title, a score that has been incorporated into an extended work, and vocal scores that have been re-recorded as an instrumental (or vice versa) all have double listings. Scores whose order of musical events was altered for a new recording do not have multiple listings.

If no first issued recording is known, then recordings from other sources (radio or television broadcasts, films, private collectors' tapes) are given, provided they are listed in any of the standard Ellington discographies or itineraries (Massagli and Volonté 1999; Stratemann 1992; Timner 1996). With the incessant stream of reissues on CD, these unissued selections may eventually become available.

Note that performances and recordings of a specific piece tended to flock together, since the orchestra usually first tried out a work in a number of concerts and broadcasts, eventually to take it into the recording studio. Once recorded, a piece typically remained in the band's book for a while. It is therefore, in general, safe to assume that roughly contemporary recordings and performances of a given title are based on the same score. But there are exceptions. Therefore, one should always compare the reference recording listed in this appendix with the version under consideration.

5. Performers. Gives the performers on a given recording. Though Strayhorn in many instances played the piano on recordings of his own material, this appendix sticks to the generic billing "Duke Ellington and His Orchestra," rather than "Billy Strayhorn with the Duke Ellington Orchestra."

6. Matrix number. Lists the matrix or master number of the recording, if known. Concerts, radio broadcasts, and TV or film soundtrack recordings as a rule have no matrix number.

7. Title of the CD or LP (re)issue (record label and number). Lists the most accessible issue or reissue, if any, preferably on CD. Since label numbers of LPs and CDs vary by country, consult Valburn (1993) or Massagli and Volonté (1999). Many LP issues of broadcasts and concerts carry scant information. Most of them are out of print. The Institute of Jazz Studies at Rutgers University (Campus at

APPENDIX B   197

Newark, New Jersey) houses virtually every commercial jazz record in an easily accessible collection. For noncommercial recordings, including tapes of rare broadcasts and concerts, the Jerry Valburn Collection at the Library of Congress (Washington, D.C.) is the best public source.

8. Relevant manuscripts. Lists the status of the surviving manuscripts used for the recording, that is, whether the manuscript is an autograph score or a set of autograph parts. Unless otherwise stated, the listed relevant manuscripts are in the hand of Billy Strayhorn. Matching copyist's parts are not listed. When the documents reside in more than one collection, this section gives a breakdown for the respective locations of the manuscripts.

9. Remarks. Gives additional information. When comparing the autograph with the recording, this breakdown usually gives measure numbers (based on the recording). Piano introductions are excluded from the count, that is, measures are counted from the beginning of the orchestral score. The entry will refer as much as possible to the actual performance, for example, "Measures 1-24 and 47-65 (the instrumental sections) are by Ellington, measures 25-46 (two vocal-choruses) are by Strayhorn." If a breakdown by measure becomes too complicated (for instance, in extended works or in works with out-of-tempo cadenzas) the recording's time codes (as displayed by a CD player, DAT recorder, or stop watch), are given, as "Webster's tenor cadenza (1 bar at 5:28-5:34, and 9 bars at 6:19-7:23) is by Strayhorn."

The final entry for each *multimovement work* lists the authors of movements not written by Strayhorn (see also Appendix D: Billy Strayhorn's Compositions).

Whenever the recorded version varies significantly from the original manuscript, this is indicated. There are three possibilities:

a) The manuscript is incomplete, that is, part of the manuscript is lost. The entry indicates which sections are missing. In most cases a manuscript is incomplete because one or more pages are missing—that is, it is not incomplete because it was not finished. Therefore, the missing pages in all likelihood are by the same author as the surviving pages.

b) The recording uses part of the manuscript. The entry indicates which sections are unused.

c) The order of the recording is at variance with the order suggested by the manuscript.

Absinthe. "Ricard," DEC. First (issued) recording: January 5, 1963. Duke Ellington
    & His Orchestra. Reprise 1701-9; issued on *Afro Bossa* (Discovery 71002).
    Relevant manuscripts: autograph score and parts.
Ac-Cent-Tchu-Ate the Positive. "Accentuate," BSC. First (issued) recording: April
    28, 1945. Duke Ellington & His Orchestra. Broadcast; issued on *Your Sat-*

urday Date with the Duke (Duke Ellington Treasury Series 03). Relevant manuscript: autograph score.

After All. "After All," BSC. First (issued) recording: February 15, 1941. Duke Ellington & His Orchestra. Victor 055287-1; issued on *Take the "A" Train: The Legendary Blanton-Webster Transcriptions* (Vintage Jazz Classics VJC 1003-2). Relevant manuscript: autograph score.

After All. No manuscript known. First (issued) recording: September 1, 1967. Duke Ellington & His Orchestra. UPAI-8538; issued on *...And His Mother Called Him Bill* (RCA Bluebird 6287-2-RB).

Agra. See *The Far East Suite* (movement 7 of 8).

Ain't Misbehavin'. "Ain't Misbehavin'," DEC. First (issued) recording: November 9, 1943. Duke Ellington & His Orchestra. Swing Treasury BB37667D C1-3; issued on *Duke Ellington World Broadcasting Series, Vol. 2* (Circle CCD102). Relevant manuscripts: autograph parts.

Ain't Nothin' Nothin' (Baby Without You). "Nothin'," DEC. First (issued) recording: April 7, 1953. Duke Ellington & His Orchestra. Cap 11416-3; issued on *The Complete Capitol Recordings of Duke Ellington* (Mosaic MDS-160). Relevant manuscripts: autograph parts. The order of the recording is at variance with the order suggested by the manuscripts.

Air-Conditioned Jungle. "Air-Conditioned Jungle" and "Air-Conditioned," BSC. First (issued) recording: January 3, 1945. Duke Ellington & His Orchestra. Circle N-3001-1; issued on *Duke Ellington World Broadcasting Series, Vol. 3* (Circle CCD103). Relevant manuscript: autograph scores by Strayhorn and Jimmy Hamilton. All thematic material is by Hamilton; the remainder is by Strayhorn.

Alice Blue Gown. "Green Sleeves/Alice Blue," DEC. First (issued) recording: March 31, 1958. Duke Ellington & His Orchestra. CO60592-16; issued on *At the Bal Masque* (Columbia LP CL-1282). Relevant manuscript: autograph score. The manuscript is incomplete: measures 1-4 are missing. The order of the recording is at variance with the order suggested by the manuscript.

All American in Jazz (track 1 of 10): *Back to School.* "Nat l'Ecole," REC. First (issued) recording: January 23, 1962. Duke Ellington & His Orchestra. CO69234-7; issued on *All American in Jazz* (Columbia 469138-2). Relevant manuscript: autograph score.

All American in Jazz (track 2 of 10): *I've Just Seen Her.* "Just Saw Her," REC. First (issued) recording: January 23, 1962. Duke Ellington & His Orchestra. CO68958-2; issued on *All American in Jazz* (Columbia 469138-2). Relevant manuscript: autograph score.

All American in Jazz (track 3 of 10): *Which Way?* "Which Way," REC. First (issued) recording: January 10, 1962. Duke Ellington & His Orchestra. CO69232; issued on *All American in Jazz* (Columbia 469138-2). Relevant manuscript: autograph score.

All American in Jazz (track 4 of 10): *If I Were You.* "If I Were," REC. First (issued) recording: January 2, 1962. Duke Ellington & His Orchestra. CO68922; issued on *All American in Jazz* (Columbia 469138-2). Relevant manuscript: autograph score. The manuscript is incomplete: the third chorus is missing.

All American in Jazz (track 5 of 10): *Once Upon A Time.* "Once Upon-A," BSC. First (issued) recording: January 2, 1962. Duke Ellington & His Orchestra. CO68921; issued on *All American in Jazz* (Columbia 469138-2). Relevant manuscript: autograph score.

All American in Jazz (track 7 of 10): *Our Children.* "Nos Enfants," REC. First (issued) recording: January 10, 1962. Duke Ellington & His Orchestra. CO69233; issued on *All American in Jazz* (Columbia 469138-2). Relevant manuscript: autograph score.

All American in Jazz (track 8 of 10): *I Couldn't Have Done It Alone.* "I Couldn't Have," REC. First (issued) recording: January 5, 1962. Duke Ellington & His Orchestra. CO68957; issued on *All American in Jazz* (Columbia 469138-2). Relevant manuscripts: autograph score and parts.

All American in Jazz (track 9 of 10): *We Speak the Same Language.* "Speak," BSC and REC). First (issued) recording: January 2, 1962. Duke Ellington & His Orchestra. CO68920; issued on *All American in Jazz* (Columbia 469138-2). Relevant manuscript: autograph score, partly in REC (mm. 1–60) and partly in BSC (mm. 61–69). Track 6, *Night Life* is by Ellington (REC); the manuscript for track 10, *What a Country*, is missing.

All Day Long. "All Day Long," DEC. First (issued) recording: April 26, 1954. Duke Ellington & His Orchestra. Cap 12579-4; issued on *The Complete Capitol Recordings of Duke Ellington* (Mosaic MDS-160). Relevant manuscripts: autograph score and parts. Also used for September 1, 1967.

All Heart. See *A Portrait of Ella Fitzgerald* (movement 2 of 4).

All I Need Is You. "All I Need," DEC. First (issued) recording: July 19, 1942. Duke Ellington & His Orchestra. Unissued broadcast from the Panther Room, Hotel Sherman, Chicago, Illinois. Relevant manuscript: autograph score.

All My Loving. "All My Loving," DEC. First (issued) recording: January 19, 1965. Duke Ellington & His Orchestra. Reprise 5094; issued on *Ellington '66* (Reprise LP R-6154). Relevant manuscript: autograph score.

All of a Sudden My Heart Sings. "Intro-Mon Ami," BSC and "Mon Ami/My Heart Sings," DEC. First (issued) recording: January 4, 1945. Duke Ellington & His Orchestra. Victor D5VB15-5; issued on *Black, Brown & Beige (The 1944–1946 Band Recordings)* (RCA Bluebird 6641-2-RB). Relevant manuscripts: autograph scores. The recording uses part of the manuscript: the introduction and a thirty-two-bar instrumental chorus were cut. The order of the recording is at variance with the order suggested by the manuscript. Also recorded as an instrumental, June 26, 1962.

All of a Sudden My Heart Sings. "Mon Ami/My Heart Sings," DEC. First (issued) recording: June 26, 1962. Duke Ellington & His Orchestra. CO75949; issued on *Midnight in Paris* (Columbia 468403-2). Relevant manuscripts: autograph scores. The recording uses part of the manuscript: a thirty-two-bar chorus was cut. The order of the recording is at variance with the order suggested by the manuscript. Also recorded as a vocal version, January 4, 1945.

All of Me. "All of Me," BSC and DEC. First (issued) recording: September 2, 1949. Duke Ellington & His Orchestra. Broadcast; issued on *Duke Ellington Live at Click Restaurant, Philadelphia* (Raretone LP 5005-FC). Relevant manuscript: autograph score (BSC) and parts (DEC).

All This and Heaven Too. "Heaven Too," DEC. First (issued) recording: November 7, 1940. Duke Ellington & His Orchestra. Dance-date; issued on *Duke Ellington and His Famous Orchestra, Fargo, North Dakota* (Vintage Jazz Classics VJC-1019/20-2). Relevant manuscripts: autograph parts. The live recording stops 2 bars into the vocal chorus, because singer Herb Jeffries was off-mike.

All Too Soon. "All Too Soon," DEC. First (issued) recording: May 28, 1954. Ben Webster with Ralph Burns's Orchestra. Norgran 1723; issued on *Music for Loving: Ben Webster with Strings* (Verve 527 774-2). Relevant manuscript: autograph score.

All Too Soon. "All Too Soon," BSC. First (issued) recording: June 27, 1957. Ella Fitzgerald with Duke Ellington & His Orchestra. VRV21063-3; issued on *Ella Fitzgerald Sings the Duke Ellington Songbook* (Verve 837 035-2). Relevant manuscript: autograph score.

Allah Bye. "Allah Bye," DEC. First (issued) recording: March 20, 1957. Duke Ellington & His Orchestra. Columbia CO57562; issued on *Duke 56/62, Vol. 1* (CBS LP 88653). Relevant manuscripts: autograph score and parts. The recording uses part of the manuscript: the eight-bar introduction was replaced by a twenty-four-bar piano-introduction; the brass answers in the first and final choruses were cut. Written between November 1940 and June 1942.

Almost Cried. See *Anatomy of a Murder* (track 8 of 13).

Amor. "Amor," BSC and DEC. First (issued) recording: July 8, 1944. Duke Ellington & His Orchestra. Broadcast; issued on *The Fabulous Forties, Vol. 3* (Rarities LP 70). Relevant manuscript: autograph score (BSC) and parts (DEC).

Anatomy of a Murder (track 1 of 13): *Main Title & Anatomy of a Murder.* Untitled, DEC. First (issued) recording: June 2, 1959. Duke Ellington & His Orchestra. Issued on *Anatomy of a Murder* (Columbia CK 65569). Relevant manuscript: autograph score. Measures 11 and 12 are by Strayhorn; the remainder is by Ellington.

Anatomy of a Murder (track 5 of 13): *Low Key Lightly.* "Polly Did Continued," DEC.

First (issued) recording: June 2, 1959. Duke Ellington & His Orchestra. Issued on *Anatomy of a Murder* (Columbia CK 65569). Relevant manuscript: autograph score. The manuscript is incomplete: [0:00–1:52] and [2:54–3:38] are missing. See also Appendix C.

Anatomy of a Murder (track 8 of 13): *Almost Cried*. "Flirtibird Down," "Almost Cried" and untitled, REC. First (issued) recording: June 1, 1959. Duke Ellington & His Orchestra. RHCO46263; issued on *Anatomy of a Murder* (Columbia CK 65569). Relevant manuscript: autograph scores. Pieced together from two scores: measures 1–6 (intro), 17–24 (bridge), and 33–38 (coda) are by Ellington; measures 7–8 (intro), 9–16 (first A) and 24–32 (second A) by Strayhorn. The recording uses parts of these manuscripts: sections of both the Ellington and Strayhorn scores are not used.

Anatomy of a Murder (track 12 of 13): *Haupê*. "Polly Rab" and "Polly Lead," REC and DEC. First (issued) recording: June 2, 1959. Duke Ellington & His Orchestra. RHCO46265; issued on *Anatomy of a Murder* (Columbia CK 65569). Relevant manuscripts: autograph scores.

Anatomy of a Murder (bonus track [not in original release]): *Polly*. "Polly Rab," "Polly Did," "Polly Did Continued," and "Polly Valse," DEC and REC. First (issued) recording: June 2, 1959. Duke Ellington & His Orchestra. RHCO46265-6; issued on *Anatomy of a Murder* (Columbia CK 65569). Relevant manuscripts: autograph scores. Pieced together from different scores: the final section [2:49–3:33] is by Ellington; the remainder is by Strayhorn. The recording uses part of these manuscripts. See also Appendix C. Tracks 2, *Flirtibird*, 3, *Way Early Subtone*, 4, *Hero to Zero*, 6, *Happy Anatomy*, 7, *Midnight Indigo*, 9, *Sunswept Sunday*, 10, *Grace Valse*, 11, *Happy Anatomy*, and 13, *Upper and Outest*, are by Ellington.

And Russia Is Her Name. "Russia," BSC. First (issued) recording: July 11, 1943. Duke Ellington & His Orchestra. Broadcast; issued on *Duke Ellington at the Hurricane Club, Vol. 02* (Hurricane LP HC-6002). Relevant manuscript: autograph score.

Anitra's Dance. See *Peer Gynt Suites Nos. 1 and 2* (movement 5 of 5).

Arabesque Cookie. See *The Nutcracker Suite* (movement 9 of 9).

Artistry in Rhythm. "Art-Rhythm," DEC. First (issued) recording: January 3, 1963. Duke Ellington & His Orchestra. Reprise 3372-11; issued on *Recollections of the Big Band Era* (Atlantic Jazz 7 90043-2). Relevant manuscript: autograph score.

As Long as I Live. "Long as I Live," BSC. First (issued) recording: November 17, 1945. Duke Ellington & His Orchestra. Broadcast; issued on *Your Saturday Date with the Duke* (Duke Ellington Treasury Series 32). Relevant manuscript: autograph score.

Åse's Death. See *Peer Gynt Suites Nos. 1 and 2* (movement 4 of 5).

At Last. "End-At Last," DEC. First (issued) recording: August 13, 1942. Duke

Ellington & His Orchestra. Unissued broadcast from the Hotel Sherman, Chicago, Illinois. Relevant manuscript: autograph score and parts. The manuscript is incomplete: it carries the final eleven bars only; Strayhorn's autograph parts, however, are complete.

Autumn Leaves. "Autumn Leaves," DEC. First (issued) recording: March 4, 1958. Duke Ellington & His Orchestra. Concert; issued on *The Private Collection, Vol. 2: Dance Concerts, California 1958* (Saja 7 91042-2). Relevant manuscript: autograph score. Ellington added the trombone chords to the last four bars of the bridge. The remainder is by Strayhorn.

Autumn Serenade. "Autumn Serenade," REC. First (issued) recording: October 13, 1945. Duke Ellington & His Orchestra. Broadcast; issued on *Your Saturday Date with the Duke* (Duke Ellington Treasury Series 26). Relevant manuscript: autograph score. The eight measures preceding the vocal chorus (baritone with trombone background) are by Ellington; the remainder is by Strayhorn.

Azalea. "AAEZLA," DEC. First (issued) recording: June 10, 1947. Duke Ellington & His Orchestra. Issued on *Capitol Transcriptions* (Capitol LP B-305). Relevant manuscript: autograph score. Also recorded on December 11, 1951, with a new intro and in a different order.

Azalea. "Azalea" and "AAEZLA," DEC. First (issued) recording: December 11, 1951. Duke Ellington & His Orchestra. CO47271-1; issued on *The Complete Duke Ellington: 1947–1952, Vol. 4* (CBS 88035). Relevant manuscripts: autograph scores and parts. The recording uses part of the manuscript: a nineteen-bar instrumental section was cut. The order of the recording is at variance with the order suggested by the manuscript. The recording of June 10, 1947, adheres to the original order.

Baghdad. "Casa-blanca," Rutgers Institute of Jazz Studies. First (issued) recording: June 13, 1944. Boyd Raeburn and His Orchestra. Issued on *Boyd Raeburn and His Orchestra: 1944* (Circle CD-22). Relevant manuscript: autograph parts by Juan Tizol. The recording uses part of the manuscript: 66 bars were cut.

Ballad for Very Sad and Very Tired Lotus Eaters. "Ballad for Very Sad and Very Tired Lotus Eaters," BSC. First (issued) recording: September 1, 1956. Johnny Hodges and the Ellington All-Stars without Duke. VRV 2976-3; issued on *Duke's in Bed* (Verve 2304383). Relevant manuscript: autograph score.

Ballet of the Flying Saucers. See *A Drum Is a Woman* (track 11 of 15).

Barney Goin' Easy. Untitled, SIDE. First (issued) recording: June 8, 1939. Barney Bigard & His Orchestra. Vocalion WM1036-A. Relevant manuscript: part.

BDB. "BDB," DEC. First (issued) recording: July 6, 1961. Duke Ellington & Count Basie with Their Orchestras. CO67615; issued on *First Time! The Count Meets the Duke* (Columbia CD CK 65571). Relevant manuscript: autograph score. The recording uses part of the manuscript: a final saxophone chorus was cut. The order of the recording is at variance with the order suggested by the manuscript.

Beautiful Friendship. "Beautiful Friendship," DEC. First (issued) recording: January 21, 1965. Duke Ellington & His Orchestra. Reprise 5094; issued on *Ellington '66* (Reprise LP R-6154). Relevant manuscripts: autograph score and parts.

Beige. See *Black, Brown and Beige* (movement 3 of 3).

Beyond Category. See: *A Portrait of Ella Fitzgerald* (movement 3 of 4).

Bill Bailey, Won't You Please Come Home. "B. Bailey," DEC. First (issued) recording: September 20, 1959. Duke Ellington & His Orchestra. Concert; issued on *Duke Ellington Live in Paris 1959* (BYG YX-2035). Relevant manuscripts: autograph parts.

Black Butterfly. "Butterfly," BSC. First (issued) recording: February 15, 1940. Cootie Williams and His Rug Cutters. Vocalion WM1143-A; issued on *Duke Ellington and His Orchestra 1939–1940* (Classics 790). Relevant manuscript: autograph score.

Black, Brown and Beige (movement 3 of 3): *Beige.* "Cy-Runs/Beige" and "Symphonette-Rhythmique," DEC. First (issued) recording: January 23, 1943. Duke Ellington & His Orchestra. Concert; issued on *The Duke Ellington Carnegie Hall Concerts, January 1943* (Prestige 2PCD 34004-2). Relevant manuscripts: autograph scores and parts. The background under Lawrence Brown's trombone solo on the waltz-theme (29 bars, 4:13–4:52 on the CD), the tenor cadenza by Webster (1 bar at 5:28–5:34, and 9 bars at 6:19–7:23) and the earlier composed *Symphonette-Rhythmique* alternately known as *Sugar Hill Penthouse* (recorded May 18, 1965) and *Symphonette* (84 bars at 7:35–10:28] are Strayhorn's. The remainder is by Ellington. The first two movements, *Black* and *Brown*, are by Ellington (DEC).

Black, Brown and Beige Pt. 4 (Come Sunday). "Come Sun," DEC. First (issued) recording: February 11, 1958. Duke Ellington & His Orchestra. RHCO40635; issued on *Black, Brown and Beige* (Columbia LP CL-1162). Relevant manuscript: autograph score.

Bli-Blip. "Bli-Blip," "Bli Blip," Bli-Blip-," "Ending," and untitled, DEC. First (issued) recording: September 26, 1941. Duke Ellington & His Orchestra. Victor 061686-1; issued on *The Blanton-Webster Band* (RCA Bluebird 5659-2-RB). Relevant manuscripts: autograph scores and parts. This recording was pieced together from five different manuscripts that were written for the theatre show *Jump for Joy*. Measures 1–20 and 93–104 are by Ellington, measures 21–36, 45–92, and 105–116 are by Strayhorn. Measures 37–44 (bridge of the vocal chorus) are missing.

Bli-Blip. "Bli+Blip," "Bli-Blip-," "Ending," untitled, DEC. First (issued) recording: November/December 1941. Duke Ellington & His Orchestra. Ellington Soundie, Victor 4904. Relevant manuscripts: autograph scores (Strayhorn) and parts (Ellington). Largely matching the earlier September 26, 1941, recording, this version carries a new first chorus by Strayhorn. The twelve-bar introduction is by Ellington, the remainder by Strayhorn.

Bli-Blip. "Bli-Blip," BSC. First (issued) recording: June 27, 1957. Ella Fitzgerald with Duke Ellington & His Orchestra. VRV21065-7; issued on *Ella Fitzgerald Sings the Duke Ellington Songbook* (Verve 837 035-2). Relevant manuscript: autograph score.

Blood Count. "Blood Count," DEC. First (issued) recording: August 28, 1967. Duke Ellington & His Orchestra. UPA1-8530-1; issued on *...And His Mother Called Him Bill* (RCA Bluebird 6287-2-RB). Relevant manuscripts: autograph score and parts.

Blossom. "Blossom," BSC and DEC. First (issued) recording: April 9, 1953. Duke Ellington & His Orchestra. Cap 11422-6; issued on *The Complete Capitol Recordings of Duke Ellington* (Mosaic MDS-160). Relevant manuscripts: autograph score (sketchbook no. 3: 18–19) and parts (DEC).

Blousons Noirs. "Blousons Noirs," DEC. First (issued) recording: April 18, 1963. Duke Ellington & His Orchestra. Issued on *The Private Collection, Vol. 4: Studio Sessions, New York 1963* (Saja 7 91044-2). Relevant manuscript: autograph score. Ellington scored the background riff in chorus 2 and 4 (largely based on Strayhorn's first chorus); the remainder is by Strayhorn.

Blue Belles of Harlem. "Blue Bells" and "Intro-Bells," BSC. First (issued) recording: January 23, 1943. Duke Ellington & His Orchestra. Concert; issued on *The Duke Ellington Carnegie Hall Concerts, January 1943* (Prestige 2PCD 34004-2). Relevant manuscript: autograph score.

Blue Bird Of Delhi. See: *The Far East Suite* (movement 2 of 8).

Blue Serge. Untitled, BSC. First (issued) recording: March 16, 1959. Mercer Ellington & His Orchestra. Issued on Coral. Relevant manuscript: autograph score. The manuscript is incomplete: it carries a rough outline of the arrangement only.

Blueberry Hill. "B. Hill," DEC. First (issued) recording: September 13, 1940. Duke Ellington & His Orchestra. Broadcast; issued on *Live from the Hotel Sherman, Chicago, Vol. 2* (Jazz Supreme 705). Relevant manuscripts: autograph parts.

Blues Ain't, The. See *My People* (track 5 of 8).

Blues A-Poppin'. "Blue," BSC. First (issued) recording: June 22, 1939. Cootie Williams & His Rug Cutters. Vocalion WM1043-A. Relevant manuscripts: autograph parts.

Blues in Orbit. "Star Blues," DEC. First (issued) recording: February 12, 1958. Duke Ellington & His Orchestra. RHCO40626-1; issued on *Blues in Orbit* (Columbia CK 44051). Relevant manuscripts: autograph scores and parts.

Blues to Be There. See *Newport Jazz Festival Suite* (movement 2 of 3).

Blues. "Blues I + II," DEC. First (issued) recording: February 7 or 8, 1956. Duke

Ellington & His Orchestra. Issued on *Duke Ellington Presents...*(Bethlehem 6004-2). Relevant manuscript: autograph score.

Blutopia. "Blutopia" and "Blutopia," BSC. First (issued) recording: December 19, 1944. Duke Ellington & His Orchestra. Concert; issued on *The Duke Ellington Carnegie Hall Concerts, December 1944* (Prestige 2PCD 24073-2). Relevant manuscript: autograph scores. The six bars following the piano break are by Ellington; the remainder is by Strayhorn. The arrangement is largely based on an unfinished Ellington score.

Boo-Dah. "Boo-Dah," DEC, and untitled, BSC. First (issued) recording: April 9, 1953. Duke Ellington & His Orchestra. Cap 11421-6; issued on *The Complete Capitol Recordings of Duke Ellington* (Mosaic MDS-160). Relevant manuscripts: autograph score and parts.

Boo-Dah. No manuscript known. First (issued) recording: June 30, 1965. Billy Strayhorn & The Riverside Drive Five. Issued on *Billy Strayhorn: Lush Life* (Red Baron AK-52760).

Boo-Dah. "Boo-Dah," DEC, and untitled, BSC. First (issued) recording: August 28, 1967. Duke Ellington & His Orchestra. Victor UPAI-8528; issued on *...And His Mother Called Him Bill* (RCA Bluebird 6287-2-RB). Relevant manuscripts: autograph score and parts. The manuscript is incomplete: an additional countermelody, used for the eight-bar introduction and the reprise, is missing.

Bounce. "Bounce," DEC. First (issued) recording: January 15, 1941. Duke Ellington & His Orchestra. Standard Radio Transcription 055250. Relevant manuscripts: autograph parts.

Brown Betty. "Brown Betty," DEC. First (issued) recording: November 13, 1948. Duke Ellington & His Orchestra. Concert; issued on *Duke Ellington and His Orchestra: Carnegie Hall November 13, 1948* (Vintage Jazz Classics VJC-1024/25-2). Relevant manuscript: autograph score (*K*Lite Vision Ease* sketchbook: 1-5). The manuscript is incomplete: the four-bar introduction is missing.

Brown Betty. "Brown Betty," DEC. First (issued) recording: May 24, 1951. Duke Ellington & His Orchestra. CO45830-1; issued on *The Complete Duke Ellington: 1947–1952, Vol. 4* (CBS 88035). Relevant manuscript: autograph score (*K*Lite Vision Ease* sketchbook: 1–5). Based on the same manuscript as November 13, 1948, with different soloists. The recording uses part of the manuscript: various sections were cut.

Brown Penny. "Brown Penny," DEC. First (issued) recording: October 2, 1947. Duke Ellington & His Orchestra. Columbia HCO2667-2; issued on *The Complete Duke Ellington: 1947–1952, Vol. 1* (CBS 67264). Relevant manuscript: autograph score. The first page of the manuscript (mm. 1–15) is missing.

Brown Penny. "B.P.," DEC. First (issued) recording: December 2, 1959. Duke

Ellington & His Orchestra. CO64442; issued on *Blues in Orbit* (Columbia CK 44051). Relevant manuscript: autograph score. The recording uses part of the manuscript: the trombone background (mm. 1–16), the clarinet lead in the cross-section voicing (mm. 26–27), the sax unison line (mm. 29), and an eighteen-bar section were cut.

Bugle Breaks. "Bugle Breaks," BSC. First (issued) recording: December 3, 1941. Duke Ellington & His Orchestra. Standard Radio Transcription 061946-1; issued on *Take the "A" Train: The Legendary Blanton-Webster Transcriptions* (Vintage Jazz Classics VJC 1003-2). Relevant manuscript: autograph score by Ellington and Strayhorn. *Bugle Breaks* consists of a cornet solo introduction followed by 10 blues-choruses. For choruses 1–4 no manuscripts survive. Chorus 5 is by Strayhorn, 6 and 7 are by Ellington, 8 is by both (Strayhorn first 4 and last 2 measures, Ellington remainder), 9–10 are by Strayhorn, with an additional sax riff (not on manuscript).

"C" Jam Blues, The. "Blues," BSC. First (issued) recording: January 21, 1942. Duke Ellington & His Orchestra. Victor 070683-1; issued on *The Blanton-Webster Band* (RCA Bluebird 5659-2-RB). Same as *Jam Session* November/December 1941.

Cabin in the Sky. "Fanfare Cabin-Sky Intro B Flat," DEC. First (issued) recording: September 29, 1942. Duke Ellington & His Orchestra. For the motion picture *Cabin in the Sky*; soundtrack issued on Hollywood Soundstage (HS 5003). Relevant manuscript: autograph score.

Call Me Irresponsible. "Irresponsible," DEC. First (issued) recording: April 15, 1964. Duke Ellington & His Orchestra. Reprise 5017; issued on *Ellington '65* (Reprise LP R-6122). Relevant manuscript: autograph score.

Call of the Canyon, The. "Canyon," BSC and DEC. First (issued) recording: November 7, 1940. Duke Ellington & His Orchestra. Dance-date; issued on *Duke Ellington and His Famous Orchestra, Fargo, North Dakota* (Vintage Jazz Classics VJC-1019/20-2). Relevant manuscripts: autograph score (BSC) and parts (DEC). The live recording stops 23 bars into the vocal chorus, because Jeffries was off-mike.

Can't Help Lovin' Dat Man. "Lovin' That Man," DEC. First (issued) recording: October 5, 1946. Duke Ellington & His Orchestra. Broadcast; issued on *Duke Ellington Treasury Series* (Duke Ellington Treasury Series 46). Relevant manuscript: autograph score. The recording uses part of the manuscript: the twelve-bar verse and an eight-bar modulatory section (mm. 49–56) were cut. See also Appendix C.

Candy. "Bon-Bon Candy," BSC. First (issued) recording: April 28, 1945. Duke Ellington & His Orchestra. Broadcast; issued on *Your Saturday Date with the Duke* (Duke Ellington Treasury Series 03). Relevant manuscript: autograph score.

Carribee Joe. See *A Drum Is a Woman* (track 6 of 15).

Carribee Joe—Part 2. See *A Drum Is a Woman* (track 14 of 15).
Charade. "Charade," DEC. First (issued) recording: May 19, 1964. Duke Ellington & His Orchestra. Reprise 5094; issued on *Ellington '66* (Reprise LP R-6154). Relevant manuscript: autograph score.
Charlotte Russe. No manuscript known. First (issued) recording: September/October 1947. Johnny Hodges & The Ellingtonians. Vogue M1016; issued on *The Johnny Hodges All-Stars with the Duke Ellington All-Stars and the Billy Strayhorn All-Stars: Caravan* (Prestige PCD 24103-2). A leadsheet in Strayhorn's hand is in REC.
Charpoy. "Charpoy," DEC. First (issued) recording: November 15, 1967. Duke Ellington & His Orchestra. WPA5-0919; issued on *...And His Mother Called Him Bill* (RCA Bluebird 6287-2-RB). Relevant manuscript: autograph score.
Chelsea Bridge. "Chelsea Bridge," BSC. First (issued) recording: February 16 or 20, 1941. Unissued broadcast from the Casa Mañana, Culver City, California. Relevant manuscript: autograph score. The only known full recording of *Chelsea Bridge* by the Ellington orchestra. Later recordings (September 17, 1941, and December 2, 1941) use different parts of the manuscript. The recording of June 30, 1945 (broadcast; issued on *Your Saturday Date with the Duke* [Duke Ellington Treasury Series 12]) moves after the bridge of the third chorus into *Something to Live For*.
Chelsea Bridge. "Chelsea Bridge," BSC. First (issued) recording: September 17, 1941. Duke Ellington & His Orchestra. Standard Radio Transcription; issued on *Take the "A" Train: The Legendary Blanton-Webster Transcriptions* (Vintage Jazz Classics VJC 1003-2). Relevant manuscripts: autograph score and parts. The recording uses part of the manuscript: the final, third chorus was cut. An unissued broadcast from the Casa Mañana (February 16 or 20, 1941) gives the full version of *Chelsea Bridge*. See also Appendix C.
Chelsea Bridge "Chelsea Bridge," BSC. First (issued) recording: December 2, 1941. Duke Ellington & His Orchestra. Victor 061687-2; issued on *The Blanton-Webster Band* (RCA Bluebird 5659-2-RB). The recording uses part of the manuscript: after the bridge of the second chorus, the orchestra jumps to the final eight bars of the third chorus, skipping the 32 bars in between. An unissued broadcast from the Casa Mañana (February 16 or 20, 1941) gives the full version of *Chelsea Bridge*.
Chelsea Bridge. "Chelsea Bridge," DEC. First (issued) recording: May 28, 1954. Ben Webster with Ralph Burns's Orchestra. Norgran 1724; issued on *Music for Loving: Ben Webster with Strings* (Verve 527 774-2). Relevant manuscript: autograph score.
Chelsea Bridge. "Chelsea Bridge," BSC. First (issued) recording: June 27, 1957. Ella Fitzgerald with Duke Ellington & His Orchestra. VRV21066-8; issued on *Ella Fitzgerald Sings the Duke Ellington Songbook* (Verve 837 035-2). Rele-

vant manuscript: autograph score. The recording uses part of the manuscript: an eight-bar introduction was cut.

Chelsea Bridge. "Chelsea Bridge," BSC. First (issued) recording: July 2, 1965. Billy Strayhorn & The Riverside Drive Five. Issued on *Billy Strayhorn: Lush Life* (Red Baron AK-52760). Relevant manuscript: autograph score.

Chim Chim Cheree. See *Mary Poppins* (track 2 of 12).

Chloë (Song of the Swamp). "Chloe," DEC. First (issued) recording: October 28, 1940. Duke Ellington & His Orchestra. Victor 053580-1; issued on *The Blanton-Webster Band* (RCA Bluebird 5659-2-RB). Relevant manuscripts: autograph score and parts.

Christmas Surprise, A. "A Song for Christmas," REC, and "Christmas Song," BSC. First (issued) recording: December 26, 1965. Billy Strayhorn with Lena Horne. Unissued concert. Relevant manuscripts: autograph scores.

Clementine. "Clementine," BSC. First (issued) recording: July 2, 1941. Duke Ellington & His Orchestra. Victor 061338-1. Epitaph 061661-1 (September 17, 1941) is issued on *The Blanton-Webster Band* (RCA Bluebird 5659-2-RB). Relevant manuscripts: autograph score and parts. The manuscript is incomplete: the saxophone background riff in the bridge of the trumpet solo chorus is missing.

Clementine. "Clementine" and "Clementine," BSC. First (issued) recording: June 26, 1957. Ella Fitzgerald with Duke Ellington & His Orchestra. VRV21049-2; issued on *Ella Fitzgerald Sings the Duke Ellington Songbook* (Verve 837 035-2). Relevant manuscript: autograph scores. Part of the manuscript was recorded as an instrumental on September 17, 1941.

Close to You. "Close," BSC and DEC. First (issued) recording: June 27, 1943. Duke Ellington & His Orchestra. Broadcast; issued on *Duke Ellington at the Hurricane Club, Vol. 01* (Hurricane LP HC-6001). Relevant manuscript: autograph score (BSC) and parts (DEC).

Coffee and Kisses. "Coffee + Kisses," BSC. First (issued) recording: April 29, 1954. Duke Ellington & His Orchestra. Concert; issued on *Happy Birthday: Duke Ellington and His Orchestra, April 29th, Vol. 4* (Laserlight Digital 15786). Relevant manuscript: autograph score (sketchbook no. 2: 10–15).

Come on Home. "Home," DEC. First (issued) recording: June 30, 1952. Duke Ellington & His Orchestra. CO47483-8; issued on *The Complete Duke Ellington: 1947–1952, Vol. 4* (CBS 88035). Relevant manuscript: autograph score. The manuscript is incomplete: the introduction, first, and fourth choruses are missing.

Come to Baby, Do. "Come to Mama," DEC. First (issued) recording: October 8, 1945. Duke Ellington & His Orchestra. Victor D5VB663-1; issued on *Black, Brown & Beige (The 1944–1946 Band Recordings)* (RCA Bluebird 6641-2-RB). Relevant manuscript: autograph score. The manuscript is incomplete: the sixteen-bar introduction is missing. The recording uses part of the manuscript: an eight-bar tutti was cut. The order of the recording is at variance with the order suggested by the manuscript.

Comme Çi, Comme Ça. "Coplin-Coplan," DEC. First (issued) recording: January 31, 1962. Duke Ellington & His Orchestra. CO69334; issued on *Midnight in Paris* (Columbia 468403-2). Relevant manuscript: autograph score.

Concerto for Cootie. "Cooty," DEC. First (issued) recording: March 15, 1940. Duke Ellington & His Orchestra. Victor 049015-1; issued on *The Blanton-Webster Band* (RCA Bluebird 5659-2-RB). Relevant manuscripts: autograph parts by Strayhorn, Ellington, and Tizol. As argued in Chapter 2, the eight-bar introduction is most likely by Strayhorn.

Congo Square. See *A Drum Is a Woman* (track 7 of 15).

Cordon Bleu. "Cordon Bleu," DEC. First (issued) recording: September 13, 1962. Duke Ellington & His Orchestra. Issued on *The Private Collection, Vol. 3: Studio Sessions, New York 1962* (Saja 7 91043-2). Relevant manuscript: autograph score.

Could It Be You. "Could It Be You," REC. First (issued) recording: April 3, 1943. Duke Ellington & His Orchestra. Broadcast; issued on *Duke Ellington* (Azure LP-431). Relevant manuscript: autograph score.

Cowboy Rumba. "C-R," DEC. First (issued) recording: September 29, 1947. Duke Ellington & His Orchestra. Columbia HCO2554-2; issued on *The Complete Duke Ellington: 1947–1952, Vol. 1* (CBS 67264). Relevant manuscript: autograph score. The order of the recording is at variance with the order suggested by the manuscript.

Cynthia's in Love. "Cynthia," BSC. First (issued) recording: August 17, 1946. Duke Ellington & His Orchestra. Broadcast; issued on *Your Saturday Date with the Duke* (Duke Ellington Treasury Series 43). Relevant manuscript: autograph score.

Dance of the Floreadores. See *The Nutcracker Suite* (movement 8 of 9).

Dancing in the Dark. "Dancing in the Dark," BSC. First (issued) recording: August 4, 1945. Duke Ellington & His Orchestra. Broadcast; issued on *Your Saturday Date with the Duke* (Duke Ellington Treasury Series 17). Relevant manuscript: autograph score.

Dancing in the Dark. "D. In the D," BSC and DEC. First (issued) recording: October 1, 1957. Duke Ellington & His Orchestra. CO59896; issued on *Ellington Indigos* (Columbia CK-44444). Relevant manuscripts: autograph score (sketchbook no. 5: 1–4) and parts (DEC).

Day Dream. "Day Dream (Small Band)," BSC and DEC. First (issued) recording: November 2, 1940. Johnny Hodges and His Orchestra. Bluebird 053603-1; issued on *The Great Ellington Units* (RCA Bluebird ND86751). Relevant manuscripts: autograph score (BSC) and parts (DEC).

Day Dream. "Day Dream," DEC. First (issued) recording: January 23, 1943. Duke Ellington & His Orchestra. Concert; issued on *The Duke Ellington Carnegie*

Hall Concerts, January 1943 (Prestige 2PCD 34004-2). Relevant manuscripts: autograph parts.

Day Dream. "Day Dream," BSC. First (issued) recording: June 24, 1957. Ella Fitzgerald with Duke Ellington & His Orchestra. VRV21033-6; issued on *Ella Fitzgerald Sings the Duke Ellington Songbook* (Verve 837 035-2). Relevant manuscript: autograph score.

Day Dream. "Day Dream," BSC. First (issued) recording: January 1961. Billy Strayhorn & The Paris String Quartet. Issued on *The Peaceful Side of Billy Strayhorn* (Capitol Jazz CDP 7243 8 52563 2 5). Relevant manuscript: autograph score.

Day In, Day Out. "Day-In-Day-Out," BSC. First (issued) recording: January 9, 1940. Duke Ellington & His Orchestra. Broadcast; issued on *The Duke in Boston* (Jazz Unlimited JUCD 2022). Relevant manuscripts: autograph score and parts. The recording uses part of the manuscript: a final modulation and six-bar coda were cut. This score was originally scored for a vocalist. For this recording trombonist Lawrence Brown played the vocal part, which starts after the modulation—as a result, the trombone background misses a voice.

Day In, Day Out. "In-Out-Day," BSC and DEC. First (issued) recording: May 27, 1960. Duke Ellington & His Orchestra. Concert; issued on *The Duke Live in Santa Monica, Vol. 1* (Queen Disk Q-069). Relevant manuscripts: autograph score (BSC) and parts (DEC).

Days of Wine and Roses, The. "W + R," DEC. First (issued) recording: January 19, 1965. Duke Ellington & His Orchestra. Reprise 5094; issued on *Ellington '66* (Reprise LP R-6154). Relevant manuscript: autograph score.

Dearly Beloved. "Dearly Beloved," DEC. First (issued) recording: December 17, 1942. Duke Ellington & His Orchestra. Broadcast; issued on *Duke Ellington and His Famous Orchestra* (Black Jack LP-3004). Relevant manuscripts: autograph parts.

Deep Night. "Deep Night," DEC. First (issued) recording: August 7, 1951. Duke Ellington & His Orchestra. Columbia CO47018-1; issued on *The Complete Duke Ellington: 1947–1952, Vol. 4* (CBS 88035). Relevant manuscript: autograph score. The recording uses part of the manuscript: a trombone duet in the bridge of the first chorus is replaced by a trumpet solo.

Deep Purple. "D.P.," BSC, DEC, and SIDE. First (issued) recording: February 7 or 8, 1956. Duke Ellington & His Orchestra. Issued on *Duke Ellington Presents...* (Bethlehem 6004-2). Relevant manuscripts: autograph score (BSC) and parts (DEC).

Deep South Suite (movement 2 of 4): *Hearsay*. "O. W. Hearsay," DEC. First (issued) recording: November 10, 1946. Duke Ellington & His Orchestra. Concert; issued on *The Great Chicago Concerts* (Music Master 65110-2). Relevant manuscript: autograph score. Movement 1, *Magnolias Dripping with*

Molasses (DEC), 3, *There Was Nobody Lookin'* (REC), and 4, *Happy-Go-Lucky-Local* (incomplete, REC) are by Ellington.

Diane. See *The Girls Suite* (movement 10 of 10).

Dirge. "Dirge," BSC. First (issued) recording: January 23, 1943. Duke Ellington & His Orchestra. Concert; issued on *The Duke Ellington Carnegie Hall Concerts, January 1943* (Prestige 2PCD 34004-2). Relevant manuscript: autograph score.

Do Nothin' Till You Hear from Me. "Do Nothin'," DEC. First (issued) recording: November 18, 1947. Duke Ellington & His Orchestra. Columbia CO38705-1; issued on *The Complete Duke Ellington: 1947–1952, Vol. 2* (CBS 68275). Relevant manuscript: autograph score. The manuscript is incomplete: the sixteen-bar instrumental introduction is missing.

Don't Be So Mean to Baby ('Cause Baby's So Good to You). "Don't Be So Mean," DEC. First (issued) recording: September 30, 1947. Duke Ellington & His Orchestra. Columbia HCO2662-1; issued on *The Complete Duke Ellington: 1947–1952, Vol. 1* (CBS 67264). Relevant manuscript: autograph score. The recording uses part of the manuscript: 24 bars of the instrumental chorus were cut. The order of the recording is at variance with the order suggested by the manuscript.

Don't Take Your Love from Me. "Don't Take My Love," DEC. First (issued) recording: November 3, 1945. Duke Ellington & His Orchestra. Broadcast; issued on *Your Saturday Date with the Duke* (Duke Ellington Treasury Series 29). Relevant manuscript: autograph score.

Don't Touch Me. "Don't Touch," BSC and DEC. First (issued) recording: June 30, 1953. Duke Ellington & His Orchestra. Cap 11622-6; issued on *The Complete Capitol Recordings of Duke Ellington* (Mosaic MDS-160). Relevant manuscripts: autograph score (BSC) and parts (DEC). The recording uses part of the manuscript: a thirty-two-bar instrumental chorus was cut.

Don't You Know I Care. "Don't You Know I Care," "DYKIC," and untitled, BSC. First (issued) recording: January 3, 1945. Duke Ellington & His Orchestra. Circle N-3004-1; issued on *Duke Ellington World Broadcasting Series, Vols. 1–5* (Circle CD 101-5). Relevant manuscripts: autograph scores. Ellington scored three bars of the instrumental passage following the vocal chorus; the remainder is by Strayhorn. The manuscript is incomplete: the four-bar introduction is missing. The recording uses part of the manuscript: eighteen bars were cut.

Donkey Serenade. "Donkey Serenade," DEC. First (issued) recording: March 31, 1958. Duke Ellington & His Orchestra. CO60750-8; issued on *At the Bal Masque* (Columbia LP CL-1282). Relevant manuscript: autograph score.

Double Ruff. "Double Ruff," DEC. First (issued) recording: July 17, 1946. Duke Ellington & His Orchestra. Capitol Transcriptions; issued on *Duke Ellington and His World Famous Orchestra: The Collection '46–47 Recordings* (Hindsight 501). Relevant manuscript: autograph score.

Down By (Wait for Me Mary). "Down-By (Wait for Me Mary)," BSC and DEC. First (issued) recording: June 1943. Duke Ellington & His Orchestra. Issued on *Duke Ellington Treasury Series* (Duke Ellington Treasury Series 46). Relevant manuscripts: autograph score (BSC) and parts (DEC).

Drop Me Off at Harlem. "Harlem," BSC. First (issued) recording: June 25, 1957. Ella Fitzgerald with Duke Ellington & His Orchestra. VRV21038-3; issued on *Ella Fitzgerald Sings the Duke Ellington Songbook* (Verve 837 035-2). Relevant manuscript: autograph score. The manuscript is incomplete: the final chord is missing.

Drum Is a Woman—Part 1, A. See *A Drum Is a Woman* (track 1 of 15)

Drum Is a Woman—Part 2, A. See *A Drum Is a Woman* (track 8 of 15).

Drum Is a Woman, A (track 1 of 15): *A Drum Is a Woman—Part 1*. "Drum Marg 1," BSC. First (issued) recording: September 17, 1956. Duke Ellington & His Orchestra. Issued on *A Drum Is a Woman* (Columbia 471320 2). Relevant manuscript: autograph score.

Drum Is a Woman, A (track 2 of 15): *Rhythm Pum-Te-Dum*. Untitled, BSC. First (issued) recording: September 24, 1956. Duke Ellington & His Orchestra. Issued on *A Drum Is a Woman* (Columbia 471320 2). Relevant manuscript: autograph score.

Drum Is a Woman, A (track 3 of 15): *What Else Can You Do with a Drum*. "Calyph," DEC. First (issued) recording: September 24, 1956. Duke Ellington & His Orchestra. Issued on *A Drum Is a Woman* (Columbia 471320 2). Relevant manuscript: autograph score.

Drum Is a Woman, A (track 6 of 15): *Carribee Joe*. "Carabae Joe," DEC. First (issued) recording: September 25, 1956. Duke Ellington & His Orchestra. Issued on *A Drum Is a Woman* (Columbia 471320 2). Relevant manuscript: autograph score. DEC and BSC house unfinished Ellington sketches for *Carribee Joe*.

Drum Is a Woman, A (track 7 of 15): *Congo Square*. "Matumbe," BSC, and "Mme Zajj Entrance," DEC. First (issued) recording: September 17, 1956. Duke Ellington & His Orchestra. Issued on *A Drum Is a Woman* (Columbia 471320 2). Relevant manuscript: autograph score. Section [0:39–2:40] is by Strayhorn, section [3:51–4:32] is by Ellington. The remainder is missing.

Drum Is a Woman, A (track 8 of 15): *A Drum Is a Woman—Part 2*. "Drums-Marg-Rab-#2," BSC. First (issued) recording: September 25, 1956. Duke Ellington & His Orchestra. Issued on *A Drum Is a Woman* (Columbia 471320 2). Relevant manuscript: autograph score. The recording uses part of the manuscript: various sections were cut.

Drum Is a Woman, A (track 11 of 15): *Ballet of the Flying Saucers*. "Zajing" and "T.V. Madame Zajj," BSC. First (issued) recording: October 23, 1956. Duke Ellington & His Orchestra. Issued on *A Drum Is a Woman* (Columbia 471320 2). Relevant manuscript: autograph score. The recording uses part of the manuscript: a twenty-two-bar section was cut.

Drum Is a Woman, A (track 14 of 15): *Carribee Joe—Part 2*. No manuscript known. First (issued) recording: September 25, 1956. Duke Ellington & His Orchestra. Issued on *A Drum Is a Woman* (Columbia 471320 2). Track 4, *New Orleans*, consists of Ellington narrative and background (no manuscript known); the manuscript for track 5, *Hey, Buddy Bolden*, is missing, but Clark Terry's trumpet solo in his own hand is in BSC (untitled); the manuscript for track 9, *You Better Know It*, is missing; track 10, *Madame Zajj*, consists of Ellington narrative with various backgrounds (no manuscripts known); the manuscript for track 12, *Zajj's Dream*, is missing; track 13, *Rhumbop*, is by Ellington and Jimmy Hamilton (DEC); the manuscript for track 15, *Finale*, is missing. An additional composition, *Pomegranate*, used for the telecast only, was recorded on March 7, 1957.

Drum Is a Woman, A: Pomegranate. "Pomgranate [sic]," DEC. First (issued) recording: March 7, 1957. Duke Ellington & His Orchestra. Issued on *Duke Ellington: Duke 56/62--Vol.3* (CBS 26306). Relevant manuscript: autograph score. The recording uses part of the manuscript: the introduction, an instrumental chorus, and a two-bar vamp were cut. See also Appendix C.

Eighth Veil, The. "8th Veil" and "Out World," DEC. First (issued) recording: March 28, 1946. Duke Ellington & His Orchestra. Capitol Transcriptions; issued on *Duke Ellington and His World Famous Orchestra: The Collection '46–47 Recordings* (Hindsight 501). Relevant manuscript: autograph scores. To Strayhorn's earlier arrangement of *Out of This World* (by Johnny Mercer and Harold Arlen, 1945) Ellington wrote a new trumpet theme, based on counterpoint in Strayhorn's original arrangement. Strayhorn added a new introduction.

Elf. "Elf," DEC. First (issued) recording: July 18, 1963. Duke Ellington & His Orchestra. Issued on *The Private Collection, Vol. 4: Studio Sessions, New York 1963* (Saja 7 91044-2). Relevant manuscripts: autograph score and parts. The recording uses part of the manuscript: an eight-bar tutti (apparently added later) was cut. Also recorded as *Isfahan (The Far East Suite*, movement 3), December 20, 1966.

Elysee. "Elysée," DEC. First (issued) recording: April 18, 1963. Duke Ellington & His Orchestra. Issued on *The Private Collection, Vol. 4: Studio Sessions, New York 1963* (Saja 7 91044-2). Relevant manuscript: autograph score.

Embraceable You. "Embraceable," DEC. First (issued) recording: March 20, 1946. Duke Ellington & His Orchestra. Capitol Transcriptions; issued on *Duke Ellington and His World Famous Orchestra: The Collection '46–47 Recordings* (Hindsight 501). Relevant manuscript: autograph score. The recording uses part of the manuscript: the tenor counterpoint in measures 8 and 15–16, as well as the entire background in the three final bars, were cut.

Entr'Acte. See *The Nutcracker Suite* (movement 5 of 9).

Entrance of Youth. No manuscript known. First (issued) recording: December 26 and 27, 1947. Duke Ellington & His Orchestra, with three winners of the Juilliard Duke Ellington Scholarship. Unissued concert recording from Carnegie Hall.

Esquire Swank. See *Magazine Suite* (movement 2 of 3).

Every Hour on the Hour (I Fall in Love with You). "Every Hour," BSC. First (issued) recording: August 7, 1945. Duke Ellington & His Orchestra. Circle N-3639-2; issued on *Duke Ellington World Broadcasting Series, Vols. 1–5* (Circle CD 101-5). Relevant manuscript: autograph score.

Everything but You. "Everything but You," DEC. First (issued) recording: August 7, 1945. Duke Ellington & His Orchestra. Circle N-3534-1; issued on *Duke Ellington World Broadcasting Series, Vols. 1–5* (Circle CD 101-5). Relevant manuscripts: autograph score and parts. The recording uses part of the manuscript: the final sixteen bars were cut.

Everything but You. "But You," DEC. First (issued) recording: June 25, 1957. Ella Fitzgerald with Duke Ellington & His Orchestra. VRV21036-6; issued on *Ella Fitzgerald Sings the Duke Ellington Songbook* (Verve 837 035-2). Relevant manuscript: autograph score.

Far East Suite, The (movement 2 of 8): *Blue Bird of Delhi.* "Mynah," DEC. First (issued) recording: December 20, 1966. Duke Ellington & His Orchestra. Victor TPA1-9150; issued on *The Far East Suite—Special Mix* (RCA Bluebird 07863-66551-2). Relevant manuscript: autograph score.

Far East Suite, The (movement 3 of 8): *Isfahan.* "Elf," DEC. First (issued) recording: December 20, 1966. Duke Ellington & His Orchestra. Victor TPA1-9152-1; issued on *The Far East Suite—Special Mix* (RCA Bluebird 07863-66551-2). Relevant manuscripts: autograph score and parts. Also recorded as *Elf* (without the later added eight-bar tutti passage), July 18, 1963.

Far East Suite, The (movement 7 of 8): *Agra.* "Agra," DEC. First (issued) recording: December 20, 1966. Duke Ellington & His Orchestra. Victor TPA1-9150; issued on *The Far East Suite—Special Mix* (RCA Bluebird 07863-66551-2). Relevant manuscript: autograph score. Movements 1, *Tourist Point of View*, 4, *Depk*, and 8, *Amad*, are by Ellington (DEC). The manuscripts for movements 5, *Mount Harissa*, 6, *Blue Pepper*, and 9, *Ad Lib on Nippon*, are missing.

Feed the Birds (Tuppence a Bag). See *Mary Poppins* (track 3 of 12).

Ferryboat Serenade. Untitled, DEC. First (issued) recording: November 7, 1940. Duke Ellington & His Orchestra. Dance-date; issued on *Duke Ellington and His Famous Orchestra, Fargo, North Dakota* (Vintage Jazz Classics VJC-1019/20–2). Relevant manuscripts: autograph score and parts.

Festival Junction. See *Newport Jazz Festival Suite* (movement 1 of 3).

Fiddle on the Diddle. See *Virgin Island Suite* (movement 3 of 4).

Five O'Clock Whistle. "Whistle," BSC. First (issued) recording: September 5, 1940.

Duke Ellington & His Orchestra. Victor 053429-1; issued on *The Blanton-Webster Band* (RCA Bluebird 5659-2-RB). Relevant manuscript: autograph score.

Flamingo. "Flamingo," DEC, untitled, BSC. First (issued) recording: December 28, 1940. Duke Ellington & His Orchestra. Victor 053781-1; issued on *The Blanton-Webster Band* (RCA Bluebird 5659-2-RB). Relevant manuscript: autograph score (partly in DEC [mm. 1–32 and 71–86] and partly in BSC [mm. 33–70]). Also used for an Ellington Soundie (Victor 4907), November/December, 1940.

Flamingo. "Flamingo," DEC. First (issued) recording: September 1, 1945. Duke Ellington & His Orchestra. Broadcast; issued on *Your Saturday Date with the Duke* (Duke Ellington Treasury Series 21). Relevant manuscripts: autograph score (sketchbook no. 4: 2–4). Closely matches the December 28, 1940s manuscript, but with an additional fourth trumpet.

Flamingo. "Flamingo," BSC and "Flamingo-Instrumental," DEC. First (issued) recording: April 9, 1953. Duke Ellington & His Orchestra. Cap 11406-9; issued on *The Complete Capitol Recordings of Duke Ellington* (Mosaic MDS-160). Relevant manuscripts: autograph score (sketchbook no. 3: 20–22) and parts (DEC).

Flippant Flurry. "Flip," REC. First (issued) recording: January 7, 1947. Duke Ellington & His Orchestra. Capitol Transcriptions; issued on *Duke Ellington and His World Famous Orchestra: The Collection '46–47 Recordings* (Hindsight 501). Relevant manuscript: autograph part. The order of the recording is at variance with the order suggested by the manuscript.

Flower Is a Lovesome Thing, A. "Lovesome Thing," DEC. First (issued) recording: February 13, 1941. Unissued broadcast from the Casa Mañana in Culver City, California. Relevant manuscripts: autograph parts. Only part of the performance survives—the recording fades out at the beginning of the second chorus: a full chorus and the coda remain unrecorded.

Flower Is a Lovesome Thing, A. "Lovesome Thing," DEC. First (issued) recording: July 17, 1946. Duke Ellington & His Orchestra. Capitol Transcriptions; issued on *Duke Ellington and His World Famous Orchestra: The Collection '46–47 Recordings* (Hindsight 501). Relevant manuscript: autograph score.

Flower Is a Lovesome Thing, A. "Flower," DEC. First (issued) recording: July 8, 1947. Duke Ellington & His Orchestra. CBS broadcast; issued on *The Undocumented Ellington—Vol. 1* (Up-to-Date 2001). Relevant manuscript: autograph score.

Flower Is a Lovesome Thing, A. No manuscript known. First (issued) recording: January 1961. Billy Strayhorn & The Paris String Quartet. Issued on *The Peaceful Side of Billy Strayhorn* (Capitol Jazz CDP 7243 8 52563 2 5).

Frankie and Johnny. "Frankie and Johnny," BSC. First (issued) recording: September 17, 1941. Duke Ellington & His Orchestra. Standard Radio Transcription; issued on *Take the "A" Train: The Legendary Blanton-Webster Transcriptions* (Vintage Jazz Classics VJC 1003-2). Relevant manuscript: autograph score. An earlier recording of May 29, 1941, with Ellington and the John Scott Trotter Orchestra—issued on Temple—largely follows this score, which appears to be written around January 1941.

Frankie and Johnny. "Frankie + Johnny," BSC, and "F + J," DEC. First (issued) recording: February 16, 1949. Duke Ellington & His Orchestra. SM573; for the short film *Symphony in Swing* (Universal Pictures); soundtrack issued on Azure audiocassette (available to members of the Duke Ellington Music Society, Belgium). Relevant manuscript: autograph score (BSC) and parts (DEC). "Frankie + Johnny" gives the eight-bar introduction and the ten-bar interlude; "F + J" carries the final 26 bars. The recording uses part of the manuscript: various sections were cut.

Frantic Fantasy. "Frantic Fantasy," DEC. First (issued) recording: January 2, 1945. Duke Ellington & His Orchestra. Circle N-2997-1; issued on *Duke Ellington World Broadcasting Series, Vols. 1–5* (Circle CD 101-5). Relevant manuscript: autograph score. Measures 41–44 are by Strayhorn, the remainder is by Ellington.

Frère Monk. "Frére [sic] Monk," DEC. First (issued) recording: September 13, 1962. Duke Ellington & His Orchestra. Issued on *The Private Collection, Vol. 3: Studio Sessions, New York 1962* (Saja 7 91043-2). Relevant manuscript: autograph score.

Friend of Yours, A. "Friend," BSC. First (issued) recording: May 26, 1945. Duke Ellington & His Orchestra. Broadcast; issued on *A Date with the Duke, Vol. 2* (Fairmont Records FA-1002). Relevant manuscript: autograph score.

Frisky. "Friskey," DEC. First (issued) recording: June 10, 1947. Duke Ellington & His Orchestra. Capitol Transcriptions; issued on *Duke Ellington and His World Famous Orchestra: The Collection '46–47 Recordings* (Hindsight 501). Relevant manuscript: autograph score. The manuscript is incomplete: the background riff in the first eight bars of the third chorus is missing.

Frou Frou. "Easy," BSC. First (issued) recording: March 27, 1959. Duke Ellington & His Orchestra. Sesac, issued on *The Duke's DJ Special, March 27, 1959* (Fresh Sound Records FSR-CD-141). Relevant manuscript: autograph score.

Garden in the Rain, A. "Garden in the Rain," DEC. First (issued) recording: October 25, 1946. Duke Ellington & His Orchestra. Broadcast; issued on *Duke Ellington & His Orchestra* (Fanfare LP-35135). Relevant manuscript: autograph score.

Ghost of Love. "Ghost of Love," BSC. First (issued) recording: March 24, 1959. Lil Greenwood with Duke Ellington & His Orchestra. Unissued RCA studio recording. Relevant manuscript: autograph score.

Girl in My Dreams Tries to Look Like You, The. "Like-You," DEC. First (issued) recording: December 28, 1940. Duke Ellington & His Orchestra. Victor 053782-1; issued on *The Blanton-Webster Band* (RCA Bluebird 5659-2-RB). Relevant manuscripts: autograph score by Ellington and Strayhorn. The vocal chorus is by Strayhorn with exception of the last two bars of the bridge; the remainder is by Ellington.

Girls, The. See *The Girls Suite* (movement 1 of 10).

Girls Suite, The (movement 1 of 10): *The Girls.* "Who?," REC. First (issued) recording: September 19, 1961. Duke Ellington & His Orchestra. RHCO70342-1; issued on *The Girls Suite/The Perfume Suite* (Columbia CK 469139-2). Relevant manuscript: autograph score. The order of the recording is at variance with the order suggested by the manuscript.

Girls Suite, The (movement 4 of 10): *Sweet Adeline.* "Adeline," REC. First (issued) recording: September 19, 1961. Duke Ellington & His Orchestra. RHCO70345-1; issued on *The Girls Suite/The Perfume Suite* (Columbia CK 469139-2). Relevant manuscript: autograph score. The recording uses part of the manuscript: a final sixteen-bar chorus was cut.

Girls Suite, The (movement 5 of 10): *Juanita.* "Juanita," REC. First (issued) recording: September 19, 1961. Duke Ellington & His Orchestra. RHCO70346-1; issued on *The Girls Suite/The Perfume Suite* (Columbia CK 469139-2). Relevant manuscript: autograph score.

Girls Suite, The (movement 10 of 10): *Diane.* "Diane," DEC. First (issued) recording: September 20, 1961. Duke Ellington & His Orchestra. RHCO70346-1; issued on *The Girls Suite/The Perfume Suite* (Columbia CK 469139-2). Relevant manuscript: autograph score. Movements 7, *Lena,* and 8, *Dinah,* are by Ellington; the manuscripts for movements 2, *Mahalia* (in all likelihood by Strayhorn), 3, *Peg O'My Heart,* 6, *Sylvia,* and 9, *Clementine* (not related to the 1941 Strayhorn composition) are missing.

Give Me the Right. Untitled, BSC. First (issued) recording: June 30, 1953. Duke Ellington & His Orchestra. Cap 11620-4; issued on *The Complete Capitol Recordings of Duke Ellington* (Mosaic MDS-160). Relevant manuscript: autograph score (BSC). The recording uses part of the manuscript: an eighteen-bar instrumental section was cut.

Go Away Blues. "Go Away Blues," DEC. First (issued) recording: March 24, 1959. Lil Greenwood with Duke Ellington & His Orchestra. Unissued RCA studio recording. Relevant manuscript: autograph score.

Goin' My Way. "Going My Way," DEC. First (issued) recording: May 20, 1944. Duke Ellington & His Orchestra. Unissued broadcast from The Hurricane, New York City. Relevant manuscript: autograph score.

Going Out the Back Way. "Dunbar Blues," DEC. First (issued) recording: July 3, 1941. Johnny Hodges & His Orchestra. Bluebird 061349-1; issued on *The Great Ellington Units* (RCA Bluebird ND86751). Relevant manuscripts: autograph parts.

Gonna Tan Your Hide. "Tan Your Hide," DEC. First (issued) recording: June 17, 1954. Duke Ellington & His Orchestra. Capitol 11406-9; issued on *The Complete Capitol Recordings of Duke Ellington* (Mosaic MD5-160). Relevant manuscript: autograph score. The recording uses part of the manuscript: 7 measures by Strayhorn and all 24 measures by Ellington were cut. The order of the recording is at variance with the order suggested by the manuscript.

Good Life, The. "Good Life," DEC. First (issued) recording: May 19, 1964. Duke Ellington & His Orchestra. Reprise 5024; issued on *Ellington '66* (Reprise LP R-6154). Relevant manuscript: autograph score.

Good Queen Bess. "Diaesus," DEC. First (issued) recording: November 2, 1940. Johnny Hodges and His Orchestra. Bluebird 053604-1; issued on *The Great Ellington Units* (RCA Bluebird ND86751). Relevant manuscripts: autograph parts.

Good-Bye. " 'Bye," BSC and DEC. First (issued) recording: November 29, 1962. Duke Ellington & His Orchestra. Reprise 3222; issued on *Recollections of the Big Band Era* (Atlantic Jazz 7 90043-2). Relevant manuscripts: autograph score (BSC) and parts (DEC).

Grievin'. "Grievin," DEC. First (issued) recording: October 14, 1939. Duke Ellington & His Orchestra. Columbia WM1093-A. Relevant manuscripts: autograph score by Ellington and parts by Strayhorn and Tizol. Ellington's manuscript does not carry the last twelve measures—Strayhorn added them to the parts, extracted by copyist Juan Tizol.

Grievin'. "Grievin," BSC. First (issued) recording: January 23, 1956. Rosemary Clooney with Duke Ellington & His Orchestra. Columbia CO55818; issued on *Blue Rose* (CBS 466444-2). Relevant manuscript: autograph score (sketchbook no. 5: 5–9). The final chord is by Ellington.

Gypsy Love Song. "Gypsy Sweet," DEC. First (issued) recording: April 1, 1958. Duke Ellington & His Orchestra. CO60752-6; issued on *At the Bal Masque* (Columbia LP CL-1282). Relevant manuscripts: autograph score and parts. The manuscript is incomplete: the final 2 measures are missing. The order of the recording is at variance with the order suggested by the manuscript.

Half the Fun. See *Such Sweet Thunder* (movement 11 of 12).

Haupê. See *Anatomy of a Murder* (track 12 of 13).

Have You Changed? "Have You Changed," DEC. First (issued) recording: December 3, 1941. Duke Ellington & His Orchestra. Standard Radio Transcription 061946-1; issued on *Take the "A" Train: The Legendary Blanton-Webster Transcriptions* (Vintage Jazz Classics VJC 1003-2). Relevant manuscript: autograph part.

Hayfoot, Strawfoot. "Hay Foot," BSC. First (issued) recording: July 28, 1942. Duke Ellington & His Orchestra. Victor 074781-1; issued on *The Blanton-Webster Band* (RCA Bluebird 5659-2-RB). Relevant manuscripts: autograph score and parts. The recording uses part of the manuscript: Cornetist Rex Stewart ad-libbed in lieu of the trumpet tutti (the final A-strain of the first chorus). Strayhorn replaced Ivie Anderson's initial vocal chorus in G♭ (preceded by a nine-bar modulation) with a new chorus in D♭.

He Makes Me Believe He's Mine. "Makes Me Know," DEC. First (issued) recording: November 11, 1947. Duke Ellington & His Orchestra. Columbia CO38375-1; issued on *The Complete Duke Ellington: 1947–1952, Vol. 2* (CBS 68275). Relevant manuscript: autograph score. The recording uses part of the manuscript: a sixteen-bar modulatory section was cut.

Hear My Plea. "Plea," BSC and DEC. First (issued) recording: July 1, 1953. Duke Ellington & His Orchestra. Cap 11625-10; issued on *The Complete Capitol Recordings of Duke Ellington* (Mosaic MDS-160). Relevant manuscripts: autograph score (BSC) and parts (DEC).

Hearsay. See *Deep South Suite* (movement 2 of 4).

Hello Little Girl. "Hello Little Girl," DEC. First (issued) recording: February 19, 1959. Duke Ellington & His Orchestra. CO62118; issued on *Duke Ellington's Jazz Party* (Columbia LP CL-1323). Relevant manuscript: autograph score. The recording uses part of the manuscript: the final chorus was cut.

Hey, Baby. "Hey Baby," BSC. First (issued) recording: January 27, 1956. Rosemary Clooney with Duke Ellington & His Orchestra. Columbia ZEP37983-5; issued on *Blue Rose* (CBS 466444-2). Relevant manuscript: autograph score.

History of Jazz in Three Minutes, A. "Miller," "History Jazz," "Dorsey," "Dizzy," and untitled, DEC and SIDE, "Jazz in 3 Min.," BSC. First (issued) recording: March 6, 1950. Duke Ellington & His Orchestra. For the short motion picture *Salute to Duke Ellington* (Universal Pictures); soundtrack issued on Azure audiocassette (available to members of the Duke Ellington Music Society, Belgium). Relevant manuscripts: autograph scores (on verso of "Violet Blue") and parts. The parts are divided in sections, titled "Clar. Cadenza," "Dixie," "Bop Lick," "Louie," "Miller," "Lombardo," "Dorsey," "Dizzy," "Hawk," and "Hamp."

Hit Me with a Hot Note (And Watch Me Bounce). "Hot Note," BSC. First (issued) recording: January 3, 1945. Duke Ellington & His Orchestra. Circle N-3004-2; issued on *Duke Ellington World Broadcasting Series, Vols. 1–5* (Circle CD 101-5). Relevant manuscript: autograph score.

Homesick—That's All. "Homesick," DEC. First (issued) recording: September 22, 1945. Duke Ellington & His Orchestra. Broadcast; issued on *Your Saturday Date with the Duke* (Duke Ellington Treasury Series 24). Relevant manuscript: autograph score.

Honeysuckle Rose. "Honey Suckle," BSC, SIDE, and DEC. First (issued) recording: December 1, 1943. Duke Ellington & His Orchestra. FDC N-1055-1; issued on *Duke Ellington World Broadcasting Series, Vols. 1–5* (Circle CD 101-5). Relevant manuscript: autograph score (BSC) and parts (SIDE and DEC).

How Blue the Night. "How Blue the Nite," BSC. First (issued) recording: June 3,

1944. Duke Ellington & His Orchestra. Broadcast; issued on *Duke Ellington* (White Label RM-297-298). Relevant manuscript: autograph score. The recording uses part of the manuscript: four bars preceding the four-bar coda were replaced with the four-bar intro.

How Could It Happen to a Dream. "Dream Happen," DEC. First (issued) recording: June 1947. Johnny Hodges & The Ellingtonians. Vogue M1014; issued on *The Johnny Hodges All-Stars with the Duke Ellington All-Stars and the Billy Strayhorn All-Stars: Caravan* (Prestige PCD 24103-2). Relevant manuscript: autograph score. The recording uses part of the manuscript: the four-bar introduction and an eight-bar tutti were cut. The order of the recording is at variance with the order suggested by the manuscript.

How High the Moon. "Hi-Moon," DEC. First (issued) recording: November 13, 1948. Duke Ellington & His Orchestra. Concert; issued on *Duke Ellington and His Orchestra: Carnegie Hall November 13, 1948* (Vintage Jazz Classics VJC-1024/25-2). Relevant manuscript: autograph score. The manuscript is incomplete: it carries the first thirty-two-bar chorus only. The recording uses part of the manuscript: the eight-bar introduction was discarded and replaced by another (manuscript missing).

I Ain't Got Nothin' but the Blues. "Nothin' but The Blues," BSC. First (issued) recording: June 25, 1957. Ella Fitzgerald with Duke Ellington & His Orchestra. VRV21040-4; issued on *Ella Fitzgerald Sings the Duke Ellington Songbook* (Verve 837 035-2). Relevant manuscript: autograph score.

I Can't Begin to Tell You. "I Can't Begin To Tell You," DEC. First (issued) recording: November 17, 1945. Duke Ellington & His Orchestra. Broadcast; issued on *Your Saturday Date with the Duke* (Duke Ellington Treasury Series 31). Relevant manuscript: autograph score.

I Could Get a Man (But the Man I Want Is Got). "Want Is Got," DEC. First (issued) recording: December 22, 1947. Duke Ellington & His Orchestra. Columbia CO38591-1; issued on *The Complete Duke Ellington: 1947–1952, Vol. 2* (CBS 68275). Relevant manuscript: autograph score. The recording uses part of the manuscript: an eight-bar repeat and a saxophone solo with backgrounds were cut.

I Couldn't Have Done It Alone. See *All American in Jazz* (track 8 of 10).

I Didn't Know About You. "I Didn't Know," BSC. First (issued) recording: January 2, 1945. Duke Ellington & His Orchestra. Circle N-2995-4; issued on *Duke Ellington World Broadcasting Series, Vols. 1–5* (Circle CD 101-5). Relevant manuscript: autograph score.

I Didn't Know About You. "Didn't Know About You," BSC. First (issued) recording: June 26, 1957. Ella Fitzgerald with Duke Ellington & His Orchestra. VRV21052-2; issued on *Ella Fitzgerald Sings the Duke Ellington Songbook* (Verve 837 035-2). Relevant manuscript: autograph score.

I Don't Stand a Ghost of a Chance with You. "Ghost of A Chance," DEC. First (issued) recording: June 1, 1946. Duke Ellington & His Orchestra. Broadcast; issued on *Your Saturday Date with the Duke* (Duke Ellington Treasury Series 38). Relevant manuscript: autograph score.

I Don't Want Anybody at All (If I Can't Have You). "Don't Want Nobody," REC and DEC. First (issued) recording: November 9, 1943. Duke Ellington & His Orchestra. Circle BB37667D C1-2; issued on *Duke Ellington World Broadcasting Series, Vols. 1–5* (Circle CD 101-5). Relevant manuscript: autograph score (REC) and parts (DEC). The parts carry the final ten-bar section missing from the score.

I Don't Want to Walk Without You, Baby. "Walk," DEC. First (issued) recording: August 29, 1942. Duke Ellington & His Orchestra. Broadcast; issued on *Duke Ellington and His Orchestra 1941–1943* (Temple LP M-554). Relevant manuscripts: autograph score and parts. The recording uses part of the manuscript: the second ending on the first A-strain and a following sixteen-bar tutti were cut.

I Fell and Broke My Heart. "Fell and Broke" and untitled, DEC. First (issued) recording: September 29, 1947. Duke Ellington & His Orchestra. Columbia HCO2656-1; issued on *The Complete Duke Ellington: 1947–1952, Vol. 1* (CBS 67264). Relevant manuscripts: autograph scores. Pieced together from two manuscripts (the second transposed from D^b to C). The recording uses part of the second manuscript: measures 1–44 and 69–84 were cut. The order of the recording is at variance with the order suggested by the manuscripts.

I Got It Bad (and That Ain't Good). "Got It Bad" and "Bad-Good," DEC. First (issued) recording: June 26, 1941. Duke Ellington & His Orchestra. Victor 061319-1; issued on *The Blanton-Webster Band* (RCA Bluebird 5659-2-RB). Relevant manuscripts: autograph score and parts. The score carries the thirty-two-bar vocal chorus; the parts carry an additional eight-bar introduction. The eight-bar alto saxophone interlude preceding the vocal recapitulation is missing. The parts carry some additional sections by Strayhorn and copyist Tizol, not used for any known recording.

I Got It Bad (and That Ain't Good). "Got it Bad" and "Bad-Good," DEC. First (issued) recording: November/December 1941. Duke Ellington & His Orchestra. Ellington Soundie, Storyville 5105. Relevant manuscripts: autograph score and parts. Largely matching the earlier June 26, 1941, recording, this version carries a new final A-strain (no manuscript known).

I Got It Bad (and That Ain't Good). "Got It Bad," DEC. First (issued) recording: May 5, 1945. Duke Ellington & His Orchestra. Broadcast; issued on *Your Saturday Date with the Duke* (Duke Ellington Treasury Series 04). Relevant manuscript: autograph score.

I Got It Bad (and That Ain't Good). "Got it Bad (Avon)," BSC and untitled, DEC. First (issued) recording: May 3, 1951. Duke Ellington & His Orchestra. MBS telecast, issued on *Hooray for Duke Ellington* (Session Disc LP 107). Relevant manuscript: autograph scores. The recording uses part of the manuscript: the untitled score replaces the first 26 bars of the BSC score.

I Got It Bad (and That Ain't Good). "Rochés Bad Got Busted," BSC. First (issued) recording: January 27, 1956. Rosemary Clooney with Duke Ellington & His Orchestra. Columbia ZEP37987; issued on *Blue Rose* (CBS 466444-2). Relevant manuscript: autograph score. Originally performed with Betty Roché (unissued broadcast, November 28, 1952) and performed as an instrumental with guest soloist Stan Getz (issued on *Stan Getz Special—Vol. 2* [Raretone LP 5012-FC], February 9, 1953).

I Got It Bad (and That Ain't Good). "Got It Bad (Hodges)," BSC. First (issued) recording: June 1957. Duke Ellington & His Orchestra. Concert; issued on *All Star Road Band* (Doctor Jazz W2X-39137). Relevant manuscript: autograph score. The manuscript is incomplete: the final two bars of the bridge and the last chord are missing.

I Got It Bad (and That Ain't Good). "I Got It Bad," BSC. First (issued) recording: June 25, 1957. Ella Fitzgerald with Duke Ellington & His Orchestra. VRV21037-6; issued on *Ella Fitzgerald Sings the Duke Ellington Songbook* (Verve 837 035-2). Relevant manuscript: autograph score. The manuscript is incomplete: the alto solo section is missing.

I Got It Bad (and That Ain't Good). "Green-Bad," BSC. First (issued) recording: July 3, 1958. Duke Ellington & His Orchestra. Concert, issued on *Duke Ellington Live at Newport 1958* (Columbia C2K-53584). Relevant manuscript: autograph score.

I Got It Bad (and That Ain't Good). "Got It Bad Verse," DEC. First (issued) recording: March 24, 1959. Lil Greenwood with Duke Ellington & His Orchestra. Unissued RCA studio recording. Relevant manuscript: autograph score. The recording uses part of the manuscript: the first 16 bars of the second chorus were cut.

I Know What You Know (I Know What You Do). Untitled, BSC. First (issued) recording: October 14, 1939. Johnny Hodges & His Orchestra. Vocalion WM1097-A. Relevant manuscript: autograph score.

I Left My Heart in San Francisco. "San-Fran," DEC. First (issued) recording: April 27, 1964. Duke Ellington & His Orchestra. Reprise 5024; issued on *Ellington '65* (Reprise LP R-6122). Relevant manuscript: autograph score.

I Left My Sugar in Salt Lake City. "Salt Lake," DEC. First (issued) recording: July 1943. Duke Ellington & His Orchestra. Unissued broadcast (WMCA). Relevant manuscripts: autograph parts.

I Let a Song Go Out of My Heart. "Let a Song," DEC. First (issued) recording: May 15, 1945. Duke Ellington & His Orchestra. Victor D5VB269-1; issued on *Black, Brown & Beige (The 1944–1946 Band Recordings)* (RCA Bluebird 6641-2-RB). Relevant manuscript: autograph score. The manuscript is incomplete: the first two choruses are missing. The recording uses

part of the manuscript: only the final twenty bars, after the vocal chorus.
I Let a Song Go Out of My Heart. "I Let a Song (2nd Chos)," DEC. First (issued) recording: January 27, 1956. Rosemary Clooney with Duke Ellington & His Orchestra. Columbia ZEP37987; issued on *Blue Rose* (CBS 466444-2). Relevant manuscript: autograph score. The manuscript is incomplete: the first and third choruses are missing.
I Love to Laugh. See *Mary Poppins* (track 6 of 12).
I Want to Live. "Live," DEC. First (issued) recording: September/October 1940. Duke Ellington & His Orchestra. Relevant manuscripts: autograph parts. Unissued broadcast from the Hotel Sherman, Chicago, Illinois.
I Wish You Love. "Wish You Love," DEC. First (issued) recording: June 26, 1962. Duke Ellington & His Orchestra. CO75582-10; issued on *Midnight in Paris* (Columbia 468403-2). Relevant manuscripts: autograph score and parts. The manuscript is incomplete: the final chord is missing.
I Wonder Why. "I.W. Harper," BSC. First (issued) recording: November 9, 1943. Duke Ellington & His Orchestra. Circle BB37667C C1-2; issued on *Duke Ellington World Broadcasting Series, Vols. 1–5* (Circle CD 101-5). Relevant manuscript: autograph score (BSC). (I.W. Harper is a bourbon whisky.)
I Wonder Why. "Wonder Why," BSC. First (issued) recording: March 24, 1959. Lil Greenwood with Duke Ellington & His Orchestra. Unissued RCA studio recording. Relevant manuscript: autograph score. The order of the recording is at variance with the order suggested by the manuscript.
I'd Do It All over Again. "I'd Do It All over," DEC. First (issued) recording: October 20, 1945. Duke Ellington & His Orchestra. Broadcast; issued on *Your Saturday Date with the Duke* (Duke Ellington Treasury Series 28). Relevant manuscript: autograph score.
I'll Buy That Dream. "Buy That Dream," DEC. First (issued) recording: October 13, 1945. Duke Ellington & His Orchestra. Broadcast; issued on *Your Saturday Date with the Duke* (Duke Ellington Treasury Series 26). Relevant manuscript: autograph score.
I'll Get By. "I'll Get By," BSC. First (issued) recording: April 13, 1944. Duke Ellington & His Orchestra. Unissued broadcast from The Hurricane, New York City. Relevant manuscript: autograph score.
I'm Checking Out, Goom-Bye. "Goom-Bye" and "Middle of Voc Goombye," DEC. First (issued) recording: June 12, 1939. Duke Ellington & His Orchestra. Columbia WM1039-A. Relevant manuscripts: autograph score by Ellington and parts by Strayhorn. The four-bar modulation following the first chorus (mm. 33–36) and the nine-bar coda are by Strayhorn; the remainder is by Ellington.
I'm Checkin' Out, Goom Bye. "Checkin' Out," BSC. First (issued) recording: January 23, 1956. Rosemary Clooney with Duke Ellington & His Orchestra. Columbia ZEP37984; issued on *Blue Rose* (CBS 466444-2). Relevant manuscript: autograph score.
I'm Getting Sentimental over You. "Gettin' Sent," DEC. First (issued) recording:

November 29, 1962. Duke Ellington & His Orchestra. ARC 3225; issued on *Recollections of the Big Band Era* (Atlantic Jazz 7 90043-2). Relevant manuscripts: autograph parts.

I'm Just a Lucky So and So. "Lucky So + So," BSC. First (issued) recording: June 26, 1957. Ella Fitzgerald with Duke Ellington & His Orchestra. VRV21050-1; issued on *Ella Fitzgerald Sings the Duke Ellington Songbook* (Verve 837 035-2). Relevant manuscript: autograph score.

I'm Just a Lucky So and So. "Lucky So + So," BSC. First (issued) recording: June 2, 1960. Duke Ellington & His Orchestra. RHCO46671; issued on *Duke 56/62, Vol. 3* (CBS 26306). Relevant manuscript: autograph score.

I'm Walkin' with My Honey. "Walkin' with My Honey," DEC. First (issued) recording: November 17, 1945. Duke Ellington & His Orchestra. Broadcast; issued on *Your Saturday Date with the Duke* (Duke Ellington Treasury Series 31). Relevant manuscript: autograph score. The manuscript is incomplete: the final sixteen bars are missing.

I've Just Seen Her. See *All American in Jazz* (track 2 of 10).

If I Were You. See *All American in Jazz* (track 4 of 10).

If You Are but a Dream. "If You Were but a Dream," BSC. First (issued) recording: April 21, 1945. Duke Ellington & His Orchestra. Broadcast; issued on *Your Saturday Date with the Duke* (Duke Ellington Treasury Series 02). Relevant manuscript: autograph score.

If You Were in My Place. "In My Place," BSC. First (issued) recording: January 23, 1956. Rosemary Clooney with Duke Ellington & His Orchestra. Columbia CO55591; issued on *Blue Rose* (CBS 466444-2). Relevant manuscript: autograph score.

In a Sentimental Mood. "S. Mood," DEC. First (issued) recording: February 1957. Duke Ellington & His Orchestra. Issued on *The Private Collection, Vol. 1: Studio Sessions Chicago 1956* (Saja 7 91041-2). Relevant manuscript: autograph score.

Indian Love Call. "Love Call," DEC. First (issued) recording: March 26, 1958. Duke Ellington & His Orchestra. CO607506-8; issued on *At the Bal Masque* (Columbia LP CL-1282). Relevant manuscript: autograph score. The recording uses part of the manuscript: a nine-bar section was cut. The order of the recording is at variance with the order suggested by the manuscript.

Indian Summer. "Indian Summer," DEC. First (issued) recording: May 18, 1951. The Coronets. Mercer Records M4035; issued on *The Johnny Hodges All-Stars with the Duke Ellington All-Stars and the Billy Strayhorn All-Stars: Caravan* (Prestige PCD 24103-2). Relevant manuscripts: autograph parts (on verso of *Swamp Drum*).

Indian Summer. "Indian Summer," BSC and DEC. First (issued) recording: February 7 or 8, 1956. Duke Ellington & His Orchestra. Issued on *Duke Ellington Presents...* (Bethlehem 6004-2). Relevant manuscripts: autograph score (BSC) and parts (DEC).

Intimacy of the Blues, The. "Hi, Figh, Fo, Fum," DEC. First (issued) recording: March 15, 1967. Duke Ellington's Sextet. Fantasy; issued on *The Combo Suite* (Fantasy F-9640). Relevant manuscript: autograph score. The originally untitled manuscript carries unused sections by Ellington; the titles were added by Ellington. Also used for November 15, 1967.

Intimacy of the Blues, The. "Hi, Figh, Fo, Fum," DEC. First (issued) recording: November 15, 1967. Duke Ellington & His Orchestra. Victor WPA5-0918; issued on...*And His Mother Called Him Bill* (RCA Bluebird 6287-2-RB). Relevant manuscript: autograph score. Based on the same manuscript as March 15, 1967.

Irresistible You. "Irresistible You," DEC. First (issued) recording: June 3, 1944. Duke Ellington & His Orchestra. Broadcast; issued on untitled LP (White Label RM-297/298). Relevant manuscripts: autograph parts.

Isfahan. See *The Far East Suite* (movement 3 of 8).

Island Virgin. See *Virgin Island Suite* (movement 1 of 4).

It Can't Be Wrong. "ICBW," BSC. First (issued) recording: June 1943. Duke Ellington & His Orchestra. Issued on *Duke Ellington Treasury Series* (Duke Ellington Treasury Series 46). Relevant manuscript: autograph score.

It Don't Mean a Thing (If It Ain't Got That Swing). "IDMAT," DEC. First (issued) recording: June 17 and 19, 1943. Duke Ellington & His Orchestra. For the motion picture *An RKO Jamboree.* Relevant manuscript: autograph score. The manuscript is incomplete: sixteen bars of the out-chorus are missing. The recording uses part of the manuscript: the ten-bar introduction was discarded. Also recorded commercially on December 1, 1943. Parts of the manuscript were used for the vocal version of May 14, 1945.

It Don't Mean a Thing (If It Ain't Got That Swing). "IDMAT," DEC. First (issued) recording: December 1, 1943. Duke Ellington & His Orchestra. Circle N-1055-1; issued on *Duke Ellington World Broadcasting Series, Vols. 1–5* (Circle CD 101-5). Relevant manuscript: autograph score. The manuscript is incomplete: sixteen bars of the out-chorus are missing. The recording uses part of the manuscript: the ten-bar introduction was discarded. Also recorded for the film *An RKO Jamboree* (June 17, 1943).

It Don't Mean a Thing (If It Ain't Got That Swing). "IDMAT," DEC. First (issued) recording: May 14, 1945. Duke Ellington & His Orchestra. Victor D5VB269-1; issued on *Black, Brown & Beige (The 1944–1946 Band Recordings)* (RCA Bluebird 6641-2-RB). Relevant manuscript: autograph score. The recording uses part of the instrumental June 17, 1943, manuscript: the first two choruses are omitted. The manuscript is incomplete: sixteen bars of the out-chorus are missing.

It Don't Mean a Thing (If It Ain't Got That Swing). "It Don't," BSC. First (issued) recording: January 27, 1956. Rosemary Clooney with Duke Ellington & His Orchestra. Columbia ZEP37988; issued on *Blue Rose* (CBS 466444-2). Relevant manuscript: autograph score. The manuscript is incomplete: the final chorus (starting at the baritone solo) and coda are missing.

It Happens to Be Me. "It Happens to Be Me," DEC. First (issued) recording: May 28, 1954. Ben Webster with Ralph Burns's Orchestra. Norgran 1722; issued on *Music for Loving: Ben Webster with Strings* (Verve 527 774-2). Relevant manuscript: autograph score.

It Shouldn't Happen to a Dream. "It Shouldn't," BSC. First (issued) recording: December 18, 1946. Duke Ellington & His Orchestra. Mu 5842-3; issued on *Happy-Go-Lucky Local* (Musicraft MVCSD-52). Relevant manuscript: autograph score.

It's a Lonesome Old Town When You're Not Around. "Lonely Town" and "Lonesome Old Town," DEC. First (issued) recording: December 11, 1962. Duke Ellington & His Orchestra. ARC 3370-10; issued on *Recollections of the Big Band Era* (Atlantic Jazz 7 90043-2). Relevant manuscript: autograph score. The recording uses part of the manuscript: a solo trombone replaced the initial two-part trombone statement.

It's Kind of Lonesome Out Tonight. "Lonesome Out," BSC. First (issued) recording: August 1, 1947. Duke Ellington & His Orchestra. Broadcast; issued on *Spotlight on Duke Ellington* (Joyce LP-4014). Relevant manuscript: autograph score.

It's Love I'm In. "Love I'm In," DEC. First (issued) recording: November 20, 1947. Duke Ellington & His Orchestra. Columbia CO38400-1; issued on *The Complete Duke Ellington: 1947–1952, Vol. 2* (CBS 68275). Relevant manuscript: autograph score. The recording uses part of the manuscript: the background of measures 1–16 has been cut.

It's Mad, Mad, Mad! "Mad!," DEC. First (issued) recording: October 1, 1947. Duke Ellington & His Orchestra. Columbia HCO2663-1; issued on *The Complete Duke Ellington: 1947–1952, Vol. 1* (CBS 67264). Relevant manuscript: autograph score. The recording uses part of the manuscript: a four-bar transition from the instrumental chorus to the vocal chorus was replaced by four bars of piano. The order of the recording is at variance with the order suggested by the manuscript.

It's Monday Every Day. "Monday Every Day," DEC. First (issued) recording: September 1, 1947. Duke Ellington & His Orchestra. Columbia HCO2596-1; issued on *The Complete Duke Ellington: 1947–1952, Vol. 1* (CBS 67264). Relevant manuscript: autograph score.

It's Monday Every Day. "Monday Every Day," BSC. First (issued) recording: November 13, 1948. Duke Ellington & His Orchestra. Concert; issued on *Duke Ellington and His Orchestra: Carnegie Hall November 13, 1948* (Vintage Jazz Classics VJC-1024/25-2). Relevant manuscript: autograph score. The manuscript is incomplete: the six-bar trombone solo section preceding the five-bar coda is missing. The recording uses part of the manuscript: a thirty-two-bar trombone solo chorus was cut.

It's Sad but True. "True-Sad," DEC. First (issued) recording: January 15, 1941. Duke Ellington & His Orchestra. Standard Radio Transcription 055250; issued on *Take the "A" Train: The Legendary Blanton-Webster Transcriptions* (Vintage Jazz Classics VJC 1003-2). Relevant manuscripts: autograph parts.

It's Square, but It Rocks. "Rocks," BSC. First (issued) recording: June 16, 1941. Duke Ellington & His Orchestra. Unissued MBS broadcast. Relevant manuscripts: autograph score (BSC) and parts (DEC).

Jam Session. "Blues," BSC. First (issued) recording: November/December 1941. Duke Ellington & His Orchestra. Ellington Soundie, Extreme Rarities 5503. Relevant manuscripts: autograph score and parts. The two out-choruses are by Strayhorn, the remainder of the composition consists of solo choruses without scored backgrounds. Ellington is possibly the composer of the theme, which was recorded by Barney Bigard and His Orchestra as *"C" Blues*, September 29, 1941, with Strayhorn as pianist. Same as *The C-Jam Blues*, January 21, 1942.

Jeep Is Jumping, The. "Jeep Is Jumping," BSC. First (issued) recording: March 28, 1946. Duke Ellington & His Orchestra. Capitol Transcriptions; issued on *Duke Ellington and His World Famous Orchestra: The Collection '46–47 Recordings* (Hindsight 501). Relevant manuscripts: autograph parts.

Johnny Come Lately. "Moe" and "Johnny Come Lately," DEC. First (issued) recording: June 26, 1942. Duke Ellington & His Orchestra. Victor 072439-1; issued on *The Blanton-Webster Band* (RCA Bluebird 5659-2-RB). Relevant manuscript: autograph score.

Johnny Come Lately. Untitled, BSC. First (issued) recording: February 1952. The Just Jazz All-Stars. Cap 9941, issued on *The Just Jazz All-Stars* (Capitol). Relevant manuscript: autograph score.

Jolly Holiday. See *Mary Poppins* (track 7 of 12).

Juanita. See *The Girls Suite* (movement 5 of 10).

Just Another Dream. Untitled, BSC. First (issued) recording: June 8, 1939. Barney Bigard & His Orchestra. Okeh WM1037-A. Relevant manuscript: autograph score. The introduction, first chorus, and second and fourth strains of the second chorus are by Strayhorn (mm. 1–36, 45–52, and 61–67); the first and third strains of second chorus are by Ellington (mm. 37–44 and 53–60).

Just as Though You Were Here. "Just as Tho," BSC. First (issued) recording: November 19, 1942. Duke Ellington & His Orchestra. Broadcast; issued on *Way Low* (Duke Records D-1015). Relevant manuscripts: autograph score and parts.

Just A-Settin' and A-Rockin'. No manuscript known. First (issued) recording: June 5, 1941. Duke Ellington & His Orchestra. Victor 061285-1; issued on *The Blanton-Webster Band* (RCA Bluebird 5659-2-RB). Though the original score is missing, various original sketches by Strayhorn survive ("Jocco," sketchbook no. 8: 8 [BSC], and untitled, sketchbook no. 1: 5 [REC]).

Just A-Settin' and A-Rockin'. "Settin' + Rockin'," BSC. First (issued) recording: January 27, 1956. Rosemary Clooney with Duke Ellington & His Orchestra. Columbia ZEP37986; issued on *Blue Rose* (CBS 466444-2). Relevant manuscript: autograph score.

Just A-Settin' and A-Rockin'. "Rockin'," BSC. First (issued) recording: January 1961. Billy Strayhorn & The Paris String Quartet. Issued on *The Peaceful Side of Billy Strayhorn* (Capitol Jazz CDP 7243 8 52563 2 5). Relevant manuscript: autograph part.

Just Squeeze Me. "Squeeze Me," BSC. First (issued) recording: November 24, 1952. Duke Ellington & His Orchestra. NBC broadcast; issued on *Duke Ellington at Birdland, 1952* (Jazz Unlimited JUCD-2036). Relevant manuscript: autograph score. The manuscript is incomplete: the background behind the vocals is missing. The recording uses part of the manuscript: the instrumental bridge was discarded.

Killin' Myself. "Killing Myself," BSC and DEC. First (issued) recording: October 16, 1939. Duke Ellington & His Orchestra. Columbia WM1106-A; issued on *Duke Ellington and His Orchestra 1939–1940* (Classics 790). Relevant manuscripts: autograph score (BSC) and parts (DEC).

Kissing Bug, The. "Kissing Bug," BSC. First (issued) recording: August 7, 1945. Duke Ellington & His Orchestra. Circle N-3538-1; issued on *Duke Ellington World Broadcasting Series, Vols. 1–5* (Circle CD 101-5). Relevant manuscript: autograph score. The recording uses part of the manuscript: mm. 1–8 and 24 bars of the instrumental chorus were cut. The order of the recording is at variance with the order suggested by the manuscript.

Lady in Red. "Lady Red," DEC. First (issued) recording: March 31, 1958. Duke Ellington & His Orchestra. CO60707-9; issued on *At the Bal Masque* (Columbia LP CL-1282). Relevant manuscript: autograph score.

Lament for Javanette. No manuscript known. First (issued) recording: November 11, 1940. Barney Bigard & His Orchestra. Victor 053622-1; issued on *The Great Ellington Units* (RCA Bluebird ND86751).

Last Time I Saw You, The. "Last Time I Saw You," DEC. First (issued) recording: November 24, 1945. Duke Ellington & His Orchestra. Broadcast; issued on *Your Saturday Date with the Duke* (Duke Ellington Treasury Series 32). Relevant manuscript: autograph score.

Lately. "Lately," DEC. First (issued) recording: August 7, 1956. Duke Ellington & His Orchestra. Columbia CO56566-1; issued on *The Studio Series, Vol. 5* (Up to Date 2005). Relevant manuscripts: autograph score and parts. Also recorded as *Half the Fun* (movement 11 of *Such Sweet Thunder*).

Laura. "Laura," DEC. First (issued) recording: February 7 or 8, 1956. Duke Ellington & His Orchestra. Issued on *Duke Ellington Presents...* (Bethlehem 6004-2). Relevant manuscript: autograph score.

Lily Belle. "Lily Belle," BSC. First (issued) recording: October 6, 1945. Duke Ellington & His Orchestra. Broadcast; issued on *Your Saturday Date with the Duke* (Duke Ellington Treasury Series 25). Relevant manuscript: autograph score. The manuscript is incomplete: the last eight bars are missing.

Limehouse Blues. "Lime House," DEC. First (issued) recording: November 13, 1948. Duke Ellington & His Orchestra. Concert; issued on *Duke Ellington and His Orchestra: Carnegie Hall November 13, 1948* (Vintage Jazz Classics VJC-1024/25-2). Relevant manuscript: autograph score.

Lonely Ones, The. "Loneley [sic] Ones," BSC. First (issued) recording: September 26, 1958. Johnny Ray with Duke Ellington & His Orchestra. CO61513; issued on *Duke 56/62, Vol. 3* (CBS 26306). Relevant manuscript: autograph score (sketchbook no. 4). The recording uses part of the manuscript: an instrumental chorus and four bars from the coda were cut.

Lonely Ones, The. "Lonely Ones," DEC. First (issued) recording: September 13, 1962. Duke Ellington & His Orchestra. Issued on *The Private Collection, Vol. 3: Studio Sessions, New York 1962* (Saja 7 91043-2). Relevant manuscript: autograph score.

Lost in Meditation. "Lost In Meditation," BSC. First (issued) recording: June 25, 1957. Ella Fitzgerald with Duke Ellington & His Orchestra. VRV21039-4; issued on *Ella Fitzgerald Sings the Duke Ellington Songbook* (Verve 837 035-2). Relevant manuscript: autograph score.

Lost in the Night. "Lost in the Night," BSC. First (issued) recording: March 27, 1959. Duke Ellington & His Orchestra. Sesac, issued on *The Duke's DJ Special, March 27, 1959* (Fresh Sound Records FSR CD-141). Relevant manuscript: autograph score.

Lost in Two Flats. "Lost in Two Flats," BSC. First (issued) recording: November 22, 1939. Barney Bigard & His Orchestra. Vocalion WM1118-A; issued on *Duke Ellington and His Orchestra 1939–1940* (Classics 790). Relevant manuscript: autograph score.

Love and I. "Love and I," BSC. First (issued) recording: January 15, 1941. Duke Ellington & His Orchestra. Standard Radio Transcription 055251; issued on *Take the "A" Train: The Legendary Blanton-Webster Transcriptions* (Vintage Jazz Classics VJC 1003-2). Relevant manuscripts: autograph score and parts.

Love Is Here to Stay. "Here to Stay," DEC. First (issued) recording: May 28, 1954. Ben Webster with Ralph Burns's Orchestra. Norgran 1721; issued on *Music for Loving: Ben Webster with Strings* (Verve 527 774-2). Relevant manuscript: autograph score.

Love Letters. "Love Letters," DEC. First (issued) recording: October 7, 1945. Duke Ellington & His Orchestra. Broadcast; issued on *One Night Stand with the Duke Return to the Zanzibar* (Joyce LP 1071). Relevant manuscript: autograph score.

Love Like This Can't Last. "Can't Last," BSC. First (issued) recording: September 17, 1941. Duke Ellington & His Orchestra. Standard Radio Transcription; issued on *Take the "A" Train: The Legendary Blanton-Webster Transcriptions* (Vintage Jazz Classics VJC 1003-2). Relevant manuscripts: autograph score and parts.

Love You Madly. "Sarah-Nat-Madly," BSC. First (issued) recording: November 15, 1951. Sarah Vaughan, Nat "King" Cole, and Duke Ellington with an unidentified orchestra. Unissued concert at the University of Michigan. Relevant manuscript: autograph score (sketchbook no. 1: 12–15).

Love You Madly. "Madly," BSC. First (issued) recording: March 24, 1959. Lil Greenwood with Duke Ellington & His Orchestra. Unissued RCA studio recording. Relevant manuscript: autograph score. The manuscript is incomplete: the eight-bar introduction and four-bar coda are missing.

Love. See *Perfume Suite* (movement 1 of 4).

Lover Man. "Lover Man," DEC. First (issued) recording: August 26, 1946. Duke Ellington & His Orchestra. Victor D6VB2115-2; issued on *Black, Brown & Beige (The 1944–1946 Band Recordings)* (RCA Bluebird 6641-2-RB). Relevant manuscript: autograph score. The recording uses part of the manuscript: the six-bar introduction and a sixteen-bar middle section were cut. See also Appendix C.

Low Key Lightly. See *Anatomy of a Murder* (track 5 of 13).

Lullaby of Birdland. "Lullaby of Birdland," BSC. First (issued) recording: November 14, 1952. Duke Ellington & His Orchestra. Concert; issued on *Duke Ellington at Birdland, 1952* (Jazz Unlimited JUCD 2036). Relevant manuscript: autograph score.

Lush Life. "Lush Life," BSC. First (issued) recording: January 1961. Billy Strayhorn & The Paris String Quartet. Issued on *The Peaceful Side of Billy Strayhorn* (Capitol Jazz CDP 7243 8 52563 2 5). Relevant manuscript: autograph score.

Magazine Suite (movement 2 of 3): *Esquire Swank.* "Esquire," BSC. First (issued) recording: July 31, 1945. Duke Ellington & His Orchestra. Circle N-3516-4; issued on *Duke Ellington World Broadcasting Series, Vols. 1–5* (Circle CD 101-5). Relevant manuscript: autograph score. The alto solo introduction and the unison brass line following the trumpet solo are by Ellington; the remainder is by Strayhorn. The manuscript is incomplete: the brass interjections following the unison brass line are missing. Movements 1, *Down Beat Shuffle*, and 3, *Metronome All Out*, are by Ellington.

Main Title & Anatomy of a Murder. See *Anatomy of a Murder* (track 1 of 13).

Manhattan Murals. "Take the 'A' Train," BSC, "A Train," and " 'A' Train (Cont.)," DEC. First (issued) recording: November 13, 1948. Duke Ellington & His Orchestra. Concert; issued on *Duke Ellington and His Orchestra: Carnegie Hall November 13, 1948* (Vintage Jazz Classics VJC-1024/25-2). Relevant manuscripts: autograph scores. Pieced together from the original January 15, 1941, manuscript and two new scores. All orchestral sections are by Strayhorn but for the first eight bars of the third chorus, which are by Ellington.

Mary Poppins (track 1 of 12): *A Spoonful of Sugar.* "Sucre," BSC. First (issued) recording: September 6, 8, or 9, 1964. Duke Ellington & His Orchestra. Reprise 2948; issued on *Duke Ellington Plays with the Original Score from Walt Disney's Mary Poppins* (Reprise R-6141). Relevant manuscript: autograph score.

Mary Poppins (track 2 of 12): *Chim Chim Cheree.* "Chim-Chim," BSC. First (issued) recording: September 6, 8, or 9, 1964. Duke Ellington & His Orchestra. Reprise 2953; issued on *Duke Ellington Plays with the Original Score from Walt Disney's Mary Poppins* (Reprise R-6141). Relevant manuscript: autograph score. Measures 1–64 are by Strayhorn, measures 65–100 are by Ellington.

Mary Poppins (track 3 of 12): *Feed the Birds (Tuppence a Bag).* "Oiseaux," BSC. First (issued) recording: September 6, 8, or 9, 1964. Duke Ellington & His Orchestra. Reprise 2950; issued on *Duke Ellington Plays with the Original Score from Walt Disney's Mary Poppins* (Reprise R-6141). Relevant manuscript: autograph score.

Mary Poppins (track 5 of 12): *Stay Awake.* "Stay Awake," BSC. First (issued) recording: September 6, 8, or 9, 1964. Duke Ellington & His Orchestra. Reprise 2949; issued on *Duke Ellington Plays with the Original Score from Walt Disney's Mary Poppins* (Reprise R-6141). Relevant manuscript: autograph score.

Mary Poppins (track 6 of 12): *I Love to Laugh.* "Laugh," BSC. First (issued) recording: September 6, 8, or 9, 1964. Duke Ellington & His Orchestra. Reprise 2956; issued on *Duke Ellington Plays with the Original Score from Walt Disney's Mary Poppins* (Reprise R-6141). Relevant manuscript: autograph score.

Mary Poppins (track 7 of 12): *Jolly Holiday.* "Jolly," BSC. First (issued) recording: September 6, 8, or 9, 1964. Duke Ellington & His Orchestra. Reprise 2958; issued on *Duke Ellington Plays with the Original Score from Walt Disney's Mary Poppins* (Reprise R-6141). Relevant manuscript: autograph score.

Mary Poppins (track 9 of 12): *The Perfect Nanny.* "P.N.," BSC. First (issued) recording: September 6, 8, or 9, 1964. Duke Ellington & His Orchestra. Reprise 2955; issued on *Duke Ellington Plays with the Original Score from Walt Disney's Mary Poppins* (Reprise R-6141). Relevant manuscript: autograph score. The remaining tracks, 4, *Let's Go Fly a Kite*, 8, *Sister Suffragette*, 10, *Step in Time (The Chimney Sweep Dance)*, 11, *The Life I Lead*, are by Ellington (all BSC). The manuscript for track 12, *Supercalifragilisticexpialidocious*, is missing.

Massachusetts. "Massachusetts," REC. First (issued) recording: August 13, 1942. Duke Ellington & His Orchestra. Unissued broadcast (NBC) from the Hotel Sherman, Chicago, Illinois. Relevant manuscript: autograph score.

Maybe I Should Change My Ways. "Philosophy—Change My Ways" and "End Change My Ways," DEC. First (issued) recording: October 6, 1947. Duke Ellington & His Orchestra. Columbia HCO2665-2; issued on *The Complete Duke Ellington: 1947–1952, Vol. 1* (CBS 67264). Relevant manuscripts: autograph scores. The first half of the second chorus (at the violin entrance) and the four-bar coda are by Strayhorn; the remainder is by Ellington. The recording uses part of the manuscripts: various sections were discarded. The order of the recording is at variance with the order suggested by the manuscripts.

Midnight in Paris, A. "AIX," and "AIX (2)," DEC. First (issued) recording: June 21, 1962. Duke Ellington & His Orchestra. CO75568; issued on *Midnight in Paris* (Columbia 468403-2). Relevant manuscript: autograph score. The recording uses part of the manuscript: eighteen bars were cut. The order of the recording is at variance with the order suggested by the manuscript. This score was originally for the Ellington-Basie recording session (July 6, 1961).

Mid-Riff. "Mid-Riff," DEC. First (issued) recording: December 19, 1944. Duke Ellington & His Orchestra. Concert; issued on *The Duke Ellington Carnegie Hall Concerts, December 1944* (Prestige 2PCD 24073-2). Relevant manuscript: autograph score.

Minuet in Blues. "Minuet in Blues," BSC. First (issued) recording: November 22, 1939. Barney Bigard & His Orchestra. Vocalion WM1117-A; issued on *Duke Ellington and His Orchestra 1939–1940* (Classics 790). Relevant manuscript: autograph score.

Mississippi Dreamboat. "Mississippi," DEC. First (issued) recording: February 27, 1939. Johnny Hodges & His Orchestra. Vocalion M975-1. Relevant manuscript: trumpet part by Strayhorn and Ellington. The manuscript is incomplete: it carries the instrumental choruses only. Ellington's part, added to the Strayhorn manuscript, is an adaptation of Strayhorn's version, of which the re-scored bridge was used for the recording.

Monk's Dream. "M.D. Intro," DEC. First (issued) recording: September 13, 1962. Duke Ellington & His Orchestra. Issued on *The Private Collection, Vol. 3: Studio Sessions, New York 1962* (Saja 7 91043-2). Relevant manuscript: autograph score. The manuscript is incomplete: the first chorus is missing.

Mood Indigo. "Mood Indigo" and "Ogidni Doom," REC and DEC. First (issued) recording: December 18, 1950. Duke Ellington & His Orchestra. CO44750-1, issued on *Masterpieces by Ellington* (Columbia LP ML-4418); reissued on *The Complete Duke Ellington 1947–1952, Vol. 5* (CBS 88082). Relevant manuscripts: autograph score (REC) and parts (DEC). The manuscript is incomplete: the third chorus is missing. The first and final choruses stem from Ellington's original 1930 version. The order of the recording is at variance with the order suggested by the manuscripts.

Moon Mist. "Moon Mist," DEC. First (issued) recording: February 1957. Duke Ellington & His Orchestra. Issued on *The Private Collection, Vol. 1: Studio Sessions, Chicago 1956* (Saja 7 91041-2). Relevant manuscript: autograph score.

More I See You, The. "The More I See You," BSC. First (issued) recording: June 2, 1945. Duke Ellington & His Orchestra. Broadcast; issued on *Your Saturday Date with the Duke* (Duke Ellington Treasury Series 08). Relevant manuscript: autograph score.

More. "More," DEC. First (issued) recording: April 16, 1964. Duke Ellington & His Orchestra. Reprise 5021; issued on *Ellington '65* (Reprise LP R-6122). Relevant manuscript: autograph score.

Morning Mood. See *Peer Gynt Suites Nos. 1 and 2* (movement 1 of 5).

Multi-Colored Blue. "M.C. Blue," DEC. First (issued) recording: July 21, 1958. Duke Ellington & His Orchestra. CO61283-3; issued on *Live at Newport 1958* (Columbia C2K-53584). Relevant manuscript: autograph score.

Multi-Colored Blue. "M. Blue," BSC. First (issued) recording: January 1961. Billy Strayhorn & The Paris String Quartet. Issued on *The Peaceful Side of Billy Strayhorn* (Capitol Jazz CDP 7243 8 52563 2 5). Relevant manuscripts: autograph score and parts.

Multi-Colored Blue. "Multicolored Blue," BSC. First (issued) recording: July 2, 1965. Billy Strayhorn & The Riverside Drive Five. Issued on *Billy Strayhorn: Lush Life* (Red Baron AK-52760). Relevant manuscript: autograph score.

My Funny Valentine. "F.V.," DEC. First (issued) recording: February 7 or 8, 1956. Duke Ellington & His Orchestra. Issued on *Duke Ellington Presents...* (Bethlehem 6004-2). Relevant manuscripts: autograph score and parts.

My Heart Tells Me. "Heart Tells Me," BSC. First (issued) recording: April 1, 1944. Duke Ellington & His Orchestra. Unissued broadcast (MBS) from The Hurricane, New York City. Relevant manuscript: autograph score.

My Ideal. "My Ideal," BSC. First (issued) recording: April 2, 1944. Duke Ellington & His Orchestra. Unissued broadcast (MBS) from The Hurricane, NYC. Relevant manuscript: autograph score. The manuscript is incomplete: the last three measures are missing.

My Last Good-Bye. "Good Bye," DEC. First (issued) recording: January 9, 1940. Duke Ellington & His Orchestra. Broadcast; issued on *The Duke in Boston* (Jazz Unlimited JUCD 2022). Relevant manuscripts: autograph parts.

My Little Brown Book. "My Little Brown Book," DEC. First (issued) recording: June 26, 1942. Duke Ellington & His Orchestra. Victor 072437-1; issued on *The Blanton-Webster Band* (RCA Bluebird 5659-2-RB). Relevant manuscripts: autograph parts. The recording uses part of the manuscript: a fourteen-bar coda was cut.

My Little Brown Book. "Book," BSC. First (issued) recording: March 24, 1959. Lil Greenwood with Duke Ellington & His Orchestra. Unissued RCA studio recording. Relevant manuscript: autograph score. The manuscript is incomplete: the two-bar introduction and four final bars are missing.

My Mother, My Father (Heritage). See *My People* (track 3 of 8).

My Old Flame. "Flame," BSC and SIDE. First (issued) recording: April 7, 1953. Duke Ellington & His Orchestra. Cap 11414-3; issued on *The Complete Capitol Recordings of Duke Ellington* (Mosaic MDS-160). Relevant manuscripts: autograph score (BSC) and parts (SIDE).

My People (track 3 of 8): *My Mother, My Father (Heritage)*. "Heritage #3," DEC. First (issued) recording: August 21, 1963. Duke Ellington & His Orchestra. Issued on *My People* (Red Baron AK-52759). Relevant manuscript: autograph score.

My People (track 5 of 8): *The Blues Ain't*. "Mauve (B.B.B. Blues)," BSC. First (issued) recording: August 20, 1963. Duke Ellington & His Orchestra. Issued on *My People* (Red Baron AK-52759). Relevant manuscript: autograph score. The vocal sections (1–3 and 5) are by Strayhorn; section 4 (the tenor solo) is by Ellington.

My People (track 8 of 8): *What Color Is Virtue?* "What Color," DEC. First (issued) recording: August 21, 1963. Duke Ellington & His Orchestra. Issued on *My People* (Red Baron AK-52759). Relevant manuscript: autograph score. The manuscript is incomplete: the chorus preceding the drum break and the final passage after the a capella choir section are missing.

Newport Jazz Festival Suite (movement 1 of 3): *Festival Junction*. "Hummer," "Break for Hummer," DEC. First (issued) recording: July 9, 1956. Duke Ellington & His Orchestra. Concert; issued on *Ellington at Newport* (Columbia 40587). Relevant manuscript: autograph score. The order of the recording is at variance with the order suggested by the manuscript.

Newport Jazz Festival Suite (movement 2 of 3): *Blues to Be There*. "Woosie," DEC. First (issued) recording: July 9, 1956. Duke Ellington & His Orchestra. Concert; issued on *Ellington at Newport* (Columbia 40587). Relevant manuscript: autograph score. The order of the recording is at variance with the order suggested by the manuscript. The third movement, *Newport Up*, is by Ellington (DEC).

Night and Day. "Night + Day," DEC. First (issued) recording: October 10, 1957. Duke Ellington & His Orchestra. CO59939; issued on *Ellington Indigos* (Columbia CK-44444). Relevant manuscript: autograph score.

Night Time. "Nite-Time," DEC. First (issued) recording: December 28, 1953. Duke Ellington & His Orchestra. Cap 12247-10; issued on *The Complete Capitol Recordings of Duke Ellington* (Mosaic MDS-160). Relevant manuscript: autograph score.

No Love, No Nothin'. "No Love," BSC. First (issued) recording: April 2, 1944. Duke Ellington & His Orchestra. Unissued broadcast (MBS) from The Hurricane, New York City. Relevant manuscript: autograph score.

No Regrets. "Regret," DEC. First (issued) recording: June 26, 1962. Duke Ellington & His Orchestra. CO75950-4; issued on *Midnight in Paris* (Columbia 468403-2). Relevant manuscript: autograph score. The recording uses part of the manuscript: the final two bars were replaced by a saxophone chord.

Nobody Knows the Trouble I've Seen. "Nobody Knows," BSC. First (issued) recording: April 14, 1945. Duke Ellington & His Orchestra. Broadcast; issued on *Duke Ellington: F. D. Roosevelt Memorial* (Ariston ARLP-12029). Relevant manuscript: autograph score.

Noir Bleu. (No manuscript known). First (issued) recording: September 29, 1941. Barney Bigard & His Orchestra. Victor 061689-1. Two other autographs in Strayhorn's hand are in BSC and DEC, respectively.

Northern Lights. See *The Queen's Suite* (movement 4 of 6).

Nutcracker Suite, The (movement 1 of 9): *Overture.* "Overture," BSC. First (issued) recording: May 26, 1960. Duke Ellington & His Orchestra. RHCO46653-5; issued on *Three Suites* (Columbia CK 46825). Relevant manuscript: autograph score.

Nutcracker Suite, The (movement 2 of 9): *Toot Toot Tootie Toot.* "The Pipes," BSC. First (issued) recording: May 31, 1960. Duke Ellington & His Orchestra. RHCO46656-6; issued on *Three Suites* (Columbia CK 46825). Relevant manuscript: autograph score. The recording uses part of the manuscript: a sixteen-bar coda was discarded.

Nutcracker Suite, The (movement 4 of 9): *Sugar Rum Cherry.* "Sugar Plum," BSC. First (issued) recording: June 3, 1960. Duke Ellington & His Orchestra. RHCO46675-2; issued on *Three Suites* (Columbia CK 46825). Relevant manuscript: autograph score. The recording uses part of the manuscript: a twenty-four-bar introduction, an eight-bar bridge, and some backgrounds were discarded.

Nutcracker Suite, The (movement 5 of 9): *Entr'Acte.* "Overture," BSC. First (issued) recording: May 26, 1960. Duke Ellington & His Orchestra. RHCO46654-6; issued on *Three Suites* (Columbia CK 46825). Relevant manuscript: autograph score. The recording uses part of the manuscript: measures 1–24 and 28–34. The order of the recording is at variance with the order suggested by the manuscript.

Nutcracker Suite, The (movement 8 of 9): *Dance of the Floreadores.* "Waltz-Trot-Fleurs," BSC. First (issued) recording: June 3, 1960. Duke Ellington & His Orchestra. RHCO46674-20; issued on *Three Suites* (Columbia CK 46825). Relevant manuscripts: autograph score and parts.

Nutcracker Suite, The (movement 9 of 9): *Arabesque Cookie.* "Naibara" and "Naibara Bottom," DEC. First (issued) recording: June 22, 1960. Duke Ellington & His Orchestra. RHCO46655-5A; issued on *Three Suites* (Columbia CK 46825). Relevant manuscripts: autograph score and parts.

Additional Strayhorn parts give the altered instrumentation. The recording uses part of the manuscript. The order of the recording is at variance with the order suggested by the manuscript. Movement 3, *Peanut Brittle Brigade*, is by Ellington; the manuscripts for movement 6, *The Volga Vouty*, and 7, *Chinoiserie*, are missing.

Oh! Lady Be Good. "Lady B," DEC. First (issued) recording: June 6, 1943. Duke Ellington & His Orchestra. Unissued broadcast (MBS) from The Hurricane, New York City. Relevant manuscripts: autograph parts.

Once There Lived a Fool. "Once Fool," BSC. First (issued) recording: March, 1952. Duke Ellington & His Orchestra. Concert; issued on *Don't Worry 'Bout Me: Duke Ellington Swinging His Big Band, Live* (Skata 502). Relevant manuscript: autograph score.

Once Upon a Dream. "Once Upon a Dream," DEC. First (issued) recording: November 20, 1947. Duke Ellington & His Orchestra. Columbia CO38399-1; issued on *The Complete Duke Ellington: 1947–1952, Vol. 2* (CBS 68275). Relevant manuscript: autograph score. The recording uses part of the manuscript: an eight-bar repeat and an eight-bar tutti were cut.

Once Upon a Time. See *All American in Jazz* (track 5 of 10).

One I Love Belongs to Someone Else, The. "One I Love," BSC. First (issued) recording: May 1942. Duke Ellington & His Orchestra. Unissued broadcast (MBS) from the Trianon Ballroom, Southgate, California. Relevant manuscripts: autograph score and parts.

Orchids for Madame. "Orchids," DEC. First (issued) recording: June 10, 1947. Duke Ellington & His Orchestra. Capitol Transcriptions; issued on *Capitol Transcriptions* (Capitol B-305). Relevant manuscript: autograph score. The recording uses part of the manuscript: the ten-bar introduction and an instrumental chorus were cut.

Orchids for Remembrance. "Orchids," DEC. First (issued) recording: July 29, 1940. Duke Ellington & His Orchestra. Broadcast; issued on *Duke Ellington: Chicago-Detroit 1940* (Jazz Moderne DE-003). Relevant manuscripts: autograph parts.

Orson. "Orson," BSC. First (issued) recording: April 7, 1953. Duke Ellington & His Orchestra. Cap 11420-5; issued on *The Complete Capitol Recordings of Duke Ellington* (Mosaic MDS-160). Relevant manuscript: autograph score. The recording uses part of the manuscript: a four-bar trumpet answer after the first strain, a five-bar modulation, and the consequent thirty-four-bar final section were cut. The order of the recording is at variance with the order suggested by the manuscript. See also Appendix C.

Our Children. See *All American in Jazz* (track 7 of 10).

Out of This World. "Out World," DEC. First (issued) recording: August 11, 1945. Duke Ellington & His Orchestra. Broadcast; issued on *Your Saturday Date with the Duke* (Duke Ellington Treasury Series 18). Relevant manuscript:

autograph score. An adaptation of this arrangement was recorded as *The Eighth Veil*, March 28, 1946.

Overture to a Jam Session. "OTJ I," "OTJ II," and "OTJ III," BSC. First (issued) recording: January 7, 1947. Duke Ellington & His Orchestra. Capitol Transcriptions; issued on *Duke Ellington and His World Famous Orchestra: The Collection '46–47 Recordings* (Hindsight 501). Relevant manuscripts: autograph scores.

Overture. See *The Nutcracker Suite* (movement 1 of 9).

Paradise. "Paradise" and "End of Paradise," DEC. First (issued) recording: November 13, 1948. Duke Ellington & His Orchestra. Concert; issued on *Duke Ellington and His Orchestra: Carnegie Hall November 13, 1948* (Vintage Jazz Classics VJC-1024/25-2). Relevant manuscript: autograph score (partly in K*Lite Vision Ease sketchbook: 11–13).

Passion Flower. "Passion Flower," DEC. First (issued) recording: July 3, 1941. Johnny Hodges & His Orchestra. Bluebird 061347-1; issued on *The Great Ellington Units* (RCA Bluebird ND86751). Relevant manuscript: autograph score.

Passion Flower. "Passion Flower" and "Passion Flower," DEC. First (issued) recording: August 7, 1945. Duke Ellington & His Orchestra. Circle N-3540-3; issued on *Duke Ellington World Broadcasting Series, Vols. 1–5* (Circle CD 101-5). Relevant manuscripts: autograph scores. The recording uses part of the manuscript: the trombone background behind the alto theme in the first sixteen bars of the theme has been replaced by the reed background from the recapitulation. The recording from March 28, 1945, uses virtually the entire manuscript.

Passion Flower. "Passion Flower" and "Passion Flower," DEC. First (issued) recording: March 28, 1946. Duke Ellington & His Orchestra. Capitol Transcriptions; issued on *Duke Ellington and His World Famous Orchestra: The Collection '46–47 Recordings* (Hindsight 501). Relevant manuscripts: autograph scores. The recording uses part of the manuscript: the trumpet background in the first ending has been cut. It can be heard on the recording from August 7, 1945, which omits different parts from the manuscript.

Passion Flower. "Passon [sic] Flower," BSC. First (issued) recording: April 19, 1947. Duke Ellington & His Orchestra. Broadcast; issued on *Duke Ellington, Vol. 4* (Stardust Records 204). Relevant manuscript: autograph score.

Passion Flower. "Passion Flower," BSC. First (issued) recording: February 1952. Just Jazz All-Stars. Cap 9940, issued on *Just Jazz All-Stars* (Capitol). Relevant manuscript: autograph score. The recording uses part of the manuscript: 18 bars were cut. The order of the recording is at variance with the order suggested by the manuscript. April 29, 1952, gives the full score.

Passion Flower. "Passion Flower," BSC. First (issued) recording: April 29, 1952. Duke Ellington & His Orchestra. Concert; issued on *The Unusual Ellington*

(Jazz Guild 1004). Relevant manuscript: autograph score. February 1952 gives the partial score.

Passion Flower. "Passion Flower," DEC. First (issued) recording: January 27, 1956. Duke Ellington & His Orchestra. Columbia CO55592-2; issued on *Blue Rose* (CBS 466444-2). Relevant manuscript: autograph score. Also used for a vocal version (October 18–20, 1965).

Passion Flower. "P. Flower," BSC. First (issued) recording: January 1961. Billy Strayhorn & The Paris String Quartet. Issued on *The Peaceful Side of Billy Strayhorn* (Capitol Jazz CDP 7243 8 52563 2 5). Relevant manuscript: autograph part.

Passion Flower. No manuscript known. First (issued) recording: June 30, 1965. Billy Strayhorn & The Riverside Drive Five. Issued on *Billy Strayhorn: Lush Life* (Red Baron AK-52760).

Passion Flower. "Passion Flower," DEC. First (issued) recording: October 18–20, 1965. Ella Fitzgerald and Duke Ellington & His Orchestra. VRV 65KV5533-9-2; issued on *Ella at Duke's Place* (Verve 529 700-2). Relevant manuscript: autograph score. Also used for an instrumental version (January 27, 1956).

Peer Gynt Suites Nos. 1 and 2 (movement 1 of 5): *Morning Mood.* "Morning," BSC. First (issued) recording: June 28, 1960. Duke Ellington & His Orchestra. RHCO46705-5; issued on *Three Suites* (Columbia CK 46825). Relevant manuscripts: autograph score and parts.

Peer Gynt Suites Nos. 1 and 2 (movement 3 of 5): *Solvejg's Song.* "Solvejg," BSC. First (issued) recording: June 29, 1960. Duke Ellington & His Orchestra. RHCO46709-8; issued on *Three Suites* (Columbia CK 46825). Relevant manuscript: autograph score.

Peer Gynt Suites Nos. 1 and 2 (movement 4 of 5): *Åse's Death.* "Åses Death," BSC. First (issued) recording: June 29, 1960. Duke Ellington & His Orchestra. RHCO46710-7; issued on *Three Suites* (Columbia CK 46825). Relevant manuscript: autograph score.

Peer Gynt Suites Nos. 1 and 2 (movement 5 of 5): *Anitra's Dance.* "Anitra," BSC. First (issued) recording: June 28, 1960. Duke Ellington & His Orchestra. RHCO46706-4; issued on *Three Suites* (Columbia CK 46825). Relevant manuscripts: autograph score and parts. Movement 2, *In the Hall of the Mountain King*, is by Ellington (DEC).

People Will Say We're in Love. "People," DEC. First (issued) recording: June 18, 1943. Duke Ellington & His Orchestra. Broadcast; issued on *The Fabulous Forties, Vol. 1* (Rarities 56). Relevant manuscripts: autograph parts.

People. "People," DEC. First (issued) recording: May 19, 1964. Duke Ellington & His Orchestra. Reprise 5095; issued on *Ellington '66* (Reprise LP R-6154). Relevant manuscript: autograph score.

Perfect Nanny, The. See *Mary Poppins* (track 8 of 12).

Perfume Suite (movement 1 of 4): *Love.* "Love #1," and "Pentonsilic," BSC. First (issued) recording: December 19, 1944. Duke Ellington & His Orchestra. Concert; issued on *The Duke Ellington Carnegie Hall Concerts, December 1944* (Prestige 2PCD 24073-2). Relevant manuscripts: autograph scores. The recording uses part of the manuscript: the final eight bars of *Love #1* and mm. 1–290 and 318–375 of *Pentonsilic* (sketchbook no. 8: 18–33) were discarded. See also Appendix C.

Perfume Suite (movement 2 of 4): *Violence* (also known as *Strange Feeling*). "Strange," "Streamers," "Strange-Hibbler-II D-," and "End of Strange," BSC. First (issued) recording: December 19, 1944. Duke Ellington & His Orchestra. Concert; issued on *The Duke Ellington Carnegie Hall Concerts, December 1944* (Prestige 2PCD 24073-2). Relevant manuscripts: autograph scores. Ellington arranged the first 28 measures of the instrumental chorus; the remainder is by Strayhorn.

Perfume Suite (movement 4 of 4): *Sophistication* (also known as *Coloratura*). "Coloratura," DEC. First (issued) recording: December 19, 1944. Duke Ellington & His Orchestra. Concert; issued on *The Duke Ellington Carnegie Hall Concerts, December 1944* (Prestige 2PCD 24073-2). Relevant manuscript: autograph score. The four bars (in eighth-note triplets) preceding Anderson's penultimate cadenza are by Strayhorn, the remainder is by Ellington. Movement 3, *Naiveté* (also known as *Dancers in Love*), is by Ellington (DEC).

Petite Waltz, The. "La Petite Valse," DEC. First (issued) recording: January 31, 1962. Duke Ellington & His Orchestra. CO69332-7; issued on *Midnight in Paris* (Columbia 468403-2). Relevant manuscript: autograph score.

Please Be Kind. "Please Be Kind," BSC. First (issued) recording: August 7, 1951. Duke Ellington & His Orchestra. Columbia CO47019-1; issued on *The Complete Duke Ellington: 1947–1952, Vol. 4* (CBS 88035). Relevant manuscript: autograph score.

Pomegranate. See *A Drum Is a Woman*.

Poor Butterfly. "Butterfly," DEC. First (issued) recording: March 24, 1958. Duke Ellington & His Orchestra. CO60592-16; issued on *At the Bal Masque* (Columbia LP CL-1282). Relevant manuscript: autograph score. The first chorus (mm. 1–32) is by Strayhorn; the second (mm. 33–72) is by Ellington. The recording uses part of the manuscript: Strayhorn's nine-bar intro was cut.

Portrait of Ella Fitzgerald, A (movement 1 of 4): *Royal Ancestry*. "P.O.E. #II," DEC. First (issued) recording: September 2, 1957. Duke Ellington & His Orchestra. VRV21381-12; issued on *Ella Fitzgerald Sings the Duke Ellington Songbook* (Verve 837 035-2). Relevant manuscripts: autograph score and parts.

Portrait of Ella Fitzgerald, A (movement 2 of 4): *All Heart*. "P.O.E. #III," DEC. First (issued) recording: September 2, 1957. Duke Ellington & His Orchestra. VRV21382-7; issued on *Ella Fitzgerald Sings the Duke Ellington Songbook* (Verve 837 035-2). Relevant manuscripts: autograph score and parts. The manuscript is incomplete: the final chord is missing. The recording uses part of the manuscript: eight bars were cut.

Portrait of Ella Fitzgerald, A (movement 3 of 4): *Beyond Category.* "P.O.E. No. I," DEC. First (issued) recording: September 2, 1957. Duke Ellington & His Orchestra. VRV21380-13; issued on *Ella Fitzgerald Sings the Duke Ellington Songbook* (Verve 837 035-2). Relevant manuscripts: autograph score and parts. Movement 4, *Total Jazz*, is by Ellington (DEC).

Prelude to a Kiss. "Kiss," DEC. First (issued) recording: October 1, 1957. Duke Ellington & His Orchestra. CO59897; issued on *Ellington Indigos* (Columbia CK-44444). Relevant manuscript: autograph score.

Pretty Girl. "Pretty Girl," DEC. First (issued) recording: December 6, 1956. Duke Ellington & His Orchestra. CO57015-1; issued on *The Studio Series, Vol. 5* (Up-to-Date LP 2006). Relevant manuscript: autograph score. The recording uses part of the manuscript: the four-bar introduction, a modulatory section, and the consequent out-chorus were cut (revisions partly by Strayhorn). Also recorded as *The Star-Crossed Lovers*, May 3, 1957. See also Appendix C.

Pretty Little One. "II," DEC. First (issued) recording: February 22, 1963. Duke Ellington's Jazz Violins. Issued on *Duke Ellington's Jazz Violin Session* (Atlantic SD 1688). Relevant manuscripts: autograph score and parts.

Prima Bara Dubla. "Double Bar," DEC. First (issued) recording: July 3, 1958. Duke Ellington & His Orchestra. Concert; issued on *Live at Newport 1958* (Columbia CL-1245). Relevant manuscript: autograph score. The backgrounds in the second and third blues-choruses (mm. 89–112) are by Ellington; the remainder is by Strayhorn.

Prisoner of Love. "Prisoner of Love," DEC. First (issued) recording: July 4, 1947. Duke Ellington & His Orchestra. Broadcast; issued on *Jam-A-Ditty* (Jazz & Jazz JJ-602). Relevant manuscript: autograph score. The manuscript is incomplete: the final four bars are missing—they were added to the manuscript by copyist Thomas Whaley.

Progressive Gavotte. "Re-bop Gavotte," DEC. First (issued) recording: November 11, 1947. Duke Ellington & His Orchestra. Columbia CO38374-1; issued on *The Complete Duke Ellington: 1947–1952, Vol. 2* (CBS 68275). Relevant manuscript: autograph score. The recording uses part of the manuscript: a sixteen-bar repeat was cut.

Pussy Willow. Untitled, REC. First (issued) recording: March 20, 1939. Duke Ellington & His Orchestra. Brunswick M997-1. A later broadcast, July 26, 1939, is issued on *The Duke in Boston* (Jazz Unlimited JUCD 2022). Relevant manuscript: autograph score. The score has seven measures of the eight-bar theme (reeds with tutti brass answer), used in the first, second, and final thirty-two-bar choruses. The remainder of the score, possibly by Ellington, is lost.

Put Yourself in My Place, Baby. "Put Yourself in My Place, Baby," DEC. First (issued) recording: September 29, 1947. Duke Ellington & His Orchestra. Columbia HCO2655-1; issued on *The Complete Duke Ellington: 1947–1952, Vol. 1* (CBS 67264). Relevant manuscript: autograph score. The manuscript is incomplete: the unison saxophone background in the vocal chorus is missing. The recording uses part of the manuscript: the first eight bars of the tutti were cut.

Queen's Suite, The (movement 4 of 6): *Northern Lights*. "N.L.," DEC. First (issued) recording: February 25, 1959. Duke Ellington & His Orchestra. CO62257; issued on *The Ellington Suites* (Pablo 2310-762). Relevant manuscript: autograph score. Movements 1, *Sunset and the Mocking Bird*, and 6, *Apes and Peacocks* are by Ellington (DEC); the manuscripts for movements 2, *Lightning Bugs and Frogs*, 3, *Le Sucrier Velours*, and 5, *A Single Petal of Rose* (in all likelihood by Ellington) are missing.

Rain Check. "Rain Check," BSC. First (issued) recording: December 3, 1941. Duke Ellington & His Orchestra. Standard Radio Transcription 061946-1; issued on *Take the "A" Train: The Legendary Blanton-Webster Transcriptions* (Vintage Jazz Classics VJC 1003-2). Relevant manuscripts: autograph score and parts.

Rain Check. No manuscript known. First (issued) recording: July 2, 1965. Billy Strayhorn & The Riverside Drive Five. Issued on *Billy Strayhorn: Lush Life* (Red Baron AK-52760).

Rain Check. "Rain Check," BSC. First (issued) recording: August 30, 1967. Duke Ellington & His Orchestra. WPA5-UPAI-8533; issued on *...And His Mother Called Him Bill* (RCA Bluebird 6287-2-RB). Relevant manuscript: autograph score. The order of the recording is at variance with the order suggested by the manuscript.

Red Roses for a Blue Lady. "Rouge-Bleu," DEC. First (issued) recording: January 21, 1965. Duke Ellington & His Orchestra. Reprise 5094; issued on *Ellington '66* (Reprise LP R-6154). Relevant manuscript: autograph score.

Rhapsody in Blue. No manuscript known. First (issued) recording: December 20, 1962. Duke Ellington & His Orchestra. Reprise 3383-8; issued on *Recollections of the Big Band Era* (Atlantic Jazz 7 90043-2). BSC houses various sketches for *Rhapsody in Blue* (untitled 40J, untitled 40K and "Rhap in Blue").

Rhythm Pum-Te-Dum. See *A Drum Is a Woman* (track 2 of 15).

Ring Around the Moon. "Ring-Moon," BSC. First (issued) recording: April 1943. Duke Ellington & His Orchestra. Broadcast (MBS); issued on *Ellington* (Azure LP-431). Relevant manuscript: autograph score. The recording uses part of the manuscript: thirty-two bars were cut.

River Seine. "La Seine," DEC. First (issued) recording: June 26, 1962. Duke Ellington & His Orchestra. CO69723-9; issued on *Midnight in Paris* (Columbia 468403-2). Relevant manuscript: autograph score. The recording uses part of the manuscript: the trombone background behind the alto saxophone solo was cut.

Rock Skippin' at the Blue Note. No manuscript known. First (issued) recording: August 7, 1951. Duke Ellington & His Orchestra. Columbia CO47021-4; issued on *The Complete Duke Ellington: 1947–1952, Vol. 4* (CBS 88035). BSC houses an earlier, unrecorded, and incomplete version, titled *Piks.*

Rocks in My Bed. "Rocks in My Bed," DEC. First (issued) recording: September 26, 1941. Duke Ellington & His Orchestra. Victor 061685-1; issued on *The Blanton-Webster Band* (RCA Bluebird 5659-2-RB). Relevant manuscript: autograph score. Measures 1–24 and 47–65 are by Ellington; measures 25–46 (the vocal choruses) are by Strayhorn. Sketches in Strayhorn's hand for the lyrics are in BSC.

Rod La Roque. "Rod La Roque," DEC. First (issued) recording: April 14, 1965. Duke Ellington & His Orchestra. Issued on *The Private Collection, Vol. 4: Studio Sessions, New York 1963* (Saja 7 91044-2). Relevant manuscript: autograph score.

Royal Ancestry. See *Portrait of Ella Fitzgerald, A* (movement 1 of 4).

Royal Garden Blues. "Royal Garden Blues," DEC. First (issued) recording: June 9, 1947. Duke Ellington & His Orchestra. Victor D6VB2131-1; issued on *Black, Brown & Beige (The 1944–1946 Band Recordings)* (RCA Bluebird 6641-2-RB). Relevant manuscript: autograph score. The manuscript is incomplete: the trumpet after-beat chords in the two final choruses and the two-bar tag are missing.

Savoy Strut. Untitled, DEC. First (issued) recording: March 21, 1939. Duke Ellington & His Orchestra. Vocalion WM1001-1 and Columbia WM1001-2. Relevant manuscript: autograph part. The manuscript is incomplete: the part has the first twenty-four-bar chorus only (mm. 3–26).

Second Time Around, The. "The 2nd Time Around," DEC. First (issued) recording: April 15, 1964. Duke Ellington & His Orchestra. Reprise 5022; issued on *Ellington '65* (Reprise LP R-6122). Relevant manuscript: autograph score.

Sentimental Journey. "Voyage Sentimentale," BSC. First (issued) recording: May 5, 1945. Duke Ellington & His Orchestra. Broadcast; issued on *Your Saturday Date with the Duke* (Duke Ellington Treasury Series 04). Relevant manuscript: autograph score.

Sepia Panorama. Untitled, DEC. First (issued) recording: July 24, 1940. Duke Ellington & His Orchestra. Victor 054625-1; issued on *The Blanton-Webster Band* (RCA Bluebird 5659-2-RB). Relevant manuscripts: autograph scores by Strayhorn (sketchbook no. 2: 18) and Ellington, parts by Strayhorn. Measures 29–36 and 61–69 stem from a Strayhorn arrangement of *Tuxedo Junction.* The remainder of the score (mm. 1–28 and 70–90) is by Ellington. See also Chapter 2.

September Song. "S. Song," DEC. First (issued) recording: October 8, 1954. Duke Ellington & His Orchestra. PCK 1309-2; issued on *We Love You Madly*

(Pickwick LP SPC-3390). Relevant manuscript: autograph score. The recording uses part of the manuscript: in the eight-bar section following the first chorus, the vocal part (originally for Kay Davis, who left the band in mid-1950) and Ray Nance's violin part have been omitted.

Since You Went Away. "Since U Went Away," BSC. First (issued) recording: May 20, 1944. Duke Ellington & His Orchestra. Unissued broadcast (MBS) from The Hurricane, New York City. Relevant manuscript: autograph score.

Skunk Hollow Blues. Untitled, BSC and DEC. First (issued) recording: October 14, 1939. Johnny Hodges & His Orchestra. Vocalion WM1096-A. Relevant manuscripts: autograph score (BSC) and parts (DEC).

Sky Fell Down, The. "Sky Fell (Ray Background)," REC. First (issued) recording: May 20, 1962. Duke Ellington & His Orchestra. Issued on *The Private Collection, Vol. 7: Studio Sessions 1957 and 1962* (Saja 7 91231-2). Relevant manuscript: autograph score. The first chorus is by Ellington; the second chorus and coda are by Strayhorn.

Sleep, Sleep, Sleep. "Sleep," BSC. First (issued) recording: December 20, 1962. Duke Ellington & His Orchestra. Reprise 3385-5; issued on *Recollections of the Big Band Era* (Atlantic Jazz 7 90043-2). Relevant manuscript: autograph score.

Smada. "Don't Take My Love," BSC and DEC. First (issued) recording: August 7, 1951. Duke Ellington & His Orchestra. Columbia CO47018-1; issued on *The Complete Duke Ellington: 1947–1952, Vol. 4* (CBS 88035). Relevant manuscript: autograph score (the first chorus is in DEC, the remainder in BSC).

Smoke Rings. "Smoker," DEC. First (issued) recording: January 4, 1963. Duke Ellington & His Orchestra. Reprise 3371-5; issued on *Recollections of the Big Band Era* (Atlantic Jazz 7 90043-2). Relevant manuscripts: autograph score and parts.

Snibor. "Robins Nest," DEC. First (issued) recording: December 27, 1947. Duke Ellington & His Orchestra. Concert; issued on *The Duke Ellington Carnegie Hall Concerts, December 1947* (Prestige 2PCD 24075-2). Relevant manuscript: autograph score. Also known as *The New Look*. The manuscript is incomplete: the twenty-bar introduction is missing.

So Little Time (The Peking Theme). "Pee King," DEC. First (issued) recording: April 16, 1964. Duke Ellington & His Orchestra. Reprise 5019; issued on *Ellington '65* (Reprise LP R-6122). Relevant manuscript: autograph score.

Solitude. "Solitude," DEC. First (issued) recording: May 15, 1945. Duke Ellington & His Orchestra. Victor D5VB270-1; issued on *Black, Brown & Beige (The 1944–1946 Band Recordings)* (RCA Bluebird 6641-2-RB). Relevant manuscript: autograph score. The recording uses part of the manuscript: the six-bar transition that leads to Al Hibbler's vocals was replaced with a two-bar Ellington-piano transition.

Solitude. "Solitude-Vocal," DEC. First (issued) recording: October 14, 1957. Duke Ellington & His Orchestra. CO59960-3; issued on *Ellington Indigos* (Columbia CK-44444). Relevant manuscript: autograph score. Originally scored as a vocal arrangement. The recording uses part of the manuscript: the orchestral backgrounds under the first half-chorus were cut.

Solvejg's Song. See *Peer Gynt Suites Nos. 1 and 2* (movement 3 of 5).

Somebody Loves Me. "Somebody Loves," BSC, DEC, and SIDE. First (issued) recording: December 1, 1943. Duke Ellington & His Orchestra. Swing Treasury N-1059-1; issued on *Duke Ellington World Broadcasting Series, Vols. 1–5* (Circle CD 101-5). Relevant manuscript: autograph score (BSC) and parts (DEC and SIDE).

Someone. "Someone," DEC. First (issued) recording: February 26, 1942. Duke Ellington & His Orchestra. Victor 071892-1; issued on *The Blanton-Webster Band* (RCA Bluebird 5659-2-RB). Relevant manuscripts: autograph scores by Ellington and Strayhorn; parts by Strayhorn. Chorus 1 (mm. 1–32) and final half-chorus (mm. 65–87) are by Ellington; chorus two (mm. 33–64, Rex Stewart's solo) is by Strayhorn. The manuscript is incomplete: the coda (mm. 88–95) is missing.

Something to Live For. "Live for #12," DEC. First (issued) recording: December 11, 1951. Duke Ellington & His Orchestra. CO47272-5; issued on *The Complete Duke Ellington: 1947–1952, Vol. 4* (CBS 88035). Relevant manuscript: autograph score. The recording uses part of the manuscript: Strayhorn's original eight-bar coda with preceding two-bar modulation was replaced by a nonmodulating ten-bar ending, which was added to the manuscript by copyist Tom Whaley (author unknown).

Something to Live For. "S.L.F," DEC. First (issued) recording: July 14, 1960. Duke Ellington Group. Issued on *Unknown Session* (CBS JC35342). Relevant manuscript: autograph score.

Something to Live For. "Something-Live For," BSC. First (issued) recording: January 1961. Billy Strayhorn & The Paris String Quartet. Issued on *The Peaceful Side of Billy Strayhorn* (Capitol Jazz CDP 7243 8 52563 2 5). Relevant manuscript: autograph score.

Something to Live For. No manuscript known. First (issued) recording: October 18–20, 1965. Ella Fitzgerald with Duke Ellington & His Orchestra. VRV 65KV5533-7; issued on *Ella at Duke's Place* (Verve 529 700-2).

Sophisticated Lady. Untitled, BSC, "Soph-La" and "Sophla," DEC. First (issued) recording: December 18, 1950. Duke Ellington & His Orchestra. CO44751-1; issued on *Masterpieces by Ellington* (Columbia LP ML-4418); reissued on *The Complete Duke Ellington 1947–1952, Vols. 5* (CBS 88082). Relevant manuscripts: autograph scores (BSC and DEC) and parts (DEC). Sections [0:11–1:00], [1:44–2:33], [2:56–3:18], [8:46–9:34], and [9:59–10:20] are by Ellington; sections [6:39–8:45] and [10:21–10:45] are by Strayhorn. The remainder is missing. The order of the recording is at variance with the order suggested by the manuscript.

Sophisticated Lady. "Soph Lady Rose—Voc," BSC. First (issued) recording: January 23, 1956. Rosemary Clooney with Duke Ellington & His Orchestra. Columbia CO55819; issued on *Blue Rose* (CBS 466444-2). Relevant manuscript: autograph score. Also used for an instrumental version (June 1957).

Sophisticated Lady. "Soph Lady Rose—Voc," BSC. First (issued) recording: June 1957. Duke Ellington & His Orchestra. Concert; issued on *The Private Collection, Vol. 2: Dance Concerts, California 1958* (Saja 7 91042-2). Relevant manuscript: autograph score. The manuscript is incomplete: the trombone background from the second bridge is missing. The recording uses part of the manuscript: all saxophone backgrounds were cut. The vocal version of January 23, 1956, uses the entire score.

Sophistication. See *Perfume Suite* (movement 4 of 4).

Speak to Me of Love. "Parlez-Moi d'Amour," BSC. First (issued) recording: January 30, 1962. Duke Ellington & His Orchestra. CO69326-10; issued on *Midnight in Paris* (Columbia 468403-2). Relevant manuscript: autograph score (sketchbook no. 6: 1–2).

Spoonful of Sugar, A. See *Mary Poppins* (track 1 of 12).

Star Dust. "Stardust," BSC and DEC. First (issued) recording: April 7, 1953. Duke Ellington & His Orchestra. Cap 11418-8; issued on *The Complete Capitol Recordings of Duke Ellington* (Mosaic MDS-160). Relevant manuscript: autograph score (sketchbook no. 3: 15–16) and parts (DEC). The twelve-bar introduction is by Ellington; the remainder is by Strayhorn.

Star-Crossed Lovers, The. See *Such Sweet Thunder* (movement 9 of 12).

Stay Awake. See *Mary Poppins* (track 5 of 12).

Stormy Weather. "Stormy Weather," DEC. First (issued) recording: October 21, 1950. The Ellingtonians with Al Hibbler. Issued on Mercer Records (M4019). Relevant manuscript: autograph score.

Stormy Weather. "Stormy Weather," BSC and DEC. First (issued) recording: April 7, 1953. Duke Ellington & His Orchestra. Cap 11418-8; issued on *The Complete Capitol Recordings of Duke Ellington* (Mosaic MDS-160). Relevant manuscript: autograph score (sketchbook no. 3: 12–15) and parts (DEC). The recording uses part of the manuscript: the eight-bar coda was cut.

Strange Feeling. "Strange Feeling-Gris," BSC. First (issued) recording: November 26, 1952. Duke Ellington & His Orchestra. Unissued NBC broadcast. Relevant manuscript: autograph score (sketchbook no. 1: 15–16). The manuscript is incomplete: the eight-bar introduction, the last two bars of the instrumental section, and the final eight-bar vocal bridge are missing.

Strange Feeling. "Feeling," BSC. First (issued) recording: January 1961. Billy Strayhorn & The Paris String Quartet. Issued on *The Peaceful Side of Billy*

Strayhorn (Capitol Jazz CDP 7243 8 52563 2 5). Relevant manuscript: autograph score.

Strange Love. "Strange Love," DEC. First (issued) recording: June 8, 1946. Duke Ellington & His Orchestra. Broadcast; issued on *Your Saturday Date with the Duke* (Duke Ellington Treasury Series 39). Relevant manuscript: autograph score.

Such Sweet Thunder (movement 1 of 12): *Such Sweet Thunder.* "Cleo," REC. First (issued) recording: April 24, 1957. Duke Ellington & His Orchestra. CO57722-3; issued on *Such Sweet Thunder* (Columbia CK 65568 2). Relevant manuscript: autograph score. Measures 1–48 and 61–72 are by Ellington; measures 49–60 are missing; and measures 73–75 are by Strayhorn.

Such Sweet Thunder (movement 7 of 12): *Up and Down, Up and Down.* "P-3," and untitled, BSC, and "P.-," DEC. First (issued) recording: April 24, 1957. Duke Ellington & His Orchestra. CO57721-12; issued on *Such Sweet Thunder* (Columbia CK 65568 2). Relevant manuscripts: autograph score (sketchbook no. 9: 1–4) and parts. The recording uses part of the manuscript: a twenty-two-bar section was cut.

Such Sweet Thunder (movement 9 of 12): *The Star-Crossed Lovers.* "Pretty Girl," DEC. First (issued) recording: May 3, 1957. Duke Ellington & His Orchestra. CO57015-4; issued on *Such Sweet Thunder* (Columbia CK 65568 2). Relevant manuscript: autograph score. The recording uses part of the manuscript: the four-bar introduction, a modulatory section, and a consequent out-chorus were cut (revisions partly by Strayhorn). Also used for December 6, 1956.

Such Sweet Thunder (movement 11 of 12): *Half the Fun.* "Lately," DEC. First (issued) recording: May 3, 1957. Duke Ellington & His Orchestra. CO56566-4; issued on *Such Sweet Thunder* (Columbia CK 65568 2). Relevant manuscript: autograph score. Recorded August 7, 1956 under its title proper. Movements 2, *Sonnet for Caesar*, 4, *Lady Mac*, 6, *The Telecasters*, 8, *Sonnet for Sister Kate*, 10, *Madness in Great Ones*, and 12, *Circle of Fourths* are by Ellington (all REC). The manuscripts for movements 3, *Sonnet to Hank Cinq*, and 5, *Sonnet in Search of a Moor* are missing.

Sugar Hill Penthouse. "Symphonette-Rhythmique," DEC. First (issued) recording: May 18, 1965. Duke Ellington & His Orchestra. D4-VC-563-1; issued on *The Private Collection, Vol. 8: Studio Sessions, 1957, 1965, 1966, 1967, San Francisco, Chicago, New York* (Saja 7 91232-2). Recorded earlier as part of *Black, Brown and Beige*, January 23, 1943. Relevant manuscripts: autograph score and parts.

Sugar Rum Cherry. See *The Nutcracker Suite* (movement 4 of 9).

Summertime. "Summertime," BSC. First (issued) recording: November 8, 1943. Duke Ellington & His Orchestra. Swing Treasury BB37652D C1-5; issued on *Duke Ellington World Broadcasting Series, Vols. 1–5* (Circle CD 101-5). Relevant manuscript: autograph score. The recording uses part of the manuscript: the five-bar introduction was cut. With additional material also used for June 2, 1945.

Summertime. "Summertime," BSC. First (issued) recording: June 2, 1945. Duke Ellington & His Orchestra. Broadcast; issued on *A Date with the Duke, Vol. 3* (Fairmont Records FA-1003). Relevant manuscript: autograph score. The manuscript is incomplete: the additions made to the earlier version (November 8, 1943) are missing.

Swamp Drum. "Brew," BSC and DEC. First (issued) recording: May 18, 1951. The Coronets. Mercer Records M4033; issued on *The Johnny Hodges All-Stars with the Duke Ellington All-Stars and the Billy Strayhorn All-Stars: Caravan* (Prestige PCD 24103-2). Relevant manuscripts: autograph score (BSC) and parts (DEC).

Sweet & Pungent. "Blues," BSC. First (issued) recording: December 2, 1959. Duke Ellington & His Orchestra. CO64446-6; issued on *Blues in Orbit* (Columbia CK 44051). Relevant manuscript: autograph score.

Sweet Adeline. See *The Girls Suite* (movement 4 of 10).

Swingin' on the Campus. Untitled, DEC. First (issued) recording: February 27, 1939. Johnny Hodges & His Orchestra. Vocalion M976-1. Relevant manuscript: autograph part. The manuscript is incomplete: the backgrounds behind Hodges's solo choruses (second and fourth chorus) are missing.

Symphomaniac, The (movement 1 of 2): *Symphonic or Bust.* "Intro Bells," BSC, and "8th Veil," DEC. First (issued) recording: November 13, 1948. Duke Ellington & His Orchestra. Concert; issued on *Duke Ellington and His Orchestra: Carnegie Hall November 13, 1948* (Vintage Jazz Classics VJC-1024/25-2). Relevant manuscripts: autograph scores. The manuscript is incomplete: three orchestral sections (at [0:25–0:45], [4:42–4:55], and [5:02–5:11]) are missing. The recording uses two earlier Strayhorn introductions—at 1:28–2:01 (mm. 1–20 of *The Eighth Veil*, Ellington replaces the trumpet lines on piano) and at 3:01–3:52 (mm. 1–14 of *Blue Belles of Harlem*). The remainder consists of piano themes and transitions by Ellington. The second movement, *How You Sound*, is by Ellington (DEC).

Symphonic or Bust. See *Symphomaniac, The* (movement 1 of 2).

Take It Slow. "Tune Up Slow," DEC. First (issued) recording: July 25, 1962. Duke Ellington & His Orchestra. Issued on *The Private Collection, Vol. 3: Studio Sessions, New York 1962* (Saja 7 91043-2). Relevant manuscript: autograph score.

Take Love Easy. "Take Love Easy," DEC. First (issued) recording: November 14, 1947. Duke Ellington & His Orchestra. Columbia CO38386-1; issued on *The Complete Duke Ellington: 1947–1952, Vol. 2* (CBS 68275). Relevant manuscripts: autograph score and parts. The recording uses part of the manuscript: the saxophone background from the first vocal chorus was replaced by a unison riff. The order of the recording is at variance with the order suggested by the manuscript.

Take the "A" Train. "Take the 'A' Train," BSC. First (issued) recording: January 15, 1941. Duke Ellington & His Orchestra. Standard Radio Transcription 055250; issued on *Take the "A" Train: The Legendary Blanton-Webster Transcriptions* (Vintage Jazz Classics VJC 1003-2). Relevant manuscripts: autograph score and parts. For the recording of February 15, 1941 (Victor 055283-1; issued on *The Blanton-Webster Band* [RCA Bluebird 5659-2-RB]), the final eight bars of the first chorus were re-scored (author unknown) and added to the parts by copyist Juan Tizol.

Take the "A" Train. "Take the 'A' Train," BSC, and " 'A' Train Ending," DEC. First (issued) recording: October 8, 1942. Duke Ellington & His Orchestra. For the motion picture *Reveille with Beverly*. Relevant manuscripts: autograph scores. Uses the entire first chorus, the four-bar modulation, and the bridge of chorus three of the January 15, 1941, score, with a newly scored coda (final 24 measures). The manuscript is incomplete: the four-bar introduction is missing. Also recorded commercially on March 28, 1946.

Take the "A" Train. "Take the 'A' Train," BSC, " 'A' Train Ending," DEC. First (issued) recording: March 28, 1946. Duke Ellington & His Orchestra. Capitol Transcriptions; issued on *Duke Ellington and His World Famous Orchestra: The Collection '46–47 Recordings* (Hindsight 501). Relevant manuscripts: autograph scores. This version uses the January 15, 1941, score with the coda from October 8, 1942.

Take the "A" Train. "A Train," BSC. First (issued) recording: June 24, 1957. Ella Fitzgerald with Duke Ellington & His Orchestra. VRV21034-5; issued on *Ella Fitzgerald Sings the Duke Ellington Songbook* (Verve 837 035-2). Relevant manuscript: autograph score.

Take the "A" Train. No manuscript known. First (issued) recording: January 1961. Billy Strayhorn & The Paris String Quartet. Issued on *The Peaceful Side of Billy Strayhorn* (Capitol Jazz CDP 7243 8 52563 2 5).

Take the "A" Train. No manuscript known. First (issued) recording: June 30, 1965. Billy Strayhorn & The Riverside Drive Five. Issued on *Billy Strayhorn: Lush Life* (Red Baron AK-52760).

Tapioca. No manuscript known. First (issued) recording: February 14, 1940. Barney Bigard & His Orchestra. Epic WM1140-A; issued on *Duke Ellington and His Orchestra 1939–1940* (Classics 790).

Tea for Two. "T for Two," BSC and DEC. First (issued) recording: November 8, 1943. Duke Ellington & His Orchestra. Circle BB37653A C2-1; issued on *Duke Ellington World Broadcasting Series, Vols. 1–5* (Circle CD 101-5). Relevant manuscripts: autograph score (BSC) and parts (DEC).

Tell Ya What I'm Gonna Do. "Gonna Fall in Love," DEC. First (issued) recording: October 8, 1945. Duke Ellington & His Orchestra. Victor D5VB662-1; issued

on *Black, Brown & Beige (The 1944–1946 Band Recordings)* (RCA Bluebird 6641-2-RB). Relevant manuscript: autograph score. The ten bars following the vocal chorus are by Ellington; the remainder is by Strayhorn. The recording uses part of the manuscript: a twenty-four-bar final section was cut.
Telstar. "Telstar," DEC. First (issued) recording: July 25, 1962. Duke Ellington & His Orchestra. Issued on *The Private Collection, Vol. 3: Studio Sessions, New York 1962* (Saja 7 91043-2). Relevant manuscripts: autograph score and parts. Also recorded as *Tigress* (January 5, 1963).
That's for Me. "That's for Me," DEC. First (issued) recording: November 3, 1945. Duke Ellington & His Orchestra. Broadcast; issued on *Your Saturday Date with the Duke* (Duke Ellington Treasury Series 30). Relevant manuscript: autograph score.
That's the Blues, Old Man. "Blues," DEC. First (issued) recording: November 2, 1940. Johnny Hodges and His Orchestra. Bluebird 053605-1; issued on *The Great Ellington Units* (RCA Bluebird ND86751). Relevant manuscripts: autograph parts.
There I Go. "There I Go," DEC. First (issued) recording: September/October, 1940. Duke Ellington & His Orchestra. Relevant manuscripts: autograph parts. Unissued broadcast from the Hotel Sherman, Chicago, Illinois.
There Shall Be No Night. "Night," DEC. First (issued) recording: September 5, 1940. Duke Ellington & His Orchestra. Victor 053427-1; issued on *The Blanton-Webster Band* (RCA Bluebird 5659-2-RB). Relevant manuscripts: autograph score and parts.
There's a Man in My Life. "Man in My Life," DEC. First (issued) recording: August 14, 1943. Duke Ellington & His Orchestra. Broadcast; issued on *Duke Ellington at the Hurricane Club, Vol. 02* (Hurricane LP HC-6002). Relevant manuscript: autograph score.
There's No You. "There's No You," DEC. First (issued) recording: July 21, 1945. Duke Ellington & His Orchestra. Broadcast; issued on *Your Saturday Date with the Duke* (Duke Ellington Treasury Series 15). Relevant manuscript: autograph score.
Things Ain't What They Used to Be. "Serenade to a P. + P.," DEC. First (issued) recording: July 3, 1941. Johnny Hodges & His Orchestra. Bluebird 061348-1; issued on *The Great Ellington Units* (RCA Bluebird ND86751). Relevant manuscripts: autograph parts.
Things We Did Last Summer, The. "Last Summer," DEC. First (issued) recording: October 25, 1946. Duke Ellington & His Orchestra. Broadcast; issued on *Duke Ellington & His Orchestra* (Fanfare LP-35135). Relevant manuscript: autograph score.
This Is Always. "This Is Always," DEC. First (issued) recording: October 11, 1946. Duke Ellington & His Orchestra. Broadcast; issued on *Duke Ellington & His Orchestra* (Fanfare LP-35135). Relevant manuscript: autograph score.

Tigress. "Telstar," DEC. First (issued) recording: January 5, 1963. Duke Ellington & His Orchestra. Reprise 1707-45; issued on *Afro Bossa* (Discovery). Relevant manuscripts: autograph score and parts. Also recorded as Telstar (July 25, 1962).

To Know You Is to Love You. "To Know You," BSC. First (issued) recording: September 26, 1958. Johnny Ray with Duke Ellington & His Orchestra. CO61513; issued on *Duke 56/62, Vol. 3* (CBS 26306). Relevant manuscript: autograph score (sketchbook no. 4). The recording uses part of the manuscript: an eight-bar instrumental passage was cut.

To Know You Is to Love You. "To Know You," DEC. First (issued) recording: September 12, 1962. Duke Ellington & His Orchestra. Issued on *The Private Collection, Vol. 3: Studio Sessions, New York 1962* (Saja 7 91043-2). Relevant manuscript: autograph score.

Tone Parallel to Harlem, A. "Ending," DEC. First (issued) recording: December 7, 1951. Duke Ellington & His Orchestra. CO50717-1; issued on *Ellington Uptown* (Columbia CK 40836). Relevant manuscript: autograph score. The final 10 measures [13:16–13:44], starting after the drum-roll, are by Strayhorn; the remainder is by Ellington.

Tonight I Shall Sleep (With a Smile on My Face). "Tonight I Shall Sleep," DEC. First (issued) recording: June 6, 1943. Duke Ellington & His Orchestra. MBS Broadcast; issued on *Ben Webster: A Tribute to a Great Jazzman* (Jazz Archives LP 15). Relevant manuscript: autograph score.

Toot Toot Tootie Toot. See *The Nutcracker Suite* (movement 2 of 9).

Top and Bottom. "Cymbals," BSC. First (issued) recording: June 22, 1939. Cootie Williams & His Rug Cutters. Okeh WM1044-A (78 rpm record). Relevant manuscripts: autograph score and parts.

Trees. "Trees," BSC. First (issued) recording: November 13, 1948. Duke Ellington & His Orchestra. Concert; issued on *Duke Ellington and His Orchestra: Carnegie Hall November 13, 1948* (Vintage Jazz Classics VJC-1024/25-2). Relevant manuscript: autograph score.

Triple Play. No manuscript known. First (issued) recording: December 27, 1947. Duke Ellington & His Orchestra. Concert; issued on *The Duke Ellington Carnegie Hall Concerts, December 1947* (Prestige 2PCD 24075-2). A Strayhorn leadsheet is in SIDE.

Tymperturbably Blue. "Boom Boom," DEC. First (issued) recording: February 25, 1959. Duke Ellington & His Orchestra. CO62118; issued on *Duke Ellington's Jazz Party* (Columbia LP CL-1323). Relevant manuscript: autograph score.

U.M.M.G. "Upper Manhattan Medical Group," DEC. First (issued) recording: February 7 or 8, 1956. Duke Ellington & His Orchestra. Issued on *Historically Speaking—The Duke* (Bethlehem BCP-60). Relevant manuscripts: autograph parts.

U.M.M.G. No manuscript known. First (issued) recording: June 30, 1965. Billy

Strayhorn & The Riverside Drive Five. Issued on *Billy Strayhorn: Lush Life* (Red Baron AK-52760).

Under Paris Skies. "Sous le Ciel," DEC. First (issued) recording: February 27, 1962. Duke Ellington & His Orchestra. CO69722; issued on *Midnight in Paris* (Columbia 468403-2). Relevant manuscripts: autograph score and parts.

Until Tonight. "Until Tonight," BSC. First (issued) recording: January 15, 1941. Duke Ellington & His Orchestra. Standard Radio Transcription 055251; issued on *Take the "A" Train: The Legendary Blanton-Webster Transcriptions* (Vintage Jazz Classics VJC 1003-2). Relevant manuscripts: autograph score and parts.

Up and Down, Up and Down. See *Such Sweet Thunder* (movement 7 of 12).

Violence. See *Perfume Suite* (movement 2 of 4).

Violet Blue. "Violet Blue," DEC. First (issued) recording: June 1947. Johnny Hodges & The Ellingtonians. Vogue M1016; issued on *The Johnny Hodges All-Stars with the Duke Ellington All-Stars and the Billy Strayhorn All-Stars: Caravan* (Prestige PCD 24103-2). Relevant manuscript: autograph score.

Violet Blue. "V. Blue," DEC. First (issued) recording: June 9, 1947. Duke Ellington & His Orchestra. Capitol Transcriptions; issued on *Duke Ellington and His World Famous Orchestra: The Collection '46–47 Recordings* (Hindsight 501). Relevant manuscript: autograph score.

Violet Blue. "Violet Blue," DEC. First (issued) recording: March 6, 1950. Duke Ellington & His Orchestra. For the short motion picture *Salute to Duke Ellington* (Universal Pictures); soundtrack issued on Azure audiocassette (available to members of the Duke Ellington Music Society, Belgium). Relevant manuscripts: autograph score and parts. The recording uses part of the manuscript: the six-bar introduction was discarded; the parts carry extra sections that were not used either. Also recorded on June 10, 1950.

Violet Blue. "Violet Blue," DEC. First (issued) recording: June 10, 1950. Duke Ellington & His Orchestra. Unissued broadcast from the Ernst Merck Halle, Hamburg, Germany. Relevant manuscripts: autograph score and parts. Also recorded in part on March 6, 1950.

Virgin Island Suite (movement 1 of 4): *Island Virgin.* "Obmil," DEC. First (issued) recording: April 14, 1965. Duke Ellington & His Orchestra. Issued on *Concert in the Virgin Islands* (Reprise LP R-6185). Relevant manuscript: autograph score.

Virgin Island Suite (movement 3 of 4): *Fiddle on the Diddle.* "Volta," BSC. First (issued) recording: April 14, 1965. Duke Ellington & His Orchestra. Issued on *Concert in the Virgin Islands* (Reprise LP R-6185). Relevant manuscript: autograph score. *Virgin Jungle* is by Ellington (DEC); the manuscript for *Jungle Kitty* is missing.

Walkin' and Singin' the Blues. "Greenwood-Blues," BSC. First (issued) recording:

August 6, 1958. Duke Ellington & His Orchestra. CO61391-5; issued on *Primping for the Prom* (CBS 62993). Relevant manuscript: autograph score. The manuscript is incomplete: the background riff in the final chorus is missing.

Way Down Yonder in New Orleans. "Orleans," DEC. First (issued) recording: November 7, 1940. Duke Ellington & His Orchestra. Dance date; issued on *Duke Ellington and His Famous Orchestra, Fargo, North Dakota* (Vintage Jazz Classics VJC-1019/20-2). Relevant manuscripts: autograph score and parts.

We Speak the Same Language. See *All American in Jazz* (track 9 of 10).

We'll Be Together Again. "Together Again," DEC. First (issued) recording: April 27, 1946. Duke Ellington & His Orchestra. Broadcast; issued on *Your Saturday Date with the Duke* (Duke Ellington Treasury Series 35). Relevant manuscript: autograph score.

What Color Is Virtue? See *My People* (track 8 of 8).

What Else Can You Do with a Drum. See *A Drum Is a Woman* (track 3 of 15).

What Good Would It Do? "What Good," DEC. First (issued) recording: December 2, 1941. Duke Ellington & His Orchestra. Victor 061942-1; issued on *The Blanton-Webster Band* (RCA Bluebird 5659-2-RB). Relevant manuscripts: autograph parts.

What More Can I Say. "What More," DEC. First (issued) recording: December 5, 1953. Duke Ellington & His Orchestra. Cap 20263-7; issued on *The Complete Capitol Recordings of Duke Ellington* (Mosaic MDS-160). Relevant manuscript: autograph score. A four-bar section [2:11–2: 22] in the final strain is by Strayhorn, the remainder is by Ellington.

What's the Good Word, Mr. Bluebird? "B. Bird," BSC and "End of B. Bird," DEC. First (issued) recording: April, 1943. Duke Ellington & His Orchestra. Unissued broadcast, from The Hurricane, NYC. Relevant manuscripts: autograph scores.

Where or When. "WOW!," DEC. First (issued) recording: October 10, 1957. Duke Ellington & His Orchestra. CO59937-1; issued on *Ellington Indigos* (Columbia CK-44444). Relevant manuscript: autograph score (sketchbook no. 4: 9–13). Scored between July 1943 and April 1944 for a vocalist. See also Appendix C.

Who Wouldn't Love You? "Who Wouldn't," DEC. First (issued) recording: August 29, 1942. Duke Ellington & His Orchestra. Broadcast, issued on *Duke Ellington and His Orchestra 1941–1943* (Temple LP M-554). Relevant manuscripts: autograph parts. The surviving recording does not start at the beginning, but at least 37 bars into the manuscript. The manuscript is incomplete: the four-bar coda is missing (it was added to the parts by copyist Juan Tizol).

Why Was I Born. "Born," BSC. First (issued) recording: March 2, 1961. Duke Ellington & His Orchestra. RHCO70036; issued on *Duke 56/62, Vol. 3* (CBS 26306). Relevant manuscript: autograph score.

Wild Man. "Wild Man," REC. First (issued) recording: July 6, 1961. Duke Ellington & Count Basie with Their Orchestras. CO67611; issued on *First Time! The Count Meets the Duke* (Columbia CK 65571 2). Relevant manuscript: autograph score. The order of the recording is at variance with the order suggested by the manuscript.

Wildest Gal in Town, The. "Wildest Gal," DEC. First (issued) recording: September 29, 1947. Duke Ellington & His Orchestra. Columbia HCO2656-1; issued on *The Complete Duke Ellington: 1947–1952, Vol. 1* (CBS 67264). Relevant manuscript: autograph score. The order of the recording is at variance with the order suggested by the manuscript.

Willow Weep for Me. "Willow," BSC. First (issued) recording: October 10, 1957. Duke Ellington & His Orchestra. CO59936-1; issued on *Ellington Indigos* (Columbia CK-44444). Relevant manuscript: autograph score (sketchbook no. 2: 15–19).

Without a Song. "W. Song," BSC and DEC. First (issued) recording: April 6, 1953. Duke Ellington & His Orchestra. Cap 11399-4; issued on *The Complete Capitol Recordings of Duke Ellington* (Mosaic MDS-160). Relevant manuscripts: autograph score (sketchbook no. 3: 6–10) and parts (DEC).

Women (They'll Get You). "W.W.W.," DEC. First (issued) recording: August 14, 1947. Duke Ellington & His Orchestra. Columbia HCO2533-1; issued on *The Complete Duke Ellington: 1947–1952, Vol. 1* (CBS 67264). Relevant manuscript: autograph score. Measures 1–28 are by Strayhorn, and measures 29–68 are by Ellington.

Wonder of You, The. "Wonder of You," DEC. First (issued) recording: November 26, 1945. Duke Ellington & His Orchestra. Victor D5VB951-1; issued on *Black, Brown & Beige (The 1944–1946 Band Recordings)* (RCA Bluebird 6641-2-RB). Relevant manuscript: autograph score.

Wrong, It Can't Be Wrong. "Wrong," BSC. First (issued) recording: April 3, 1943. Duke Ellington & His Orchestra. Broadcast; issued on *Duke Ellington* (Azure LP-431). Relevant manuscript: autograph score.

Yesterdays. "Yesterdaze," BSC and DEC. First (issued) recording: May 12, 1945. Duke Ellington & His Orchestra. Broadcast; issued on *Your Saturday Date with the Duke* (Duke Ellington Treasury Series 05). Relevant manuscripts: autograph score (BSC) and parts (DEC).

You and I. "U + I," DEC. First (issued) recording: December 3, 1941. Duke Ellington & His Orchestra. Standard Radio Transcription BS061946-1; issued on *Take the "A" Train: The Legendary Blanton-Webster Transcriptions* (Vintage Jazz Classics VJC 1003-2). Relevant manuscript: autograph part.

You Don't Love Me No More. "No More," DEC. First (issued) recording: March 24, 1959. Lil Greenwood with Duke Ellington & His Orchestra. Unissued RCA studio recording. Relevant manuscript: autograph score.

You Never Know the Things You Miss. "Never Know the Things You Miss," BSC.

First (issued) recording: January 3, 1945. Duke Ellington & His Orchestra. Circle N-3004-2; issued on *Duke Ellington World Broadcasting Series, Vols. 1–5* (Circle CD 101-5). Relevant manuscript: autograph score.

You Think of Ev'rything. Untitled, BSC and DEC. First (issued) recording: September 10, 1940. Duke Ellington & His Orchestra. Broadcast; issued on *Live from the Hotel Sherman, Chicago, Vol. 1* (Jazz Supreme 704). Relevant manuscripts: autograph score (BSC) and parts (DEC).

Your Love Has Faded. "Love Has Faded," BSC and DEC. First (issued) recording: October 14, 1939. Johnny Hodges & His Orchestra. Okeh WM1098-A. Relevant manuscripts: autograph score (BSC) and parts (DEC).

Your Love Has Faded. "Your Love Has Faded," "Your Love Is Faded" and untitled, DEC. First (issued) recording: October 16, 1939. Duke Ellington & His Orchestra. Columbia WM1107-A; issued on *Duke Ellington and His Orchestra 1939–1940* (Classics 790). Relevant manuscripts: autograph scores by Strayhorn (sketchbook no. 3: 33) and Ellington; autograph parts by Strayhorn. Ellington scored the introduction and instrumental chorus, Strayhorn the vocal chorus and eight-bar coda.

Your Love Has Faded. "Faded," DEC. First (issued) recording: March 20, 1957. Duke Ellington & His Orchestra. Columbia CO57522-9; issued on *Duke 56/62* (CBS). Relevant manuscript: autograph score.

Your Love Has Faded. "Love Faded," DEC. First (issued) recording: December 11, 1961. Johnny Hodges with Billy Strayhorn & His Orchestra. Issued on *Billy Strayhorn and The Orchestra* (Verve). Relevant manuscripts: autograph score and parts.

Appendix C

Billy Strayhorn's Works on Record (Posthumously Premiered)

The following is an inventory of music by Strayhorn (both originals and arrangements) premiered on record posthumously, with the exception of the Ellington orchestra's recordings for ...*And His Mother Called Him Bill*, which are included in Appendix B.

In a number of instances, the works listed below were recorded earlier by the Ellington orchestra, but in an abridged form. These works are cross-referenced with the entries in Appendix B.

The entries below follow the format detailed in the introduction to Appendix B.

Anatomy of a Murder. "Polly No. 1," "Polly Did," and "Polly Did Continued," DEC and REC. First (issued) recording: October 1998. The Dutch Jazz Orchestra. *So This Is Love: More Newly Discovered Works of Billy Strayhorn* (Challenge Records CHR 70091). Relevant manuscripts: autograph scores and parts. Parts of this score were used for *Low Key Lightly* (see Appendix B).

Autumn in New York. "AINY" and "Autumn in New York," BSC and DEC. First (issued) recording: October 1999. The Dutch Jazz Orchestra. *You Go to My Head: Strayhorn and Standards* (Challenge Records CHR 70090). Relevant manuscripts: autograph scores and parts.

Bagatelle. "Bagatelle," DEC. First (issued) recording: January 1995. The Dutch Jazz Orchestra. *Portrait of a Silk Thread: Newly Discovered Works of Billy Strayhorn* (Challenge Records CHR 70089). Relevant manuscripts: autograph score and parts.

Blue Heart. "Blue Heart," DEC. First (issued) recording: October 1998. The Dutch Jazz Orchestra. *So This Is Love: More Newly Discovered Works of Billy*

Strayhorn (Challenge Records CHR 70091). Relevant manuscripts: autograph score and parts.

Blue House. "Blue House," DEC. First (issued) recording: October 1998. The Dutch Jazz Orchestra. *Something to Live For: The Dutch Jazz Orchestra Plays the Music of Billy Strayhorn* (Challenge Records CHR 70092). Relevant manuscripts: autograph score.

Blue Star. "Blue Star," BSC and DEC. First (issued) recording: January 1995. The Dutch Jazz Orchestra. *Portrait of a Silk Thread: Newly Discovered Works of Billy Strayhorn* (Challenge Records CHR 70089). Relevant manuscripts: autograph scores, leadsheet, and parts.

Boll Weevil Ballet. "Boll Weavol," BSC and DEC. First (issued) recording: October 1999. The Dutch Jazz Orchestra. *So This Is Love: More Newly Discovered Works of Billy Strayhorn* (Challenge Records CHR 70091). Relevant manuscripts: autograph scores.

Can't Help Lovin' Dat Man. "Lovin' That Man," DEC. First (issued) recording: October 1999. The Dutch Jazz Orchestra. *You Go to My Head: Strayhorn and Standards* (Challenge Records CHR 70090). Relevant manuscripts: autograph score and parts. Parts of this score were used for October 5, 1946 (see Appendix B).

Cashmere Cutie. "Cashmere Cutie," BSC and DEC. First (issued) recording: January 1995. The Dutch Jazz Orchestra. *Portrait of a Silk Thread: Newly Discovered Works of Billy Strayhorn* (Challenge Records CHR 70089). Relevant manuscripts: autograph scores (BSC and DEC), leadsheet and parts (DEC).

Chelsea Bridge. "Chelsea Bridge," BSC. First (issued) recording: October 1998. The Dutch Jazz Orchestra. *Something to Live For: The Dutch Jazz Orchestra Plays the Music of Billy Strayhorn* (Challenge Records CHR 70092). Relevant manuscripts: autograph score. Parts of this score were used for September 17, 1941, and December 2, 1941 (see Appendix B).

Everything Is Copasetic. "Copasetic," BSC. First (issued) recording: April 2000. The Dutch Jazz Orchestra. *Something to Live For: The Dutch Jazz Orchestra Plays the Music of Billy Strayhorn* (Challenge Records CHR 70092). Relevant manuscripts: autograph score.

Fantastic Rhythm. "Fantastic Rhythm," DH. First (issued) recording: October 1999. The Dutch Jazz Orchestra. *Something to Live For: The Dutch Jazz Orchestra Plays the Music of Billy Strayhorn* (Challenge Records CHR 70092). Relevant manuscripts: autograph score.

Fantastic Rhythm: Let Nature Take Its Course. Untitled, REC. First (issued) recording: April 2000. The Dutch Jazz Orchestra. *Something to Live For: The Dutch Jazz Orchestra Plays the Music of Billy Strayhorn* (Challenge Records CHR 70092). Relevant manuscripts: autograph score.

Feet on the Beat. "Feet on the Beat," BSC. First (issued) recording: October 1998.

The Dutch Jazz Orchestra. *So This Is Love: More Newly Discovered Works of Billy Strayhorn* (Challenge Records CHR 70091). Relevant manuscripts: autograph score.

Flame Indigo. "Flame Indigo," DEC. First (issued) recording: October 1998. The Dutch Jazz Orchestra. *So This Is Love: More Newly Discovered Works of Billy Strayhorn* (Challenge Records CHR 70091). Relevant manuscripts: autograph score.

Fol-De-Rol-Rol. "Fol De Rol," BSC. First (issued) recording: October 1998. The Dutch Jazz Orchestra. *So This Is Love: More Newly Discovered Works of Billy Strayhorn* (Challenge Records CHR 70091). Relevant manuscripts: autograph score (BSC) and parts (DEC).

Hip. "Hip," BSC. First (issued) recording: April 2000. The Dutch Jazz Orchestra. *Something to Live For: The Dutch Jazz Orchestra Plays the Music of Billy Strayhorn* (Challenge Records CHR 70092). Relevant manuscripts: autograph score and parts.

Hipper-Bug. "Hipper-Bug," BSC. First (issued) recording: April 2000. The Dutch Jazz Orchestra. *Something to Live For: The Dutch Jazz Orchestra Plays the Music of Billy Strayhorn* (Challenge Records CHR 70092). Relevant manuscripts: autograph score.

Hues, The. "The Hues," DEC. First (issued) recording: January 1995. The Dutch Jazz Orchestra. *Portrait of a Silk Thread: Newly Discovered Works of Billy Strayhorn* (Challenge Records CHR 70089). Relevant manuscripts: autograph score. Arranged for the recording by Walter van de Leur.

I'll Remember April. "Avril, je me vous souviendrais," DEC. First (issued) recording: October 1999. The Dutch Jazz Orchestra. *You Go to My Head: Strayhorn and Standards* (Challenge Records CHR 70090). Relevant manuscripts: autograph score.

I've Got the World on a String. "World on a String," DEC. First (issued) recording: October 1999. The Dutch Jazz Orchestra. *You Go to My Head: Strayhorn and Standards* (Challenge Records CHR 70090). Relevant manuscripts: autograph score.

Jo. "Jo," DEC and SIDE. First (issued) recording: October 1999. The Dutch Jazz Orchestra. *So This Is Love: More Newly Discovered Works of Billy Strayhorn* (Challenge Records CHR 70091). Relevant manuscripts: autograph score and parts.

Lament for an Orchid. "Lament for an Orchid," BSC and DEC. First (issued) recording: January 1995. The Dutch Jazz Orchestra. *Portrait of a Silk Thread: Newly Discovered Works of Billy Strayhorn* (Challenge Records CHR 70089). Relevant manuscripts: autograph score (BSC) and parts (DEC).

Lana Turner. "Lana Turner," DEC. First (issued) recording: January 1995. The Dutch Jazz Orchestra. *Portrait of a Silk Thread: Newly Discovered Works of Billy Strayhorn* (Challenge Records CHR 70089). Relevant manuscripts:

autograph score and parts. The score does not carry the melody—it was taken from the copyright registration file, titled *Francesca* (DEC).

Leave Me Be. "Leave Me Be," BSC. First (issued) recording: April 6–9, 1998. UMO Jazz Orchestra featuring Annika Hultman, Ulf Johansson, and Larry Coryell. Finland Svenska Radio (FSR CD02). Relevant manuscripts: autograph leadsheet. Arranged for the recording by Eero Koivistoinen.

Love Has Passed Me By, Again. "LHPMBA," BSC. First (issued) recording: January 1995. The Dutch Jazz Orchestra. *Portrait of a Silk Thread: Newly Discovered Works of Billy Strayhorn* (Challenge Records CHR 70089). Relevant manuscripts: autograph score and lead sheet.

Love of Don Perlimplín for Belisa in Their Garden, The: Love, Love. "Love, Love," BSC. First (issued) recording: April 2000. The Dutch Jazz Orchestra. *Something to Live For: The Dutch Jazz Orchestra Plays the Music of Billy Strayhorn* (Challenge Records CHR 70092). Relevant manuscripts: autograph score.

Love of Don Perlimplín for Belisa in Their Garden, The: Sprite Music. "Sprite Music," BSC. First (issued) recording: October 1999. The Dutch Jazz Orchestra. *Something to Live For: The Dutch Jazz Orchestra Plays the Music of Billy Strayhorn* (Challenge Records CHR 70092). Relevant manuscripts: autograph score.

Love of Don Perlimplín for Belisa in Their Garden, The: The Flowers Die of Love. Untitled, BSC. First (issued) recording: April 2000. The Dutch Jazz Orchestra. *Something to Live For: The Dutch Jazz Orchestra Plays the Music of Billy Strayhorn* (Challenge Records CHR 70092). Relevant manuscripts: autograph score.

Love of Don Perlimplín for Belisa in Their Garden, The: Wounded Love. "Wounded Love," BSC. First (issued) recording: April 6–9, 1998. UMO Jazz Orchestra featuring Annika Hultman, Ulf Johansson, and Larry Coryell. Finland Svenska Radio (FSR CD02). Relevant manuscripts: autograph leadsheet. First recording of the song with its original lyrics.

Lover Man. "Lover Man," DEC. First (issued) recording: October 1999. The Dutch Jazz Orchestra. *You Go to My Head: Strayhorn and Standards* (Challenge Records CHR 70090). Relevant manuscripts: autograph score and parts. Parts of this score were used for August 26, 1946 (see Appendix B).

Lozit. "Lozit," BSC and DEC. First (issued) recording: October 1999. The Dutch Jazz Orchestra. *So This Is Love: More Newly Discovered Works of Billy Strayhorn* (Challenge Records CHR 70091). Relevant manuscripts: autograph score (BSC) and parts (DEC).

Lush Life. "Lonely Again," BSC. First (issued) recording: October 1999. The Dutch Jazz Orchestra. *So This Is Love: More Newly Discovered Works of Billy Strayhorn* (Challenge Records CHR 70091). Relevant manuscripts: autograph score.

Man I Love, The. "The Man I Love," BSC and DEC. First (issued) recording: October 1999. The Dutch Jazz Orchestra. *You Go to My Head: Strayhorn and Standards* (Challenge Records CHR 70090). Relevant manuscripts: autograph score and parts.

Matinee. "Matinee," DEC. First (issued) recording: October 1998. The Dutch Jazz Orchestra. *So This Is Love: More Newly Discovered Works of Billy Strayhorn* (Challenge Records CHR 70091). Relevant manuscripts: autograph score.

Maybe. "Untitled," BSC. First (issued) recording: October 1993. Lena Horne. *We'll Be Together Again* (Blue Note 7243 8 28974 2 2).

Moon River. "Moon River," BSC. First (issued) recording: October 1999. The Dutch Jazz Orchestra. *You Go to My Head: Strayhorn and Standards* (Challenge Records CHR 70090). Relevant manuscripts: autograph score.

Night and Day. "N. + Day," DEC and SIDE. First (issued) recording: October 1999. The Dutch Jazz Orchestra. *You Go to My Head: Strayhorn and Standards* (Challenge Records CHR 70090). Relevant manuscripts: autograph score and parts.

On the Wrong Side of the Rail Road Tracks. "R. R. Track," DEC. First (issued) recording: October 1998. The Dutch Jazz Orchestra. *Something to Live For: The Dutch Jazz Orchestra Plays the Music of Billy Strayhorn* (Challenge Records CHR 70092). Relevant manuscripts: autograph score.

Oo, You Make Me Tingle. "OO!!," BSC. First (issued) recording: April 6–9, 1998. UMO Jazz Orchestra featuring Annika Hultman, Ulf Johansson, and Larry Coryell. Finland Svenska Radio (FSR CD02). Relevant manuscripts: autograph leadsheet. Arranged for the recording by Jarmo Savolainen.

Orson. "Orson," BSC. First (issued) recording: October 1998. The Dutch Jazz Orchestra. *So This Is Love: More Newly Discovered Works of Billy Strayhorn* (Challenge Records CHR 70091). Relevant manuscripts: autograph score (BSC). Parts of this score were used for April 7, 1953 (see Appendix B).

Paramaribo. "Parimaribo [sic]," BSC. First (issued) recording: April 6–9, 1998. UMO Jazz Orchestra featuring Annika Hultman, Ulf Johansson, and Larry Coryell. Finland Svenska Radio (FSR CD02). Relevant manuscripts: autograph leadsheet. Arranged for the recording by Ralf Nyqvist.

Penthouse on Shady Avenue, A. "Penthouse," REC. First (issued) recording: April 2000. The Dutch Jazz Orchestra. *Something to Live For: The Dutch Jazz Orchestra Plays the Music of Billy Strayhorn* (Challenge Records CHR 70092). Relevant manuscripts: autograph score.

Pentonsilic. "Pentonsilic," BSC and DEC. First (issued) recording: January 1995. The Dutch Jazz Orchestra. *Portrait of a Silk Thread: Newly Discovered Works of Billy Strayhorn* (Challenge Records CHR 70089). Relevant manuscripts: autograph score (BSC) and parts (DEC). Parts of this score were used for *Perfume Suite* (movement 1 of 4): *Love* (see Appendix B).

Pomegranate. "Pomgranate [sic]," DEC. First (issued) recording: October 1998. The Dutch Jazz Orchestra. *So This Is Love: More Newly Discovered Works of*

Billy Strayhorn (Challenge Records CHR 70091). Relevant manuscripts: autograph score and parts. Parts of this score were used for March 7, 1957 (see Appendix B).

Portrait of a Silk Thread. "Portrait of a Silk Thread," DEC. First (issued) recording: January 1995. The Dutch Jazz Orchestra. *Portrait of a Silk Thread: Newly Discovered Works of Billy Strayhorn* (Challenge Records CHR 70089). Relevant manuscripts: autograph score and parts.

Pretty Girl. "Pretty Girl," DEC. First (issued) recording: October 1998. The Dutch Jazz Orchestra. *Something to Live For: The Dutch Jazz Orchestra Plays the Music of Billy Strayhorn* (Challenge Records CHR 70092). Relevant manuscripts: autograph score. Parts of this score were used for December 6, 1956, and May 3, 1957 (see Appendix B).

Remember. "Remember," REC. First (issued) recording: October 1999. The Dutch Jazz Orchestra. *So This Is Love: More Newly Discovered Works of Billy Strayhorn* (Challenge Records CHR 70091). Relevant manuscripts: autograph score.

Sacre Supreme, Le. "Sacre Supreme," BSC and DEC. First (issued) recording: January 1995. The Dutch Jazz Orchestra. *Portrait of a Silk Thread: Newly Discovered Works of Billy Strayhorn* (Challenge Records CHR 70089). Relevant manuscripts: autograph scores.

Skylark. "Sky-Lark," DEC. First (issued) recording: October 1999. The Dutch Jazz Orchestra. *You Go to My Head: Strayhorn and Standards* (Challenge Records CHR 70090). Relevant manuscripts: autograph score and parts.

So This Is Love. "So This Is Love," BSC and REC. First (issued) recording: October 1999. The Dutch Jazz Orchestra. *So This Is Love: More Newly Discovered Works of Billy Strayhorn* (Challenge Records CHR 70091). Relevant manuscripts: autograph leadsheet. Arranged for the recording by Jerry van Rooijen.

Suite for the Duo. First (issued) recording: 1968. The Dwike Mitchell-Willie Ruff Duo. *Strayhorn* (Mainstream LP). Relevant manuscripts: autograph scores in the possession of Dwike Mitchell.

Swing Dance. "Swing Dance," BSC. First (issued) recording: October 1998. The Dutch Jazz Orchestra. *So This Is Love: More Newly Discovered Works of Billy Strayhorn* (Challenge Records CHR 70091). Relevant manuscripts: autograph score.

Tiffany. "Tiffany," BSC. First (issued) recording: October 1998. The Dutch Jazz Orchestra. *So This Is Love: More Newly Discovered Works of Billy Strayhorn* (Challenge Records CHR 70091). Relevant manuscripts: autograph score.

Tonk. "Tonk," BSC and DEC. First (issued) recording: January 1995. The Dutch Jazz Orchestra. *Portrait of a Silk Thread: Newly Discovered Works of Billy Strayhorn* (Challenge Records CHR 70089). Relevant manuscripts: autograph score (BSC) and parts (DEC).

Valse (lento sostenuto). "Valse (lento sostenuto)," BSC. First (issued) recording: October 1998. The Dutch Jazz Orchestra. *So This Is Love: More Newly Discovered Works of Billy Strayhorn* (Challenge Records CHR 70091). Relevant manuscripts: autograph score.

Where or When. "WOW!," DEC. First (issued) recording: October 1998. The Dutch Jazz Orchestra. *You Go to My Head: Strayhorn and Standards* (Challenge Records CHR 70090). Relevant manuscripts: autograph score and parts. This score was recorded as an instrumental on October 10, 1957 (see Appendix B).

Wounded Love. "Wounded Love," BSC, DEC, and SIDE. First (issued) recording: January 1995. The Dutch Jazz Orchestra. *Portrait of a Silk Thread: Newly Discovered Works of Billy Strayhorn* (Challenge Records CHR 70089). Relevant manuscripts: autograph score, leadsheet, and parts (DEC and SIDE).

You Go to My Head. "You Go to My Head," DEC. First (issued) recording: October 1999. The Dutch Jazz Orchestra. *You Go to My Head: Strayhorn and Standards* (Challenge Records CHR 70090). Relevant manuscripts: autograph score.

You're the One. "You're The One," DEC. First (issued) recording: October 1993. Lena Horne. *We'll Be Together Again* (Blue Note 7243 8 28974 2 2).

Appendix D

Billy Strayhorn's Compositions

Appendix D lists all of Strayhorn's known compositions, as well as those attributed to him, whether recorded or not. Authorship is established on the basis of original manuscripts and their provenance. As much as possible, other sources, such as interviews, articles, spoken introductions at concerts, credits on LPs and record labels, as well as copyright registrations have been taken into consideration.

The date gives the year of *composition*, as close as possible, again based on autographs, recordings, interviews, articles, and manuscript provenance. Still, dates listed are approximate. If the copyright date deviates from the date of composition, this is listed as well.

The attribution of authorship in this list willingly stays on the conservative side: in case of any reasonable doubt a work is not listed. For that reason some four dozen vocal tunes credited to Ellington but apparently only existent as Strayhorn manuscripts have been omitted, since musically they provide insufficient proof of Strayhorn's authorship.

Because of the thin line between composition and arrangement, the truly joint works (the handful of pieces that both composers evidently worked on together) are treated on a case-by-case basis. Even though Strayhorn contributed to *Black, Brown and Beige* and *Harlem*, it would be an overstatement to list him as *co-composer* for these works, since they were conceived by Ellington. Yet, when Strayhorn added significantly to an Ellington work, be it thematically, harmonically, or structurally, the piece gets listed as a co-composition. Thus, the unfinished Ellington work *Blutopia*, expanded by Strayhorn into a full playable work, is listed as a co-composition, whereas *Blue Belles of Harlem* is not listed: unlike *Blutopia*, *Blue Belles* was a finished, self-contained Ellington composition before Strayhorn reworked it. *C-Jam Blues*, on the other hand, is listed as a co-composition, because Strayhorn expanded the earlier *C Blues*, first credited to Ellington.

A significant number of compositions remained unrecorded during Strayhorn's life. Listed here are only those unrecorded works that seem to be finished, self-contained compositions, that is, compositions that consist of a melodically and harmonically rounded-out statement. Consequently, some two hundred sketches are not listed.

As much as possible, each entry gives the original or oldest known title, together with all relevant alternate titles. Discographers tend to list all known alternate titles, but that is not the purpose here. Strayhorn's *Johnny Come Lately*, for instance, had been recorded and copyrighted under that title before it got listed as *Stomp* in the January 1943 Carnegie Hall program. That alternate title is of little relevance here and is therefore not given. By contrast, the original autograph for *Johnny Come Lately* has an earlier title (*Moe*) which is therefore listed.

Movements from suites are listed under the respective suite's title.

"A" Blues. Billy Strayhorn. 1962. Copyright registered posthumously (2000).
Absinthe. See *Lament for an Orchid.*
After All. Billy Strayhorn. 1941. Copyright registered 1942.
Agra. See *Far East Suite* (movement 7).
Air-Conditioned Jungle. Billy Strayhorn and Jimmy Hamilton. 1945. Copyright registered in the names of Duke Ellington and Jimmy Hamilton.
AIX. See *A Midnight in Paris.*
All Aboard. See *Anchors Aweigh.*
All Day Long. Billy Strayhorn. 1951. Copyright registered 1955. Alternate title: *Lavender Lift.*
All Heart (movement 2 of *A Portrait of Ella Fitzgerald*). See *Entrance of Youth.*
All Roads Lead Back to You. See *Charlotte Russe.*
Allah Bye. Billy Strayhorn. 1942. Copyright registered 1960.
Alouette. See *On the Riviera.*
Amad. See *Far East Suite* (movement 8).
Anatomy of a Murder:

> *Polly's Theme.* Billy Strayhorn. 1959. Copyright registered as *Haupê* and *Low Key Lightly* in the name of Duke Ellington. Alternate titles: *Polly # 1, Polly A Train, Polly Did, Polly Did Continued, Polly Lead, Polly Mix,* and *Polly Prime.* Copyright registered posthumously as *Themes from Anatomy of a Murder* (1994).

Anchors Aweigh. Billy Strayhorn and Honi Coles (unidentified sections). 1962. All copyrights registered posthumously (2000). Known titles:

> *Anchors Aweigh.*
> *Bon Voyage—Welcome Aboard.* Alternate title: *All Aboard.*

Cook and Brown.
Drill.
Everything Is Copasetic. Alternate titles: *The Copasetics Song* and *Copasetic.*
New Low Down.
Swing Dance. Copyright registered posthumously (1998).

Anitra's Dance. See *Peer Gynt Suites Nos. 1 and 2* (movement 5).
Arabesque Cookie. See *Nutcracker Suite* (movement 9).
Åse's Death. See *Peer Gynt Suites Nos. 1 and 2* (movement 4).
BDB. Billy Strayhorn. 1961. Copyright registered in the names of Duke Ellington and Billy Strayhorn (1964).
Baby Clementine. See *Clementine.*
Bagatelle. Billy Strayhorn. 1957. Copyright registered posthumously (1994).
Balcony Serenade. See *Perfume Suite* (movement 1).
Ballad for Very Tired and Very Sad Lotus Eaters. Billy Strayhorn. 1956. Copyright registered 1964.
Ballet of the Flying Saucers. See *A Drum Is a Woman.*
Barefoot Stomper. Author(s) not established (score has not been located). Undated. Copyright registered in the names of Duke Ellington and Billy Strayhorn (1965).
Barney Goin' Easy. Duke Ellington and Billy Strayhorn. 1939. Copyright registered as *I'm Checkin' Out—Goom Bye* (1939), in the names of Duke Ellington and Billy Strayhorn (words and music).
Beauty and Talent. See *Rose-Colored Glasses.*
Beggar's Holiday. See *Themes from Beggar's Holiday.*
Beyond Category. See *A Portrait of Ella Fitzgerald* (movement 3).
Big Fat Alice's Blues. Author(s) not established (no score has been located). Undated. Copyright registered in the names of Duke Ellington and Billy Strayhorn (1965).
Big White Mountain. See *Saturday Laughter.*
Bioscope Song. See *Saturday Laughter.*
Bip. Billy Strayhorn. 1949. Copyright registered posthumously as *Blues in Purple* (1996).
Blood Count. Billy Strayhorn. 1966. Copyright registered 1967. Alternate title: *Blue Cloud* (no relation to the similarly titled second movement of the *North by Southwest Suite*).
Blossom. Johnny Mercer (words), Duke Ellington and Billy Strayhorn (music). 1954.
Blousons Noirs. Billy Strayhorn. 1962. Copyright registered posthumously (2000). Credited at the time of its release (1988) to Duke Ellington.
Blue Bird of Delhi. See *Far East Suite* (movement 2).
Blue Cloud. See *Blood Count.*

Blue Cloud. See *North by Southwest Suite* (movement 2, *Boo Loose*).
Blue Heart. Billy Strayhorn. 1946. Copyright registered as *Paradise* (1949).
Blue House. Billy Strayhorn. 1941. Copyright registered posthumously (1996).
Blue Mural from Two Perspectives, A. Billy Strayhorn. 1965. Also known as *A Blue Mural from Two Points of View*. No copyright has been filed (score has not been located).
Blue Orchid. Billy Strayhorn. 1942.
Blue Pepper. See: *Far East Suite* (movement 6).
Blue Star. Billy Strayhorn. 1941. Copyright registered posthumously (1994).
Blues I + II. Billy Strayhorn. 1956. Alternate title: *Blues*. Copyright registered posthumously (2000). Credited at the time of its release to Duke Ellington.
Blues in Orbit. See *Star Blues*.
Blues in Purple. See *Bip*.
Blues to Be There. See *Newport Jazz Festival Suite* (movement 2).
Blues. See *Blues I + II*.
Blukie. Billy Strayhorn. 1957. Copyright registered posthumously (2000).
Blutopia. Duke Ellington and Billy Strayhorn. 1944. Copyright registered in the name of Duke Ellington.
Boll Weevil Ballet. See *Themes from Beggar's Holiday*.
Bon Soir Madame. See *On the Riviera*.
Bon Voyage—Welcome Aboard. See *Anchors Aweigh*.
Boo Loose. Billy Strayhorn. 1966. Alternate titles: *Boo-Lose; Boo Lose; Pretty Little One*. See also *North by Southwest Suite* (movement 2).
Boo-Dah. Billy Strayhorn (words and music). 1954.
Bounce. Billy Strayhorn. 1941. Copyright registered posthumously (2000).
Boom Boom. Billy Strayhorn. 1959. Copyright registered as *Tymperturbably Blue*, in the names of Duke Ellington and Billy Strayhorn (1959).
Brother Big Eyes. See *Rose-Colored Glasses*.
Brown Betty. Billy Strayhorn. 1948. Copyright registered in the names of Duke Ellington and Billy Strayhorn (1951). In a spoken introduction Ellington credits the work to Strayhorn.
Brown Penny. See *Themes from Beggar's Holiday*.
Bugle Breaks. Duke Ellington, Mercer Ellington, and Billy Strayhorn. 1941. Copyright registered 1945.
But. See *Themes from Jump for Joy* (1959).
C-Jam Blues. Duke Ellington and Billy Strayhorn. 1941. Copyright registered in the name of Duke Ellington (1942).
Can It Be. Leonard Feather (words) and Billy Strayhorn (music). No copyright filed (score has not been located). As per Tempo Music Catalogue.
Can-Can. See *On the Riviera*.
Carribee Joe. See *A Drum Is a Woman*.

Cashmere Cutie. Billy Strayhorn. 1957.

Chalmeau. Harry Carney and Billy Strayhorn. 1946.

Charlotte Russe. Billy Strayhorn. 1945. Copyright registered as *Hominy* in the name of Billy Strayhorn (1945). Newly registered as *All Roads Lead Back to You* (1946), in the names of Allan Roy (words) and Duke Ellington and Billy Strayhorn (music). Alternate title: *Lotus Blossom.*

Charpoy. See *Lana Turner.*

Chelsea Bridge. Billy Strayhorn. 1941.

Chinoiserie. See *Nutcracker Suite* (movement 7).

Chippy. Billy Strayhorn. Undated. Copyright registered posthumously (2000).

Christmas Surprise, A. See *A Song for Christmas.*

Circle. Duke Ellington and Billy Strayhorn. 1964.

Circle. See *Felix.*

Circle of Fourths. See *Such Sweet Thunder* (movement 12).

Clementine. Billy Strayhorn. 1941. Copyright registered 1942. Newly registered as *Baby Clementine* (1958), in the names of Ruth Roberts, Bill Katz, and Stanley Clayton (words), and Billy Strayhorn (music).

Coffee and Kisses. Billy Strayhorn. 1953. Copyright registered posthumously (2000). Credited at the time of its release to F. Hollander and R. Freed, who wrote a different piece by the same title in 1938.

Coles and Atkins. See *Copasetics Dances.*

Coloratura. See *Perfume Suite* (movement 4).

Concerto for Piano and Percussion. Billy Strayhorn. 1934. No copyright has been filed (no score has been located).

Congo Square. See *A Drum Is a Woman.*

Cook and Brown. See *Anchors Aweigh.*

Cookie. See *Copasetics Dances.*

Copasetic. See *Anchors Aweigh.*

Copasetics Cruise. Billy Strayhorn. 1957. Multimovement *Copasetics Dance.* No individual titles known (no score has been located).

Copasetics Dances. For the annual *Copasetics Dance,* written between 1951 and 1960, the titles remain unknown, as do most of their individual numbers. The following titles by Billy Strayhorn belong either to one of these lost shows or to any of the known *Copasetics Dances* (*Anchors Aweigh; Copasetics Cruise; Down Dere; On the Riviera*):

> *Coles and Atkins.*
> *Cookie.*
> *Don't Mind if I Do* (no score has been located).
> *Everybody.*
> *Everything Is Coming Up.*
> *Finale* (three finales survive—they have been copyrighted posthumously as *Finale 1, Finale 2,* and *Finale 3*).

Limbo.
Opening (four openings survive—they have been copyrighted posthumously as *Opening 1, Opening 2, Opening 3,* and *Opening 4*).
Phace.
Work Song.

Copasetics Song, The. See *Anchors Aweigh.*
Cordon Bleu. Billy Strayhorn. 1962. Copyright registered posthumously in the name of Duke Ellington (1988).
Cottage on the Hill. See *Rose-Colored Glasses.*
Cream for Supper. See *Themes from Beggar's Holiday.*
Cue's Blue Now. Johnny Hodges and Billy Strayhorn. 1959. Copyright registered 1965.
Dance of the Floreadores. See *Nutcracker Suite* (movement 8).
Day Dream. Billy Strayhorn. 1939. Copyright registered in the names of Duke Ellington and Billy Strayhorn (1940). Newly registered (1941) in the names of John LaTouche (words) and Duke Ellington and Billy Strayhorn (music).
Deep South Suite. 1946. All copyrights registered in the names of Duke Ellington and Billy Strayhorn (1947), unless stated otherwise:

> Movement 1, *Magnolias Dripping with Molasses.* Duke Ellington. Copyright registered in the name of Duke Ellington (1947).
> Movement 2, *Hear Say.* Billy Strayhorn. Alternate titles: *Hearsay* and *O. W. Hearsay.*
> Movement 3, *There Was Nobody Lookin'.* Duke Ellington.
> Movement 4, *Happy-Go-Lucky-Local.* Duke Ellington.

Depk. See *Far East Suite* (movement 4).
Dew. Billy Strayhorn. 1942.
Diamond Jubilee Song. Duke Ellington and Billy Strayhorn. 1940.
Dirge. Billy Strayhorn. 1943. Copyright registered posthumously (2000).
Doing the Doo (Du). Billy Strayhorn. Undated. Copyright registered posthumously (2000).
Don't Believe Everything You Hear. See *Themes from Jump for Joy* (1959).
Don't Mess Around with the Women. See *Fantastic Rhythm.*
Don't Mind if I Do. See *Copasetics Dances.*
Don't Take My Love. See *Ugly Ducklin'.*
Double Ruff. Billy Strayhorn. 1946. Copyright registered 1947.
Down Beat Shuffle. See *Magazine Suite* (movement 1).
Down Dere. Billy Strayhorn. 1963. Multimovement *Copasetics Dance.* No individual titles known. Copyright registered posthumously (2000).
Drawing Room Blues. Billy Strayhorn. 1948.
Drill. See *Anchors Aweigh.*

Drum Is a Woman—Parts 1 and 2. See *A Drum Is a Woman*.
Drum Is a Woman, A. 1956. All copyrights registered in the names of Duke Ellington and Billy Strayhorn (1957):

> *A Drum Is a Woman—Part 1 and 2*. Billy Strayhorn.
> *Ballet of the Flying Saucers*. Billy Strayhorn.
> *Carribee Joe*. Billy Strayhorn.
> *Congo Square*. Billy Strayhorn.
> *Finale*. Author(s) not established (no score has been located).
> *Hey, Buddy Bolden*. Clark Terry, possibly others.
> *Madame Zajj*. Author(s) not established (no score has been located).
> *New Orleans*. Author(s) not established (no score has been located).
> *Pomegranate*. Billy Strayhorn.
> *Rhumbop*. Duke Ellington and Jimmy Hamilton.
> *Rhythm-Pum-Te-Dum*. Billy Strayhorn.
> *What Else Can You Do with a Drum*. Billy Strayhorn.
> *You Better Know It*. Author(s) not established (no score has been located).
> *Zajj's Dream*. Author(s) not established (no score has been located).

Dues. Billy Strayhorn. 1958. Copyright registered as *Prima Bara Dubla*, in the names of Duke Ellington and Billy Strayhorn (1958). Alternate title: *Double Bar*.
Eighth Veil, The. Duke Ellington and Billy Strayhorn. 1946. Copyright registered 1949. Adapted from *Out of This World* (Johnny Mercer and Harold Arlen).
Elf. Billy Strayhorn. 1963. Copyright registered in the names of Duke Ellington and Billy Strayhorn (1964). Alternate title: *Isfahan*. See *Far East Suite* (movement 3).
Elysee. Billy Strayhorn. 1964.
Entr'Acte. See *Nutcracker Suite* (movement 5).
Entrance of Youth. Billy Strayhorn. 1947. Copyright registered as *All Heart* (movement 2 of *A Portrait of Ella Fitzgerald*) in the names of Duke Ellington and Billy Strayhorn (1957). In a spoken introduction (December 26 and 27, 1947) Ellington credits the work to Strayhorn (no score has been located).
Esquire Swank. See *Magazine Suite* (movement 2).
Everybody. See *Copasetics Dances*.
Everything Is Coming Up. See *Copasetics Dances*.
Everything Is Copasetic. See *Anchors Aweigh*.
Fanfare Cabin in the Sky. Billy Strayhorn. 1942. For the motion picture *Cabin in the Sky*. Copyright registered posthumously (2000).
Fanfare Jump for Joy. See *Themes from Jump for Joy* (1941).
Fantastic Rhythm. See *Fantastic Rhythm*.

Fantastic Rhythm. Billy Strayhorn (words and music). 1935. All copyrights registered posthumously (2000), unless stated otherwise. Known titles:

Don't Mess Around with the Women (no score has been located).
Fantastic Rhythm.
Harlem Rhumba (no score has been located).
I'll Never Have to Dream Again.
I've Got the Blues in My Love Song (no score has been located).
It Must Be a Dream (no score has been located).
Let Nature Take Its Course. Copyright registered posthumously (1994). Also used for *Themes from Beggar's Holiday* and *Rose-Colored Glasses.*
Life Ain't Nothing but Rhythm. Alternate title: *The Rhythm Man.*
My Little Brown Book. Copyright registered 1944.
Office Scene.
Overture. Copyright registered posthumously (1994).
The Sob Sisters.
We Are the Reporters (no score has been located).

Far East Suite. All copyrights registered in the names of Duke Ellington and Billy Strayhorn, unless stated otherwise. Known titles:

Movement 1, *Tourist Point of View.* Duke Ellington. 1966.
Movement 2, *Bluebird of Delhi.* Billy Strayhorn. 1964. Original title: *Mynah.*
Movement 3, *Isfahan.* See *Elf.*
Movement 4, *Depk.* Duke Ellington. 1964.
Movement 5, *Mount Harissa.* Author(s) not established (no score has been located). No copyright filed.
Movement 6, *Blue Pepper.* Author(s) not established (no score has been located). 1966. Copyright registered in the name of Duke Ellington (1967).
Movement 7, *Agra.* Billy Strayhorn. 1964.
Movement 8, *Amad.* Duke Ellington. 1964.

Far Eastern Weekend. Louie Bellson, Seymour Press, and Billy Strayhorn. 1957.
Feather Roll Blues. Billy Strayhorn. 1947. Copyright registered posthumously (2000).
Felix. Billy Strayhorn. 1961. Alternate title: *Circle.* Copyright registered posthumously (2000).
Ferb. Billy Strayhorn. 1942. Copyright registered posthumously (2000).
Festival Junction. See *Newport Jazz Festival Suite* (movement 1).
Fiddle on the Diddle. See *Virgin Islands Suite.*
58 St. Suite. Duke Ellington and Billy Strayhorn. 1965.

Finale. See *A Drum Is a Woman.*
Finale. See *Copasetics Dances.*
Flame Indigo. See *Themes from Jump for Joy* (1941).
Flippant Flurry. Billy Strayhorn. 1946. Copyright registered in the name of Duke Ellington (1947).
Flower Is a Lovesome Thing, A. Billy Strayhorn. 1939. Copyright registered 1941. Alternate titles: *Nocturne; Passion.*
Flowers Die of Love, The. See *The Love of Don Perlimplín for Belisa in Their Garden.*
Fluid Jive. See *Lament for an Orchid.*
Fol-De-Rol-Rol. See *Themes from Beggar's Holiday.*
Francesca. See *Lana Turner.*
Frère Monk. Billy Strayhorn. 1962. Copyright registered posthumously in the name of Duke Ellington (1988).
Frou-Frou. See *So Easy.*
Full of Shadows. See *Saturday Laughter.*
Girls Suite, The. 1961. Copyright registered posthumously (2000):

> Movement 1, *Girls.* Billy Strayhorn. Original title: *Who?*
> Movement 5, *Juanita.* Billy Strayhorn.

Girls Want a Hero. See *Themes from Beggar's Holiday.*
Girls. See *The Girls Suite.*
Gonna Tan Your Hide. Billy Strayhorn. 1954. Copyright registered 1957. Newly registered in the name of Duke Ellington (1962).
Got No Time. See *Rose-Colored Glasses.*
Great Day, A. See *Rose-Colored Glasses.*
Grievin'. Duke Ellington and Billy Strayhorn. 1939.
Half the Fun. See *Such Sweet Thunder* (movement 11).
Halfway to Dawn. Billy Strayhorn. 1947. Copyright registered posthumously (2000). Titled posthumously—the original title is unknown.
Happy-Go-Lucky-Local. See *Deep South Suite* (movement 4).
Harlem Rhumba. See *Fantastic Rhythm.*
Haupê. See *Anatomy of a Murder.*
He Outfox the Fox. See *Saturday Laughter.*
Hear Say. See *Deep South Suite* (movement 2).
Hearsay. See *Deep South Suite* (movement 2).
Helen's Theme. See *Orson.*
Here a Man Sees Nothing. See *Saturday Laughter.*
Hey, Buddy Bolden. See *A Drum Is a Woman.*
Hi-Ya. Johnny Hodges and Billy Strayhorn. 1956. Copyright registered in the name of Johnny Hodges (1957).
Hip. Billy Strayhorn. 1941. Copyright registered posthumously (2000).

Hipper-Bug. Billy Strayhorn. 1941. Copyright registered posthumously (2000).
History of Jazz in Three Minutes, A. Jimmy Hamilton and Billy Strayhorn. 1950. Copyright registered posthumously (2000). Credited at the time of its release alternately to Duke Ellington and to Duke Ellington and Billy Strayhorn.
Hominy. See *Charlotte Russe.*
Honchi-Chonch. Duke Ellington and Billy Strayhorn. 1940.
Hues, The. Billy Strayhorn. 1960. Copyright registered posthumously (1994).
Hummer. See *Newport Jazz Festival Suite* (movement 1: *Festival Junction.*
I Am Angry. See *Saturday Laughter.*
I Can Dream. Billy Strayhorn. Undated. No copyright has been filed (score has not been located). As per Tempo Music Catalogue.
I Don't Mind. Duke Ellington (music) and Billy Strayhorn (words). 1942.
I Get Lonely for a Plaything. See *Saturday Laughter.*
I Like Singing. See *Saturday Laughter.*
I Remember. Billy Strayhorn. Undated. No copyright has been filed (score has not been located). As per Tempo Music Catalogue.
I'll Never Have to Dream Again. See *Fantastic Rhythm.*
I'm Checkin' Out—Goom Bye. See *Barney Goin' Easy.*
I'm Still Begging You. John Raymond Wood (words and music) and Billy Strayhorn (music). 1934.
I've Got the Blues in My Love Song. See *Fantastic Rhythm.*
If I Can't Have You. Billy Strayhorn (words and music). 1942. Copyright registered posthumously (2000). Also used for *Rose-Colored Glasses.*
If It Can't Be You. Billy Strayhorn (words and music). 1957. Copyright registered posthumously (2000).
If We Were Any More British, We Couldn't Talk at All. See *Themes from Jump for Joy* (1959).
Imagine My Frustration. Billy Strayhorn (words), Duke Ellington and Gerald Wilson (music). 1966.
In a Blue Summer Garden. Duke Ellington and Billy Strayhorn. 1951. Copyright registered posthumously (2000). Shares thematic material with *Woosie* (movement 2 of *Newport Festival Suite*).
In the Hall of the Mountain King. See *Peer Gynt Suites Nos. 1 and 2* (movement 3).
Intimacy of the Blues. Billy Strayhorn. 1964. Originally untitled. Copyright registered posthumously (1968).
Isfahan. See *Far East Suite* (movement 3): *Elf.*
Island Virgin. See *Virgin Island Suite.*
It Is Saturday. See *Saturday Laughter.*
It Must Be a Dream. See *Fantastic Rhythm.*
J. P. Williamson. See *Saturday Laughter.*
Jasmine. Billy Strayhorn. 1945. Copyright registered posthumously (1994).

Jazz Festival Suite. See *Toot Suite.*
Jennie Lou Stomp. See *Ugly Ducklin'.*
Jo. Billy Strayhorn. 1940. Copyright registered posthumously (2000).
Johnny Come Lately. Billy Strayhorn. 1942.
Jump for Joy (1941). See *Themes from Jump for Joy* (1941).
Jump for Joy (1959). See *Themes from Jump for Joy* (1959).
Jump-Cats Hall. Billy Strayhorn. Undated. Copyright registered posthumously (2000).
Jungle Kitty. See *Virgin Island Suite.*
Just A-Settin' and A-Rockin'. Duke Ellington and Billy Strayhorn. 1941. Copyright registered 1944. Newly registered as *Just A-Sittin' and A-Rockin'* in the names of Lee Gaines (words) and Duke Ellington and Billy Strayhorn (music).
Just A-Sittin' and A-Rockin'. See *Just A-Settin' and A-Rockin'.*
Just in Case. Billy Strayhorn. Undated. Copyright registered posthumously (2000).
Keep Your Feet on the Beat. See *On the Riviera.*
Killin' Myself. Billy Strayhorn. 1939. Copyright registered posthumously (2000).
Kissing Bug, The. Rex Stewart and Billy Strayhorn (music). 1945. Newly registered in the names of Joya Sherrill (words) and Rex Stewart and Billy Strayhorn (music).
Lady Mac. See *Such Sweet Thunder* (movement 4).
Lament for an Orchid. Billy Strayhorn. 1941. Copyright registered as *Absinthe* (1963). Alternate titles: *Fluid Jive; Water-Lily; Ricard.*
Lament for Javanette. Barney Bigard and Billy Strayhorn. 1940. Copyright registered 1941.
Lana Turner. Billy Strayhorn. 1944. Copyright registered as *Francesca* (1946). Newly registered as *Charpoy* (1968).
Lately. Billy Strayhorn. 1956. Copyright registered as *Half the Fun* (movement 11 of *Such Sweet Thunder*) in the names of Duke Ellington and Billy Strayhorn (1957).
Later I'll Know. Aaron Bridgers, Perry Fuller, Marguerite Star, and Billy Strayhorn. 1945. Copyright registered posthumously (2000).
Lavender Lift. See *All Day Long.*
Lay-By. See *Suite Thursday* (movement 4).
Le Sacre Supreme. See *Sacre Supreme, Le.*
Le Vieux Piano. See *Vieux Piano, Le.*
Leave Me Be. Billy Strayhorn (words and music). Undated. Copyright registered posthumously (2000).
Let Nature Take Its Course. See *Fantastic Rhythm.*
Let's Have a Ball. Billy Strayhorn. 1950. No copyright registered (no score has been located). As per Hajdu (1996, 119–120).

Leticia. Billy Strayhorn. 1943. The later *Strange Feeling* (movement 2 of *Perfume Suite*) is based on this work. Copyright registered posthumously (2000).
Life Ain't Nothing but Rhythm. See *Fantastic Rhythm.*
Limbo. See *Copasetics Dances.*
Little Brown Book. See *My Little Brown Book.*
Little Stray-Horn. Billy Strayhorn. 1944.
Lonely Co-Ed. Duke Ellington and Billy Strayhorn. 1939. Newly registered in the names of Edgar Leslie (words) and Duke Ellington and Billy Strayhorn (music), 1943.
Looking for a Male. See *Rose-Colored Glasses.*
Lost in Two Flats. Billy Strayhorn. 1939. Copyright registered 1940.
Lotus. See *Charlotte Russe.*
Lotus Blossom. See *Charlotte Russe.*
Love Came. Duke Ellington (words), Billy Strayhorn (music). 1965.
Love Has Passed Me By, Again. See *Rose-Colored Glasses.*
Love Like This Can't Last. Billy Strayhorn. 1941. Copyright registered 1945. Newly registered 1954, by Tempo Music, Inc.
Love of Don Perlimplín for Belisa in Their Garden, The. Billy Strayhorn (music). 1953. Based on *El amor de Don Perlimplín por Belisa en su jardín* by Federico García Lorca. All copyrights registered posthumously (2000), unless stated otherwise. Known titles:

> *Flowers Die of Love, The.* Originally untitled.
> *Sprite Music.*
> *Love, Love.* Originally untitled.
> *Wounded Love.* Copyright registered posthumously as *Three and Six* (1969) and as *Wounded Love* (1995).

Love, Love. See *The Love of Don Perlimplín for Belisa in Their Garden.*
Love. See *Perfume Suite,* Movement 1.
Lovelinessence. Billy Strayhorn. 1959. Copyright registered posthumously (2000).
Low Key Lightly. See *Anatomy of a Murder.*
Lozit. Billy Strayhorn. 1942. Copyright registered posthumously (2000).
Lush Life. Billy Strayhorn. Ca. 1935. Copyright registered 1949.
M.H. and R. Johnny Hodges and Billy Strayhorn. 1962. Copyright registered posthumously (1968).
Madame X. Billy Strayhorn and Willie Smith. 1943.
Madame Zajj. See *A Drum Is a Woman.*
Madness in Great Ones. See *Such Sweet Thunder* (movement 10).
Magazine Suite. 1945:

> Movement 1, *Down Beat Shuffle.* Duke Ellington.
> Movement 2, *Esquire Swank.* Duke Ellington and Billy Strayhorn.

Copyright registered in the names of Duke Ellington and Johnny Hodges (1946).

Movement 3, *Metronome All Out*. Duke Ellington. Copyright registered in the names of Duke Ellington and Billy Strayhorn (1946).

Malay Camp on Saturday. See *Saturday Laughter*.
Man Beneath, The. See *Saturday Laughter*.
Manhattan Murals. See *Take the "A" Train*.
Matinee. Billy Strayhorn. 1947. Copyright registered posthumously (1997).
Maybe. Billy Strayhorn. 1961.
Me, You and Dudley. Billy Strayhorn (music) and Don George (words). Undated. Copyright registered posthumously (2000).
Merry Ha! Ha!, The. Bob Russell (words) and Billy Strayhorn (music). 1947.
Metronome All Out. See *Magazine Suite* (movement 3).
Mid-Riff. Billy Strayhorn. 1944. Alternate titles: *Midriff* and *Raindrop Stomp*.
Midnight in Paris, A. Billy Strayhorn. 1961. Copyright registered 1963. Original title *AIX*.
Midriff. See *Mid-Riff*.
Minuet in Blues. Billy Strayhorn. 1939. Copyright registered in the name of Barney Bigard.
Misfit Blues. See *Suite Thursday* (movement 1).
Morning Mood. See *Peer Gynt Suites Nos. 1 and 2* (movement 1).
Mount Harissa. See *Far East Suite* (movement 5).
Multicolored Blue. Billy Strayhorn. 1950. An expanded vocal version of the earlier, instrumental *Violet Blue*. Copyright registered 1958.
My Arms. See *Saturday Laughter*.
My Home Lies Quiet. See *Saturday Laughter*.
My Little Brown Book. See *Fantastic Rhythm*.
My Love Is as a Fever. See *Sonnet for Caesar* (movement 2 of *Such Sweet Thunder*).
My People:

Purple People. Billy Strayhorn. 1963. All other movements are by Duke Ellington.

My Resistance Is Low. Undated. Don George (words), Cat Anderson, Duke Ellington, and Billy Strayhorn (music). Copyright registered posthumously (2000).
Mynah. See *Blue Bird of Delhi* (movement 2 of *Far East Suite*).
Mysterious Chick. Author(s) not established (no score has been located). Copyright registered in the names of Duke Ellington and Billy Strayhorn (1965).
Natives Are Restless Tonight, The. See *Themes from Jump for Joy* (1959).
Never Meet. Billy Strayhorn. No copyright has been filed (score has not been located). As per Tempo Music Catalogue.

New Look, The. See *Snibor.*
New Low Down. See *Copasetics Dances.*
New Orleans. See *A Drum Is a Woman.*
New Shoes. See *Saturday Laughter.*
Newport Jazz Festival Suite. 1956. All copyrights registered in the names of Duke Ellington and Billy Strayhorn:

>Movement 1: *Festival Junction.* Billy Strayhorn. Original title: *Hummer.*
>Movement 2: *Blues to Be There.* Billy Strayhorn. Original title: Woosie. Shares thematic material with *In a Blue Summer Garden.*
>Movement 3: *Newport Up.* Duke Ellington.

Newport Up. See *Newport Jazz Festival Suite* (movement 3).
Night Time. Doris Julian (words), Duke Ellington and Billy Strayhorn (music). 1954.
No One Knows. Billy Strayhorn. 1954. Copyright registered 1967.
Nocturne. See *A Flower Is a Lovesome Thing.*
Noir Bleu. Billy Strayhorn. 1941. Copyright registered 1947.
North by Southwest Suite. Billy Strayhorn. 1966–67. Copyright registered posthumously as *Suite for the Duo* (1995).

>Movement 1, *Up There.* 1966. Alternate title: *Skippy.*
>Movement 2, *Boo Loose.* Ca. 1963. Alternate titles: *Boo-Lose, Boo Lose, Pretty Little One,* and *Blue Cloud.*
>Movement 3, *Pavane Bleu No. 2.* 1966.

Northern Lights. See *Queens Suite.*
Nutcracker Suite. 1960. All copyrights registered posthumously in the names of Duke Ellington and Billy Strayhorn (1995). Adapted from *The Nutcracker Suite,* by Peter Ilyitch Tchaikovsky (Opus 71a, 1892):

>Movement 1, *Overture.* Billy Strayhorn.
>Movement 2, *Toot Toot Tootie Toot.* Billy Strayhorn. Original title: *The Pipes.*
>Movement 3, *Peanut Brittle Brigade.* Duke Ellington. Original title: *March.*
>Movement 4, *Sugar Rum Cherry.* Billy Strayhorn. Original title: *Sugar Plum.*
>Movement 5, *Entr'Acte.* Billy Strayhorn. Original title: *Overture.*
>Movement 6, *The Volga Vouty.* Author(s) not established (no score has been located).
>Movement 7, *Chinoiserie.* Author(s) not established (no score has been located).
>Movement 8, *Dance of the Floreadores.* Billy Strayhorn. Original title: *Waltz-Trot-Fleurs.*

Movement 9, *Arabesque Cookie*. Billy Strayhorn. Original title: *Naibara*.

Obmil. See *Island Virgin (Virgin Islands Suite)*.
On the Riviera. See *On the Riviera*.
On the Riviera. Roy Branker (words) and Billy Strayhorn (music). 1961. Multi-movement *Copasetics Dance*. All copyrights registered posthumously (2000). Known titles:

> *Alouette*.
> *Bon Soir Madame*.
> *Can-Can* (no score has been located).
> *Keep Your Feet on the Beat*.
> *On the Riviera* (no score has been located).
> *Opening*.

On the Verge. Billy Strayhorn. Undated. Copyright registered posthumously (2000).
On the Wrong Side of the Railroad Tracks. See *Themes from Beggar's Holiday*.
Once upon a Dream. Bill Cottrell and T. Hee (words), Duke Ellington and Billy Strayhorn (music). 1962.
Only Yesterday. See *Saturday Laughter*.
Oo! (You Make Me Tingle). See *Rose-Colored Glasses*.
Ool-Ya-Coo. See *Rose-Colored Glasses*.
Opening. See *Copasetics Dances*.
Opening. See *On the Riviera*.
Opening Jump for Joy. See *Themes from Jump for Joy* (1941).
Orson. Billy Strayhorn. 1950. Based on *Helen's Theme*, which was written for an Orson Welles production of *Faust* (titled *Le Temps Court*). Copyright registered in the names of Duke Ellington and Billy Strayhorn (1956).
Overture to a Jam Session. Billy Strayhorn. 1947. Copyright registered in the name of Duke Ellington (1947).
Overture. See *Fantastic Rhythm*.
Overture. See *Nutcracker Suite* (movement 1).
Paki. Duke Ellington. 1964. Copyright registered in the names of Duke Ellington and Billy Strayhorn.
Paradise. See *Blue Heart*.
Parimaribo [sic]. Don George (words) and Billy Strayhorn (music). Undated. Copyright registered posthumously (2000).
Paris Blues. Harold Flender and Billy Strayhorn (words), Duke Ellington (music). 1961. Copyright registered 1962.
Passion. See *A Flower Is a Lovesome Thing*.
Passion Flower. Billy Strayhorn. 1939. Copyright registered 1944. Newly regis-

tered in the names of Milton Raskin (words) and Billy Strayhorn (music), 1965.
Pavane Bleu No. 2. See *North by Southwest Suite* (movement 3).
Peanut Brittle Brigade. See *Nutcracker Suite* (movement 3).
Peer Gynt Suites Nos. 1 and 2. 1960. All copyrights registered in the names of Duke Ellington and Billy Strayhorn (1995). Adapted from *The Peer Gynt Suites Nos. 1 and 2* (opus 46 and opus 55) by Edvard Grieg (1888):

> Movement 1, *Morning Mood.* Billy Strayhorn.
> Movement 2, *Solvejg's Song.* Billy Strayhorn.
> Movement 3, *In the Hall of the Mountain King.* Duke Ellington.
> Movement 4, *Åse's Death.* Billy Strayhorn.
> Movement 5, *Anitra's Dance.* Billy Strayhorn.

Penthouse on Shady Avenue, A. Billy Strayhorn. 1934. Copyright registered posthumously (1996). Possibly related to *Fantastic Rhythm.*
Pentonsilic. Billy Strayhorn. 1941. Copyright registered posthumously (1994). Part of this work was registered as *Sonata* (movement 1 of *Perfume Suite.*
Perfume Suite:

> Movement 1, *Love.* Billy Strayhorn. 1944. Partly based on *Pentonsilic.* Copyright registered as *Sonata* (1945). Alternate titles: *Under the Balcony* and *Balcony Serenade.*
> Movement 2, *Strange Feeling.* Billy Strayhorn. 1943. Copyright registered in the names of Duke Ellington and Billy Strayhorn (words and music) (1945). Based on *Leticia.*
> Movement 3, *Dancers in Love.* Duke Ellington. 1944.
> Movement 4, *Coloratura.* Duke Ellington and Billy Strayhorn. Copyright registered in the name of Duke Ellington (1945).

Phace. See *Copasetics Dances.*
Pianistically Allied. See *Tonk.*
Poke. Billy Strayhorn. 1960. Copyright registered posthumously (1994).
Polly's Theme. See *Anatomy of a Murder.*
Pomegranate. See *A Drum Is a Woman.*
Portrait of a Silk Thread. Billy Strayhorn. 1945. Copyright registered posthumously (1995).
Portrait of Ella Fitzgerald, A. All copyrights registered in the names of Duke Ellington and Billy Strayhorn:

> Movement 1, *Royal Ancestry.* Billy Strayhorn. 1957.
> Movement 2, *All Heart.* See *Entrance of Youth.*
> Movement 3, *Beyond Category.* Billy Strayhorn. 1957.
> Movement 4, *Total Jazz.* Duke Ellington. 1957.

Pretty Girl. Billy Strayhorn. 1956. Newly registered as *The Star-Crossed Lovers (Such Sweet Thunder*, Movement 9) in the names of Duke Ellington and Billy Strayhorn (1957).
Pretty Little One. See *Boo Loose.*
Pretty Little Girl. See *Pretty Girl.*
Prima Bara Dubla. See *Dues.*
Progressive Gavotte. See *Re-Bop Gavotte.*
Purple People. See *My People.*
Pussy Willow. Duke Ellington and Billy Strayhorn. 1939. Copyright registered in the name of Duke Ellington (1939).
Put-Tin. Duke Ellington. 1964. Copyright registered in the names of Duke Ellington and Billy Strayhorn.
Queens Suite:

> Movement 4, *Northern Lights.* Billy Strayhorn. 1959. Movements 1–3 and 5–6 are by Duke Ellington.

Rain Check. Billy Strayhorn. 1941. Copyright registered 1942. When published in 1942 by Tempo Music, *Rain Check* became *Raincheck*.
Raincheck. See *Rain Check.*
Raindrop Stomp. See *Mid-Riff.*
Re-Bop Gavotte. Billy Strayhorn. 1947. Copyright registered as *Progressive Gavotte* (1948).
Ready, Go! See *Toot Suite* (movement 6).
Red Carpet (Part 1). See *Toot Suite* (movement 3).
Red Carpet (Part 2). See *Toot Suite* (movement 4).
Red Carpet (Part 3). See *Toot Suite* (movement 5).
Red Garter. See *Toot Suite* (movement 1).
Red Shoes. See *Toot Suite* (movement 2).
Rhumbop. See *A Drum Is a Woman.*
Rhythm-Pum-Te-Dum. See *A Drum Is a Woman.*
Ricard. See *Lament for an Orchid.*
Rock Skippin' at the Blue Note. Billy Strayhorn. 1951. Copyright registered in the names of Duke Ellington and Billy Strayhorn (1952).
Rocks in My Bed. See *Themes from Jump for Joy* (1941).
Rod La Roque. Billy Strayhorn. 1965. Copyright registered posthumously (2000). Credited at the time of its release to Duke Ellington.
Rose Bud. Billy Strayhorn and Juan Tizol. 1942.
Rose-Colored Glasses. 1954. Unless stated otherwise, no copyrights have been filed (scores have not been located). Known titles (as per Hajdu 1996, 128–133):

> *Beauty and Talent.* Billy Strayhorn (words and music).
> *Brother Big Eyes.* Billy Strayhorn (words and music).

Cottage on the Hill. Billy Strayhorn (words and music).
Got No Time. Billy Strayhorn (words and music).
Great Day, A. Billy Strayhorn (words and music).
Hey Cherie. Luther Henderson (words and music).
Hip Hoe Down Mambo. Luther Henderson (words and music).
If I Can't Have You. See *If I Can't Have You* (1942).
It All Depends on Your Point of View. Luther Henderson (words and music).
Let Nature Take Its Course. See *Fantastic Rhythm*.
Looking for a Male. Billy Strayhorn (words and music).
Love Has Passed Me By, Again. Billy Strayhorn (words and music). Copyright registered posthumously (1994).
Oo! (You Make Me Tingle). Billy Strayhorn. Copyright registered in the names of Duke Ellington and Billy Strayhorn (1955).
Ool-Ya-Coo. Billy Strayhorn (words and music).
Rose-Colored Glasses. Billy Strayhorn (words and music).
Still in Love with You. Billy Strayhorn (words and music). Copyright registered posthumously (2000).
Well, Well. Luther Henderson (words and music).
You, You, You. Luther Henderson (words and music).

Royal Ancestry. See *A Portrait of Ella Fitzgerald* (movement 1).
Sacre Supreme, Le. Billy Strayhorn. 1944. Copyright registered posthumously (1994).
Satin Doll. Johnny Mercer (words), Duke Ellington and Billy Strayhorn (music). 1958. The first copyright registration (1958) credits Mercer Ellington and Billy Strayhorn as lyricists and Ellington as composer; a second registration (1960) credits Mercer as lyricist solely and Duke Ellington and Billy Strayhorn as composers.
Saturday Laughter. Herbert Martin (words), Duke Ellington and Billy Strayhorn (music). 1958. Alternate titles: *Renaissance Man; Mine Boy*. Based on a novel by Peter Abrahams. Authorship for individual movements not established (see Hajdu 1996, 180–181, 183). Unless stated otherwise no copyrights have been filed. Known titles:

Big White Mountain.
Bioscope Song.
Full of Shadows. Copyright registered in the name of Duke Ellington (1966).
He Outfox the Fox.
Here a Man Sees Nothing. Copyright registered as *Man Sees Nothing* in the name of Duke Ellington (1966).
I Am Angry.

> *I Get Lonely for a Plaything.*
> *I Like Singing.* Copyright registered in the name of Duke Ellington (1966).
> *It Is Saturday.*
> *J. P. Williamson.* Copyright registered in the name of Duke Ellington (1966).
> *Malay Camp on Saturday.* Copyright registered as *Malay Camp,* in the name of Duke Ellington (1966).
> *My Arms.*
> *My Home Lies Quiet.* Copyright registered in the name of Duke Ellington (1966).
> *New Shoes.* Copyright registered in the name of Duke Ellington (1966).
> *Only Yesterday.*
> *Skokiaan Queens.*
> *Man Beneath, The.* Copyright registered in the name of Duke Ellington.
> *They Say (That People Turn into Stars When They Die).* Copyright registered in the name of Duke Ellington (1966).
> *This Man.* Copyright registered in the name of Duke Ellington (1966).
> *You Are Beautiful.* Copyright registered in the name of Duke Ellington (1966).
> *You Are Lonely.*
> *You Walk in My Dreams.*

Schwiphtiey. See *Suite Thursday* (movement 2).
Sepia Panorama. Duke Ellington and Billy Strayhorn. 1940. Partly based on a Strayhorn arrangement of *Tuxedo Junction,* by Erskine Hawkins, William Johnson, Julian Dash, and Buddy Feyne, 1939 (see Chapter 2). Copyright registered in the name of Duke Ellington.
September Rain. Lorraine Feather and Billy Strayhorn. Undated. As per ASCAP listing. No copyright has been filed (score has not been located).
Shadow Shuffle. Billy Strayhorn. 1944. Copyright registered posthumously (2000). Alternate title: *Silver.*
Show 'Em You Got Class. See *Themes from Jump for Joy* (1959).
Skippy. See *North by Southwest Suite* (movement 1).
Skokiaan Queens. See *Saturday Laughter.*
Smada. See *Ugly Ducklin'.*
Snibor. Billy Strayhorn. 1947. Copyright registered 1959. Original title: *Robin's Nest.* Alternate title: *The New Look.*
So Easy. Billy Strayhorn. 1959. Copyright registered as *Frou-Frou* (1965), in the name of Lil Young—Strayhorn's mother's maiden name.

So the Good Book Says. See *Themes from Jump for Joy* (1959).
So This Is Love. Billy Strayhorn. 1934. Copyright registered posthumously (1968).
Solvejg's Song. See *Peer Gynt Suites Nos. 1 and 2* (movement 2).
Something to Live For. Billy Strayhorn. 1937. Copyright registered in the names of Duke Ellington and Billy Strayhorn (1939).
Sonata. See *Pentonsilic* and *Perfume Suite* (movement 1).
Song for Christmas, A. Dean Bartlett (words), Duke Ellington and Billy Strayhorn (music). 1965. Copyright registered 1967. Alternate title: *A Christmas Surprise.*
Sonnet for Caesar. See *Such Sweet Thunder* (movement 2).
Sonnet for Sister Kate. See *Such Sweet Thunder* (movement 8).
Sonnet in Search of a Moor. See *Such Sweet Thunder* (movement 5).
Sonnet to Hank Cinq. See *Such Sweet Thunder* (movement 3).
South Wind. Duke Ellington and Billy Strayhorn (words and music). Undated. Copyright registered posthumously (2000).
Sprite Music. See *The Love of Don Perlimplín for Belisa in Their Garden.*
Star Blues. Billy Strayhorn. 1958. Copyright registered as *Blues in Orbit.*
Star-Crossed Lovers, The (movement 9 of *Such Sweet Thunder*). See *Pretty Girl.*
Still in Love with You. See *Rose-Colored Glasses.*
Strange Feeling. See *Leticia* and *Perfume Suite* (movement 2).
Stray's—Plays. Billy Strayhorn. Undated. Copyright registered 1967.
Strayhorn's Latest. Billy Strayhorn. 1938. Copyright registered posthumously (2000).
Such Sweet Thunder. See *Such Sweet Thunder* (movement 1).
Such Sweet Thunder. All copyrights registered in the names of Duke Ellington and Billy Strayhorn (1957):

>Movement 1, *Such Sweet Thunder.* Duke Ellington and Billy Strayhorn.
>Movement 2, *Sonnet for Caesar.* Duke Ellington.
>Movement 3, *Sonnet to Hank Cinq.* Copyright registered as *Hank Cinq.* Author(s) not established (no score has been located).
>Movement 4, *Lady Mac.* Duke Ellington.
>Movement 5, *Sonnet in Search of a Moor.* Author(s) not established (no score has been located).
>Movement 6, *The Telecasters.* Duke Ellington.
>Movement 7, *Up and Down, Up and Down (I Will Lead Them Up and Down).* Billy Strayhorn.
>Movement 8, *Sonnet for Sister Kate.* Duke Ellington.
>Movement 9, *The Star-Crossed Lovers.* See *Pretty Girl.*
>Movement 10, *Madness in Great Ones.* Duke Ellington.

Movement 11, *Half the Fun*. See *Lately*.
Movement 12, *Circle of Fourths*. Duke Ellington.

Sugar Hill Penthouse. See *Symphonette Rhythmique*.
Sugar Rum Cherry. See *Nutcracker Suite* (movement 4).
Suite for the Duo. See *North by Southwest Suite*.
Suite Thursday. 1960. All copyrights registered posthumously in the names of Duke Ellington and Billy Strayhorn (1995):

> Movement 1, *Misfit Blues*. Author(s) not established (no score has been located).
> Movement 2, *Schwiphtiey*. Author(s) not established (no score has been located).
> Movement 3, *Zweet Zurzday*. Duke Ellington.
> Movement 4, *Lay-By*. Duke Ellington.

Sunny Day Honey. Billy Strayhorn (words and music). 1952. Copyright registered posthumously (2000).
Swamp Drum. Billy Strayhorn. 1951. Original title: *Brew*. Copyright registered 1952.
Sweet and Pungent. Billy Strayhorn. 1959. Original title: *Blues*. Copyright registered 1964.
Swing. Billy Strayhorn. 1940.
Swing Dance. See *Anchors Aweigh*.
Symphomaniac, The. 1948:

> Movement 1, *Symphonic or Bust*. Duke Ellington and Billy Strayhorn. Based on fragments from earlier Strayhorn arrangements (*Blue Belles of Harlem* and *Out of This World / The Eighth Veil*). Copyright registered posthumously (2000).
> Movement 2, *How You Sound*. Duke Ellington.

Symphonette Rhythmique. Billy Strayhorn. 1941. Copyright registered as *Sugar Hill Penthouse* (part of *Black, Brown and Beige*) in the name of Duke Ellington.
Symphonie. Billy Strayhorn. 1945. Copyright registered posthumously (2000).
Tail-Spin. Billy Strayhorn. Undated. Copyright registered posthumously (2000).
Take 'Em Slow. Billy Strayhorn. 1942.
Take It Slow. Billy Strayhorn. 1942.
Take It Slow. Billy Strayhorn. 1962. Copyright registered posthumously (2000). Original title: *Tune Up Slow*.
Take the "A" Train. Billy Strayhorn. 1939. Copyright registered 1941. Alternate title: *Manhattan Murals*.
Tapioca. Billy Strayhorn. 1940. Copyright registered posthumously (2000).

APPENDIX D   283

Telecasters, The. See *Such Sweet Thunder* (movement 6).
Telstar. Billy Strayhorn. 1962. Copyright registered as *Tigress.*
Thé. Billy Strayhorn. 1964. Copyright registered posthumously (2000).
Themes from Beggar's Holiday. 1947. All copyrights registered posthumously (2000), unless stated otherwise. Eleven more untitled compositions were registered posthumously (2000) as *Song 1, Song 2, Song 3, Song 4, Song 5, Song 6, Song 7, Song 8, Song 9, Song 10, Song 11.* Known titles by Strayhorn:

> *Boll Weevil Ballet.* Billy Strayhorn.
> *Brown Penny.* John LaTouche (words) and Billy Strayhorn (music). 1946. Copyright registered in the names of Duke Ellington and John LaTouche (1949).
> *Cream for Supper.* Billy Strayhorn.
> *Fol-De-Rol-Rol.* Billy Strayhorn.
> *Girls Want a Hero.* John LaTouche (words) and Billy Strayhorn (music).
> *Let Nature Take Its Course.* See *Fantastic Rhythm.*
> *On the Wrong Side of the Railroad Tracks.* John LaTouche (words), Duke Ellington and Billy Strayhorn (music). Copyright registered in the names of Duke Ellington and John LaTouche.
> *Thirteen Boxes of Rayon Skirts.* John LaTouche (words) and Billy Strayhorn (music).
> *Through All the Employments.* John LaTouche (words) and Billy Strayhorn (music).
> *We'll Scratch Out His Eyes.* John LaTouche (words) and Billy Strayhorn (music).
> *Wedding Ballet.* Billy Strayhorn.
> *You Wake Up and Breakfast on a Cigarette.* John LaTouche (words) and Billy Strayhorn (music).

Themes from Jump for Joy. (1941). Known titles by Strayhorn:

> *Fanfare.* Billy Strayhorn. Copyright registered posthumously (2000).
> *Flame Indigo.* Billy Strayhorn. Copyright registered posthumously (1994).
> *Opening.* Billy Strayhorn. Copyright registered posthumously (2000).
> *Rocks in My Bed.* Duke Ellington and Billy Strayhorn. Copyright registered in the name of Duke Ellington (1941).
> *Uncle Tom's Cabin Is a Drive-In Now.* Duke Ellington and Billy Strayhorn. Copyright registered posthumously (2000).

Themes from Jump for Joy (1959). Unless stated otherwise, all copyrights registered in the names of Sid Kuller (words) and Duke Ellington (music):

But. Sid Kuller (words), Duke Ellington and Billy Strayhorn (music).

Don't Believe Everything You Hear. Sid Kuller (words), Duke Ellington and Billy Strayhorn (music).

Entrance Music for Comedians. Billy Strayhorn. Copyright registered posthumously (2000) in the name of Billy Strayhorn.

If We Were Any More British, We Couldn't Talk at All. Sid Kuller (words), Billy Strayhorn (music). Copyright registered in the names of Sid Kuller (words), Duke Ellington and Billy Strayhorn (music).

Natives Are Restless Tonight, The. Sid Kuller (words), Duke Ellington and Billy Strayhorn (music).

Show 'Em You Got Class. Sid Kuller (words), Duke Ellington and Billy Strayhorn (music).

So the Good Book Says. Sid Kuller (words), Billy Strayhorn (music). Copyright registered in the names of Sid Kuller (words), Duke Ellington and Billy Strayhorn (music).

Three Shows Nightly. Sid Kuller (words), Duke Ellington and Billy Strayhorn (music).

Walk It Off. Sid Kuller (words), Billy Strayhorn (music). Copyright registered in the names of Sid Kuller (words), Duke Ellington and Billy Strayhorn (music).

When I Trilly with My Filly. Sid Kuller (words), Duke Ellington and Billy Strayhorn (music).

There Was Nobody Lookin'. See *Deep South Suite* (movement 3).

They Say (That People Turn into Stars When They Die). See *Saturday Laughter.*

Thirteen Boxes of Rayon Skirts. See *Themes from Beggar's Holiday.*

This Man. See *Saturday Laughter.*

Three and Six. See *The Love of Don Perlimplín for Belisa in Their Garden: Wounded Love.*

Three Flights Up. Billy Strayhorn. 1941. Copyright registered posthumously (2000).

3:10 Blues. Billy Strayhorn. 1963. Copyright registered 1964.

Through All the Employments. See *Themes from Beggar's Holiday.*

Tiffany. Billy Strayhorn. 1955. Copyright registered posthumously (2000).

Tigress. See *Telstar.*

Tonk. Billy Strayhorn. 1940. Copyright registered in the names of Duke Ellington and Billy Strayhorn (1940). Newly registered in 1954 by Tempo Music Corporation. Alternate title: *Pianistically Allied.*

Too Late. Billy Strayhorn. 1957. Copyright registered posthumously (1996). Originally untitled.

Toot Suite. 1958. All copyrights registered in the names of Duke Ellington and Billy Strayhorn (1959):

Movement 1, *Red Garter*. Duke Ellington.
Movement 2, *Red Shoes*. Duke Ellington.
Movement 3, *Red Carpet (Part 1)*. Duke Ellington.
Movement 4, *Red Carpet (Part 2)*. Billy Strayhorn.
Movement 5, *Red Carpet (Part 3)*. Duke Ellington.
Movement 6, *Ready, Go!* Author(s) not established (no score has been located).

Toot Toot Tootie Toot. See *Nutcracker Suite* (movement 2).
Total Jazz. See *A Portrait of Ella Fitzgerald*.
Tourist Point of View. See *Far East Suite* (movement 1).
Trails. Billy Strayhorn. 1958. Copyright registered posthumously (2000).
Triple Play. Billy Strayhorn. 1947. Copyright registered 1949.
Tymperturbably Blue. See *Boom Boom*.
U.M.M.G. See *Upper Manhattan Medical Group*.
Ugly Ducklin'. Billy Strayhorn. 1935. Copyright registered as *Jennie Lou Stomp* in the name of Billy Strayhorn (1944). Newly registered as *Smada*, in the names of Duke Ellington and Billy Strayhorn (1951). Alternate title: *Don't Take My Love*.
Uncle Tom's Cabin Is a Drive-In Now. See *Themes from Jump for Joy* (1941).
Under the Balcony. See *Perfume Suite* (movement 1).
Up and Down, Up and Down (I Will Lead Them Up and Down). See *Such Sweet Thunder* (movement 7).
Upper Manhattan Medical Group. Billy Strayhorn. 1956. Also known as U.M.M.G.
Upside Looking. Billy Strayhorn. Undated. No copyright has been filed (score has not been located). As per Tempo Music Catalogue.
Until Tonight. Billy Strayhorn. 1941. Copyright registered posthumously (2000).
Valse #2. Billy Strayhorn. 1935. Copyright registered posthumously (1996).
Valse (Lento Sostenuto). Billy Strayhorn. 1935. Copyright registered posthumously (1996).
Vict. Duke Ellington. 1964. Copyright registered in the names of Duke Ellington and Billy Strayhorn.
Vieux Piano, Le. Billy Strayhorn. Late 1950s. Copyright registered posthumously (2000).
Violet Blue. Billy Strayhorn. 1945. Copyright registered 1947. Newly registered as part of *Multicolored Blue* (1958).
Virgin Islands Suite. 1965. All copyrights registered in the names of Duke Ellington and Billy Strayhorn:

Movement 1, *Island Virgin*. Billy Strayhorn. Original title: *Obmil*.
Movement 2, *Virgin Jungle*. Duke Ellington.
Movement 3, *Fiddle on the Diddle*. Billy Strayhorn. Original title: *Volta*.

Movement 4, *Jungle Kitty*. Author(s) not established (no score has been located).

Volga Vouty, The. See *Nutcracker Suite* (movement 6).
Volta. See *Virgin Islands Suite: Fiddle on the Diddle.*
Walk It Off. See *Themes from Jump for Joy* (1959).
Watch Your Cue. Johnny Hodges and Billy Strayhorn. 1965.
Water-Lily. See *Lament for an Orchid.*
We Are the Reporters. See *Fantastic Rhythm.*
We'll Scratch Out His Eyes. See *Themes from Beggar's Holiday.*
Wedding Ballet. See *Themes from Beggar's Holiday.*
Welcome Aboard. See *Anchors Aweigh.*
What Else Can You Do with a Drum. See *A Drum Is a Woman.*
When I Trilly with My Filly. See *Themes from Jump for Joy* (1959).
Who? See *Girls Suite* (movement 1): *Girls.*
Wish I Knew What Happened. Duke Ellington and Billy Strayhorn. Undated. Copyright registered posthumously (2000).
Without Rhythm. Billy Strayhorn. 1941. Copyright registered posthumously (2000).
Woosie. See *Newport Jazz Festival Suite* (movement 2): *Blues to Be There.*
Work Song. See *Copasetics Dances.*
Wounded Love. See *The Love of Don Perlimplín for Belisa in Their Garden.*
Wrong Number. Billy Strayhorn. 1942.
Xmas Present. Billy Strayhorn. 1942.
You Are Beautiful. See *Saturday Laughter.*
You Are Lonely. See *Saturday Laughter.*
You Better Know It. See *A Drum Is a Woman.*
You Lovely Little Devil. 1934. John Raymond Wood (words) and Billy Strayhorn (music).
You Wake Up and Breakfast on a Cigarette. See *Themes from Beggar's Holiday.*
You Walk in My Dreams. See *Saturday Laughter.*
You're the One. Billy Strayhorn. 1955.
Your Love Has Faded. Billy Strayhorn. 1937. Copyright registered in the name of Duke Ellington (1939).
Zajj's Dream. See *A Drum Is a Woman.*
Zonk. Billy Strayhorn 1960. Copyright registered posthumously (1995).
Zweet Zurzday. See *Suite Thursday* (movement 3).

Notes

INTRODUCTION

1. There are many books on Ellington. *Beyond Category: The Life and Genius of Duke Ellington*, by John Hasse (1993), introduces the general reader to its subject, while *The Duke Ellington Reader*, edited by Mark Tucker (1993), provides excellent background material.

CHAPTER 1

1. All biographical data taken from Hajdu 1996.
2. *Valse* has been recorded posthumously (see Appendix C).
3. *Fantastic Rhythm* and *Let Nature Take Its Course* have been recorded posthumously (see Appendix C).
4. Remarkably enough, most of the surviving material for *Fantastic Rhythm* turned up after sixty years in the Ruth Ellington Collection, acquired in 1995 by the Smithsonian Institution from Ellington's sister, Ruth Ellington-Boatwright. Strayhorn possibly brought these materials with him when he first came to New York and stayed with her in the apartment Ellington shared with his family. Strayhorn may also have put these scores in the hands of Tempo Music, Ellington's music publication firm administered by his sister, perhaps to have Tempo file the copyrights—they remained unregistered.
5. The incomplete manuscript counts forty-eight measures, for a small band consisting of two altos (doubling on clarinets), a tenor, two trumpets, and rhythm. Two instrumental parts survive (both REC), one for the first alto and one for the first trumpet, each counting 132 bars.
6. *Let Nature Take Its Course* has been recorded posthumously (see Appendix C).
7. *A Penthouse on Shady Avenue* has been recorded posthumously (see Appendix C).
8. *So This Is Love* has been recorded posthumously (see Appendix C).
9. Tempo Music filed the copyright more than a year after Strayhorn's death.
10. With remarkable ease Strayhorn exploits chromatic ambiguities in *So This Is Love*,

exemplified by the enharmonic modulation that ends the verse (Example 1-6, m. 11). The F♯mi$^{(maj7)}$ on the fourth beat is retroactively heard as a non-root E♭mi9($^\flat$5), the delay for the dominant A♭.

11. The discussion and music examples for *Lush Life* are based on later autographs ("Lush Life," BSC and DEC).
12. Nat "King" Cole accompanied by Pete Rugolo's Orchestra, March 29, 1949 (3751-3D; issued on Capitol 57-606).
13. John Coltrane Quintet: January 10, 1958, issued on *John Coltrane: Lush Life* (Prestige LP7188) and reissued on *John Coltrane: The Complete Prestige Recordings* (Prestige CD VICJ40017-34). Coltrane recorded the piece again on March 7, 1963, issued on *The John Coltrane Quartet and Johnny Hartman: The Gentle Side of John Coltrane* (Impulse ASH9306/Impulse CD GRD107).
14. Issued on *Billy Strayhorn: Lush Life* (Red Baron AK 52760).
15. The manuscript carries a crossed-out title: *Smoky City* (REC). *Ugly Ducklin'* bears a striking melodic similarity to *Blue Moonlight*, a composition by Dana Suesse (1911–1987, composer of *You Oughta Be in Pictures*) recorded in 1939 by Paul Whiteman's Orchestra. The relationship between both compositions, if any, is unclear.
16. From the album *My Favorite Things*, 1960 (Atlanta 1361).
17. Respectively from the albums *Kind of Blue*, 1959 (Columbia CL1355), and *Sketches of Spain*, 1959–1960 (Columbia CS 8271).
18. First recorded by Boyd Raeburn and His Orchestra for Lang-Worth Transcriptions, June 1944. Reissued on Circle CD CCD-22.
19. All these original compositions are documented by the band books of Strayhorn's fellow Mad Hatters Charles "Buzz" Mayor and Jerome Eisner (DH), which also contain numerous arranged standards, often associated with the Benny Goodman group. *Something to Live For* survives in various incomplete sets of instrumental parts in Strayhorn's hand (untitled manuscript, REC), all predating 1939.
20. *Remember* has been recorded posthumously (see Appendix C).

CHAPTER 2

1. For a detailed description see Hajdu 1996, 49–53.
2. The lyric he referred to may be the one Strayhorn set to an earlier instrumental work credited to Ellington, *T.T. on Toast* (no manuscript known), recorded by the orchestra December 19, 1938, twelve days after the two composers first met. Although the exact date of its creation is unknown, Strayhorn's manuscript with melody and lyrics, *Lady in Doubt* (DEC), was certainly written before the orchestra embarked on its European tour on March 23, 1939—Ellington scribbled the itinerary on verso. Melodically, *Lady in Doubt* has some striking similarities to Strayhorn's later *Chelsea Bridge*. Strayhorn arranged *Lady in Doubt* for the 1944–46 band (DEC).
3. According to Hajdu (1996, 34), the original title for *Lush Life* was *Life Is Lonely*.
4. *Lonely Again* contains the chorus of *Lush Life* (the section starting with "Life is lonely again"), with an additional four-bar introduction. It is not known where and how in this particular case Strayhorn planned the verse (if at all), and which instrument was to play the lead in that verse: the Ellington orchestra never recorded this score. The unusual key of G for *Lonely Again* (all other versions of *Lush Life* are in D♭) suggests that Strayhorn envisioned the work as a vocal piece, to be sung by the band's vocalist Ivie Anderson and possibly to be followed by an

orchestral out-chorus. *Lonely Again* has been recorded posthumously as an instrumental (see Appendix C). Strayhorn's only other known big band version of *Lush Life*, apparently for the 1948 Carnegie Hall performance with singer Kay Davis, also gives the second section only (that score was not used either, and Davis and Strayhorn performed the work as a duet instead). Strayhorn wrote a number of leadsheets for *Lush Life*, often for friends. After Parisian-Americans Aaron Bridgers, pianist, and Nye Pharr, painter, complained to Strayhorn that the piece was "very complex," Strayhorn told them " 'perhaps, but actually you can play the chorus with three fingers.'" As Bridgers (1997) recollects: "Naturally we [Bridgers and Pharr] were anxious to see and hear it. So he played it and scored it and dedicated it to Nye." The score, titled "Lush Life, Three Finger Version" (again in D♭), is currently in the possession of Bridgers, together with a full ten-finger version in the same key.

5. Further clues for assigning this early date to both scores may be found in Strayhorn's music handwriting, which matches that of his 1938 manuscripts. The scores furthermore show markings that Ellington never used ("Trum." where Ellington would write "Cors" for trumpets, "Hodges" for "Rab" and "Bigard" for "Barney")—apparently Strayhorn had never laid eyes on an Ellington manuscript.

6. Strayhorn (1962) named *Savoy Strut* and *You Can Depend on Me* as his first arrangements for this Hodges date. *Savoy Strut* (DEC) was recorded a month later, on March 21, 1939. *You Can Depend on Me* is possibly *You Can Count on Me* recorded by a Hodges-led small band on June 2, 1939 (no manuscript known). Feather (1943, 13) named the same titles, together with *Like a Ship in the Night*. Ellington arranged the big band version of *You Can Count on Me* (DEC) for the June 12 session.

7. The only known instances of this so-called Henderson style in the recent Ellington repertoire occurred in *A Jazz Potpourri* (recorded December 19, 1938) and in certain portions of the earlier *The Gal from Joe's* (first recorded on January 13, 1938).

8. As with *Lush Life*, there are no manuscripts that can establish with certainty this early date of *Take the "A" Train*—the score for the famous 1941 version is certainly written later. Still, Hajdu (1996, 55–56) cites various sources reporting Strayhorn had written the piece prior to joining the Ellington organization in New York. As copyist Thomas Whaley (1965) told members of the New York Duke Ellington Jazz Society (now TDES, Inc.), "Strayhorn in 1939, see, Strayhorn joined...and Strayhorn had this number, *The 'A' Train*, then" (emphasis his).

9. Ellington recycled part of an earlier, unrecorded arrangement of Leslie Edgar's and Joseph A. Burke's *Robins and Roses*, which is also the manuscript's title (REC).

10. Strayhorn explained the idea of "on the man writing" as follows: "You have to deal with individual characteristics. Like, [Harold] 'Shorty' Baker, who has a certain trumpet sound. If you're writing for a brass section and you want his sound, you give him the lead part. The rest follow him. Or if you want Johnny Hodges' color or Russell Procope's color in the reeds, you write the lead part for either of them" (Coss 1962, 40). While most other orchestras had designated lead players (one per section), Ellington had picked musicians that could all play lead, which allowed this type of scoring.

11. Though the first manuscript for *Day Dream* is lost, BSC and DEC have Strayhorn autographs for seven different, later versions, including an unrecorded score from 1940 for the orchestra. Since that score refers to Ben Webster and Cootie Williams, it was created no later than November 1940. This belies Giddins's suggestion that *Day Dream* builds on Ellington's 1941 composition *I Got It Bad (and*

That Ain't Good). (Both works are materially so different that even if Ellington's piece had preceded Strayhorn's there would have been little ground to see a connection between them.) The copyright for *Day Dream* was registered that same year in the names of Duke Ellington and Billy Strayhorn.

12. The later *Chelsea Bridge* uses a similar harmonic and melodic construction—its melody centers around major sevenths against planing minor sixth chords.
13. Another source for Rollins's *Airegin* (and Strayhorn's *Day Dream?*) might be Ida Cox's *Nobody Knows You When You're Down and Out* (made famous by Bessie Smith). The melody of the bridge of *Nobody Knows You*, though not modulating, comes surprisingly close to the passages examined here—Rollins is known for drawing inspiration from the older blues repertoire.
14. Miles Davis: *Porgy and Bess* (Columbia LP CL 1274); reissued on *Miles Davis and Gil Evans: The Complete Studio Recordings* (Columbia CD 67397).
15. On November 7, 1940, two fans recorded the first full typical dance date of the band, in Fargo, North Dakota, reissued on: *Duke Ellington and His Famous Orchestra, Fargo, North Dakota* (Vintage Jazz). Of the forty-three different titles performed at the concert, ten were never recorded commercially—all pop songs, and virtually all arranged by Strayhorn.
16. Feather (1943, 13) names a number of small-band arrangements by Strayhorn for which the manuscripts are currently lost, such as *Dream Blues* and *The Rabbit's Jump*, both recorded September 1, 1939, and *Watch the Birdie*, recorded February 14, 1940. He further states that Strayhorn's "own favorite among his small-band works was Cootie's *Black Beauty* on Vocalion." This score is in fact by Ellington (DEC); Strayhorn may have referred to his arrangement of *Black Butterfly*, another recording by Cootie Williams and his Rug Cutters on Vocalion.
17. See, for instance, *The Girl in My Dreams Tries to Look Like You*, *Rocks in My Bed*, and an unrecorded version of *Bli-Blip* (all DEC).
18. A copyright leadsheet in DEC, entitled *Lick Chorus*, contains the melody for the famous saxophone chorus from *Cotton Tail*. The manuscript, by copyist John Sanders who worked for Ellington from 1954 on, curiously credits the chorus to Ellington and Strayhorn. The copyright was filed July 20, 1940, in the name of Duke Ellington.
19. An Ellington manuscript for *Bojangles*, containing the sixteen-bar section that follows Webster's solo, is in BSC. Ellington may have given Strayhorn the manuscript in order to expand it into a full composition. However, the final work (no manuscript known) does not bear any of Strayhorn's musical characteristics.
20. All original manuscripts for *Concerto for Cootie* are lost, apart from three instrumental parts in the hand of extractor Juan Tizol (DEC). This might contradict Strayhorn's involvement, since Tizol reportedly refused to extract Strayhorn's scores. With the exception of a handful of *joined* Ellington-Strayhorn works, such as *The Girl in My Dreams Tries to Look Like You* or *Rocks in My Bed* (both in DEC), Tizol never seems to have copied out any Strayhorn scores. Yet, the entire guitar part, most of the bass part, and two final bars on the other parts are in Strayhorn's hand—the only Ellington scores Strayhorn is known to have extracted were those they had collaborated on. Strayhorn's hand on these parts thus suggests his involvement in *Concerto for Cootie*. More circumstantial evidence of Strayhorn's involvement is given by a later score of the introduction, "Intro Concerto Cooty" (BSC), written around October 1942, when the trumpet section expanded to four voices with the addition of Harold "Shorty" Baker. On Baker's arrival, Strayhorn reworked a number of his earlier scores, including the introduction plus the two

final bars for *Concerto for Cootie*, to accommodate the extra voice. For that later version he also extracted the instrumental parts.

21. In the introduction to his published transcription of *Sepia Panorama*, Schuller (1995, iv) is more positive about the work's merits, stating that it "is one of several hundred miniature masterpieces Ellington created during his...career." As noted before, Schuller's transcription of the *Tuxedo Junction* section used for *Sepia Panorama* is seriously flawed. For a more detailed analysis of *Sepia Panorama*, as well as reproductions of Ellington's and Strayhorn's autographs, see Van de Leur (2000, 240–243).

22. The original orchestral version of *Tonk* has been recorded posthumously (see Appendix C). After performing it incidentally as a four-handed party treat in the 1940s, Ellington and Strayhorn commercially recorded a version of *Tonk* in 1950, issued on *The Billy Strayhorn Trio: Great Times* (Mercer Records LP-1001).

23. Ulanov (1946, 238) mentions an unrecorded Strayhorn piano concerto. Whether he refers to *Tonk* or to another (incomplete and untitled) piano concerto found in BSC is not known.

24. See DeVeaux (1997, 105–110) for a detailed discussion of tritone-related dominants and their usage in jazz.

25. The vocalise and the consecutive trombone and alto solos (not in the autograph) have been added for reference to the music examples given here. The remainder derives directly from the manuscript.

CHAPTER 3

1. Works copyrighted in Mercer Ellington's name were *John Hardy's Wife* (arranged, and possibly composed, by his father ["John Hardy," REC]), *Jumpin' Punkins*, *Moon Mist*, and *Blue Serge* (no manuscripts known, the latter arranged by Ellington according to Strayhorn [1962]), and *Things Ain't What They Used to Be*, first recorded by Johnny Hodges and His Orchestra, in a Strayhorn arrangement. A fifth titular Mercer Ellington composition, *The Girl in My Dreams Tries to Look Like You* ("Like-You," DEC), dates from December 1940, and was co-arranged (possibly co-composed) by Ellington and Strayhorn.

2. At the January 15, 1941, session for Standard Radio Transcriptions, the orchestra also recorded *Until Tonight* (BSC and DEC), a feature Strayhorn had written for his friend Ben Webster. At the time, no copyright was registered. *Until Tonight* is not known to have been performed since.

3. The transcription published by the Smithsonian Institution's Jazz Masterworks Editions erroneously has two altos and two tenors in this passage. In his introduction, Schuller decides against two altos, a tenor, and a baritone, because of "the high A in mm. 43, 52, and 67, which even the great Harry Carney could not have managed so lightly and effortlessly in 1941" (Schuller 1993). The chord in the saxophones, however, is not an Ami7, as Schuller's transcription would have it, but an $A^b\text{mi}^{(\text{maj}7)}$, a decisively more modern chord, with a high A^b for the baritone that falls in its range.

4. Possibly, Ellington wrote not all of *Daybreak Express*. Around 1929, Jimmy Hilliard (who also worked under the pseudonym Hilly Edelstein) "started to do arrangements for the Duke Ellington ork. Among others was an arrangement on a tune written by Duke and Jimmy called *Stevedore Serenade*. There was another arrangement, on ['Jelly Roll' Morton's] *Milenburg Joys*, done by Jimmy for Duke, which the latter changed around a bit and called *Sleepy Town Express* [sic]" (Hoefer 1945, 12).

Both *Daybreak Express* and *Milenburg Joys* are based on the *Tiger Rag* chord progression, which served as a harmonic framework for many compositions before Gershwin's *I Got Rhythm* became the favored model. According to Ann Keubler (2000), the parts for *Milenburg Joys* (DEC) are in Hilliard's hand. They carry the final choruses of *Daybreak Express*.

5. Strayhorn's score suggests that he indeed envisioned this chord as a tritone-related, altered E7. Blanton, however, plays a B♭ on the second half of beat three, giving the chord an altered B♭7 flavor.

6. McHugh's theme, however, does not touch on the characteristic flatted-fifth in bar three. Aware of their shared chord progressions, Charles Mingus made a recording that simultaneously featured the themes of *Take the "A" Train* and *Exactly Like You* (May 25, 1960, issued on *Charles Mingus: Mingus Revisited*, Mercury MG20627).

7. According to Strayhorn (1962), when he had finished *The Jumping Jive* (Summer 1939), "Tizol refused to copy my scores: they were like hen-scratching. So I did my own copying." Indeed, the legibility of Strayhorn's scores from 1939 leave much to be desired, but his music writing improved dramatically during the next year. The ample space Strayhorn gave to Tizol in *Chelsea Bridge*, *Rain Check*, and the unrecorded *Blue Star* and *Lozit* (the latter a trombone feature clearly dedicated to Tizol) as well as their collaborative work on a Tizol tune named *Rose Bud*—after the trombonist's wife—belies any animosity between the two men. Still, over three hundred (partly incomplete) sets of instrumental parts in Strayhorn's hand survive (the majority in DEC and SIDE), more than half with their matching Strayhorn scores. Although for the remainder the original score is lost, these parts are as much proof of his authorship as his autograph scores. Strayhorn was not one of the orchestra's designated copyists, and therefore there is not a single Ellington score with a set of matching Strayhorn parts, with the sole exception of a handful of their earliest *collaborative* arrangements from 1939 (*Grievin'*, *I'm Checkin' Out*, *Goom Bye*, *Like a Ship in the Night*, *A Lonely Co-Ed*, and *Your Love Has Faded*) and one from 1940: *Sepia Panorama*. After that, Strayhorn never again extracted his employer's scores. The proverbial exception to the rule is Strayhorn's set of instrumental parts to Ellington's arrangement for *Danke Schoen*, the only known instance.

8. Similarly, a rumor circulates among musicians that Ellington composed Ray Nance's masterly solo on *"A" Train*. Again, there is no trace of evidence. Nance's solo is built on embellishments and variations of the theme, put in his part by Strayhorn as a point of departure.

9. The full version of *Chelsea Bridge* has been recorded posthumously (see Appendix C).

10. James McNeill Whistler (1834–1902) painted several Impressionistic canvases (most of them currently housed at the Smithsonian Institution's Freer Gallery, Washington, D.C., and the Tate Gallery, London) depicting scenes of London's Chelsea Embankment, such as *Nocturne: Blue and Gold—Old Battersea Bridge*. Although Chelsea Bridge is an actual London bridge, two bridges east of Old Battersea Bridge, it was not one of Whistler's subjects. As Strayhorn's lover Aaron Bridgers told *Momentum* (1997, 4), Strayhorn—fully aware of the original painting's title—"thought that *Chelsea Bridge* sounded better: he did know the difference." Other Whistler paintings bore titles such as *Arrangement in Grey and Black*, *Caprice in Purple and Gold*, *Symphony in White*, and *Harmony in Gold*. This assignation of musical terminology is rooted in Whistler's conviction that his works stood as metaphors for music (Whistler 1890).

11. Vallas (1933, 112) notes that Whistler "was a favorite with Debussy, and their art has often been compared. The comparison is...legitimate."
12. These same parallel moving chords can also be found in Horace Silver's *Nica's Dream* (1960).
13. This term was suggested to me by jazz-theoretician Boudewijn Leeuwenberg.
14. Strayhorn's piano introduction is transcribed from the original recording. It is not in the autograph.
15. This $B^{\flat}mi6^{(maj7)}$ could suggest that the theme starts with an $E^{\flat}9^{(\flat 5)}$, in fact encountered in many "fake books" (e.g., Aebersold 1995, 4). Strayhorn, however, assigned the bass an F and a $B^{\flat}$, which rules out this harmonization.
16. Strayhorn's second piano interlude, which was to set up the third chorus, remains unknown. At the February broadcast recording (without Strayhorn) the assigned space is however clearly audible: the whole band rests (including Ellington) while bassist Jimmie Blanton hastens to fill the gap with some ad-lib runs.
17. The unissued first recording of *Chelsea Bridge* (February 16 or 20, 1941) takes up 4 minutes and 14 seconds, at a tempo of M.M. ♩ = 103. The Standard Radio Transcription of September 17 is significantly slower at a tempo of almost M.M. ♩ = 90, and takes up a little over three minutes for two of the three choruses. These so-called radio transcriptions, produced for distribution to radio stations only, imposed relatively few limits on duration, as the 33-1/3 rpm 16-inch transcription-discs could register up to 15 minutes of playing time: *Chelsea Bridge* could have been recorded entirely. At the somewhat faster tempo of almost M.M. ♩ = 95 of the commercial Victor recording of December 2 (2 minutes and 52 seconds), the entire score of *Chelsea Bridge* would have taken up four-and-a-half minutes, definitely too long for a regular 78 (which lasted around 3 minutes and 30 seconds). The obvious solution here would have been to record the first two choruses fully, and play only the first half of the final chorus, similar to the structure of *Take the "A" Train*. At a slightly faster tempo of M.M. ♩ = 96 this would have adequately filled a 78, would have used all the important material of the score (the second half of the last chorus did not present any new material) and would have preserved a more satisfactory structure.
18. An unusual publication of a Strayhorn score in *Down Beat* (Strayhorn 1968), which was "copied...from individual parts, a conductor's score not being extant" (ibid.), prints the full three choruses of the original Strayhorn score. Yet, a fourth trumpet part in the score indicates that the *Down Beat* score was culled from a later version—Strayhorn's original includes three trumpets only. The published manuscript is at variance with the Casa Mañana broadcast, the most important omission being exactly the trombone-against-reeds passage (mm. 43–50 in the score, mm. 60–68 on the broadcast recording).
19. According to Tucker (1993a, 110), this validation of Ellington's work started as early as 1932, when the Australian-born classical composer Percy Grainger "ranked Ellington as one of the greatest composers in the history of music, sharing honors with J. S. Bach and Frederick Delius." Soon the jazz field adopted this legitimization and "the Ellington-Delius comparison was by now [1943] commonplace" (Tucker 1993a, 165).
20. After being cited by Homzy (1992, 6), Dance (1993a) withdrew his early criticism on Strayhorn. This resulted in a severe attack on Dance from Leonard Feather (1993) with an equally acrid rebuttal by Dance (1993b).
21. Evans worked with Thornhill's orchestra from late 1941 until it disbanded in the fall of 1942. The orchestra regrouped in 1946, with Evans as main arranger. For

the second edition of the Thornhill orchestra, Evans looked more at the newly emerging bebop.

The legendary *Birth of the Cool* sessions were recorded for Capitol Records on January 21 and April 22, 1949, and March 9, 1950, by different ensembles under stewardship of Miles Davis (reissued in 1996 on Capitol CDP7 92862 2).

22. Similarly, in his multimovement *Open Letter to Duke* (issued on *Mingus Ah Um*; reissued on *Better Git It in Your Soul*—the reissue includes original versions of *Mingus Ah Um* and *Mingus Dynasty* [Columbia CG30628])—Mingus built one of the movements, *Nouroog*, on the theme of *Passion Flower*. *This Subdues My Passion* and *Minor Intrusion* have been issued on *Charlie Mingus* (Everest FS235), *Profile of Jackie* has been issued on *Pithecanthropus Erectus* (Atlantic SD8809), and *Duke Ellington's Sound of Love* has been issued on *Changes One and Two* (Atlantic 60108).

23. A final brass chord entering on the second half of the bar can be found among others in *Love Has Passed Me By*, *Again*, *Lana Turner*, and in his arrangements of *Yesterdays*, *Where or When*, *We'll Be Together Again*, or *I Don't Stand a Ghost of a Chance with You*.

24. Titles put aside included the Pittsburgh compositions *My Little Brown Book* ("L.B.B.," DEC) and *Ugly Ducklin'*, both re-scored for the full band and the latter retitled to *Don't Take My Love* (REC, on verso of Ellington's arrangement of *John Hardy's Wife*; Strayhorn's score is crossed out); the slow tempo, highly dissonant *Blue House* (DEC); a medium tempo trumpet feature called *Hip* (BSC and DEC); the modernist, angular *Hipper-Bug* (BSC); the ballads *Blue Star* (BSC and DEC) and *Lament for an Orchid* (BSC); an elaborate full-band version of Strayhorn's earlier *Day Dream* (BSC); the pensive *Noir Bleu* (BSC, recorded later that year in a small-band version by Barney Bigard and His Orchestra); a trombone feature for Juan Tizol called *Lozit* (BSC); the up-tempo, hard-swinging *Jo* (DEC); two pieces in a more "classical" vein, named *Etude* (DEC) and *Symphonette-Rhythmique* (DEC); the less convincing and somewhat patchy *Allah Bye* (DEC); and *Pentonsilic* (BSC). All these manuscripts can be dated through names of personnel: they either refer to Jimmie Blanton (who left in September 1941) or Barney Bigard, who played with Ellington until June 1942, while in most cases they also refer to Ray Nance, who joined in November 1940, further narrowing down the time frame. *Blue House*, *Hip*, *Hipper-Bug*, *Lament for an Orchid*, *Blue Star*, *Lozit*, *Jo*, and *Pentonsilic* have been recorded posthumously (see Appendix C).

25. When Strayhorn composed *Pentonsilic*, he and Ellington reportedly were involved with two film projects, one with Orson Welles, tentatively titled *It's All True*, and one with Boris Morros, named *Tales of Manhattan* (Stratemann 1992, 193–195). *Pentonsilic* may have been intended for either, though it could also be a production number for *Jump for Joy* or for an unknown, unproduced stage show that was envisioned to include the Ellingtonians.

26. Collier's terminology ("rainforest," "leanness and strength") has racist connotations as well.

27. Works Strayhorn composed or arranged for *Jump for Joy* (on his own or in collaboration with Ellington) include the title song (untitled, DEC, and "First-Chos-Joy," BSC), *Sharp Easter*, *Bli-Blip*, *Rocks in My Bed* (all three DEC, joint manuscripts), *Uncle Tom's Cabin Is a Drive-In Now* ("U.T. Cabin," DEC, joint manuscript), *Flame Indigo* (DEC), *Bugle Breaks* (BSC, joint manuscript), *The Chocolate Shake* ("Choc-Shake-Verse," DEC), two versions of *I Got It Bad (and That Ain't Good)* ("Bad-Good," DEC, and "Bad-Good-Vocal," BSC), and four versions of *The Brown-Skin*

Gal in the Calico Gown ("B-Skin," "Introduction," and untitled, all DEC, and "B. Skin Gal," BSC). All these works have been credited solely to Ellington, with the exception of *Bugle Breaks*, for which Strayhorn shares credits with Ellington and Mercer Ellington. A number of unidentified scores and sketches for *Jump for Joy* survive as well, including dance routines, medleys, fanfares, openers, and introductions, all reflecting the continuous revisions of the show ("B. S. Gal," "H. Stick," "U. T. Cabin," "Joy," "Bugle Next," "Fanfare Jump-Joy," and "Calico Before This," all BSC).

28. Works arranged by Strayhorn include *Cindy with the Two Left Feet* ("Two Left Feet," DEC), *Cymbal Sockin' Sam, The Emperor's Bones, If Life Were All Peaches and Cream,* and *The Tune of the Hickory Stick* (untitled manuscripts, BSC). For the last two titles (and *Sharp Easter*) BSC also possesses the original conductor's scores, together with those for *I've Got a Passport from Georgia, Nothin',* and *We're the Sun-Tanned Tenth of the Nation*, suggesting that Strayhorn arranged the latter three as well (no further manuscripts known).

29. *Flame Indigo* has been recorded posthumously (see Appendix C).

30. Although the original program (Ellington 1973, 177–179) credits Paul Webster for lyrics to *Flame Indigo*, the work appears to be an instrumental. Neither lyricist Webster, who said he only vaguely remembered working with Ellington on the piece, nor singer Jeffries, who supposedly sang the number in the show, later could recall the melody or even any lyrics (Willard 1988, 27). Moreover, where the program listed vocalists for all the other vocal numbers, no singer or singers, or other cast members, were named for *Flame Indigo*. With its chromatic melody spanning an octave and a minor sixth, the piece would have been virtually impossible for an average singer to sing (and it is not likely that Strayhorn envisioned Jeffries returning to his falsetto-style singing).

31. Only one Ellington score for a segment from *I Got It Bad* (DEC) has been preserved. It refers to Ella Fitzgerald. The score is not known to be recorded.

32. RCM Soundies (for Roosevelt, Coslow, and Mills) were short music-films—video clips *avant la lettre*—that could be viewed for five cents in commercial viewing machines, placed in some 4,000 public venues nationwide. Of the five Ellington Soundies made, four were (uncredited) Strayhorn arrangements: *I Got It Bad, Flamingo, Bli-Blip,* and *C-Jam Blues*.

33. The original 1941 parts for *Johnny Come Lately* are titled "Moe" (most of the score, including the title page, is lost). Moe was Strayhorn's nickname for Jimmie Blanton—the work may have been a tribute to the bass player who was by then terminally ill.

Chapter 4

1. Elaborating on the distinction between composition and arrangement, Strayhorn explained that "sometimes you're just involved with a tune. You sit at the piano and write what represents a lead sheet....After it's done, Duke and I decide who's going to arrange it. Sometimes we both do it, and he uses whatever version is best" (Coss 1962, 23). There's indeed a group of "tunes" (often with lyrics) that appear to have been worked out along these lines, such as the songs for *Beggar's Holiday*, for which in some instances both wrote arrangements of the same song. Still, it appears that in most cases Strayhorn was the arranger of such material. Ellington, on the other hand, appears to have never arranged a Strayhorn composition, with some exceptions, such as *Polly's Theme*, Strayhorn's contribution to

Anatomy of a Murder (recorded as *Haupê* and *Low Key Lightly*). Ellington used Strayhorn's theme for *Grace Valse* and *Midnight Indigo*. Even so, their "tunes" still bore their individual imprints: "you can always tell an Ellington song," Strayhorn said (Coss 1962, 40).

2. Four-bar introductions can be found in, among others, *Azalea, Homesick—That's All, I Don't Want Anybody at All (If I Can't Have You), The Wonder of You, As Long as I Live*, and *The Last Time I Saw You*. Eight-bar introductions can be found in, among others, *Can't Help Lovin' Dat Man, I'll Buy That Dream, Dancing in the Dark* (1945 version), *Don't Be So Mean to Baby, I Can't Begin to Tell You, Love Letters, We'll Be Together Again*, and *Put Yourself in My Place, Baby*.

3. *The Man I Love* and *Night and Day* have been recorded posthumously (see Appendix C).

4. Codas built on thematic material can be found in, among others, *A Garden in the Rain, Autumn Serenade, Dancing in the Dark* (1945 version), *Homesick—That's All, I Could Get a Man (But the Man I Want Is Got)*, and *This Is Always*.

5. Codas that repeat the introduction can be found in, among others, *Could It Be You, I Can't Begin to Tell You, I'll Buy That Dream, Love Letters, Strange Love*, and *The Last Time I Saw You*.

6. An incidental Strayhorn score is fashioned along the more conventional lines of theme-solos-tutti, such as *Once Upon a Dream* (whose tutti passage was cut for the recording), and *It's Love I'm In*.

7. This return to the key of the exposition distinguishes scores with a temporary modulation from the many scores of the swing era that used two keys. In those scores a vocal chorus was typically followed by an instrumental chorus in a different key (and vice versa).

8. Strayhorn's arrangement of *Where or When* has been recorded posthumously in its original vocal version (see Appendix C).

9. In his autograph, Strayhorn specifies the key change two bars earlier (m. 57), enharmonically spelling the chords in D^b. For clarity, I have chosen to let the key change coincide with the bar where the new key is reached.

10. The broadcast (October 5, 1946) was issued on *Your Saturday Date with the Duke* (Duke Ellington Treasury Series 46).

11. Strayhorn's arrangement of *Can't Help Lovin' Dat Man* has been recorded posthumously in its entirety as an instrumental (see Appendix C).

12. *Blue Heart* and *Portrait of a Silk Thread* have been recorded posthumously (see Appendix C).

13. The title on the autograph reads "Overture to a J.S. at M.," the "M." in all probability standing either for Minton's Playhouse or for Monroe's Uptown House, both famous after-hour spots frequented by the young bebop players and those "in the know." Strayhorn belonged to the latter group.

14. *Lana Turner* was first copyrighted as *Francesca*, and retitled *Charpoy* by Strayhorn in the 1960s. The oft-cited "wordplay" *Anal Renrut* (Homzy 1992, 6), found on some of the instrumental parts, was not Strayhorn's but copyist Whaley's. Strayhorn and Lana Turner were friends.

15. A "blindfold test" with the author's family and friends inspired exactly these metaphors. Frank Janssen, for instance, described the arrangement of *Where or When* as a landscape which from high up looked like a unified whole, but at a closer distance turned out to be highly accented, with steep abysses that cut through sloping grounds (Frank Janssen, oral communication, February 2000). Such a metaphoric description is personal and subjective, but a remarkable num-

ber of people use similar images when listening to Strayhorn. Performers of Strayhorn's music are no exception, although some, such as altoist Albert Beltman, experience Strayhorn's music in entirely emotional terms (Albert Beltman, oral communication, February 2000).

16. For a more detailed analysis of *I Never Felt This Way Before*, as well as reproductions of Ellington's autograph, see Van de Leur (2000, 233–240).
17. See for instance *Love and I*, *Irresistible You*, *Passion Flower*, *Strange Love*, and *A Flower Is a Lovesome Thing*, as well as later arrangements of *Indian Summer*, *Dancing in the Dark* (1957 version), *Brown Penny*, *Blue Bird of Delhi*, and *Blood Count*.
18. A clarinet over (muted) trumpets can be found also in *Take the "A" Train* (1957 version) and *Day Dream* (1957 version), among others.
19. A subtle instrumental effect occurs in measures 7 and 8 of *The Eighth Veil*, when the saxophones first join and then replace the trombones in their doubling of the trumpet line, quickly altering the weight of the phrase. Similar instances occur in *Orson*, *Day Dream* (1957 version), and *Pretty Girl*.
20. Dissonant chords cushioning the melody can be found also in *Blue Star* (mm. 2 and 4) or *Lover Man* (mm. 11–12), among others.
21. In close-position voicing, all chord-tones are placed directly under the melody, while open-position voicing allows for wider intervals between chord-tones. Especially when harmonizing a line, Ellington tended to use more close-position voicing, which yields a so-called thickened line. Of course there are many exceptions to these general tendencies—neither composer limited himself to any given technique.
22. It seems that Strayhorn largely conceived a piece in his head before writing it down (hence the linearity in his music) where Ellington tended to engage himself (and his orchestra) in a process of trial and error (as further documented by his autograph scores and incidental recordings of his rehearsals with the band). See also Chapter 6.
23. This arrangement opens with a curious section in waltz-time. As lyricist Sid Kuller explained, one of the pieces from *Jump for Joy*, titled *Old-Fashioned Waltz*, "was eventually abbreviated into an effective old-gives-way-to-the-new introduction to *Bli-Blip*" (cited in Willard 1988, 27).
24. This version of *Polly's Theme* has been recorded posthumously in its entirety as *Anatomy of a Murder* (see Appendix C).
25. Among the numerous examples of pieces that have passages with a single-line counterpoint are *Day In, Day Out*, *There Shall Be No Night*, *There's No You*, *Lover Man*, and *A Garden in the Rain*.
26. *Lover Man* has been recorded posthumously in its entirety (see Appendix C).
27. Similar repeated chords occur in *Goin' My Way*, *Homesick—That's All*, *Cynthia's in Love*, *If You Are but a Dream*, *Lily Belle*, *Love Letters*, *Lover Man*, *Passion Flower*, *Tell Ya What I'm Gonna Do*, *Wrong, Can It Be Wrong*, and *What's the Good Word, Mr. Bluebird* as well as in earlier Blanton-Webster work such as *Chloë (Song of the Swamp)*, *Day In, Day Out*, *The Five O'Clock Whistle*, and *Way Down Yonder in New Orleans*.
28. According to Dameron's biographer Ian MacDonald, Strayhorn and Dameron worked together informally around late 1949 (MacDonald, 1998).
29. *Snowfall*, *Donna Lee*, and *Robbins' Nest* have been reissued on *Claude Thornhill and His Orchestra: The Transcription Performances 1947* (HEP CD 60); *Our Delight* has been reissued on *The Smithsonian Collection of Recordings: Big Band Jazz, Vol. 4* (Smithsonian RD 030-4).

30. *Street of Dreams* and *Some Peaceful Evening* were both recorded by Boyd Raeburn and His Orchestra in June 1944 for Lang-Worth Transcriptions, and have been reissued on *Boyd Raeburn and His Orchestra: 1944* (Circle CD CCD-22).

    Through a curious coincidence, Raeburn's "boyds" at the same session recorded an actual Strayhorn score. In April 1944, Juan Tizol had left Ellington to join Harry James's orchestra, which at the time was largely working on the West Coast. There, Tizol must have run into Raeburn and given or sold him his latest piece, *Casablanca*, written for his former employer. (The Ellingtonians performed the piece in public only once: at an MBS broadcast from the Hurrican Club, June 27, 1943.) Raeburn's orchestra recorded Tizol's piece as *Baghdad*, reissued on *Boyd Raeburn and His Orchestra: 1944* (Circle CD CCD-22). The parts for *Casablanca*, in Tizol's hand, are housed at the Rutgers Institute of Jazz Studies (W. E. Schremp Collection) and indeed carry the names of Ellington's personnel. While the arrangement is erroneously credited on the CD release to Tizol, who is not known to have ever arranged his own compositions, the arrangement of *Baghdad* is audibly by Strayhorn. Since Tizol must have had the score in his possession when he left Ellington, Strayhorn's autograph is in neither the Duke Ellington nor Billy Strayhorn Collections.

31. *Temptation, Dalvatore Sally, More Than You Know*, and *I Only Have Eyes for You* have been reissued on *Boyd Raeburn and His Orchestra: The Transcription Performances—1946* (HEP CD 42), and *Body and Soul* has been reissued on *Boyd Raeburn and His Orchestra: Jubilee Performances—1946* (HEP CD 1).

32. *Boyd Meets the Duke* has been reissued on *Boyd Raeburn and His Orchestra: 1944, Concerto for Duke* has been reissued on *Boyd Raeburn and His Orchestra: The Transcription Performances—1946* (HEP CD 42).

33. Handy's spoken introduction to an untitled "tone poem" in four movements, composed in 1946, further seems to echo Ellington. The tone poem includes *Dalvatore Sally, Hey Look—I'm Dancing, Grey Suede, Special Maid*, and *Keef* (the latter written by Flo Handy but arranged by her husband). The tone poem has been reissued on *Boyd Raeburn and His Orchestra: Jubilee Performances—1946* (HEP CD 1).

CHAPTER 5

1. V-Disc was a nonprofit record label established during the recording ban (October 1943). By extension the name was also used for the discs themselves. The AFM agreed that its members could participate in V-Disc's recording sessions, provided the records were not sold (they were distributed free of charge to the Armed Forces Radio Services) and that the masters were ultimately destroyed.

2. According to Homzy (1993, 103, 103n25), "a score of this section [*Sugar Hill Penthouse*] titled *Symphonette* has been found in the Duke Ellington Collection. Written on four staves in the typical Ellington manner, the manuscript seems to be partly in the hand of copyist Tom Whaley and partly in the hand of Billy Strayhorn.... Perhaps what we have here in *Black, Brown and Beige* is a recopied portion of Ellington's score because the original was given away or lost." The Duke Ellington Collection houses no manuscript that matches this description. There is, however, a full copyist's score by Whaley (partly in ink and partly in pencil, hence the attribution to two different authors?) that must be a copy of Strayhorn's original, now lost (only his autograph parts survive). In many similar instances, the Duke Ellington Collection contains only the copyist's score of a Strayhorn original as well as the autograph parts (e.g., *U.M.M.G.* and *Boo-Dah*).

3. As established later, Ellington did use earlier material, such as a portions from his *Concerto for Clinkers* (from *Jump for Joy*), extensive quotations from his *Ridin' on a Blue Note*, as well as an earlier piano solo called *Bitches' Ball*.
4. In the third segment of *Black*, however, Ellington introduces further thematic material before returning to the earlier themes.
5. As the second selection in the "Strayhorn group," the Carnegie program announced a new work entitled *Nocturne*. A contemporary manuscript by that title in the Billy Strayhorn Collection suggests that *Nocturne* was an arrangement of the previously composed, introspective *A Flower Is a Lovesome Thing*. Ellington probably sensed that the consecutive performance of two slow-tempo pieces might require a little too much from his audience and on second thought dropped the work.
6. In the second half of the concert the orchestra furthermore performed *Day Dream*, not included in the "Strayhorn group" but announced as "another Strayhorn arrangement" (Ellington 1943).
7. The instrumental parts for Van Eps's arrangement are in the repository of the Paul Whiteman Collection at Williams College, Massachusetts—Whiteman never recorded the suite.
8. The opening of Kolodin's article is a good example of the typical set of false criteria and misjudgments that have often been applied to jazz:

> The respectable segment of the jazz world gathered for one of its periodic sessions of self-inspection under the counselship of Paul Whiteman in Carnegie Hall on Sunday evening, the celebrated leader thus presenting his "Eighth Experiment in Modern American Music."
>
> Respectability in this case was signified by the orchestra of nearly sixty men and the fact that almost all the music was written out. However, as a concession to the swing vogue, Mr. Whiteman invited two of its leading practitioners—the clarinetist Artie Shaw and the great trumpeter Louis Armstrong—to demonstrate their talents. (Kolodin 1938, 16)

9. A later commission by Whiteman befell virtually the same fate. Ellington's *Blutopia*, written for Whiteman in 1944 and premiered by Ellington at his second appearance at Carnegie Hall (December 19, 1944) underwent similar revisions by Strayhorn. Ellington had partly scored the work for the orchestra but passed the uncompleted four-page manuscript on to Strayhorn, with the request to "Develope [sic] Ending According to Time" (Ellington n.d.[b], 4). Instead of merely developing an ending, Strayhorn largely rewrote the piece. He expanded a two-bar motif that closed Ellington's score to a full-blown secondary theme, and replaced a large part of Ellington's voicings with denser settings, for instance by adding a dissonant clarinet lead to most of the reed chords. (Ellington would reuse this two-bar piano motif in later works, e.g., in *Long Time Blues*, issued on *The Private Collection, Vol. 1* [LMR CD 83000], and *Hey, Baby*, issued on *Blue Rose* [CBS 466444-2].) The structural revisions display unmistakable Strayhorn idiosyncrasies, from the modulation that foreshadows the secondary riff to the coda that layers motivic material from both themes. Apparently, the revisions were to Ellington's satisfaction: he performed Strayhorn's arrangement *in toto* at its Carnegie premiere.
10. At his second concert at Carnegie Hall (December 11, 1943) Ellington stated: "We thought we wouldn't play it (*Black, Brown and Beige*) in its entirety tonight because it represents an awfully long and a very important story. And in that I don't think that too many people are familiar with the story, we thought it would be better to

11. wait until that story was a little more familiar before we did the whole thing again" (issued on *Carnegie Hall Concert*, Ember Records EMBD 2001).
11. Though the work is credited to Ellington and Strayhorn, the inclusion of *Strange Feeling* in his only solo concert, in 1965, and on his solo album *The Peaceful Side* further corroborates that it is a Strayhorn original.
12. *The Deep South Suite* was premiered at the Civic Opera House in Chicago (November 10, 1946) and featured later that month in Carnegie Hall (November 23, 1946). Strayhorn shares credits with Ellington for *Happy-Go-Lucky-Local*. Only part of the score survives, in Ellington's hand; the famous theme later used by Jimmy Forrest for *Night Train* is missing. (Jimmy Forrest was in the orchestra's saxophone section in August 1946, when the *Deep South Suite* was on the repertory. Forrest used his part for *Happy-Go-Lucky-Local* to write a piece called *Night Train*—a suit over copyrights was settled out of court.) Strayhorn further shares credits for Ellington's piano solo *There Was Nobody Looking* (no apparent Strayhorn involvement), and *Hear Say* (no Ellington involvement). As was the case with Strayhorn's earlier contributions to the *Perfume Suite*, the da capo *Hear Say* bore no programmatic relationship to the Deep South. The original score is titled "O.W." As the autograph reveals, these initials most likely stand for screen writer and film director Orson Welles: exploring the possibilities for an anagram title, Strayhorn jotted "ORSON WELLS [sic] NOSRO SLLEW" on his autograph score (Strayhorn n.d. [a], 5).
13. The orchestra shared the bill with a roster of other groups for the Carnegie Hall appearances in the 1950s (Stratemann 1992, passim).
14. Ellington shares credits for *Do Nothing Till You Hear from Me* and *Don't Get Around Much Anymore* with lyricist Bob Russell, while the registration for *I'm Beginning to See the Light* lists Harry James, Johnny Hodges, and Don George as co-authors.
15. Mary Lou Williams's autograph parts are in DEC, while most of her scores are in the repository of the Institute for Jazz Studies at Rutgers University, Newark.
16. A handful of notebooks with originals and arrangements by Jimmy Hamilton are in DEC; two of his scores are in BSC.
17. From the early beginnings of jazz, composers built their pieces on the chord sequences (known as the "changes") of existent pieces, using familiar pieces such as the *Tiger Rag* and *I Got Rhythm* as vehicles for new works. The bebop composers expanded this practice as their compositions consisted of new thematic material added to the changes of the harmonically more challenging pieces from the Tin Pan Alley and Broadway repertoires.
18. For most of these scores, copyist Thomas Whaley created instrumental parts carrying the names of Ellingtonians, indicating that Strayhorn wrote these pieces to be performed by the Ellington orchestra. *Portrait of a Silk Thread, Le Sacre Supreme, Lana Turner*, and *Blue Heart* have been recorded posthumously (see Appendix C). Duke Ellington and His Orchestra recorded later arrangements of *Blue Heart* and *Lana Turner*, retitled *Paradise* and *Charpoy*, respectively (see Appendix B).
19. *Entrance of Youth*, not included in the issued registration of the two Carnegie Hall concerts (December 26 and 27, 1947), featured the first Juilliard School of Music winners of a newly instated *Duke Ellington Scholarship*: Warren Ross (flute), Paul Rudolph (French horn), and Elaine Jones (piano). The theme of the piece was later reused for *All Heart*, the second movement of *A Portrait of Ella Fitzgerald*.
20. At least twenty-three scores survive, including titles that were eventually recorded during the late 1940s: *Take Love Easy, Women (They'll Get You), Maybe I Should*

Change My Ways (all with some Ellington involvement), *Brown Penny*, and *He Makes Me Believe He's Mine* (reminiscent of Fats Waller's *Ain't Misbehavin'*). Other Strayhorn contributions remained unrecorded: *Thirteen Boxes of Rayon Skirts, Through All the Employments* [sic], *We'll Scratch Out His Eyes, You Wake Up and Breakfast on a Cigarette* (all BSC), *When I Walk with You, On the Wrong Side of the Railroad Tracks* (co-written with Ellington), *Girls Want a Hero, I Wanna Be Bad,* and *Cream for Supper* (all DEC). Strayhorn took care of some of the obligatory production numbers as well, including *Boll Weevil Ballet* (BSC and DEC), *Vamp, Wedding Ballet,* and *Fol-De-Rol-Rol* (all BSC). The full orchestral versions of *On the Wrong Side of the Railroad Tracks, Boll Weevil Ballet,* and *Fol-De-Rol-Rol* have been recorded posthumously (see Appendix C). Eleven more songs, carrying script numbers only, in all likelihood were scrapped before the show opened. In addition to this host of new material, Strayhorn sought to interpolate at least one of his *Fantastic Rhythm* compositions. For a while, *Let Nature Take Its Course* was part of the trial performances, but the song was taken out before the show hit Broadway.

21. Strayhorn played piano on most of the commercial recordings of material from *Beggar's Holiday*, a sure sign of his involvement in the creation of these works. For instance, he is clearly present on the commercial recording of *Brown Penny* (October 2, 1947) where he cites Sergei Rachmaninov's (1873–1943) *Second Piano Concerto* (1901) in his piano break that leads to the coda.

Chapter 6

1. This absence of proper credits has led to ill-informed criticism, such as in Eddie Lambert's *Duke Ellington: A Listener's Guide* (Lambert 1999). In a separate chapter dedicated to Strayhorn, Lambert strikes an overall dismissive tone, faulting Strayhorn's compositions for, among other things, "overelaboration," "a soggy sentimentality," "a lack of consistency," and "a tendency…toward a rather self-conscious modishness," which "had a debilitating effect on the music of the Ellington band" (Lambert 1999, 278–279). In the main body of his text, however, (which deals with the Ellington band recordings), Lambert bestows extensive praise on several of Strayhorn's uncredited contributions to the orchestra's repertory. For instance, Lambert calls the arrangements for *Masterpieces by Ellington* "commanding" and "a unique achievement" (ibid., 155), while he finds *Up and Down* "one of the great triumphs of [*Such Sweet Thunder*]" (ibid., 194). Clearly, he is unaware of Strayhorn's authorship in these and other instances, as he often wrongly credits Ellington. According to Lambert, "Strayhorn's compositions for the Ellington band number only about 40 pieces written over a period of 28 years" (ibid., 285). Appendix D lists all known Strayhorn compositions (more than four hundred—roughly three hundred were a matter of public record when Lambert wrote his book).

2. On his copyist's score, John Sanders credits Ellington and Strayhorn jointly for *Ready, Go!*, the final movement of *Toot Suite*. Strayhorn's contribution to this movement remains unknown. Like *Red Carpet (Part 2)*, it does not build on the other material in the suite. An earlier piece called *Bassment* further contradicts Strayhorn's story, since it contains essentially the same material as *Red Carpet (Part 2)*. It is of course possible that Strayhorn's new movement in the end wasn't used by Ellington and was replaced by the aforementioned *Bassment*. This would still weaken the anecdote: why replace a section that blended perfectly with the rest of the suite with one that did not?

3. Lambert paraphrases Norman Granz, who supervised the recording of *A Portrait of Ella Fitzgerald*: "On the night before [the suite] was to be recorded, Ellington had not written a note. He turned up for the session with a few things scribbled on the backs of envelopes, and with the aid of his copyists and his special kind of musical shorthand, the band managed to turn out a four-movement suite" (Lambert 1999, 195–196). However, as in so many cases, detailed scores and parts for all four movements survive (see Appendix B). While the parts may have been extracted in the studio, it is unlikely that the scores (three by Strayhorn and one by Ellington) were prepared on the spot.
4. Of course, Ellington's writing style and aesthetics matched—that is, even without editing he tended to write sudden transitions. As such, the marked caesuras which stem from changing the order of musical events are premeditated.
5. Relatively few sketches or drafts preceding his scores survive.
6. Ellington's adage "when it sounds good, it is good" fails to consider the subjectivity of aesthetic judgment.
7. Among the arrangements that suffered serious cuts are *It Don't Mean a Thing* (1943 version), *I Let a Song Go Out of My Heart* (1945 version), *Solitude* (1945 version), *Everything but You* (1945 version), *Come to Baby, Do, Orchids for Madame, Embraceable You, It Is Love I'm In, Once upon a Dream, I Could Get a Man*, and *Put Yourself in My Place, Baby*.
8. See Appendix B for reference recordings of the works listed.
9. "We stopped using the word jazz in 1943," Ellington said; "that was the point when we didn't believe in categories" (Nicholson 1999, 247). For Strayhorn "jazz" was "only a potpourri of vowels and consonants" (Ellington and Strayhorn, 1960).
10. Typically, there were significant delays between a work's creation and Tempo's copyright registration, which further compromised the accuracy of the publisher. In 1966, for instance, more than eight years after Ellington and Strayhorn wrote music for the unperformed theater work *Saturday Laughter*, Tempo undertook action to copyright the show's numbers. Although all of the scores evidently were in Ellington's library (they are now in DEC), Tempo filed copyrights for roughly half of them (with Ellington listed as sole composer), leaving the others unprotected (see Appendix D).
11. Strayhorn's *Coffee and Kisses* was credited at the time of its release (see Appendix B) to F. Hollander and R. Freed, who wrote a different piece by the same title in 1938.

CHAPTER 7

1. The exact financial setup between Ellington and Strayhorn remains unknown, and it is possible that Strayhorn continued to receive benefits from the organization in addition to royalties generated by his compositions. Ellington could be quite loyal to former band members. Drummer Sonny Greer, for instance, was on the payroll until Ellington's death in 1974, even though he had left the band in 1951. Nevertheless, those close to Strayhorn reported that the break did have financial consequences (it also came at a time when the Ellington himself was under severe financial pressures).
2. *El Amor de Don Perlimplín con Belisa en su jardín—Aleluya erótica en quatro quadros* (1931).
3. *Sprite Music, The Flowers Die of Love*, and *Love, Love* have been recorded posthumously (see Appendix C). *Wounded Love* was recorded as an instrumental by Johnny Hodges, retitled *Three and Six*, reissued on *Lush Life: The Billy Strayhorn Songbook* (Verve 314 529 908-2).

4. Amor, amor/que estoy herido./Herido de amor huido/herido/muerto de amor./Decid a todos que ha sido/el ruiseñor./Bisturí de cuatro filos/garganta rota y olvido./Cógeme la mano, amor,/que vengo muy mal herido,/herido de amor huido,/¡herido!/¡muerto de amor!
5. Monteverdi's Venetian laments stem from two operas written in Venice, *Il Ritorno d'Ulisse in Patria* (Ulysses' Homecoming, 1641) and *L'Incoronazione di Poppea* (The Coronation of Poppea, 1642), largely fashioned along lines laid down in his still lost opera *Arianna* (1608), of which only the famous lament survives.
6. Roughly applying the techniques used for the reed section to a small five-part string ensemble seems the obvious thing to do, and in fact is recommended in most arranger's handbooks.
7. Strayhorn wrote a number of compositions for instrumental combinations that deviated from the standard big-band lineup, but this music was never performed or recorded during his lifetime. One wonders to what extent that may have bothered him. While Ellington was content to move on after a single performance of his latest composition, ready to tackle the next challenge, Strayhorn seems to have found satisfaction in exploring orchestral possibilities on music paper. Over the course of his career he wrote numerous, often detailed, scores and sketches for a wide variety of instrumental combinations that apparently were not available to him and thus remained unrecorded. The absence of instrumental parts in most instances further corroborates that he did not seek actual performance. Compositions and arrangements written in this vein consist of scores for various woodwind ensembles (including clarinets, bass clarinets, flutes, bassoons, and an incidental oboe) often with strings (violins, violas, and cellos—no double basses) and at times expanded with brass instruments. They may include parts for timpani, or a harp, and at times make use of a standard jazz-band rhythm section. The largest and most elaborated group of works are those for regular big band with additional string section. In most cases these are vocal arrangements, suggesting that he conceived them for Lena Horne: *Baby Don't You Cry, I Must Have That Man, My Dream of You, Nevada, No One but You,* and *Where Is Love.* The lineup indicates that these scores were not for the Ellington orchestra, since they call for four trombones and a guitar, and often contain written out piano parts, not found on any other score for Strayhorn's regular forum. Almost a decade after the recordings with Webster, Strayhorn would once more work with strings for the 1961 recordings of the mistitled LP *The Peaceful Side* (as the LP's producer Alan Douglas later stated, "It was my title, and it was never right...it was really the inside of Billy Strayhorn" [Hajdu 1996, 212]) with the remarkable addition of a six-part vocal choir. The ten selections on that album are all Strayhorn originals, written in the 1930s and early 1940s, and feature the composer at the piano, with subtle backdrops by strings and voices. Technically, these arrangements open no new perspectives, but the recording provides a unique opportunity to hear Strayhorn's delicate piano playing.
8. As Henderson told Hajdu (1996, 141–142) Ellington succeeded in discouraging the two composers from pursuing their musical partnership.
9. Surviving production numbers for the various Copasetics dances are *Opening Bon Voyage, Welcome Aboard, Opening Copasetics,* and *Finale* (all BSC).
10. For the 1961 Copasetics Dance, Roy Brankers wrote (part of) the lyrics. *Feet on the Beat, Swing Dance,* and *Everything Is Copasetic* have been recorded posthumously (see Appendix C)
11. Still, the mock-vaudeville Copasetics shows at times called for music in a wholly

different league. Strayhorn's *Welcome Aboard*, for instance, caricatures commercial Broadway productions, with grotesque chorus lines and the obvious tempo change to a half-time toward the end of the song for the grand finale.

12. The earlier use of his Pittsburgh compositions *Ugly Ducklin'*, *Your Love Has Faded*, *Something to Live For*, *Let Nature Take Its Course*, and *My Little Brown Book* similarly illustrates that for Strayhorn his compositions did not belong to separate worlds.

13. These later arrangements of *Wounded Love* and *Love Has Passed Me By, Again* were recorded posthumously (see Appendix C).

CHAPTER 8

1. It is possible that Ellington and Strayhorn renewed their partnership before that. Two Strayhorn arrangements consistent with the lineup used for the *Aquacade* (big band with additional strings and a harp) survive: *You Go to My Head* and *I've Got the World on a String*. On stage, Ellington was replaced at the piano by Woody Kessler, formerly Sammy Kaye's pianist, which might explain the atypical inclusion of a piano part in Strayhorn's scores. Both arrangements were recorded posthumously (see Appendix C).

2. Back in the Ellington fold in the second half of the 1950s, Strayhorn and Hodges continued their partnership on a number of LPs: *Creamy* (Norgran, 1955), *Ellingtonia 56* (Norgran, 1956), *Duke's in Bed* (Verve, 1956), *The Big Sound* (Verve, 1957), and *Cue for Saxophone* (Decca, 1959).

3. The idea of *A Drum Is a Woman* harks back to earlier, similar Ellington attempts at recounting the history of jazz, such as *It Is All True*, a film initiated by actor-director Orson Welles in 1941. Welles's plans stalled when RKO-Pathé fired him in 1942. Strayhorn's own *Fantastic Rhythm* had a quasi-historical episode as well: *The Rhythm Man* recounts the invention of rhythm and syncopation. For *A Drum Is a Woman*, Strayhorn wrote *A Drum Is a Woman (Part 1 and 2)*, *Rhythm Pum-Te-Dum*, *What Else Can You Do with a Drum*, *Carribee Joe (Part 1 and 2)*, *Congo Square*, and *Ballet of the Flying Saucers*.

4. According to Hajdu (1996, 156), the title was Strayhorn's. Irving Townsend claims it was his find (Townsend 1960, 321).

5. These sketches are on verso of "IDMAT," BSC.

6. According to the manuscript's title, "Cleo," the first movement of *Such Sweet Thunder* initially intended to portray Cleopatra.

7. Ellington had arrived later due to commitments elsewhere with the band.

8. New songs for *Jump for Joy* were *So the Good Book Says*, *The Natives Are Restless Tonight*, *But, Don't Believe Everything You Hear*, *Walk It Off*, and *If We Were Any More British We Couldn't Talk at All* (all in BSC and DEC), and *When I Trilly with My Filly*, *Show 'Em You Got Class*, and *Three Shows Nightly* (all DEC).

9. Some fifteen copyist's scores for *Saturday Laughter* are in DEC (identified by Ann Kuebler), as well as an autograph inventory of titles by Strayhorn. Since the music lacks any specific individuality, it is impossible to ascertain who wrote what, but the scores seem to give one clue: ten have detailed piano accompaniment, strikingly similar to other Strayhorn piano-vocal scores, while five consist of melody against chord symbols, not characteristic of Strayhorn. Strayhorn's handwriting can be found on two of the copyist's scores, where he provided additions.

10. Stratemann (1992, 406) lists the various alternate titles for *Polly's Theme* in DEC, but he does not identify the author.

11. "The Beatles have done several excellent things," Strayhorn said, adding, "I don't mean that as a total endorsement, because I haven't liked everything they have done" (Dance 1967, 19).
12. Of Ellington's contributions only the muscular *March* (issued as *The Peanut Brittle Brigade*) survives, while the manuscripts of the *Chinese Dance* and *Russian Dance* (respectively *Chinoiserie* and *The Volga Vouty*) are lost. Of these two only the latter seems to be by Ellington. Strayhorn wrote the remaining scores.

CHAPTER 9

1. Often the chord is erroneously given as a D♭dim or a D♭mi7$^{(♭5)}$, both incomplete spellings of altered dominants on A, lacking the G and the C (see, e.g., Aebersold 1995, 3).
2. In classical theory this chord is known as the second inversion German sixth chord (e.g., Ulehla 1966, 134–135). Its history dates back to the classical period in western-European music (late eighteenth century) where as a result of voice leading it appeared almost exclusively in its first inversion. The chord played a prominent role in nineteenth-century European music as well as in later idioms whose harmony drew largely on classical genres, including American popular song. In jazz theory this German sixth chord is commonly known as the tritone-related (or upper-chromatic) double-dominant and treated more independently, that is, its occurrence is not necessarily the result of a horizontal movement of voices.
3. Examples of a similar independent use of tritone-related double-dominants may be found in *Out of Nowhere* (G6 to E♭9 and back in measures 3–6), or in Gil Evans's arrangement of *Moon Dreams* (measures 4–5) which has D9$^{(♭5)}$-E♭9-G^{maj7}, the dominant proper surprisingly preceding the tritone-related double-dominant. For a full transcription and analysis of *Moon Dreams*, see Albjerg (2000, 1–15).
4. Arpeggiated chords, either ascending or descending, appear in many of Strayhorn's works: *Isfahan* (descending major seventh), *Johnny Come Lately* (ascending diminished), *Rain Check* (descending minor sevenths and dominant sevenths), and in the counterpoint of *All Heart* (descending altered dominant).
5. Dizzy Gillespie's recording of *U.M.M.G.* with the Ellington orchestra has been issued on *Duke Ellington's Jazz Party* (Columbia LP CL-1323).
6. Both the surviving score and a separately prepared piano leadsheet give different readings of the theme. Since the orchestral score appears to have a number of thematic ellipses, where Strayhorn in all likelihood envisioned piano fills, I have taken the leadsheet here as the primary source for the theme.
7. The edits on the score are in Strayhorn's hand. The four-bar introduction to *Pretty Girl* was also discarded. For the recording of *Such Sweet Thunder*, Ellington convincingly replaced intro and coda with piano runs over powerful chords.
8. As discussed in Chapter 6, it is unlikely that Strayhorn himself edited his scores in rehearsal.
9. Blues-based Strayhorn compositions include *Festival Junction* and *Blues to Be There* (the first two movements of the *Newport Jazz Festival Suite*), *BDB* (for the album with the combined Basie and Ellington orchestras), *Blues I + II* (recorded as *Blues*), *Beyond Category* (from *A Portrait of Ella Fitzgerald*), *Blues in Orbit*, *Sweet and Pungent*, *Tymperturbably Blue*, *Cordon Bleu*, *Frère Monk*, and *Blousons Noirs* (see Appendix B for recording references).
10. The predecessor to this *Day Dream* arrangement is the 1952 score of *I Got It Bad*

for singer Betty Roché (and recorded commercially with Rosemary Clooney, in January 1956), which draws on a similar approach.

11. *Day Dream*'s opening passage with its barely moving harmonies brings to mind Felix Mendelssohn's famous "fairy chords" which frame his *Overture to a Midsummer Night's Dream*. Strayhorn may have had the piece on his music stand at the time, since he was working on *Such Sweet Thunder*, a suite inspired by Shakespeare characters. An earlier instance of "fairy chords" in Strayhorn's writing can be found in his 1943 arrangement of *Blue Belles of Harlem*.
12. This version of *Pretty Girl* was recorded posthumously (see Appendix C).
13. *Wounded Love* was recorded posthumously (see Appendix C).
14. Up and down, up and down,/I will lead them up and down./I am feared in field and town,/Goblin, lead them up and down. (*A Midsummer Night's Dream*: III.2.496–99.)
15. In the various scenes of the play, Puck fools different couples, such as Demetrius and Helena, Lysander and Hermia, Theseus and Hyppolyta, Oberon and Titania, and Bottom and Titania. Like the play, Strayhorn's piece opens with a group of three protagonists. It appears that bass and drum play their conventional role of keeping time.
16. Unfortunately, the reissue of *Such Sweet Thunder* on CD (Columbia CK 655568 2) in 1999 (the Ellington birthday centennial year), has a different take than the one used for the original LP—it lacks Terry's quotation. The original LP has been reissued on CD as well (Columbia 469140 2).
17. It is possible that this group refers to the "mechanicals," a group of comic figures in the play: Peter Quince, Nick Bottom, Francis Flute, Tom Snout, Snug, and Robin Starveling (actually six characters, one more than in Strayhorn's group).
18. Although Sturm (1995, 28 and 153) assumes that this is a "collaborative arrangement" and that the cross-section introduction is "probably Ellington's," the entire arrangement is Strayhorn's.
19. Fitzgerald mostly sticks to the original rhythm, at times elongating some of the note values.

CHAPTER 10

1. The March on Washington took place mere days before the closure of a show called *My People* (September 2, 1963), Ellington's oblique expression of support for the civil rights movement. Ellington maintained that *My People* was "definitely not political[; it] has social significance, but the accent will be on entertainment" (Stratemann 1992, 474). The seventeen-piece pit band for *My People* went by the name of the Billy Strayhorn Orchestra and was led alternately by pianist-arranger Jimmy Jones and by the orchestra's namesake, who had also arranged part of the production's music, and composed an incidental song. *My People* was largely a reworking of Ellington's earlier *Black, Brown and Beige*.
2. The manuscript scores of *Mount Harissa* and *Blue Pepper* are lost—both works seem largely conceived by Ellington.
3. Given both the urban location in India (New Delhi) and the time of year (September), Strayhorn's visitor in all likelihood belonged to the Common or Indian Mynah species (Acridotheres tristis), a jaunty brownish bird with a glossy black head. This mynah has a sociable, adaptable, and opportunistic character and may be found anywhere in India, from remote villages to large towns (see Butterfield, n.d.).
4. See, e.g., "Agra—The City of Taj Mahal."

5. Joe Henderson's recording of *Isfahan* (in 1992; issued on *Lush Life: The Music of Billy Strayhorn* [Verve 314-511-779-2]), inspired other jazz performers to add the piece to their repertories.
6. Strayhorn puts this line to brilliant use in the subsequent bars. After it has circled around the chord's minor thirteenth (C♭) for color, the counterpoint resolves to C in measure four (Example 10-3), thereby implying that the alto's second phrase builds on its initial D♭ major seventh, and thus fully capitalizing on the harmonic ambiguity.
7. Ellington had used a similar title (*Figh, Fo, Fumm*) for a different work in 1958.
8. Homzy's (1992, 23) assessment that "Billy Strayhorn's first assignment for and last contribution to Ellington were collaborations" is off the mark. Ellington's arrangement of Strayhorn's theme does not qualify as a collaboration.
9. This reference to bass trombonist Connors rules out claims that *Blood Count* dates "from the late 1940s" (Homzy 1992, 7).
10. In all likelihood, Strayhorn had completed the recorded version of *Blood Count* before the orchestra left New York for a European tour on January 13, 1967. The Ellingtonians are known to have rehearsed the work in Milan, February 25.
11. In addition to *Something to Live For* and *A Flower Is a Lovesome Thing*, Jimmy Jones arranged *Azure* and *The Brown-Skin Gal in the Calico Gown* for *Ella at Duke's Place*. The Verve CD reissue wrongly credits Jones as the arranger of *Passion Flower*, which was in fact an earlier Strayhorn arrangement (see also Nicholson 1999, 371). Jones later stated that he arranged only four numbers, which rules out his involvement with *I Like the Sunrise*, though the CD liner notes do credit him. According to Jones, Gerald Wilson arranged a piece as well.
12. The chronology remains unclear. Ruff's detailed description of the genesis of the suite (Ruff 1991, 3–11) repeatedly indicates that Strayhorn wrote the work early in 1967, yet the Library of Congress's copyright registrations for *Up There*, *Boo Loose*, and *Pavane Bleu No. 2* are dated March 7, 1966 (the registration numbers on the copyrights seem to rule out that the Copyright Office listed a wrong date). Even if Strayhorn and the Mitchell-Ruff duo worked on the piece a year earlier it very likely still is Strayhorn's final known composition, since the two different scores of *Blood Count* suggest that that work was written before March 1966. Although in theory Strayhorn could have copyrighted the suite in 1966 and reworked it into a feature for the duo afterward, the first movement especially seems too idiomatic to be written for any other instrument than the French horn.
13. The Riverside Drive Five can be heard on *Billy Strayhorn: Lush Life* (Red Baron AK-52760).
14. Ruff (1991, 8) refers to the work as "Billy Strayhorn's *Suite for Horn and Piano*."
15. An assumption made by both Hajdu (1996, 253) and Homzy (1992, 6). Hajdu corrected this oversight in the third printing of his book.
16. "Dort, wo du nicht bist, dort ist das Glück" (translation by Paul Hindemith). From *Der Wanderer*, text by Georg Philipp Schmidt von Lübeck, set to music by Franz Schubert (Dietz 493).
17. Though he had earlier written works that were not geared toward performance or recording (see Chapter 7), those compositions appeared to be a matter of exercise or amusement. By contrast, the *North by Southwest Suite* was a personal statement, written, moreover, for specific musicians whom Strayhorn took the trouble to instruct in person. Dwike Mitchell and Willie Ruff recorded the suite in 1968 as *Suite for the Duo* (see Appendix C).

CONCLUSION

1. Ellington's eulogy for Strayhorn has been reprinted in Ellington 1973, 159–161, and Hajdu 1996, 257.
2. In fact, Ellington did not have access to much of his collaborator's material. After Strayhorn's death, a large part of his scores and sketches were held in the repository of his estate in Pittsburgh and thus were inaccessible to the Ellington organization. (Gregory Morris, executor of Billy Strayhorn's estate, provided Ellington with scores from Strayhorn's files for the recording of...*And His Mother Called Him Bill*.) Although a portion of Strayhorn's material was in the music library of the Ellington orchestra, the orchestra did not record or perform any pieces it had not recorded or performed during Strayhorn's life. Furthermore, the unused Strayhorn music in Ellington's files was largely finished, since Strayhorn tended to bring completed scores to the orchestra. Probably, Brown's assessment must be seen in the light of a long-standing resentment that had developed between him and Ellington, and which culminated in a violent confrontation between the two. After the incident (late in 1969) Brown gave Ellington his notice, and stopped playing the trombone altogether (see, e.g., Dietrich 1995, 181–182).
3. The Billy Strayhorn Project Featuring the Michael Hashim Quartet: *Lotus Blossom* (Stash Records ST-CD-533); Joe Henderson: *Lush Life* (Verve 314-511-779-2); Fred Hersch: *Passion Flower* (Nonesuch Records).

APPENDIX A

1. The only exceptions were the published scores of *Black, Brown and Beige* (Ellington 1963) and *Chelsea Bridge* (Strayhorn 1970, 90–100).

References

"A Duke Named Ellington." 1988. Two-part TV documentary. Santa Monica. Videotape in the repository of the Duke Ellington Collection, Smithsonian Institution, Washington, D.C.
"Agra—The City of Taj Mahal." *Homepage of Incore*. (www.incore.com/india/up.agra.html).
Aebersold, Jamey, ed. 1995. *Jazz Play-a-Long Vol. 66: Billy Strayhorn*. New Albany, Indiana: Jamey Aebersold.
Albjerg, Erik. 2000. "From Mellow-Textured Mood Music into Dissonance: Gil Evans's 1948 Arrangement of *Moon Dreams*." *Tijdschrift voor Muziektheorie* (February): 1–15.
Atkinson, Brooks. 1946. "Beggar's Holiday." *New York Times* (January 27): 13.
Bagar, Robert. 1943. "Duke Marks 20th Year as Musician." *New York World-Telegram* (January 25): 9.
Berliner, Paul F. 1994. *Thinking in Jazz: The Infinite Art of Improvisation*. Chicago and London: University of Chicago Press.
"Billy Strayhorn's Arranging Hints." 1942. *Music & Rhythm* (May): 27.
"Billy Strayhorn on Pianists." 1943. *Metronome* (March): 29, 66.
Binchet, J.-P. and Philippe Carles. 1966. "Antibes 007. Billy Strayhorn." *Jazz Magazine* 134 (September): 48–49.
Bridgers, Aaron. 1997. Personal communication. August 27.
Bruyninckx, W. 1985. *Jazz. The Vocalists 1917–1986: Singers and Crooners*. Mechelen, Belgium: [Copy Express].
Butterfield, Kathy. n.d. "Mynah Bird Species." *Mynah Bird Home Page* (www.mynahbird.com/articles/species).
Caine, Daniel. 1986. "A Crooked Thing: A Chronicle of *Beggar's Holiday*." *The New Renaissance* 23 (Fall): 75–100.
———. 1997. Letter to the Editor. *TDES New York Chapter Newsletter* (March): 7.
"CD Reviews." 1996. *Down Beat* (December): 58–77.
Collier, James Lincoln. 1987. *Duke Ellington*. New York: Oxford University Press.
"Copasetics Dance." 1960. *Amsterdam News* (September 24): 15.
"Copasetics Have Swinging Affair." 1961. *Amsterdam News* (October 7): 18.
"Copasetics 'Kill' Viewers with Fast Moving Show." 1962. *Music Review* (October 6): 18.

Coss, Bill. 1962. "Ellington & Strayhorn, Inc." *Down Beat* (June 7): 22–23, 40.
Crouch, Stanley. 1988. Program notes for a concert held on August 10, 1988, at Alice Tully Hall, Lincoln Center for the Performing Arts, New York. Rpt. in *The Duke Ellington Reader*, edited by Mark Tucker, 440–445. New York: Oxford University Press, 1993 (page citations are to the reprint edition).
Dance, Stanley. 1967. "A Matter of Inspiration & Interpretation." *Down Beat* (February 23): 18–19.
———. 1993a. Letter to the Editor. *TDES New York Chapter Newsletter* (January): 6.
———. 1993b. Letter to the Editor. *TDES New York Chapter Newsletter* (March): 6.
DeVeaux, Scott. 1993. "*Black, Brown and Beige* and the Critics." *Black Music Research Journal* 13, no. 2: 125–146.
———. 1997. *The Birth of Bebop: A Social and Musical History*. Berkeley and Los Angeles: University of California Press.
Dietrich, Kurt. 1995. *Duke's 'Bones: Ellington's Great Trombonists*. Rottenburg, Germany: Advance Music.
Ellington, Duke. n.d.[a]. *Boola*. Autograph sketch. In the repository of the Duke Ellington Collection, Smithsonian Institution, Washington, D.C.
———. n.d.[b]. *Blutopia*. Manuscript score. In the repository of the Duke Ellington Collection, Smithsonian Institution, Washington, D.C.
———. 1943. Spoken introduction, *Black, Brown and Beige: The Duke Ellington Carnegie Hall Concerts, January 1943*. Prestige CD 2PCD-34004-2.
———. 1944. Spoken introduction. *The Perfume Suite: The Duke Ellington Carnegie Hall Concerts, December 1944*. Prestige CD 2PCD-24073-2.
———. 1957. Spoken introduction. *Ella Fitzgerald Sings the Duke Ellington Songbook*. Verve CD 837 035-2.
———. 1963. *Black, Brown and Beige Suite*. Published score. New York: Tempo Music Inc. (Distributed by Campbell Connelly, London).
———. 1964. Spoken introduction. *Jazz 625—Duke Ellington in Concert*. Television program. London: BBC Television, February 20.
———. 1973. *Music Is My Mistress*. New York: Da Capo Press.
Ellington, Duke, and Billy Strayhorn. 1960. Unpublished interview. June. Audiocassette, author's collection.
Ellington, Mercer, and Stanley Dance. 1978. *Duke Ellington in Person: An Intimate Memoir*. New York: Da Capo Press.
Feather, Leonard. 1943. "Billy Strayhorn—The Young Duke." *Jazz Magazine* 5-6: 13–14, 31.
———. 1960. *The Encyclopedia of Jazz*. New York: Da Capo Press. Rpt. 1984.
———. 1965. Liner notes for *Ellington '65, Hits of the 60's: The Great Duke Ellington Band Swings Today's Hits*. Reprise Records RS-6122.
———. 1977. Liner notes for *Black, Brown and Beige: The Duke Ellington Carnegie Hall Concerts, January 1943*. Prestige CD 34004-2 or LP P-34004.
———. 1993. Letter to the Editor. *TDES New York Chapter Newsletter*. (March): 7.
García Lorca, Federico. 1931. *El Amor de Don Perlimplín con Belisa en su jardín—Aleluya erótica en quatro quadros*. Rpt. in Federico García Lorca *Five Plays*, translated by James Graham-Lujan and Richard L. O'Connell. London: Penguin Books, 1970.
Giddins, Gary. 1998. *Visions of Jazz: The First Century*. New York: Oxford University Press.
Granz, Norman. 1957. Liner notes for *Ella Fitzgerald Sings the Duke Ellington Song Book*. Reissued on Verve CD 837 035-2 (1988).
Hajdu, David. 1992. Unpublished interview with Herb Jeffries. January 26. Audio cassette, David Hajdu collection.

———. 1996. *Lush Life: A Biography of Billy Strayhorn*. New York: Farrar, Straus & Giroux.
———. 1997. Personal communication. April 16.
Harrington, Richard. "He Wrote the Songs: Billy Strayhorn, Out of Ellington's Shadow." *The Washington Post* (July 24): B7.
Hasse, John E. 1993. *Beyond Category: The Life and Genius of Duke Ellington*. New York: Simon and Schuster.
Haufman, Bo. 1999. "Herb Jeffries: The Bronze Buckaroo." *Blue Light* (July/August/September): 7–8.
Hentoff, Nat. 1965. "This Cat Needs No Pulitzer Prize." *The New York Times Magazine* (September 12): 64–66, 68, 70, 72, 74, 76. Rpt. in *The Duke Ellington Reader*, edited by Mark Tucker, 362–368. New York: Oxford University Press, 1993 (page citations are to the reprint edition).
Hodeir, André. "A Masterpiece: *Concerto for Cootie*." In *Jazz: Its Evolution and Essence*, translated by David Noakes. New York: Grove Press, 1956; rev. ed., 1979. Rpt. in *The Duke Ellington Reader*, edited by Mark Tucker, 276–288. New York: Oxford University Press, 1993 (page citations are to the reprint edition).
Hoefer, George. 1945. "Hilliard's Jazz Hips Chicago Radio." *Down Beat* (April 15): 3, 12.
Hoefsmit, Sjef. 1993. "Chronology of Ellington's Recordings and Performances of *Black, Brown and Beige*, 1943–1974." *Black Music Research Journal*, 13 no. 2: 161–173.
Holley, Eugene. 1996. "Billy Strayhorn Revisited." *Down Beat*. (September): 10–11.
Homzy, Andrew. 1992. "Me and You." *The Village Voice (Jazz Supplement: The Billy Strayhorn Suite)*, 37 (June 23): 5–7.
———. 1993. "*Black, Brown and Beige* in Ellington's Repertoire, 1943–1973." *Black Music Research Journal* 13 no. 2: 87–110.
Hossiason, José. 1988. "Billy Strayhorn." In *The New Grove Dictionary of Jazz*, edited by Barry Kernfeld. London: Macmillan. Rpt. 1991 and 1994 (page citations are to the reprint edition).
"Interview with Aaron Bridgers." 1997. *Momentum*, Vol. 2, No. 6 (May): 2–4.
Jablonski, Edward. 1987. *Gershwin: A Biography*. New York: Doubleday.
Jewell, Derek. [1977] 1986. *Duke: A Portrait of Duke Ellington*. London: Pavillion.
Keys, Gary. Prod., dir. 1980. *Memories of the Duke*. Film. Gary Keys Productions in association with Videovision, Time-Life Films and Bill Panzer.
Knauer, Wolfram. 1990. "'Simulated Improvisation' in Duke Ellington's *Black, Brown and Beige*." *The Black Perspective in Music* 18: 20–38.
Kolodin, Irving. 1938. "Holiday Music: Paul Whiteman Conducts Dance Band in Carnegie Hall—Benefit for Refugees." *The New York Sun* (December 27): 16.
———. 1943. Program notes for *Duke Ellington and His Orchestra: Twentieth Anniversary Concert, Carnegie Hall, January 23*. Rpt. in *The Duke Ellington Reader*, edited by Mark Tucker, 161–165. New York: Oxford University Press, 1993 (page citations are to the reprint edition).
Kuebler, Ann K. 1997a. E-mail to the author. August 14.
———. 1997b. E-mail to the author. June 19.
Lamb, John. Interview for the Smithsonian Institution Oral History Project (NMAH AC#368: tape 2, side B).
Lambert, Eddie. 1999. *Duke Ellington: A Listener's Guide*. Lanham, Maryland and London: Scarecrow Press.
Lendvai, Erno, and Alan Bush (Introduction). 1971. *Béla Bartók: An Analysis of His Music*. London: Kahn and Averill.
"List of Favorites." 1952. *Down Beat* (November 5):2–4. Rpt. in *The Duke Ellington Reader*, edited by Mark Tucker, 268–269. New York: Oxford University Press, 1993.

Lagerwerf, Frits, and Hans Mantel. 1999. "Ellington, Strayhorn and Marsalis: The Creative Process." *Big Band*, November/December: 10–15. Article is in Dutch. Translation by the author.
MacDonald, Ian. 1998. E-mail to the author. December 29.
Massagli, Luciano, and Giovanni M. Volonté. 1999. *The New DESOR: An Updated Edition of "Duke Ellington's Story on Records."* Vols. 1 and 2. Milano: Musica Jazz.
Meeker, David. 1981. *Jazz in the Movies*. New York: Da Capo Press.
Muranyi, Joseph P. 1956. Liner notes for *Duke Ellington Presents...*Bethlehem, BET 6004-2.
Nicholson, Stuart. 1999. *Reminiscing in Tempo: A Portrait of Duke Ellington*. London: Sidgwick & Jackson.
Nielsen, Ole J., ed. n.d. *Jazz Records 1942–80*. Vol. 6: Ellington. Copenhagen: Stainless/Wintermoon.
Palmer, Robert. 1967. Liner notes for...*And His Mother Called Him Bill*. RCA-Bluebird, 6287-2-RB.
Peress, Maurice. 1993. "My Life with *Black, Brown and Beige*." *Black Music Research Journal* 13, no. 2: 147–160.
Priestley, Brian. 1982. *Mingus: A Critical Biography*. New York: Da Capo Press.
———. 1993. "*Black, Brown and Beige*." Rpt. in *The Duke Ellington Reader*, edited by Mark Tucker, 186–204. New York: Oxford University Press, 1993 (page citations are to the reprint edition).
Raben, Erik, ed. 1993. *Jazz Records 1942–1980: A Discography*. Copenhagen: Jazz Media Aps.
Rattenbury, Ken. 1992. *Duke Ellington, Jazz Composer*. New Haven and London: Yale University Press.
Rayno, Don. 1997. Personal communication. July 11.
Rosen, Charles. 1971. *The Classical Style: Haydn, Mozart, Beethoven*. New York: The Viking Press.
Rust, Brian. 1975. *The American Dance Band Discography, 1917–1942*. 2 Vols. New Rochelle, N.Y.: Arlington House.
Ruff, Willie. 1991. *A Call to Assembly: The Autobiography of a Musical Storyteller*. New York: Penguin Books.
Schoenberg, Loren. 1997. Presentation for TDES, Inc., New York, March. Audiocassette. In the repository of the Ruth Ellington Collection, Smithsonian Institution, Washington, D.C.
Schuller, Gunther. [1968] 1986. *Early Jazz: Its Roots and Musical Development*. New York: Oxford University Press.
———. 1988. "Third Stream." In *New Grove Dictionary of Jazz*, Barry Kernfeld, ed. New York: Macmillan, 1199. Rpt. 1991 and 1994 (page citations are to the reprint edition).
———. 1989. *The Swing Era: The Development of Jazz*. New York: Oxford University Press.
———. 1993. Performance and editorial notes to *Take the "A" Train*. Transcription. Washington, D.C.: Jazz Masterworks Editions (Smithsonian Institution).
———. 1995. *Sepia Panorama*. Transcription. Washington, D.C.: Jazz Masterworks Editions (Smithsonian Institution).
———. 1996. Liner notes for *The Birth of the Third Stream*. Columbia 485103 2.
———. 1998. Presentation for Ellington '98. Chicago (May). Videotape, author's collection.
Stratemann, Klaus. 1992. *Duke Ellington, Day by Day and Film by Film*. Copenhagen: Jazz-Media Aps.

Strayhorn, Billy. 1952. "The Ellington Effect." *Down Beat* (November 5): 2. Rpt. in *The Duke Ellington Reader*, edited by Mark Tucker, 269–270. New York: Oxford University Press, 1993.

———. 1960. "Sweet (Suite) Thursday." Unpublished synopsis of John Steinbeck's *Sweet Thursday*. In the repository of the Duke Ellington Collection, Smithsonian Institution, Washington, DC.

———. 1962. Talk for the Duke Ellington Jazz Society. New York (March). Audiocassette. In the repository of the Ruth Ellington Collection, Smithsonian Institution, Washington, D.C.

———. 1970. *Chelsea Bridge*. Score. In *Music '70: 15th Down Beat Yearbook*: 90–100.

Stuart Ryan, David. 1988. *India, a Guide to the Experience*. London: Kozmile Press.

Sturm Fred. 1995. *Changes over Time: The Evolution of Jazz Arranging*. New York: Advance Music.

"Swee' Pea...Is Still Amazed at Freedom Allowed in Writing for Ellington Orchestra." 1956. *Down Beat* (May 30): 15.

Tempo Music, Inc. n.d. *A Catalogue of Music by Duke Ellington, Billy Strayhorn...*New York: Tempo Music, Inc.

———. 1967a. *Supplement No. 1 to Tempo Music, Inc. Catalog, 1967*. New York: Tempo Music, Inc.

———. 1967b. *Additions to Catalog Supplement as of 15 Sept. 1967*. New York: Tempo Music, Inc.

Timner, W. E. 1996. *Ellingtonia: The Recorded Music of Duke Ellington and His Sidemen*, 4th ed. Lanham, Md., and London: Institute of Jazz Studies and Scarecrow Press.

Townsend, Irving. 1960. "When Duke Records." *Just Jazz* 4. Rpt. in *The Duke Ellington Reader*, edited by Mark Tucker, 319–324. New York: Oxford University Press, 1993 (page citations are to the reprint edition).

Tucker, Mark. 1986. "Duke Ellington 1940–42." Liner notes, *The Blanton-Webster Band*. RCA Bluebird.

———. 1991. *Ellington: The Early Years*. Urbana: University of Illinois Press.

———. 1993a. *The Duke Ellington Reader*. New York: Oxford University Press.

———. 1993b. "The Genesis of *Black, Brown and Beige*." *Black Music Research Journal* 13, no. 2: 67–86.

———. 1999. "Jazz in the Sixties—Duke Ellington in His Sixties." Liner notes, *Duke Ellington: The Reprise Studio Recordings*. Mosaic Records.

Ulanov, Barry. 1944. "Ellington's Carnegie Hall Concert a Glorified Stage Show." *Metronome* (January): 8, 48. Rpt. in *The Duke Ellington Reader*, edited by Mark Tucker, 210–212. New York: Oxford University Press, 1993 (page citations are to the reprint edition).

———. 1946. *Duke Ellington*. New York: Da Capo Press. Rpt. 1975 (page citations are to the reprint edition).

Ulehla, Ludmila. 1966. *Contemporary Harmony: Romanticism Through the Twelve-Tone Row*. New York: Free Press.

Valburn Jerry. 1981. Liner notes for *Duke Ellington and his Orchestra: Your Saturday Date with the Duke*. (Duke Ellington Treasury Series 01).

———. 1993. *Duke Ellington on Compact Disk: An Index and Text of the Recorded Work of Duke Ellington on Compact Disk*. Hicksville, N.Y.: Marlor Productions.

Vallas, Léon. 1933. *Claude Debussy: His Life and Works*, translated by Maire and Grace O'Brien. New York: Oxford University Press. Rpt. New York: Dover, 1973 (page citations are to the reprint edition).

Van de Leur, Walter. 1993. *Duke Ellington and Billy Strayhorn: Their Collaboration for the "Blanton-Webster Band," 1939–1941.* Unpublished Master's thesis, University of Amsterdam.

———. 2000. "Scores of Scores: Einige Anmerkungen zu Manuskripten der Billy-Strayhorn-und Duke-Ellington-Sammlungen in den USA." Translated and edited by Wolfram Knauer, in *Duke Ellington und die Folgen.* Darmstadt: Jazz-Institut Darmstadt and Wolke Verlag.

———. 2001. "The 'American Impressionists' and the 'Birth of the Cool.'" *Tijdschrift voor Muziektheorie* (January): 18–26.

Whaley, Thomas. 1965. Talk for the Duke Ellington Jazz Society. New York (March). Audiocassette. In the repository of the Ruth Ellington Collection, Smithsonian Institution, Washington, D.C.

Whistler, James Abbott McNeill. 1890. *The Gentle Art of Making Enemies.* London: W. Heinemann.

Wilder, Alec. 1972. *American Popular Song: The Great Innovators, 1900–1950.* New York: Oxford University Press.

Willard, Patricia. 1988. "Jump for Joy." Liner notes. Washington, D.C.: Smithsonian Institution Press and Smithsonian Collection of Recordings, DMK 1-0722.

Wilson, John S. 1965. "Strayhorn: Alter Ego for the Duke." *New York Times* (June 6): section 2, 13.

Worth, Paul. 1962. "Paul Worth Presents a Portrait of Duke Ellington." Radio interview. Los Angeles: KBCA radio (January 6). Audiocassette, author's collection.

Credits

Below are the copyright credits for the music examples reproduced in this book. These credits do not necessarily reflect my assessment of the actual author(s) and dates for the works cited.

Every possible effort has been made to contact copyright holders of original material contained in this volume.

Ballad for Very Tired and Very Sad Lotus Eaters. Billy Strayhorn. Copyright © 1964 (renewed) and assigned to Tempo Music, Inc., and Famous Music Corporation in the U.S.A. All rights for the world outside the U.S.A. administered by Music Sales Corporation (ASCAP). International copyright secured. All rights reserved. Reprinted by permission.

Blood Count. Billy Strayhorn. Copyright © 1967 (renewed) by Music Sales Corporation (ASCAP) and Tempo Music, Inc. All rights administered by Music Sales Corporation. International copyright secured. All rights reserved. Reprinted by permission.

Bluebird of Delhi, from *The Far East Suite*. Duke Ellington and Billy Strayhorn. Copyright © 1964 (renewed) by Music Sales Corporation (ASCAP) and Tempo Music, Inc., and Famous Music Corporation. All rights outside the U.S.A. administered by Music Sales Corporation. International copyright secured. All rights reserved. Reprinted by permission.

Boo Loose, from the *North by Southwest Suite*. Billy Strayhorn. Copyright © 1966 (renewed) by Music Sales Corporation (ASCAP) and Tempo Music, Inc. All rights administered by Music Sales Corporation. International copyright secured. All rights reserved. Reprinted by permission.

Can't Help Lovin' Dat Man. Oscar Hammerstein (words), Jerome Kern (music). Copyright © 1927 (renewed) by T.B. Harms Company.

Cashmere Cutie. Billy Strayhorn. Copyright © 1957 (renewed) by Music Sales Corporation (ASCAP) and Tempo Music, Inc. All rights administered by Music Sales Corporation. International copyright secured. All rights reserved. Reprinted by permission.

Chelsea Bridge. Billy Strayhorn. Copyright © 1941 (renewed) by Billy Strayhorn Songs, Inc., and Tempo Music, Inc. All rights administered by Billy Strayhorn Songs, Inc.

International copyright secured. All rights reserved. Reprinted by permission.

Day Dream. Billy Strayhorn and Duke Ellington. Copyright © 1941 (renewed) by Billy Strayhorn Songs, Inc., Tempo Music, Inc., EMI Catalogue Partnership, EMI Robbins Catalog Inc., and EMI United Partnership Ltd., U.S.A. International copyright secured. Worldwide print rights controlled by Warner Bros Publications Inc./IMP Ltd. Reproduced by permission of International Music Publications Ltd. All rights reserved. Reprinted by permission.

Eighth Veil, The. Duke Ellington and Billy Strayhorn. Copyright © 1949 (renewed) and assigned to Tempo Music, Inc., and Famous Music Corporation in the U.S.A. All rights for the world outside the U.S.A. administered by Music Sales Corporation (ASCAP). International copyright secured. All rights reserved. Reprinted by permission.

Fantastic Rhythm. Billy Strayhorn. Copyright © 1997 by Billy Strayhorn Songs, Inc. International copyright secured. All rights reserved. Reprinted by permission.

Flamingo. Ed Anderson (words) and Ted Grouya (music). Copyright © 1941 by Music Sales Corporation (ASCAP), and Tempo Music, Inc. © Renewed by Edwin H. Morris & Company, a division of MPL Communications Inc., and Grouya Publishing. All rights for Grouya Publishing administered by the Songwriters Guild of America. International copyright secured. All rights reserved. Reprinted by permission.

Flowers Die of Love, The. Billy Strayhorn. Copyright © 1998 by Billy Strayhorn Songs, Inc. International copyright secured. All rights reserved. Reprinted by permission.

Garden in the Rain, A. James Dyrenforth and Carroll Gibbons. Copyright © 1928 (renewed) by Campbell Connelly, Inc. International copyright secured. All rights reserved. Reprinted by permission.

Isfahan, from *The Far East Suite.* Duke Ellington and Billy Strayhorn. Copyright © 1964 (renewed) by Music Sales Corporation (ASCAP) and Tempo Music, Inc., and Famous Music Corporation. All rights outside the U.S.A. administered by Music Sales Corporation. International copyright secured. All rights reserved. Reprinted by permission.

Let Nature Take Its Course. Billy Strayhorn. Copyright © 1997 by Billy Strayhorn Songs, Inc. International copyright secured. All rights reserved. Reprinted by permission.

Love, Love. Billy Strayhorn. Copyright © 1998 by Billy Strayhorn Songs, Inc. International copyright secured. All rights reserved. Reprinted by permission.

Lover Man. Ram Ramirez, J. Davis, and J. Sherman. Copyright © 1941 by MCA Music Publishing.

Lush Life. Billy Strayhorn. Copyright © 1949 (renewed) by Music Sales Corporation (ASCAP) and Tempo Music, Inc. All rights administered by Music Sales Corporation. International copyright secured. All rights reserved. Reprinted by permission.

Northern Lights. Billy Strayhorn. Copyright © 1959 (renewed) by Music Sales Corporation (ASCAP) and Tempo Music, Inc. All rights administered by Music Sales Corporation. International copyright secured. All rights reserved. Reprinted by permission.

Orson. Duke Ellington and Billy Strayhorn. Copyright © 1956 (renewed) and assigned to Tempo Music, Inc., and Famous Music Corporation in the U.S.A. All rights for the world outside the U.S.A. administered by Music Sales Corporation (ASCAP). International copyright secured. All rights reserved. Reprinted by permission.

Overture. Billy Strayhorn. Copyright © 1997 by Billy Strayhorn Songs, Inc. International copyright secured. All rights reserved. Reprinted by permission.

Paradise (Blue Heart). Billy Strayhorn. Copyright © 1949 (renewed) by Music Sales Corporation (ASCAP) and Tempo Music, Inc. All rights administered by Music Sales Corporation. International copyright secured. All rights reserved. Reprinted by permission.

Passion Flower. Billy Strayhorn. Copyright © 1944 (renewed) by Billy Strayhorn Songs, Inc., and Tempo Music, Inc. All rights administered by Billy Strayhorn Songs, Inc. International copyright secured. All rights reserved. Reprinted by permission.

Pavane Bleu No. 2, from the *North by Southwest Suite*. Billy Strayhorn. Copyright © 1966 (renewed) by Music Sales Corporation (ASCAP) and Tempo Music, Inc. All rights administered by Music Sales Corporation. International copyright secured. All rights reserved. Reprinted by permission.

Penthouse on Shady Avenue, A. Billy Strayhorn. Copyright © 1997 by Billy Strayhorn Songs, Inc. International copyright secured. All rights reserved. Reprinted by permission.

Portrait of a Silk Thread. Billy Strayhorn. Copyright © 1995 by Billy Strayhorn Songs, Inc. International copyright secured. All rights reserved. Reprinted by permission.

Pretty Girl. Billy Strayhorn. Copyright © 1956 (renewed) by Music Sales Corporation (ASCAP) and Tempo Music, Inc. All rights administered by Music Sales Corporation. International copyright secured. All rights reserved. Reprinted by permission.

Rain Check. Billy Strayhorn. Copyright © 1941 (renewed) by Billy Strayhorn Songs, Inc., and Tempo Music, Inc. All rights administered by Billy Strayhorn Songs, Inc. International copyright secured. All rights reserved. Reprinted by permission.

Smada (Ugly Ducklin'). Duke Ellington and Billy Strayhorn. Copyright © 1951 (renewed) by Music Sales Corporation (ASCAP) and Tempo Music, Inc. All rights administered by Music Sales Corporation. International copyright secured. All rights reserved. Reprinted by permission.

So This Is Love. Billy Strayhorn. Copyright © 1968 (renewed) by Music Sales Corporation (ASCAP) and Tempo Music, Inc. All rights administered by Music Sales Corporation. International copyright secured. All rights reserved. Reprinted by permission.

Strange Feeling. Duke Ellington and Billy Strayhorn. Copyright © 1945 (renewed) by Music Sales Corporation (ASCAP) and Tempo Music, Inc. All rights administered by Music Sales Corporation. International copyright secured. All rights reserved. Reprinted by permission.

Swing Dance. Billy Strayhorn. Copyright © 1997 by Billy Strayhorn Songs, Inc. International copyright secured. All rights reserved. Reprinted by permission.

Take the "A" Train. Billy Strayhorn. Copyright © 1941 (renewed) by Billy Strayhorn Songs, Inc., and Tempo Music, Inc. All rights administered by Billy Strayhorn Songs, Inc. International copyright secured. All rights reserved. Reprinted by permission.

Three and Six (Wounded Love). Billy Strayhorn. Copyright © 1969 (renewed) by Music Sales Corporation (ASCAP) and Tempo Music, Inc. All rights administered by Music Sales Corporation. International copyright secured. All rights reserved. Reprinted by permission.

Tonk. Duke Ellington and Billy Strayhorn. Copyright © 1940 EMI Catalogue Partnership, EMI Robbins Catalog, Inc., and EMI United Partnership Ltd., U.S.A. Worldwide print rights controlled by Warner Bros. Publications, Inc./IMP Ltd. Reproduced by permission of International Music Publications Ltd. All rights reserved. Reprinted by permission.

Tuxedo Junction. Erskine Hawkins, William Johnson, Julian Dash and Buddy Feyne. Copyright © 1939, 1940 (renewed) by Music Sales Corporation (ASCAP) and Rytvoc, Inc. All rights outside the U.S.A. administered by Music Sales Corporation. International copyright secured. All rights reserved. Reprinted by permission.

Up and Down, Up and Down. Duke Ellington and Billy Strayhorn. Copyright © 1957 (renewed) and assigned to Tempo Music, Inc., and Famous Music Corporation in the U.S.A. All rights for the world outside the U.S.A. administered by Music Sales Corporation (ASCAP). International copyright secured. All rights reserved. Reprinted by permission.

Up There, from the *North by Southwest Suite*. Billy Strayhorn. Copyright © 1966 (renewed) by Music Sales Corporation (ASCAP) and Tempo Music, Inc. All rights administered by Music Sales Corporation. International copyright secured. All rights reserved. Reprinted by permission.

Upper Manhattan Medical Group. Billy Strayhorn. Copyright © 1956 (renewed) by Music Sales Corporation (ASCAP) and Tempo Music, Inc. All rights administered by Music Sales Corporation. International copyright secured. All rights reserved. Reprinted by permission.

Valse. Billy Strayhorn. Copyright © 1997 by Billy Strayhorn Songs, Inc. International copyright secured. All rights reserved. Reprinted by permission.

Where or When. Lorenz Hart (words), and Richard Rodgers (music). Copyright © 1937 (renewed) Chappell & Co. Rights for the extended renewal term in the U.S.A. controlled by WB Music Corporation o/b/o The Estate of Lorenz Hart and The Family Trust u/w Richard Rodgers and The Family Trust u/w Dorothy F. Rodgers (administered by Williamson Music). International copyright secured. All rights reserved. Reprinted by permission.

Your Love Has Faded. Duke Ellington and Billy Strayhorn. Copyright © 1939 EMI Catalogue Partnership, EMI Robbins Catalog, Inc., and EMI United Partnership Ltd., U.S.A. Worldwide print rights controlled by Warner Bros. Publications, Inc./IMP Ltd. Reproduced by permission of International Music Publications Ltd. All Rights reserved. Reprinted by permission.

Index

Note: Pages with illustrations and musical examples are indicated in *italics* at the end of entries. For individual song titles see also Appendices B, C, and D.

Absinthe, 61
Ad Lib on Nippon, 167
African-American musical influences, 174
Afro Bossa (album), 112
The Afro-Eurasian Eclipse, 181
After All, 45, 54, 58
After Bird Jungle, xxi
Agra, 167, 169
Air-Conditioned Jungle, 97, 114
Airegin, 30, 290n. 13
albums. *See* recordings
alcoholism, 5
Alexander, Jane Patton, 5
All American (theater show), 137
All Day Long, 116, 142, 191
All Heart, 135
All Too Soon, 151
Allah Bye, 61
Amad, 167
American Broadcasting Company (ABC), 96
American Federation of Musicians (AFM), 85, 187
An American in Paris, 7
American Society of Composers and Publishers (ASCAP), 44
Amor, 67
Anacostia Museum, 186
Anatomy of a Murder: album, 112; composition, xxii, 106, 137, 152; film, 80
Anchors Aweigh (theater show), 128
...And His Mother Called Him Bill (album), 179, 255
Anderson, Cat, 94, 96–97, 189
Anderson, Edmund, 38
Anderson, Ivie: arrangements for, 30; departure from Ellington Orchestra, 54; *I Got It Bad (and That Ain't Good)*, 62;

Lonely Again (Lush Life), 288–89n. 4; *Killin' Myself*, 33; *Your Love Has Faded*, 21
Aquacade (show), 131
The Arabian Dance, 139
Are You Sticking, 45
Armed Forces Radio Service (AFRS), 96
Armstrong, Louis, 22, 299n. 8
arrangements by Strayhorn (listed), 197–261
arranging techniques: Ellington's, 103; "Henderson style," 26, 49, 289n. 7; role of piano, 65; Strayhorn's, 65, 67–70, 103, 138, 139; thickening of lines, 33, 155; through-imitation, 33, 34. *See also* composition techniques
Artists Theatre, 121–22
ASCAP (American Society of Composers and Publishers), 44
Åse's Death, 139
Asian musical influences, 168–69
At the Bal Masque (album), 136
autograph scores: collections, ix–x; expression markings, 191; individuality, xxii; Presentation Albums, 186;
purpose, 189; as source material, xx–xxii, 194; Strayhorn and Ellington compared, 107–8, 109, 185; surviving, 63, 300–301n. 20. *See also* transcriptions
Avakian, George, 133
axis theory, 29, 48, 75. *See also* Lendvai, Ernö

Bach, Johann Sebastian, 60
Baker, David, 183

Baker, Harold, 88, 148
Bakiff, 108
Ballad for Very Tired and Very Sad Lotus Eaters, 31, 145–46, *145*, *146*
ballads, 11, 21, 27, 31, 146–51
Ballet of the Flying Saucers, xxi
band books, 188, 288n. 19
Bargy, Roy, 91
Barney Bigard and His Orchestra, 33, 63
Barney Goin' Easy, 33
Bartók, Béla, 6, 29
Basie, William "Count," 57
Basin Street East, 18
The Beatles, 305n. 11
bebop: *Bluebird of Delhi*, 169; composers compared, 82–83; Ellington Orchestra members, 131;
harmony, 19, 142–45, 163–64, 300n. 17; popularity, 117; *Take the "A" Train*, 48–49; Upper Manhattan Medical Group, 142–45, 163
Beethoven, Ludwig van, 60
Beggar's Holiday (theater show): collaborative effort, 97–99; copyright, 115; inclusion of Strayhorn, 87;
lack of recordings, xviii; multipart scores, xxi; music included, 12
The Beggar's Opera, 97–98
Beltman, Albert, 296–97n. 15
Benny Goodman Orchestra, 155. *See also* Goodman, Benny
Berger, David, 183
Berlin, Irving, 22, 95
Bess, Oh Where's My Bess, 30
Bethlehem (record label), 131–33
Beyond Category, 135

Biegler, Paul, 137
Bigard, Barney, 25, 26, 36, 57, 191
Bill Ludwig Orchestra, 21
Billy Strayhorn Collection, ix–x, 185
"The Billy Strayhorn Suite," 49, 183
biographies, xvi–xvii, xxii
bird calls, 155–56, 158
Birth of the Cool (album), 53, 293–94n. 21
bi-thematic design, 90
Black, Brown and Beige: A Tone Parallel to the History of the Negro in America: collaborative effort, 87–89, 99; compared to *Pentonsilic*, 89–90; copyrights, 115; Duke Ellington Collection, 298n. 2; form, 89–90, 93, 108–9; initial sketches, 89; mood, 140; reception 92–93; recordings, 93; Strayhorn's contribution, 87–89, 90
Blanton, Jimmie: addition to Ellington Orchestra, 33; *Chloë (Song of the Swamp)*, 36; departure from Ellington Orchestra, 63; nickname, 295n. 33; solos, 35
Blanton-Webster Band, 33, 48, 58–59, 63–64, 112
The Blessed and the Damned (theater show), 111
Bli-Blip, 79
Blood Count, 31, 82, 152, 170–71, 171, 172
Blue Belles of Harlem, xxi, 91–92, 94–95
Bluebird of Delhi, 152, 155, 167–68, 306n. 3, 168
Blue Cloud, 171, 173
Blue Heart, 73, 82–83, 83
Blue House, 60–61, 189, 191, 190
Blue Pepper, 167
Blue Rose, xxii, 131
Blue Serge, 291n. 1
Blue Skies, 95
Blue Star, 60
blues: *Blues I + II*, 133; *Blues In Orbit*, 151; *Boo Loose*, 176; "C" *Blues*, 63; *C-Jam Blues*, 63; *Pretty Little One*, 176; *Rocks in My Bed*, 62
Blues a-Poppin, 31
blues-based compositions, 305n. 9
Blues in Orbit: album, 137; composition), xxi, 151
Blutopia, xxi, 99, 115, 299n. 9
BMI (Broadcast Music Inc.), 44
Body and Soul, 84
Bojangles, 35, 290n. 19

Boll Weevil Ballet, 98
Boo Loose, 173–74, 176, 307n. 12, 176
Boo-Dah, 142, 146
Boola (opera), 87
Borne, Hal, 62
Boyd, Charles, 18
Boyd Meets the Duke, 84
Boyd Raeburn and His Orchestra, 83–84, 298n. 30
Braggin' in Brass, 112
Brahms, Johannes, 60
The Breeze and I, 31
Bridgers, Aaron: on complexity of *Lush Life*, 288–89n. 4; move to Paris, 98; split with Strayhorn, 120; with Strayhorn, 33, 87, 118
Broadcast Music Inc. (BMI), 44
Bronx, New York, 47
Brown, Cleo, 57
Brown, Lawrence: *Black, Brown and Beige*, 88; *Blue House*, 189; confrontation with Ellington, 308n. 2; defection from Ellington Orchestra, 120; solos, 26; on Strayhorn compositions, 3, 181
Brown Betty, 97, 115
Brunswick (record label), 26
Buddy Malone Orchestra, 21
Burns, Ralph, 126
Burton, Gary, 6
Bushkin, Joe, 57

Cabin in the Sky (film), 87
call-and-response, 55–57
Calloway, Cab, 30–31
Can It Be, 115
Cannery Row (Steinbeck), 140
Can't Help Lovin' Dat Man, 69, 110, 71
Capitol (record label), 116, 131
Caravan, 27, 135
Carnegie Hall performances: *Black, Brown and Beige*, 299–300n. 10; effect on Strayhorn, 100; inclusion of Strayhorn, 87; *Lush Life*, 288–89n. 4; "Strayhorn group," 299n. 5; suite format, 93–94; works included, 90–92
Carney, Harry, 34, 37, 155, 169, 144
Carribee Joe, 152
Casa Mañana (ballroom), 44, 50, 54
Casablanca, 298n. 30
Cashmere Cutie, 146–48, 157, 164, 169, 147, 158
Catlin, Charlotte, 5
"C" *Blues*, 63
CBS (Columbia Broadcasting System), 44

Century/Franklin Warehouse, 185
Charlotte Russe, 97, 115
Chelsea Bridge: chromaticism, 50; departure from Ellington style, 64; harmony, 6, 52–53, 146; form, 51–53, 58, 59, 74; instrumentation, 53, 76, 126; introduction, 51; modulation, 12; performances, 45; recordings, 57, 101, 293n. 17; theme, 51–52, 83, 288n. 2, 52; voicing, 103
childhood (Strayhorn's), 3
Chloë (Song of the Swamp), 36
Chopin, Frédéric, 58
chords: altered, 77; arpeggiated, 305n. 4; bell-, 48; bitonal, 151, 168; block-, 72; broken, 5, 168; double-diminished seventh, 143, 145; extended, 77; "fairy chords," 306n. 11; polychords, 38, 55, 77, 152, 156–57, 56, 153, 158; quartal, 25, 34–35, 55, 57, 155, 35, 55, 158; sequences, 300n. 17; substitutions, 62, 119; tritone-related, 28, 302n. 2–3; whole-tone, 28, 30
chromaticism: *Agra*, 169; *Bluebird of Delhi*, 168; *Chelsea Bridge*, 50; *Concerto for Cootie*, 34; counterpoint, 57, 91–92, 161; enharmonic change, 69; enharmonic modulation, 287–88n. 10; *Fantastic Rhythm*, 10; *Flame Indigo*, 295n. 30; harmonies, 50–51, 60–61; *Lush Life*, 17; *Mood Indigo* (1950 version), 119; *Orson*, 149; *Passion Flower*, 28; *A Penthouse on Shady Avenue*, 14; *Rocks in My Bed*, 62; *So This Is Love*, 16, 287–88n. 10; Strayhorn's use of, 21, 28, 77; *Take the "A" Train*, 48; *Ugly Ducklin'*, 19; *Up and Down, Up and Down*, 161
civil rights movement, 165, 306n. 1
C-Jam Blues, 63–64, 115
clarinet bird calls, 155–56, 158
Clarinet Lament, 36
classical music influence, xv, 3, 18, 60
Claude Thornhill and His Orchestra, 53, 83
Clayton, Buck, 120
Clementine, 45, 54, 101
Clooney, Rosemary, xxii, 131–33, 151
codas: *Blue Heart*, 82; *Cashmere Cutie*, 157, 158; *Day Dream*, 156–57, 158; *Dirge*, 90; *The Eighth Veil*, 68; *It's Monday Every Day* (1947 version), 68; *Orson*, 111, 149, 149; *Overture*

INDEX

(*Nutcracker Suite*), 138; Overture to a Jam Session, 73; *Pretty Girl*, 150; *There's a Man in My Life*, 68; *Where or When*, 82
Coffee and Kisses, 116
Cole, Nat "King," 18, 57, 116
Coleman, Bill, 165
collaboration: described, 89, 93, 109–10, 292n. 7; Feather on, 104–5; with Hamilton, 97, 167; Homzy on, 307n. 8; with Mercer Ellington, 27, 61; rapport between Strayhorn and Ellington, 105–6; specific songs, 99
Coloratura, 94
Coltrane, John, 18, 20
Columbia (record label), 117, 131, 137
Columbia Broadcasting System (CBS), 44
Come Sunday, 89
complexity of Strayhorn works, 60, 73, 288–89n. 4
compositions by Strayhorn (listed), 197–261, 264–86
composition techniques: classical, 60; compared to arrangement, xxi, 65, 68–70, 96, 295–96n. 1; development, 59–60, 68–74, 90, 103, 164; economy of means, 8, 42, 77; Ellington's, xvii–xviii, 34–35, 78, 103, 107–109, 302n. 4; faux reprise, 7, 119, 148; linear composition, 59–60; multilinear writing, 152; role of piano, 58; Strayhorn's, 28, 78, 103, 109, 114, 128, 164, 171; Third Stream compositions, 60, 164; through-composition, 54, 58, 74, 92, 111, 146–47, 151. *See also* arranging techniques; form
Concerto for Cootie, 34, 74, 154, 290–91n. 20
Concerto for Duke, 84
Concerto for Piano and Percussion, 6, 7, 10
Concerto in F, 37
Concerts of Sacred Music, 181
Connors, Chuck, 171
Cook, Charles "Cookie," 127
cool jazz, 142, 163–64
Cooper, Buster, xix
Copasetic Dances, 182, 188
Copasetics, 127–29, 142, 304n. 11
copyright issues: *Black, Brown and Beige*, 115; *C-Jam Blues*, 115; copyright registrations, 114–15, 133, 139, 304n. 12; *Day Dream*, 289–90n. 11; *The Eighth Veil*, 97; Hamilton on, 120; *Harlem*,

115; *Jump for Joy*, 115; *Let Nature Take Its Course*, 115; Mercer Ellington, 99, 115; *Orson*, 115; *Overture to a Jam Session*, 97, 114; *Pavane Bleu No. 2*, 307n. 12; *The Perfume Suite*, 115; recording ban, 44–45; shared credit, 27; *Something to Live For*, 47, 114; Tempo Music, Inc. (publisher), 114–15, 133, 139, 173, 302n. 10; *Tymperturbably Blue*, 115; *Up There*, 307n. 12; *Upside Looking*, 115
Coslow, Sam, 22
Cotton Tail, 34, 49
Count Basie, 57
counterpoint: *Blood Count*, 82; *Blue Belles of Harlem*, 91; chromatic, 7, 82; *Day Dream*, 82, 153; dissonant, 52, 81; *A Garden in the Rain*, 80, 81; *Isfahan*, 82, 170, 170; "Klangfarbenmelodik" (timbre melody), 79–80, 106, 79, 80; *Lover Man*, 81, 81; *The Man I Love*, 67; *Mood Indigo* (1950 version), 119; multi-linear writing, 152; *Night and Day* (1940 version), 67; *Out of This World*, 96–97; *Pentonsilic*, 58; *Pretty Girl*, 154, 157; *Rain Check*, 57; single-line, 80–82; study of, 5; *Take the "A" Train*, 82, 162, 162; *Up and Down, Up and Down*, 159–61
creative process, 109
Creole Rhapsody, 112
criticisms of Strayhorn, 59, 301n. 1
Crouch, Stanley, 140

Dalvatore Sally, 84
Dameron, Tadd, 83
Dance, Stanley, 53
dance engagements, 45, 290n. 15
Dance of the Floreadores, 129
Dancers in Love, 94
Danish Radio, xviii
Danke Schoen, 292n. 7
David, Mack, 31
Davis, Kay, 69–70, 97, 288–89n. 4
Davis, Miles, 20, 53, 293–94n. 21
Daybreak Express, 47, 112, 291–92n. 4
Day Dream: arrangement, 36, 152–56, 154–55, 156; coda, 156–57, 158; counterpoint, 82, 153; creation date, 27, 289–90n. 11; harmony, 30, 163, 158; instrumentation, 154–55, 156; introduction, 152, 153; recordings, 133, 135; theme, 30, 30, 154–55; voicing, 152–56, 154–55, 158

Day in, Day Out, 34
death of Strayhorn, 179
Debussy, Claude, 29, 50–51, 58–59
Deep Purple, 133
Deep South Suite, 94, 300n. 12
Degas Suite, 181
D'Emilio, Anthony Edward, 21
Depk, 167
Der Wanderer, 174
Dirge, 90, 91
dissonance, 6, 75–77, 81, 152–53
Dizzy Gillespie and His Orchestra, 83
Donna Lee, 83
Don't Be So Mean, 111
Don't Mess Around with the Women, 9
Don't Take My Love, 20, 294n. 24
Don't Take Your Love from Me, 67
Dooji Wooji, 26
Dorsey, Jimmy, 31
Double Ruff, 97
Down Beat (magazine), 43, 106, 113–14, 293n. 18
Down There (theater show), 188
A Drum Is a Woman (television show), xxi–xxii, 107, 133–34, 304n. 3
Duke Ellington and His Orchestra: Columbia contract, 137; "the Ellington effect," 113–14; Fargo, North Dakota, 46; influence on Strayhorn compositions, 103; international travels, 27, 167; Pittsburgh, Pennsylvania, 19; popularity, xv–xvii, 43, 163; recordings, 184, 132, 166; repertory, 107, 187–88; Strayhorn's influence, 181–82. *See also* Ellington, Edward Kennedy "Duke"; *specific musicians*
Duke Ellington Collection: autograph scores, ix–x; instrumental pieces, 61; at Smithsonian, xix; sources, 186–93; Symphonette, 298n. 2
Duke Ellington Estate, 186
Duke Ellington Presents (album), 133
Duke Ellington's Sound of Love, 54
Duke's in Bed (album), 145
Dusk, 53, 60
Dutch Jazz Orchestra, xx, 183

East St. Louis Toodle-Oo, 49
Echoes of Harlem, 27, 36
Edition Peters, 139
edits of Strayhorn's compositions, 110–13, 115–16. *See also* collaboration

education, 18
"effeteness" of Strayhorn's music, 59
The Eighth Veil: coda, 68; collaborative effort, 97, 99; harmony, 77, 78; instrumentation 76, 78; introduction, 67, 76, 94, 97, 78; *Symphonic or Bust*, 95; theme, 78
Eisner, Jerome, 288n. 19
Eldridge, Jean, 26
Elf, 167, 169. *See also Isfahan*
Ella Fitzgerald Sings the Duke Ellington Songbook (album), 101, 135
Ellington, Edward Kennedy "Duke": after Strayhorn's death, 179–81; autographs, 191–93; *Chelsea Bridge*, 52; composition style, 110; confrontation with Brown, 308n. 2; Duke Ellington estate, 186; editing Strayhorn's compositions, 110–13; "the Ellington effect," 113–14; estate, 186; handwriting, 193, *192*; influence on Strayhorn, 23, 57; loyalty of, 302n. 1; primary jazz figure, xv–xvi; recognition of Strayhorn's contribution, 141, 194–95; recording sessions, 132, 166; renewed partnership, 304n. 1; with Strayhorn, 86, 102; stylistic comparison with Strayhorn, xvii–xviii, 77–78, 103, 107–9; support of civil rights movement, 306n. 1; use of formal balance, 60; writing style, 302n. 4. *See also* Duke Ellington and His Orchestra; Duke Ellington Collection
Ellington, Mercer: collaboration with Strayhorn, 27, 61; copyright issues, 38, 99, 114, 115, 291n. 1; custody of Strayhorn autographs, 185; donations to Danish Radio, xviii; introduction of Bridgers and Strayhorn, 33; on loss of Strayhorn, 181; recording ban, 45; use of Strayhorn material, 186
Ellington at Newport (album), 133
"the Ellington effect," 113–14
Ellington Indigos (album), 68–69, 136
Ellington Jazz Party (album), 137
Ellington '65 (album), 137, 165
Ellington '66 (album), 137, 165–66
Ellington-Boatwright, Ruth, 114, 287n. 4
Entrance of Youth, 97, 135, 300n. 19
Esch, Bill, 19

Esquire Swank, 94, 114
estates: Duke Ellington estate, 186; manuscript collections, ix–x, x, xix, 61, 185–93, 197, 287n. 4, 298n. 2; Strayhorn Estate, ix, 50, 185
European artistic influences: art music, xvi; classical music, xv, 3, 18, 60; French Impressionism, 50–51, 106; in *North by Southwest Suite*, 174; Romantic idiom, 7–8; suite format, 92–94
Evans, Gil: on *Chelsea Bridge*, 53; compared to Strayhorn, 83; influence on Strayhorn, 164; modal jazz, 20; Strayhorn's influence, 182; with Thornhill orchestra, 293–94n. 21
Exactly Like You, 48, 292n. 6
experimentation, 83
expression markings, 191

Fain, Sammy, 31
Fantastic Rhythm: song, 10–11, 38, 10; theater show, 9–14, 16, 18–19, 21, 287n. 4
Far East Suite, 95, 103, 167, 169–70
father (Strayhorn's), 3
Faust (theater show), 111, 148
Feather, Leonard: on *Dirge*, 90–91; on *Jumpin' Jive*, 31; on Strayhorn-Ellington collaboration, 100–101, 104–5; on Strayhorn's work, 21–22, 23
Feet on the Beat, 129
Fiddle on the Diddle, 167
Fields, Dorothy, 48
Fields, Frank, 120
film projects, 80, 87, 294n. 25, 295n. 32
Fitzgerald, Ella: *All Too Soon*, 151; with Ben Webster, 135; *Day Dream*, 152, 156; *Ella Fitzgerald Sings the Duke Ellington Songbook* (album), 101, 135; with Jimmy Jones, 172; A Portrait of Ella Fitzgerald, 101, 135; *Something to Live For*, 21; *Take the "A" Train*, 106
The Five O'Clock Whistle, 36
Flame Indigo, 20, 62, 295n. 30, 39
Flamingo: arrangement, 38–40, 59, 64, 39–42; form, 38, 42–43, 164; harmony, 38, 163, 164; introduction, 38, 68, 39; modulations, 39–40, 39–42; recordings, 57–58; rhythm, 38; text setting, 38, 40, 43
Flippant Flurry, 97, 114

Flirtibird, 137
A Flower Is a Lovesome Thing, 20, 30, 45, 54, 172
The Flowers Die of Love, 122, *122*
Fol-De-Rol-Rol, 98
form: *Blue Heart*, 71, 73; *Bluebird of Delhi*, 168–69; *Cashmere Cutie*, 146–47, 164; *Chelsea Bridge*, 51–53, 58, 74; circular, 42, 68; composition of, 8; "crescendo," 53; da capo, 8, 73, 138, 169; developmental sections, 68, 70, 72–73, 74, 153, 72–73, 155; Ellington's approach to, 60, 74–75, 107–9, 110, 113; expositions, 38, 68, 72, 159; *Flamingo*, 38, 42–43, 164; *Hear Say*, 71, 73; *I'll Buy That Dream*, 68; *I Never Felt This Way Before*, 75; irregularity of, 16, 21, 54, 67, 73, 96; linearity, 59–60; *Love Like This Can't Last*, 54; *Lush Life*, 16; mid-chorus modulation, 12, 16; modulatory release, 12; *Mood Indigo* (1950 version), 119; *My Little Brown Book*, 12; *Orson*, 148–49; *Overture to a Jam Session*, 71, 74; *Pentonsilic*, 58–59, 89–90; *Portrait of a Silk Thread*, 72–73, 72–73; *Pretty Girl*, 150; *Rain Check*, 55; *Sepia Panorma*, 35; *So This Is Love*, 14–16, 74; *Something to Live For*, 21; Strayhorn's approach to, 34–35, 36, 67, 74–75, 109, 110, 113; suite format, 92–95, 99; *Take the "A" Train*, 48; ternary, 7, 68, 70–74, 119; transitions, 73, 74, 75; tutti passages, 67, 68, 70, 158; *Up and Down, Up and Down*, 164; *Where or When*, 68, 74; *The Wonder of You*, 68; *Your Love Has Faded*, 21. *See also* codas; composition techniques; introductions
Fowler, Oliver "Boggy," 9
Frankie and Johnny, 92, 115
French impressionism, 50–51
Froeba, Frank, 57

A Garden in the Rain, 80–81, *81*
Garner, Errol, 57
Gay, John, 97–98
Gershwin, George, 6–7, 16, 30, 37
Gershwin, Ira, 16
The Giddybug Gallop, 45
Gillespie, Dizzy, 20, 83, 145, *166*
The Girl in My Dreams Tries to Look Like You, 38, 291n. 1
Goldberg, Francis "Goldie," 136, 165

INDEX

Gonna Tan Your Hide, 116
Gonsalves, Paul, 106, 119
Good Night, My Beautiful, 31
Good-Bye, 155
Goodman, Benny, 34, 49, 155
Gordon, Mack, 94
Gould, Morton, 91
Goutelas Suite, 181
Grace Valse, 137
Grainger, Percy, 293n. 19
Granz, Norman, 101, 126, 129, 135, 302n. 3
Great South Bay Jazz Festival, 104–5
Greenwood, Lil, 136–37
Greer, Sonny, 120
Grieg, Edvard, 137, 139
Grievin', 33, 47
Gross, Walter, 91
Grouya, Ted, 38
Grove, Bill, 165, 179
Guy, Freddy, 191

Hajdu, David, x, xxii, 114, 183
Half the Fun, 134
Hamilton, Jimmy: arrangements, 95; *Bluebird of Delhi*, 168; collaborative works, 97, 167; *Day Dream*, 155; *Midsummer Night's Dream*, 134; *Schwiphtiey*, 139; on Strayhorn's copyright problems, 120
handwriting, 191, *192*, *193*
Handy, George, 83–84, 182, 298n. 33
Happy-Go-Lucky-Local, 47
Harlem, 92, 115
Harlem, New York City, 47
Harlem Airshaft, xxi, 34–35, 78, 140
Harlem Rumba, 9
Harlem stride, 37–38
harmony: *Ballad for Very Tired and Very Sad Lotus Eaters*, 145–46, *145*; bebop, 19; *Bess, Oh Where's My Bess*, 30; *Boo Loose*, 176; *Cashmere Cutie*, 146, *147*; *Chelsea Bridge*, 6, 52–53, 146; *Concerto for Cootie*, 34; *Concerto for Piano and Percussion*, 6; *Day Dream*, 30, 163; *Fantastic Rhythm*, 10, *10*; *Flame Indigo*, 62; *Flamingo*, 38, 163, 164; *A Flower Is a Lovesome Thing*, 30; harmonic ostinato, 19–20, 30, 62, 121; harmonic variation, 7; *Isfahan*, 170, *170*; *Lush Life*, 17–18, *17*, *18*; *Orson*, 149, *149*; *Overture (Fantastic Rhythm)*, 11, *11*; *Passion Flower*, 20, 28, 146, *28*, *29*; *A Penthouse on Shady Avenue*, 14, *14*; *Portrait of a Silk Thread*, 77; *Pretty Girl*, 150; *The Rape of a Rhapsody*, 19; *Rain Check*, 6, 55, 57; *Rocks in My Bed*, 62–63; *So This Is Love*, 14–15, 28–29, 145, 16; study of, 5, 65; *Take the "A" Train*, 6, 47–48, 163; *Tonk*, 37, 37; *Ugly Ducklin'*, 19, 20, 62, 20; *Upper Manhattan Medical Group*, 143–45, 146, 163, *143*, *145*; widened tonality, 163. See also axis theory; chords; modulations
Harry James's orchestra, 298n. 30
Hart, Lorenz, 135
Hashim, Michael, 183
Haupê, 137
Hawkins, Coleman, 49
Hawkins, Erskine, 34
Haydn, Joseph, 60
Hayfoot, Strawfoot, 115
Hayton, Lennie, 98–99
He Makes Me Believe He's Mine, 70, 110
health issues (Strayhorn), 165–67, 171–72
Hear Say, 67, 73, 79, 115
Helen's Theme, 111. See also Orson
hemiolas, 6
Henderson, Fletcher, 19, 289n. 7
Henderson, Joe, 183
Henderson, Luther, 120, 185
Henderson, Rick, 120
"Henderson style," 289n. 7
Herman, Woody, 126
Hero to Zero, 106
Hersch, Fred, 183
Hey, Buddy Bolden, 134
Hibbler, Al, 11
High, Figh, Fo, Fumm, 171
Hill, Leticia, 94
Hilliard, Jimmy, 291–92n. 4
Hines, Earl, 57
Hipper-Bug, 60
Historically Speaking-The Duke (album), 133
Hodges, Johnny: ballads, 27, 145, 147–51; *Isfahan*, 169; *A Midsummer Night's Dream*, 134; *Passion Flower*, 29; return to Ellington Orchestra, 131; small-band work, 57; solos, 26, 40, 119; work outside Ellington Orchestra, 116, 120; works scored for, 25, 27
Hollander, Frederick, 22
Homewood district (Pittsburgh), 3–5, 4
hominy, 115
homophobia, 59
homosexuality, 33, 59
Homzy, Andrew, 49, 50, 90, 307n. 8
Honey Boy Minor and His Buzzing Bees, 21
Horne, Lena, 87, 98–99, 165
Horowitz, Vladimir, 138
How You Sound, 95
The Hurricane (nightclub), 95

Ibsen, Henrik, 139
I Can Dream, 115
I Can't Begin to Tell You, 67
I Got It Bad (and That Ain't Good), 62, 64, 131, 136, 188, 289–90n. 11
I Got Plenty of Nuthin', 16
I Got Rhythm, 12
I Know What You Know, 31
I Love You, 16
I Never Felt This Way Before, 74–75, 78, 108
I Only Have Eyes for You, 84
I Remember, 115
If I Can't Have You, 127
If You Were There, 21
I'll Buy That Dream, 68
I'll Never Have to Dream Again, 9, 11, 13
I'll Remember April, 67
I'm Beginning to See the Light, 108, 135
I'm Checking Out, Goom-Bye, 33, 47
I'm Slapping 7th Avenue with the Sole of My Shoe, 108
I'm Stepping Out with a Memory Tonight, 31
I'm Still Begging You, 8
Impressionism, 50–51, 292n. 10
Impressions of the Far East, 170. See also *Far East Suite*
In the Hall of the Mountain King, 139
In a Sentimental Mood, 27
Indian musical influences, 60, 168–69
Ingrid's Lament, 139
Institute of Jazz Studies (Rutgers University), 197
instrumentation: *All Too Soon*, 126, 151; as expression of form, 61; baritone, 77, 153–55, 189, 154–55; *Bluebird of Delhi*, 168; *Blues In Orbit*, 151; *Chelsea Bridge*, 53, 76, 126; clarinet, 155, 158; *Concerto for Piano and Percussion*, 6; cross-section, 25, 27, 61, 64, 103, 129, 159; definition of, 75; *The Eighth Veil*, 76, 78; "the Ellington effect," 113–14; *Entrance of Youth*, 97; French horn, 172; in Boyd Raeburn's orchestra, 83; in Claude Thornhill's orchestra, 83; instrumental combinations,

INDEX

instrumentation (cont.)
76, 106, 158, 303n. 7; "jungle-style," 36, 106; *Lonely Again (Lush Life)*, 25; *Love Is Here to Stay*, 126; mallet instruments, 6–7; "on the man writing," 25, 27, 103, 114, 289n. 10; piano, 65; *Rain Check*, 76; *Sophisticated Lady*, 151; strings, 126; *Take the "A" Train*, 162; thickening of lines, 33, 155; trombones, 36, 42, 55, 153; *Up and Down, Up and Down*, 159–61; violin, 73. See also voicing
The Intimacy of the Blues, 170
introductions: *Bli-Blip*, 79; *Blue Belles of Harlem*, 91, 94; *Chelsea Bridge*, 51; *Day Dream*, 152, 153; *The Eighth Veil*, 67, 94; *Flamingo*, 38, 68, 39; length of, 67, 296n. 2; *The Man I Love*, 67; *Night and Day* (1940 version), 67; *Orson*, 111; *Overture to a Jam Session*, 67, 73; piano, 49–50; *Pretty Girl*, 154, 157; spoken, 89–90, 93–94, 135, 298n. 33; Strayhorn's approach to, 67–68; *Take the "A" Train*, 49–50, 106; *Where or When*, 68, 74, 82, 82
Isfahan: counterpoint, 82, 152, 170, 170; harmony, 170, 170; Hodges, 31; recordings, 167; theme, 169–70, 170. See also *Elf Island Virgin*, 167
It Don't Mean a Thing (If It Ain't Got That Swing), 12
It Happens to Be Me, 126
It Must Be a Dream, 9, 11
It's All True (film), 294n. 25
It's Monday Every Day, 68

Jack the Bear, 34, 35, 108
Jackson, Mahalia, 80
Jackson, Quentin "Butter," 119
Jam Session, 63
James, Danny, 114
James, Harry, 298n. 30
Janssen, Frank, 296–97n. 15
Jazz Festival Suite, 105
Jazz Masterworks Orchestra (Smithsonian Institution), 183
The Jazz Scene (album), 126
Jeffries, Herb, 11, 36, 38, 43
Jenkins, Freddie, 185
Jenkins, Gordon, 155
Jenny Lou Stomp, 20, 115
Jerry Valburn Collection, ix, 197
John Hardy's Wife, 294n. 24
Johnny Come Lately, 63, 91
Johnny Hodges and His Orchestra, 26, 31, 291n. 1

Jones, Elaine, 300n. 19
Jones, Herbie, 185
Jones, Jimmy, xviii, 172, 307n. 11
Jones, Quincy, 187
Jones, Ricky Lee, 18
Jump for Joy (1941 theater show): arrangements for, 64, 79; compared to *Beggar's Holiday*, 98; copyright, 115; described, 61; Ellington on, 92–93; *Flame Indigo*, 62; *I Got it Bad (and That Ain't Good)*, 62; lack of recordings, xviii; *Rocks in My Bed*, 62–63; works included, 294n. 25, 294–95n. 27–28
Jump for Joy (1959 theater show), xviii, 136–37, 304n. 8
The Jumpin' Jive, 30–31, 292n. 7
Jumpin' Punkins, 291n. 1
"jungle-style," 36, 106
Just A-Settin' and A-Rockin', 101

Kennedy, Roger, 186
Kessler, Woody, 304n. 1
Keubler, Ann, 291–92n. 4
Killian, Al, 193
Killin' Myself, 33
Kinard, John, 186
King, Martin Luther, Jr., 165
The Kissing Bug, 97
"Klangfarbenmelodik" (timbre melody), 79–80, 106, 79
Ko-Ko, 34, 60
Kolodin, Irvin, 100
Kostelanetz, Andre, 31
Kuller, Sid, 61, 136

Lady in Doubt, 288n. 2
Lamb, John, 188
Lament for an Orchid, 61
Lamento d'Arianna, 125
Lana Turner, 74, 191, 296n. 14
Lanauze, Yvonne, 119
La Petite Valse, 138
Larkin, Milton, 127
Last of Penthouse, 88
Lately, 134
LaTouche, John, 98, 152
Laura, 133
Lay By, 139
Lecuona, Ernesto, 31
legacy of jazz music, xv
Lendvai, Ernö, 28–29, 48
Le Sacre Supreme, 20
Le Temps Court (theater show), 111
Leticia, 94
Let Nature Take Its Course, 9, 12, 74, 115, 127, 13
Lewis, John, 43, 88, 164
Library of Congress, ix–x, xv, 115, 197, 307n. 12

Life Ain't Nothing but Rhythm, 9, 16, 115
Like a Ship in the Night, 26
Lincoln Center Jazz Orchestra, 183
Lincoln Center of the Performing Arts, xv
Liszt, Franz, 58
Little Light Stomp, 91
live performances, 95, 189
Logan, Arthur, 142, 165
Logan, Marian, 165
Lonely Again, 23, 25, 288–89n. 4. See also *Lush Life*
A Lonely Co-Ed, 33
Lorca, Federico García, 121, 125, 129, 182
Lost in Two Flats, 33
Lotus Blossom, 97, 115, 181
Louis Armstrong and His Orchestra, 22
Love, 94
love as subject of compositions, 15, 94, 122, 123
Love Has Passed Me By, Again, 126, 129–30
Love Is Here to Stay, 126
Love Letters, 70
Love Like This Can't Last, 45, 54
Love, Love, 122, 123
The Love of Don Perlimplín (play), 121–25, 129, 182
Lover Man, 81, 81
Low Key Lightly, 80, 106, 137
LP format, 119–20
Lunceford, Jimmie, 19
Lush Life: after Strayhorn's death, 182; arrangement, 21, 288–89n. 4; chromaticism, 17; composed in Pittsburgh, 182; form, 16; harmony, 17–18, 29, 17, 18; lyrics, 17, 17, 18; inspiration on others, 54; recordings, 18, 101, 116; text setting, 17–18; theme, 16; "Three Finger Version," 288–89n. 4
Lush Life: A Biography of Billy Strayhorn (Hajdu), xxii
lyrics: *Can't Help Lovin' Dat Man*, 71; *Day Dream*, 154–55; *Flamingo*, 40; *Lady in Doubt*, 288n. 2; *Love, Love*, 123; *Lover Man*, 81; *Lush Life*, 17, 17, 18; *A Penthouse on Shady Avenue*, 13–14, 14; *So This is Love*, 14–16; *Something to Live For*, 174, 177; Strayhorn ballads, 21; *Where or When*, 69–70; *Wounded Love*, 123–24. See also text setting

Maderna, Bruno, 122
Mad Hatters, 20–21, 31, 188, 288n. 19

INDEX

Magazine Suite, 94
Main Stem, 63
The Man I Love, 67
Manhattan Murals, 32, 99, 191, 193, 192
manuscript collections: Billy Strayhorn Collection, ix–x, 185; David Hajdu Collection, x; Duke Ellington Collection, ix–x, xix, 61, 185–93, 298n. 2; Ruth Ellington Collection, ix–x, 287n. 4; Sidemen's Parts (Duke Ellington Collection), x
manuscripts: Bojangles, 290n. 19; Concerto for Cootie, 290–91n. 20; expression markings, 191; Lick Chorus, 290n. 18; original, ix–x; relevant manuscripts, 197; Tempo Music, Inc. (publisher), 186, 287n. 4. See also Appendices A–C; manuscript collections
March on Washington, 306n. 17
Marsalis, Wynton, xvii, 183
Mary Poppins (album), 137, 165
Masterpieces by Ellington (album), 117–18, 142
matrix numbers, 196
Mayor, Charles "Buzz," 288n. 19
McHugh, Jimmy, 48
McVicker, Carl, 5
melody, see themes
Mendelssohn-Bartholdy, Felix, 134
Midnight Indigo, 106, 137
A Midnight in Paris (album), 137
Mid-Riff, xxi, 97, 116, 128
A Midsummer Night's Dream (Shakespeare), 134, 159–61, 306n. 14, 306n. 15
Milenberg Joys, 291–92n. 4
Milhaud, Darius, 6
Miller, Glenn, 31, 34, 49
Miller, Sydney, 62
Mills, Irving, 33
Milton Larkin orchestra, 129
Mingus, Charles, xix, 54, 292n. 6, 294n. 22
Mingus Revisited (album) 292n. 6
Minor Intrusion, 54
Minton's Playhouse, 296n. 13
Minuet in Blues, 33
Misfit Blues, 139
Mississippi Dreamboat, 26
Mitchell, Dwike, 172–73
Mitchell-Ruff Duo, 172–73, 307n. 12
Modern Jazz Quartet, 164
modulations: After All, 54; Bluebird of Delhi, 168; Can't Help Lovin' Dat Man, 69, 109, 71; Chelsea Bridge, 12; Chloë (Song of the Swamp), 36; Concerto for Cootie, 70; enharmonic, 69, 287–88n. 10; Flamingo, 39–40, 39–42; He Makes Me Believe He's Mine, 70, 109; Lana Turner, 74; Let Nature Take Its Course, 12; Love Letters, 70; Love Like This Can't Last, 54; modulatory release, 12; Now I Know, 70; Orson, 111; Pentonsilic, 58; Pretty Girl, 150; So This Is Love, 287–88n. 10; Sophisticated Lady (1950 version), 119; Take the "A" Train, 6, 48; temporary modulation, 68–70, 73, 74, 110, 296n. 7; There Shall Be No Night, 36; There's No You, 70; This Is Always, 70; Tonight I Shall Sleep, 110; Where or When, 68–69, 69–70
Monroe's Uptown House, 296n. 13
Mood Indigo, 90, 117, 119
"mood pieces," 95
Moon Love, 31
Moon Mist, 95, 291n. 1
Moonlight Harbor Band, 9, 19, 25
More Than You Know, 84
Morgen, Joe, 135–36
Morning Mood, 139
Morris, Gregory A., 185
Morros, Boris, 294n. 25
mother (Strayhorn's), 3
Mount Harissa, 167
Mozart, Wolfgang Amadeus, 60
Mulligan, Gerry, 164
Multi-Colored Blue, 97
multimovement works, 197
Music and Rhythm (magazine), 65–66, 70, 74
Music for Loving (album), 126
Music for String Instruments, Percussion, and Celesta, 6
musical-dramatic techniques: narratives, 74, 109; subtexts, 11, 15, 17, 124; temporary reflection, 12, 74; text expression, 125
musical productions, 9
My Favorite Things, 20
My Funny Valentine, 133
My Last Good-Bye, 34
My Little Brown Book, 9–12, 21, 36, 74, 294n. 24
My People (theater show), xviii

Naiveté, 94
Nance, Ray: addition to Ellington Orchestra, 126; Blue House, 191; handwritten parts, 50; A Midsummer Night's Dream, 134; solos, 26, 47–49, 292n. 8
Nanton, Joe, 26
National Museum of American History, xix, 186
Neal, Dorcas, 120
Neal, Frank, 120
Never Meet, 115
New York Sun (newspaper), 91
Newport Jazz Festival Suite, 106, 133
Night and Day, 67–68
A Night in Tunisia, 20
Night Time, 116
Nobody Knows You When You're Down and Out, 290n. 13
Nocturne, 90, 299n. 5
Nocturnes, 51
The North by Southwest Suite, 172–78, 307–8n. 17
Northern Lights, 151–52, 151
Norvo, Red, 7
notation, xx
Now I Know, 70
"Nuages," 51
The Nutcracker Suite: album, 112; composition, 119, 129, 137–39, 194

Office Scene, 9
"Oiseaux Tristes," 51
Old Man Blues, 60
"on the man writing," 25, 27, 103, 114, 289n. 10
On the Wrong Side of the Rail Road Tracks, 98
Oo, You Make the Tingle, 126–27
Open Letter to Duke, 294n. 22
oral tradition, xviii
orchestral works, xxi, 79–80
orchestras, repertory, 183. See also specific orchestras
orchestration. See instrumentation
original manuscripts, ix–x
Orson: chromaticism, 149; coda, 111, 149, 149; copyright, 115; edits, 116; form, 148–49; harmony, 149, 164, 149; modulations, 111; performances, xx; theme, 111, 148–49, 148
Our Delight, 83
Out of This World, 96–97
Overture (Fantastic Rhythm), 9, 11, 11
Overture (Nutcracker Suite), 138
Overture to a Jam Session: autograph score, 109; coda, 73; copyright, 97, 114; form, 71, 74; introduction, 67; performances, xx; rhythm, 73; Symphonic or Bust, 95; violin, 126

Passion Flower: arrangement, 133; chromaticism, 28; harmony, 20, 27–29, 146, 28, 29; rhythm, 28; theme, 28, 77, 28, 29
Pastel Period (radio show), 95

Pavane Bleu No. 2, 173, 176–77, 307n. 12, 177
Peer Gynt Suites 1 & 2, xvii, 137, 139
Pennfield Drugs (Pittsburgh), 5
A Penthouse on Shady Avenue, 10, 12–14, 14
Pentonsilic: autograph score, 109; compared to *Hear Say*, 73; compared to *Work Song*, 89–90; complexity, 60; context, 294n. 25; counterpoint, 58; form, 58–59, 89–90; instrumentation, 64; modulations, 58; theme, 58, 89
Perdido, 135
Peress, Maurice, 88
performances, variation in, xix–xx
The Perfume Suite, 93–94, 115
Perkins, Bill, 187
Pharr, Nye, 288–89n. 4
piano: arranging tool, 65; concertos, 36; introductions, 49–50; keyboard technique, 57–58; solos, 57, 94, 97; Strayhorn on, 66, 301n. 21; styles, 37–38; transitions, 88
piano-vocal scores, 8, 9–10, 122, 10, 14, 16, 17, 18, 122, 123, 124
Pittsburgh, Pennsylvania, 3–5, 21
Pittsburgh Musical Institute, 18, 60
plays, 121–25
Polly's Theme, 80, 137, 80
polyphony. *See* counterpoint
Poor Butterfly, 80
popular music, 3, 5, 34, 68
Porgy and Bess (opera), 16, 30
Porter, Cole, 16, 135
A Portrait of Ella Fitzgerald, 101, 135
Portrait of a Silk Thread, 72–77, 72–73, 76
Portrait of a Silk Thread: Newly Discovered Works of Billy Strayhorn (CD), 183
Poulenc, Francis, 37, 123
Powell, Mel, 57
Preminger, Otto, 137
Presentation Albums, 186
Pretty Girl, 31, 134, 150, 154, 157. *See also The Star-Crossed Lovers*
Pretty Little One, 174, 176
Priestley, Brian, 54, 109
The Private Collection (album), xviii
Procope, Russell, 117–19, 193
Profile of Jackie, 54
Progressive Gavotte, 97
Pussy Willow, 26, 114

Queenie Pie (opera buffa), 181
Queen's Suite, 151

racism and racial segregation, 19
radio industry: radio transcriptions, 112, 291n. 2, 293n. 17; recording ban, 44–45, 85–87, 95; recording sessions, 132, 166. *See also* recordings
Raeburn, Boyd, 83–84, 182
ragas, 60, 169
Rain Check: counterpoint, 57; departure from Ellington style, 64; form, 55, 59; harmony, 6, 55, 57; recording, 45; theme, 54; title, 54; tutti, 55; voicing, 76
The Rape of a Rhapsody, 19
Ravel, Maurice, 51, 58, 59
Ready, Go!, 105
Recollections of the Big Band Era (album), 137
record labels: Bethlehem, 131–33; Brunswick, 26; Capitol, 116, 131; Columbia, 117, 131, 137; Verve, 135; Victor, 33, 38; Vocalion, 26
recordings: albums, 137; dance dates, 290n. 15; matching Strayhorn arrangements to, 195; radio transcriptions, 293n. 17; record formats, 111–12, 117–20; recording ban, 85–87, 95; recording sessions, 132, 166; re-recording, 196
Red Carpet (Part 1 and Part 3), 105
Red Garter, 105
Red Shoes, 105
Reinhardt, Django, 98
Remember, 22
Reminiscing in Tempo, 27, 112
Rene, Otis, 62
repertory orchestras, 183
Rex Edwards Orchestra, 21–22, 25
Rex Stewart & His Fifty-Second Street Stompers, 26
Rhapsody in Blue, 7
rhythm: *Blue Heart*, 82, 83; *Dirge*, 90; *Fantastic Rhythm*, 10; *Flamingo*, 38; in Strayhorn's piano playing, 56; *Overture to a Jam Session*, 73; *Passion Flower*, 28; *Rain Check*, 55; repeated, 82, 83; *Upper Manhattan Medical Group*, 142–43, 163
The Rhythm Man, 9
The River (ballet), 107
Riverside Drive Five, 172
An RKO Jamboree (film), 87
Robbins Music Corporation (publisher), 114
Robbins' Nest, 83

Robinson, Bill "Bojangles," 127
Rockin' in Rhythm, 135
Rocks in My Bed, 62, 115
Rod La Roque, 31, 172
Rodgers, Richard, 135
Rollins, Sonny, 30, 290n. 13
Romanticism, 174
Ronstadt, Linda, 18
Rooney, Mickey, 62
Rose-Colored Glasses (theater show), 12, 126, 129
Rosen, Charles, 60
Ross, Warren, 300n. 19
Royal Ancestry, 135
royalties, 85. *See also* copyright issues
Rudolph, Paul, 300n. 19
Ruff, Willie, 172–73, 307n. 12
Rutgers University, 197
Ruth Ellington Collection, ix–x, 287n. 4

Sanders, John, 185, 290n. 18, 301n. 2
Satie, Erik, 37, 58
Saturday Laughter (theater show), xxii, 136, 304n. 9
Schoenberg, Arnold, 79
Schubert, Franz, 174
Schwiphtiey, 139
scales: Aeolian, 52; diatonic, 20; Indian modes, 168–69; whole-tone, 50, 79
scores. *See* arrangements by Strayhorn; autograph scores; compositions by Strayhorn
Scott, Hazel, 57
Scrima, Michael, 6, 19, 21
Sears, Al, 108, 193
segregation, 19
Sepia Panorama: collaborative effort, 35, 99; conceptual approach, 78, 108; copyright, 114; Ellington Orchestra theme, 35, 47; transcriptions, xix, 291n. 21. *See also Tuxedo Junction*
September Song, 116
Shakespearean Suite, 134. *See also Such Sweet Thunder*
Shaw, Artie, 299n. 8
sheet music, xviii–xix
Shefter, Bert, 91
Sherrill, Joya, 97
Sidemen's Parts (Duke Ellington Collection), x
sight reading, xviii–xix
The Silent Fight, 9
sketches, xxi
Skunk Hollow Blues, 31
Smada, 20, 115, 116. *See also Ugly Ducklin'*

small-band arrangements, 26–31, 63–64, 290n. 16
Smith, Eve, 119
Smith, Willie "The Lion," 57
Smithsonian Institution, ix, xv, xix, 183, 186
Snibor, 97, 116
Snowfall, 83
The Sob-Sisters, 9
social themes in Strayhorn works, 92–93
Solea, 20
Solitude, 27, 117, 119
solos: ad-lib, xx; Ben Webster, 26, 35, 60; "C" *Blues*, 63; Jimmie Blanton, 35; Johnny Hodges, 26, 40, 119; Juan Tizol, 26; Lawrence Brown, 26; piano, 57, 94, 97; Ray Nance, 26, 47–49; reeds, 77, 82
Solvejg's Song, 139
Some Peaceful Evening, 83, 298n. 30
Something to Live For: arrangements, 22, 172; band books, 288n. 19; compared to *Pavane Bleu*, 177–78; composed in Pittsburgh, 182; copyright, 47, 114; form, 21; lyrics, 174, 177; recording, 26–27; score, 23, 25
Sonata for Two Pianos and Percussion, 6
So This Is Love: chromaticism, 16, 287–88n. 10; compared to *Love Like This Can't Last*, 54; composed in Pittsburgh, 182; *Fantastic Rhythm*, 9–10; form, 14–16, 74; harmony, 14–15, 28–29, 145, 16; lyrics, 14–16; modulations, 287–88n. 10; text setting, 14–15
So What, 20
Sophisticated Lady, 117–19, 133, 151
Sophistication, 94
Soundies. *See* film projects
Spiritual Theme, 89
Sprite Music, 122, 123
Standard Radio Transcriptions, 53, 112
Stanley Theatre, 23
The Star-Crossed Lovers, 134–35, 150. *See also Pretty Girl*
Steinbeck, John, 139–40
Stevedore Serenade, 291–92n. 4
Stewart, Rex, 26, 50, 97
Still in Love with You, 126
Stillman, Al, 31
Stomp, 90, 91–92. *See also Johnny Come Lately*
Strange Feeling, 32, 79, 94, 79
Strause, Charles, 137
Stravinsky, Igor, 38, 43

Strayhorn, Billy. Note: As Strayhorn is the subject of the book, references to his work and life are throughout index. Please check under specific topics in addition to the following: arrangements (recordings listed), 197–261; with Bridgers, 118; with Carney, 144; compositions (listed), 264–86; compositions (recordings listed), 197–261; with Ellington, 86, 102; in Homewood district, 4; musical form, xx; at piano, 66; portrait, 24, 180; recording sessions, 132, 166
Strayhorn, James Nathaniel, 3
"the Strayhorn Effect," 119, 182
Strayhorn Estate, ix, 50, 185
"Strayhorn group," 299n. 5, 299n. 6
Strayhorn's Latest, 21
Street of Dreams, 83, 298n. 30
stride piano style, 37–38
string ensembles, 126
studio recordings, 26, 38
"Stunt Day," 9
Such Sweet Thunder, 95, 103, 107, 134, 150, 159
Sugar Hill Penthouse, 88
suite format, 92–95, 99, 103
Suite for the Duo, 172–73
Suite Thursday, 139–40
Sunswept Sunday, 106
Sweet Duke, 36
Sweet Thursday (Steinbeck), 139–40
Swing Dance, 128, 128, 129
Swinging on the Campus, 26
swing music, 49, 67, 83, 151
The Symphomaniac, 94
Symphonette-Rhythmique, 88, 298n. 2
Symphonic or Bust, 94–95
symphonic style, 37

Taj Mahal, 169
Take the "A" Train: after Strayhorn's death, 182; arrangement, 135, 162–163, 162; attempts to date, 289n. 8; autograph, 50, 191; bebop, 48–49; chromaticism, 48; counterpoint, 82, 162, 162; departure from Ellington style, 64; Ellington Orchestra theme, 35, 47; form, 48; harmony, 6, 47–48, 163; Henderson style, 26; instrumentation, 162; introduction, 49–50, 106; Mingus's use, 54, 292n. 6; modulations, 6, 48; performances,

194–95; popularity, 182–83, 194–95; recordings, 45–47, 101, 194–95, 292n. 6; theme, 47–48, 50; train imagery, 48. *See also Manhattan Murals*
Tales of Manhattan (film), 294n. 25
The Tattooed Bride, 94, 117
Tatum, Art, 19, 57–58
Tchaikovsky, Peter Ilyitch, 31, 137–39
Tempo Music, Inc. (publisher): handling of copyrights, 114–15, 133, 139, 173, 302n. 10; Strayhorn manuscripts, 186, 287n. 4
Temptation, 84
Terry, Clark, 104, 151, 159–61, 188–89
text setting: *Fantastic Rhythm*, 10; *Flamingo*, 38, 40, 43; *I Got it Bad (and That Ain't Good)*, 62; *Let Nature Take its Course*, 12; *Love, Love*, 122–23; *Lush Life*, 17–18; *My Little Brown Book*, 12; *A Penthouse on Shady Avenue*, 14; *So This Is Love*, 14–15; *Wounded Love*, 124
That's for Me, 67
theater projects. *See Beggar's Holiday; Fantastic Rhythm; Jump for Joy; The Love of Don Perlimplín; Rose-Colored Glasses*
Theme for Helen, 148. *See also Orson*
themes: *Agra*, 169; *Ballad for Very Tired and Very Sad Lotus Eaters*, 146, 145, 146; bi-thematic design, 74, 90; *Black, Brown and Beige*, 88, 89; *Blood Count*, 171, 171; *Bluebird of Delhi*, 168, 168; *Boo Loose*, 176–77, 176; *Cashmere Cutie*, 146, 147; *Chelsea Bridge*, 51–52, 83, 52; *Day Dream*, 30, 30, 154–55; *Dirge*, 90; *Flame Indigo*, 295n. 30; *Isfahan*, 169–70, 170; *Lush Life*, 16; *Orson*, 111, 148–49, 148; *Passion Flower*, 28, 28, 29; *Pavana Bleu No. 2*, 176–77, 177; *Pentonsilic*, 58, 89; *Pretty Girl*, 150; *Rain Check*, 54; *Rocks in My Bed*, 62; secondary themes, 52, 58, 73, 74, 83, 91, 97, 168; *Strange Feeling*, 94; *Take the "A" Train*, 47–48, 50; thematic variation, 7; *Ugly Ducklin'*, 19, 20, 20; *Up There*, 174–75, 175, 176; *Upper Manhattan Medical Group*, 143, 143
There Shall Be No Night, 36
There's a Man in My Life, 68
There's No You, 70

INDEX

Things Ain't What They Used to Be, 291n. 1
"thinking with the ear," 67
Third Stream compositions, 60, 164
This Is Always, 70
This Subdues My Passion, 54
Thornhill, Claude, 83, 164, 182
Those Bells, 91
Tiger Rag, 291–92n. 4
timbre melody, 79–80, 106
Time (magazine), 133
Tin Pan Alley songs, 8, 12
Tizol, Juan: Baghdad, 298n. 30; Caravan, 135; Casablanca, 298n. 30; Chelsea Bridge, 52–53; copyist, 50, 185, 290–91n. 20, 292n. 7; Lonely Again, 25; Lozit, 292n. 7; Orson, 148; Rain Check, 57; refusal to copy Strayhorn scores, 290–91n. 20, 292n. 7; Rose Bud, 292n. 7; solos, 26
"tone poem," 298n. 33
Tonight I Shall Sleep, 67, 110
Tonk, 36–38, 59, 64, 291n. 22, 37
Toot Suite, 105
Total Jazz, 135
Tourist Point of View, 167
Townsend, Irving, 107–8
Track 360, xxi, 47
"train pieces," 47–49, 48
transcriptions: creation, xviii–xix; published, 291n. 3; radio transcriptions, 291n. 2, 293n. 17; Sepia Panorama, xix, 291n. 21
transitions, 36, 75
Träumerei, 138
Triple Play, 97
True Confession, 22
"trumpet concerto," 74
Trumpet-No-End, 95
T.T. on Toast, 288n. 2
Tucker, Mark, 54–57
Turner, Joe, 62
Tuxedo Junction, 34, 35
Tymperturbably Blue, 115

Ugly Ducklin', 19–20, 62, 96, 294n. 24, 20. See also Smada
U.M.M.G. (Upper Manhattan Medical Group), 142–46, 163, 143, 145
unions, 85

Until Tonight, 291n. 2
Up and Down, Up and Down 134, 152, 159–61, 159, 160, 161
Up There, 173, 174–77, 307n. 12, 175, 176
Upper Manhattan Medical Group (U.M.M.G.), 142–46, 163, 143, 145
Upside Looking, 115
U.S. Steel Hour (television show), 134

Valburn, Jerry. See Jerry Valburn Collection
Valse, 7–8, 7
Valses Nobles et Sentimentales, 51
Van Eps, Fred, 91
Vance, Dick, 120
variation in performances, xix–xx
V-discs, 85, 112, 298n. 1
Venetian laments, 125
Verve (record label), 135
vibraphones, 7
Victor (record label), 33, 38
The Village Voice (weekly), 49, 183
Violence, 94
Violet Blue, 97
vocal arrangements, 30, 38–39, 74–75. See also specific singers
Vocalion (record label), 26
vocal music, 288–89n. 4
voicing: Chelsea Bridge, 103; close-position, 77, 297n. 21; contrary motion, 77, 161; definition of, 75; dissonant, 6, 76; drop-two voice leading, 57; harmonized lines, 77; The Jumpin' Jive, 31; "Klangfarbenmelodik" (timbre melody), 79–80, 106, 79, 80; open-position, 297n. 21; Portrait of a Silk Thread, 76, 77, 76. See also instrumentation

Waller, Thomas "Fats," 57
waltzes, 7–8, 11, 122–22
Warren, Harry, 94
wartime influence on music, 83, 85, 96
We Are the Reporters, 9
We Love You Madly (television show), 187
Webster, Ben: addition to Ellington orchestra, 33; Black, Brown and Beige, 88; with Ella Fitzgerald, 135; with Ellington Orchestra, 46; Music for Loving (album), 126; noted in autographs, 191; solos, 26, 35, 60; Take the "A" Train, 47
Webster, Paul, 61, 62, 295n. 30
Wein, George, 133
Welcome Aboard (theater show), 188
Welles, Orson, 111, 294n. 25
Westinghouse High School (Pittsburgh), 5–6, 8–10, 11
Whaley, Thomas: collaboration with Strayhorn, 136; on Ellington's flexibility, 107; manuscript collection, 185–86, 191–93; scores copied, 300n. 18
Where Are You, 94
Where or When: coda, 82; form, 68, 74; introduction, 82; modulation, 68–69, 69–70
Whistler, James McNeill, 50, 292n. 10
Whiteman, Paul, 91, 299n. 8, 299n. 9
Wilder, Alec, 96
Will the Big Bands Ever Come Back? (album), 137, 155
Willard, George, 84
Willard, Patricia, 61
Williams, Cootie, 26, 31, 34, 36
Williams, George, 83
Williams, Mary Lou, 57, 95
Wilson, Gerald, 120
Wilson, Teddy, 19, 57–58
The Wonder of You, 68
Wood, Raymond, 8
Woody'n You, 145
Work Song, 88, 89–90
Wounded Love, 122–25, 129, 155, 124

xylophones, 6–7

Yellen, Jack, 31
You Lovely Little Devil, 8
Young, Lester, 49, 164
Young, Lillian, 3
Your Love Has Faded, 21, 31–32, 47, 114, 32
Your Saturday Date with the Duke (radio show), 96

Milton Keynes UK
Ingram Content Group UK Ltd.
UKHW020903231124
451466UK00003B/66